D1054377

H

BLUE RIDGE & SMOKY MOUNTAINS

DEBORAH HUSO

BLUE RIDGE & SMOKY MOUNTAINS

VIRGINIA

TENNESSEE

Clinch River

Norris Lake

Cherokee Lake

Holston River

Kingsport

11W

26

Johnson City

11E

321

Morristown

Greenville

25W

75

11W

11E

25

25E

321

Cherokee National Forest

19W

KNOXVILLE

40 75

40

129

441

Sevierville

Douglas Lake

French Broad River

26

23

Mars Hill

25

Burnsville

Mount Mitchell State Park

Tennessee River

SEE DETAIL

Pigeon Forge

321

40

19

Mount Mitchell 6,684ft ▲

411

Maryville

321

Gatlinburg

Pisgah National Forest

Weaverville

FOLK ART CENTER ★

Black Mountain

Great Smoky Mountains

441

Maggie Valley

ASHEVILLE

Swannanoa

National Park

Cherokee

19

Waynesville

Canton

26

ALT 74

Bat Cave

Cherokee

National

Forest

129

Fontana Lake

Cherokee

Waterrock Knob ✦

74

23

276

Mt. Pisgah

74

Chimney Rock

Dillsboro

Sylva

BLUE RIDGE PARKWAY

Mt. Pisgah ▲

Pisgah National Forest

64

Hendersonville

NORTH CAROLINA

74

19

Nantahala

National Forest

Franklin

Brevard

CARL SANDBURG HOME NATIONAL HISTORIC SITE ★

Murphy

64

441

23

SOUTH CAROLINA

25

276

Greenville

85

76

Chattahoochee

National Forest

Clayton

Sumter National Forest

178

Easley

19

129

GEORGIA

129

123

76

Clemson

76

29

25

0   10 mi

0   10 km

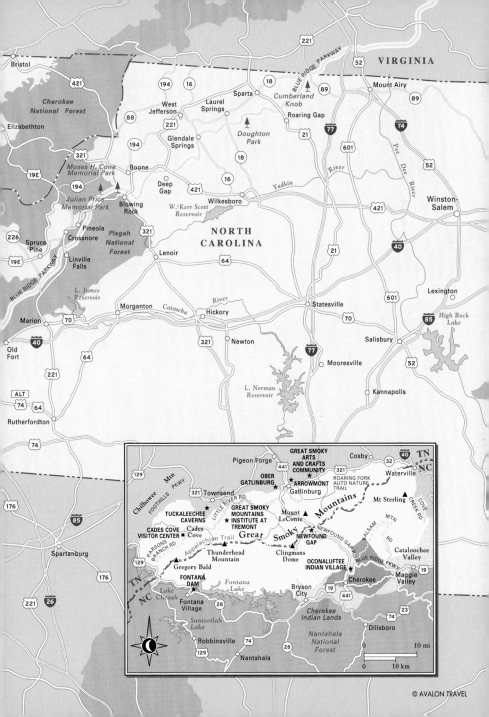

Contents

Discover Blue Ridge & Smoky Mountains

Stretching 469 miles from Shenandoah National Park in Virginia to the Great Smoky Mountains National Park in North Carolina, the Blue Ridge Parkway is often billed as "America's favorite scenic drive." This beautiful mountain byway is in many ways an engineering wonder: The Linn Cove Viaduct, one of the road's most photographed scenes, is only one of six viaducts, 26 tunnels, and 168 bridges on the Parkway.

Through North Carolina, the Parkway courses along the highest peaks east of the Mississippi River, curling around an International Biosphere Reserve at Grandfather Mountain and passing in the shadow of Mount Mitchell, the highest mountain in the East at 6,784 feet. From there it circles around the city of Asheville, which grew prosperous courting northeastern millionaires like George Vanderbilt, then into the beautiful wilderness of the Pisgah and Nantahala National Forests.

The Parkway ends at the Oconaluftee River entrance to the Great Smoky Mountains National Park, which straddles the border between North Carolina and Tennessee. The Smokies, too, boast some of the highest mountains in the East, with 16 peaks reaching over 6,000 feet. The park has more than half a million acres of forest, making it one of the largest unbroken wilderness areas on the East Coast, and its biodiversity is so great that some scientists consider walking from the park's lowest to highest elevation to be ecologically equivalent to traveling the 2,000

miles between the start point of the Appalachian Trail in Georgia and its end in Maine.

The Blue Ridge Parkway is the most-visited unit of the National Park Service with some 20 million motorists coursing along its curves annually, and the Great Smoky Mountains National Park is the country's most-visited national park with 10 million visitors a year. Being within a two-day drive of half the U.S. population ensures the popularity of both parks but also speaks to the necessity of minimizing human impacts on a much-beloved landscape.

Those impacts can be seen everywhere, as the cities and towns that surround both parks grow larger and busier every year. Asheville has undergone substantial revitalization in recent years, while on the Tennessee side of the Smokies the growth of tourist towns like Gatlinburg and Pigeon Forge seems limited only by the protected land that borders them. Nevertheless, the towns add their own special character to these mountains, offering insight into the heritage of the people who have lived and continue to live here.

Planning Your Trip

▶ WHERE TO GO

North Carolina High Country

Stretching from North Carolina's north-west corner south to the mining regions around Spruce Pine and Little Switzerland, the High Country is a vast area of mountainous landscape hugging the Blue Ridge Parkway from Cumberland Knob to Mount Mitchell. The region is defined in large part by tourism, particularly in the area around Blowing Rock and Boone, as well as by quiet rural landscapes and villages like those found below the slopes of Bluff Mountain.

Asheville Area

The only city for miles around, Asheville wears its mountain urbanism like a mantle, sporting a revitalized downtown historic district loaded with preserved art deco architecture and an arts scene that is at once funky and fine. It is a city where anything goes, and its casual atmosphere is a reflection of the fact that most people who live here and visit here are looking for

IF YOU HAVE...

- **FIVE DAYS:** Travel Blue Ridge Parkway from Boone to Cherokee.
- **ONE WEEK:** Add Great Smoky Mountains National Park.
- **TWO WEEKS:** Add Mount Airy, Asheville, Gatlinburg, and Pigeon Forge.

view of Black Mountains, to the north of Asheville

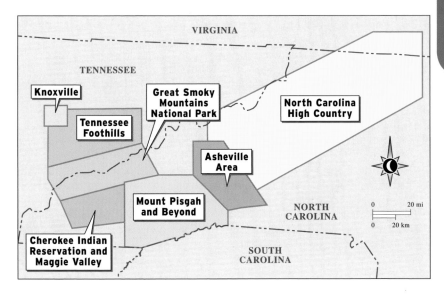

a metropolis in a land of milk and honey, which it may very well be, bordered as it is by the Black Mountains to the north and the Smokies to the west.

Mount Pisgah and Beyond

Perhaps the real land of milk and honey is in the region around Mount Pisgah, whose name actually comes from the Bible's book of Deuteronomy, in which the Lord shows Moses the Promised Land from the sacred mountain. The landscape around Mount Pisgah and to the south is loaded with wilderness, being home, in fact, to North Carolina's largest wilderness area, the Shining Rock Wilderness. Yet even in the midst of all the lush forested mountainsides are thriving little towns with arts scenes that will amaze you.

Cherokee Indian Reservation and Maggie Valley

In the midst of the Qualla Boundary, as the Cherokee Indian Reservation is known, is Cherokee. Situated along the banks of the Oconaluftee River, this is the home of the Eastern Band, the descendants of those who managed to avoid taking the tragic Trail of Tears west to what is now Oklahoma. Cherokee's proximity to the Great Smoky Mountains National Park has given it a burgeoning tourism industry based in large part on the heritage of its people, who still practice the arts of their ancestors and even speak, read, and write the tribe's native tongue.

Great Smoky Mountains National Park

The half a million acres of the Great Smoky Mountains National Park are a wilderness wonderland waiting to be discovered, quite literally. Though sliced by the Newfound Gap Road, much of this park is roadless, accessible only by its 800 miles of hiking trails. Here are towering mountains (by Eastern standards at least), dozens of waterfalls, beautiful mountain balds, and miles upon miles of clear trout streams, as well as a thriving wildlife population ranging from the park's ubiquitous black bears to its more than two dozen species of salamander.

Tennessee Foothills

The Tennessee Foothills on the Smokies' western edge are a landscape of contradictions. Here is the largest community of resident artisans anywhere in the United States, many of them practicing historic Appalachian crafts, yet only minutes away are some of the most over-the-top tourist attractions outside Las Vegas. This pull between past and present is a defining feature of the region and one that manages to comingle peacefully in some places, the theme park of Dollywood being a surprising example.

Knoxville

The largest city in east Tennessee, Knoxville is probably best known for its local music scene as well as for its significance to World War II. The nearby Oak Ridge National Laboratory was a key research site of the Manhattan Project. Home to the University of Tennessee as well as to a slowly burgeoning downtown historic district centered around the music scene of Gay Street, Knoxville today is a small but cosmopolitan Southern city on the rise.

Gatlinburg Trolley, in the Tennessee Foothills

▶ WHEN TO GO

The Smokies and Blue Ridge Parkway region are busiest in both mid-summer and in fall color season, with the peak visitation months being July and October. If your goal is to avoid crowds, go in winter or early spring. While the weather will definitely be cooler (and probably downright cold at high elevations), winter and early spring will give you the opportunity to enjoy more long-distance views without leaves on the trees.

However, if your goal is to enjoy some of the blooming flora that have long attracted visitors to these mountains, you can begin to experience it in mid-May with the onset of the mountain laurel bloom. The show continues with flame azalea, followed by Catawba

Rosebay rhododendron

rhododendron, and then Rosebay rhododendron well into mid-July.

▶ BEFORE YOU GO

Getting There

Most visitors drive to the region, but you can also fly to Knoxville or Asheville.

The Blue Ridge Parkway is organized by milepost, making it pretty easy to figure out where sights and hikes are. There are Blue Ridge Parkway visitors centers and/or services at Doughton Park, Moses H. Cone Memorial Park, Linville Falls, Crabtree Meadows, Craggy Gardens, Folk Art Center, Mount Pisgah, and Waterrock Knob. The largest cities and towns along the Blue Ridge Parkway include Mount Airy, Boone, Blowing Rock, and Asheville.

Main entry points and visitors centers for the Great Smoky Mountains National Park are at Gatlinburg and Cherokee. Main entrances to the park are on Route 441 just north of Cherokee, North Carolina, and Route 441 south of Gatlinburg, Tennessee. Stop at the Oconaluftee Visitor Center on

the North Carolina side or the Sugarlands Visitor Center on the Tennessee side to obtain additional maps and directions. Request the Great Smoky Mountains Trail Map for detailed road and trail information, including directions to the less-frequented areas mentioned in this guide.

What to Take

Be prepared for quick changes in weather and temperature due to elevation changes and the general rainy climate, particularly in the Smokies. Always have rain gear handy, dress in layers, have good hiking boots, and, if you plan to do a lot of hiking, energy snacks and water for the trail. Always stay on designated trails.

Keep your distance from wildlife at all times. Bring binoculars or a zoom lens, so you can enjoy and photograph wildlife without getting too close.

Explore Blue Ridge & Smoky Mountains

▶ BLUE RIDGE PARKWAY IN THREE DAYS

Three days will allow you a good overview of the Blue Ridge Parkway while still being able to drive at a leisurely pace. This road trip covers about 200 miles, starting at Cumberland Knob and ending at the highest point on the Parkway at Richland Balsam.

Day 1

Pack a picnic lunch, and begin your road trip at Cumberland Knob just south of the state line between North Carolina and Virginia. Head south toward Doughton Park. Here you can take a short walk to Wildcat Rocks to enjoy spectacular views into the Doughton Park backcountry. Then drive up to the Bluff Mountain picnic area. From here, you can take a short hike up the grassy slope of Bluff Mountain to a nice view into the valleys below. Afterwards, enjoy lunch in the scenic picnic area. Continue south, being sure to check out the Appalachian crafts at the Northwest Trading Post near Milepost 260.

Next head down to E. B. Jeffries Park. If you're a hiker, you can enjoy a one-mile trek to a beautiful waterfall here. Stay the night in Boone or Blowing Rock.

Day 2

The next morning, start your day with a visit to the Parkway Craft Center at Moses H. Cone Memorial Park. Then take the easy loop hike around the beautiful shores of Price Lake to the south. You'll get your first glimpses of Grandfather Mountain from here.

Next head across the Linn Cove Viaduct and take a side trip to Grandfather Mountain, where you'll likely spend the rest of the afternoon exploring the Wildlife Habitat and Mile-High Swinging Bridge. If you have time at the end of the day, take one of the many hikes around Linville Falls. Spend the night at Eseeola Lodge in Linville.

Day 3

As you head south of Linville Falls the next morning, be sure to make a quick stop at the Orchard at Altapass to buy some apples or locally made cider, and see if there is a bluegrass band playing on the stage. Then continue on your way, enjoying the scenery as you come into the Black Mountain range. Make a side trip here to Mount Mitchell State Park

view of Grandfather Mountain from Price Lake

Linville Falls

and climb the paved path to the observation tower for what will, hopefully, be 360-degree views. Make your way toward Asheville, stopping by the Folk Art Center to explore the gallery and pick up a handmade souvenir. Next it's on to Mount Pisgah, where you can grab a late lunch at the Pisgah Inn before continuing your road trip through some of the high lonesome balds to the south. Your last stop on this journey will be at the overlook on Richland Balsam, the highest point on the Parkway at 6,047 feet.

▶ TOP HIKES OFF THE PARKWAY

While the vast majority of visitors who travel the Blue Ridge Parkway spend most of their time in an automobile, pausing occasionally at overlooks to take in the views, there are countless hiking trails accessible right off the Parkway that will provide you with even more remarkable scenery. Below are some of my top picks. Most of them are appropriate only for those who are avid hikers and accustomed to lots of up-and-down terrain.

Bluff Mountain Trail

This 7.5-mile trail offers a full day's hike (you might want to arrange for a car shuttle) with almost constant long-distance views as it parallels the Parkway. The hike is accessible from various points in the Doughton Park area, but you can start at the Brinegar Cabin at Milepost 238.5.

From Brinegar Cabin, the trail passes through dense pine forest, eventually opening into a meadow with lovely views of grassy high-elevation fields. After about two more miles you'll come to one of the prettiest stretches along the trail as you gain your first view of mountain summits stretching out endlessly in front of you. Then you'll proceed through boulder fields, past the developed area around the Doughton Park Coffee Shop, and ascend into beautiful woods loaded with

Bluff Mountain Trail at Doughton Park

rhododendron. Past the picnic area the trail is wide and sunny, crossing a broad meadow that, in early summer, will likely be alive with wildflowers. At the summit, roughly 3.5 miles into your trek, you'll enjoy more long-distance views across the Blue Ridge and down into the cove of Grassy Gap.

If you choose to continue beyond the summit you'll enjoy ever-increasing long-distance views as you ascend a rough cliff overlooking the steep walls of Cove Creek Valley and experience stunning vistas with the final one coming at the Basin Cove Overlook (Milepost 244.7), which provides a view of the barren granite face of Stone Mountain and is the end of your hike.

Tanawha Trail

The entire length of the Tanawha Trail is more than 13 miles, requiring a long day of fast-paced hiking, but it's worth it if you're an experienced hiker. This trail will not only offer you the best views of the Linn Cove Viaduct, but it will also provide regular opportunities for long-distance vistas, making every uphill climb rewarding. The trail begins at the Beacon Heights parking area at Milepost 304.8.

Because the Tanawha Trail traverses the fragile ecosystem of Grandfather Mountain it is elaborate in much the way the Linn Cove Viaduct is, crossing extravagant arching bridges and long stretches of boardwalk to prevent hikers from damaging the flora below. In fact, this single trail cost almost $250,000 to build.

If you'd like to hike some of the trail but don't have time to take in the full length, you can hike from Wilson Creek overlook to Rough Ridge. This section offers several viewpoints of the Linn Cove Viaduct.

Linville Falls

There are several trails of varying lengths at Linville Falls (Milepost 316.3), all of them accessible from behind the Linville Falls Visitors

THE PARKWAY IN BLOOM: LOOKING FOR WILDFLOWERS

Late spring and early summer are especially popular times to visit the Blue Ridge Parkway, in large part because of all the blooms. There are few better ways to spend an afternoon than taking a meandering drive down the Parkway through tunnels of pink and white rhododendrons, blushing mountain laurel, and the eye-catching displays of flame azalea. While these tried and true favorites are the big draw in springtime along America's favorite drive, there are many more wild blooming things to be found on these lovely mountainsides.

One of the best stretches of road to explore for wildflowers is between Grandfather Mountain (Milepost 305) and Craggy Gardens (Milepost 365). And while a slow-paced drive will bring one within viewing distance of wild columbine as well as blossoming trees like frothy dogwoods, rosy-purple redbuds, and serviceberries, leg-stretcher hikes along the way will prove even more fruitful for flower-gazing.

Grandfather Mountain (Milepost 305) is among the best spots on the Parkway for seeing unusual and even endangered flower species like Gray's lily. The roadside overlooks between the entrance gate and summit parking area offer the easiest spots from which to view wildflowers, including tiny white-flowered wood strawberries, fern-leafed Sweet Cicely, the fringed bell-shaped petals of Starry Campion, and spiky Bluebeard-lily. The **Black Rock Trail** in particular offers a short hike through

habitat rich with spring blooming flowers and interpretive signs along the way that describe the native flora and fauna.

Just south of Grandfather Mountain at Milepost 317, several trails dart off into the woods from the **Linville Falls Visitors Center,** most of them short and moderate hikes that provide access to overlooks for viewing the heavy spring overflow of **Linville Falls** as it cascades through narrow gorge walls, spraying the rocky cliffs with flower-feeding moisture that sustains the Rosebay rhododendron.

Along the damp, dark forest floor one may spot trillium, bloodroot, Spring beauty, and the puffy bulbous blooms of Dutchman's Breeches. Sweet little violets in rainbows of colors and tiny white chickweed blooms also carpet woody areas on Parkway trails.

The **Crabtree Falls** hike at Milepost 350 offers many opportunities for viewing some of these same wildflowers, with an especially dense population of trillium. A gushing waterfall provides a special treat at the base of the trail, but the hike back up to the parking area is steep.

Those who come for the rhododendron, however, must pay a visit to **Craggy Gardens** (Milepost 365), where pink and lavender Catawba rhododendron are at their finest by mid-June. There's nothing quite like breathing deep the heady scent of these soft clusters of blossoms and walking into a tender tunnel of waxy-leafed thickets.

mountain laurel

trillium

flame azalea

Center. The hiking opportunities range from short walks to trails of up to a mile, providing many different viewing opportunities of Linville Falls and Linville Gorge.

One of the best is the hike to Chimney View and Erwin's View. Chimney View has two overlooks accessible via a series of steps. The upper Chimney View provides a full portrait of the upper falls and limited look at the lower. The lower Chimney View provides a panorama of the plunge basin where the Linville River curls through a tunnel of limestone, swirling into white foam, before dropping again at the lower falls. At Erwin's View, you'll enjoy a full panorama of the falls.

Craggy Pinnacle Trail

Accessible at Milepost 364, the Craggy Pinnacle Trail offers a trek of just under a mile

the trail to Craggy Pinnacle

to the top of a heath bald known as Craggy Pinnacle. To have the full experience of Craggy, hike the trail in late May through June to see the mountain's tremendous lavender displays of Catawba rhododendron. At the summit of Craggy Pinnacle (5,892 ft.), you'll be treated to 360-degree views of the surrounding mountains as well as some good photographic opportunities of the Parkway both south and north.

The Pisgah Summit Trail

Accessible from Milepost 407.7, the hike to summit of Mount Pisgah is just over a mile and a half. The trail starts out mostly level and full of wildflowers such as lilies, trillium, and goldenrod. A cascading spring greets you after half a mile, then the trail begins to ascend and grow steeper, requiring some scrambling over rocks and tree roots. Hundreds of rock steps lead up to the 360-degree view at the top of Mount Pisgah, where the elevation reaches 5,721 feet. From the wooden viewing platform—on a clear day—you'll enjoy a blue sea of mountains as far as the horizon.

Waterrock Knob Trail

If you want to see some of the best views along the Parkway, then take a steep but relatively short hike of just under a mile to the top of Waterrock Knob Trail at Milepost 451.2.

A steep quarter mile on a paved trail takes you to the visitor platform, but don't stop there: The views from the summit of Waterrock Knob (6,292 ft.) are worth the effort. New views lurk around every corner as you climb, and from the top you'll see the summits of Clingmans Dome (6,643 ft.), Mount LeConte (6,593 ft.), and Mount Guyot (6,621 ft.), the highest peaks in the Great Smoky Mountains National Park.

► A BLUE RIDGE ROAD TRIP

Traveling the Blue Ridge Parkway from top to bottom is one of my favorite ways to take a relaxing, laid-back journey, and while most motorists on the Parkway do just sections of the famous byway or drive from one end to the other in a couple of days, to truly experience all this great American roadway has to offer you need to take your time. Here's a 10-day itinerary for traveling the Parkway from where it crosses into North Carolina at Cumberland Knob (Milepost 217.5) to its end at Cherokee (Milepost 469).

Day 1

Begin your journey at Cumberland Knob and head south for several miles, enjoying the long blue views into the North Carolina Piedmont to the southeast and into the land of Christmas tree farms to the west. Take a side trip at Milepost 230 toward Roaring Gap to Stone Mountain State Park, and get an up-close glimpse of the bald-faced mountain you've likely been watching from the Parkway. Then get back on the Parkway, heading toward Doughton Park. Stop by the Brinegar Cabin for insights into what Appalachian life was like at the turn of the 20th century. Check in to the Bluffs Lodge on Bluff Mountain in time to watch the sunset from the porch.

Day 2

The next morning, rise early and take one of the many long and beautiful hikes offered at Doughton Park, whether that's the Bluff Mountain Trail or one of the many backcountry trails in Basin Cove. At the end of a long day of hiking you might want to take a short drive south on the Parkway along the rolling bluffs here at Doughton Park, perhaps taking in the sunset from an overlook, before taking a well-deserved rest. Stay a second night at Bluffs Lodge.

views to the southeast from the Blue Ridge Parkway south of Cumberland Knob

horses at Moses H. Cone Memorial Park

Day 3

On your third day, stop by the Northwest Trading Post at Milepost 258.6 and browse through locally made crafts, and then head into Glendale Springs on Highway 16 to see the Churches of the Frescoes. Continue your side trip off the Parkway to the town of West Jefferson to visit its many art galleries. Don't forget to pick up some locally made cheese at the Ashe County Cheese Company while you're there. If you have some extra time, drive up to the top of nearby Mount Jefferson and take a hike to a view. Spend the night at the Rocking Chair Inn just outside West Jefferson.

Day 4

Rise early for a brisk hike at E. B. Jeffries Park (Milepost 272). The Cascades Trail will take you about a mile downhill to incredibly up-close views of a gorgeous waterfall. Next head into Boone for some browsing at the Mast General Store and other shops along the town's Main Street before taking in the outdoor drama *Horn in the West*. Make the Village Inns of Blowing Rock your home base for your two-day tour of the Boone and Blowing Rock area.

Day 5

On your fifth day, start off with a visit to the Parkway Craft Center at Moses H. Cone Memorial Park, and then stroll around some of the park's 25 miles of carriage trails. Then head a few minutes south for an easy, level hike around Price Lake at Julian Price Memorial Park. Spend the afternoon enjoying the shops in nearby Blowing Rock.

Day 6

Today you'll get to drive across the Parkway's most famous icon, the Linn Cove Viaduct. Stop at the Linn Cove Viaduct Visitor Center to learn about this bridge's unique construction. Then take a side trip to Grandfather Mountain, where you will easily spend the rest of the day exploring the park's Nature Museum and Wildlife Habitat (where you can feed the resident black bears) and crossing the Mile-High Swinging Bridge. If you have the time, Grandfather Mountain also has several lovely hiking trails. Stay the night at the luxurious Eseeola Lodge in Linville.

Day 7

Next morning, start the day with a relatively easy hike on one of the trails at

SOUTHERN MOUNTAIN ROMANCE

The Blue Ridge and Smoky Mountains aren't just destinations for outdoors enthusiasts, avid hikers, and motorists seeking a scenic drive. They're also an especially nice place to get away from it all and rekindle romance. More than a few luxury lodgings in these mountains offer the ultimate in escape for couples while also providing access to some romantic attractions.

A LAKE LURE GETAWAY

Named one of the most beautiful lakes in the world by *National Geographic*, Lake Lure, about a 45-minute drive east of Asheville, has been a draw for weekenders for more than 75 years, and its shores are dotted with vacation homes ranging from quaint fishing cottages to sprawling mansions. While lakefront property here comes dear, you and your beloved can enjoy a weekend on the water with no fuss at the **Lodge on Lake Lure.** The lodge is the lake's only waterfront accommodation and was originally constructed in the 1930s as a retreat for the North Carolina Highway Patrol. Since then the lodge has undergone a complete transformation into a luxury inn, featuring rooms with furniture and eclectic antiques from South Africa, the owner's homeland, and private balconies and light-capturing floor-to-ceiling windows encircling deep claw-foot soaking tubs. The lodge's old romance still remains, with its wormy chestnut-paneled walls and floors of original oak and pine.

You can spend the day lounging in your spacious lakefront room, pampering yourselves in luxury bathrooms, taking a sunset cruise on the lake, or indulging in a couple's massage. If utter relaxation isn't your cup of tea, then take a day trip to nearby **Hendersonville** to explore all the shops in the historic district and then catch an evening performance at the **Flat Rock Playhouse. Chimney Rock Park** is also just down the road.

SUNRISE OVER THE SMOKIES

While most couples will want to sleep in during their weekend getaway, those staying at the **Timber Rose English Lodge** outside Gatlinburg, Tennessee, should set their alarms for dawn. The verandas of the Timber Rose's five suites offer sumptuous sunrise views eastward toward the Greenbrier Pinnacle, as the first light of day draws like a mauve ribbon over the blue-gray peaks of the Smokies. On fall mornings the temperatures hover just above freezing, but couples can nestle comfortably in the hot bubbling water of their own private hot tubs as the sun draws higher and higher into the sky above the mountains. In autumn, the folds of the mountains change subtly under the ever-expanding light of day, first dimly purple, then rising into the full brilliance of gold, amber, and red. Built to resemble an English estate lodge, this couples-only retreat offers rooms with Victorian antiques and wood-burning fireplaces. It's only minutes outside the bustling Tennessee entrance to the Great Smoky Mountains National Park at Gatlinburg, but the Timber Rose seems eons away from anywhere.

The Timber Rose is situated in the center of an often-overlooked cultural treasure of these mountains: the **Great Smoky Arts and Crafts Community.** Established in 1937, it is the largest independent organization of artisans in the United States with some 100 studios and shops. And if an afternoon hike or scenic drive is more to your liking, the Timber Rose is also only minutes from the **Great Smoky Mountains National Park.**

touring Lake Lure by boat

Linville Falls to see incredible views of the plunging cascade and the gorge that surrounds it. From here head south and stop by the Orchard at Altapass to buy some locally harvested fruit and check out the region's geology at the Museum of North Carolina Minerals (Milepost 331). Take a quick jaunt into Little Switzerland, visit the Swiss Shops, and enjoy lunch with a view at The Switzerland Inn. Then continue south to Mount Mitchell State Park to enjoy views from the highest peak east of the Mississippi at 6,684 feet above sea level. If you're up for some rugged camping, stay the night at Mount Mitchell State Park; otherwise head back toward Little Switzerland for the evening for an overnight at the Switzerland Inn.

Day 8

Continue your journey along the Parkway as it winds its way through the towering Black Mountains. Stop for a quick but steep hike to the top of Craggy Pinnacle, a heath bald offering more 360-degree views. Then spend the rest of the afternoon exploring the artistry of local craftspeople at the Folk Art Center and making a trip into Asheville to visit the galleries downtown. Spend the night at one of the bed-and-breakfasts in Asheville's Montford District, perhaps the Black Walnut Bed and Breakfast.

Day 9

If you're curious about what the inside of the largest private residence in North America looks like, you might want to spend the day at Biltmore, the sprawling estate George Vanderbilt built at the turn of the 20th century. It will require a full day. If you prefer to keep exploring the great outdoors, however, then continue south to Mount Pisgah (Milepost 408.6), where you can take a hike to the summit or just enjoy a lunch with incredible views at the Pisgah Inn. Then continue south to the area known as

Yellowstone Falls at Graveyard Fields

Graveyard Fields for a relatively easy hike to view Yellowstone Falls. Stay overnight at the Pisgah Inn.

Day 10

On the final day of your journey you will likely enjoy some of the best views as you cross the highest point on the Parkway (6,047 ft.) at Richland Balsam. Then head to Waterrock Knob (Milepost 451.2) for even more stunning vistas from the observation platform here or at the summit if you don't mind a steep hike. The last leg of your journey on the Parkway will take you through the Cherokee Indian Reservation to the roadway's end in the town of Cherokee. Here you should definitely pay a visit to the Museum of the Cherokee Indian as well as the Qualla Arts and Crafts Mutual across the street. The best lodgings in Cherokee are at Harrah's Casino.

▶ THE THREE-DAY BEST OF THE SMOKIES

Sadly enough, most people do the Great Smoky Mountains National Park in a day. You should give it at least three days to get a true feel for what this half-million-acre park has to offer as well as to get a taste of the history and culture of the surrounding communities. Here are my top picks for a long-weekend tour.

Day 1

Start your day in Cherokee. Visiting the Museum of the Cherokee Indian will give you a grounding in the human history of the Smokies before entering the national park. Then take the Newfound Gap Road across the park, a 30-mile trek from Cherokee to Gatlinburg. Along the way be sure to stop and visit the Mountain Farm Museum and Mingus Mill to learn about the European American settlers who called these mountains home. From the Newfound Gap Road you can also take a spur road to Clingmans Dome, the highest mountain in the park at 6,643 feet, and then enjoy the view from Newfound Gap. Your road trip will end in Gatlinburg, where you can spend the evening strolling the town. Be sure to enjoy a nighttime ride up the Gatlinburg Sky Lift.

Day 2

The next morning, start your day with an auto tour along the Roaring Fork Motor Nature Trail, a less-traveled part of the national park that will give you the opportunity to go inside several historic homes that once made up the Roaring Fork community. You may also see some black bears along this route. Exit the park at the end of your tour, and spend the afternoon exploring the Great Smoky Arts and Crafts Community in Gatlinburg, the largest resident gathering of independent artisans in the United States.

Day 3

On your last day, head back into the national park at the Sugarlands entrance at Gatlinburg, and take a right onto Little River Road, a winding journey of about 25 miles along the scenic Little River. Stop for a moderate paved hike to the lovely cascade of Laurel Falls, and then continue your journey west to Cades Cove. Cades Cove has the park's largest collection of preserved Appalachian structures, and you can take an 11-mile loop tour of the beautiful valley. This is also one of the best places in the park to see black bears, particularly if you visit close to sunset.

▶ WILD AND RUGGED SMOKIES

While it's true that most of the 10 million people who enter the Great Smoky Mountains National Park each year only get out of their cars to photograph the views, these mountains can't be fully appreciated without some work—some very fun work, however. If you're an active outdoors person, try these recommendations for exploring the Smokies in four days—while barely setting foot in your car.

Day 1

You'll start your fun in the Smokies by getting to know the rivers…and their rapids. Sign up with a local outfitter to go whitewater rafting down the Pigeon River on the national park's northern border. The rapids on the Pigeon River range from Class I to Class IV, so you'll get a good mix of adventure without feeling like you're taking your life into your hands the whole time.

Plus, you'll have some time to just float and enjoy the riverside scenery on the park's northern border. You'll likely be pretty tired after paddling for a couple of hours, so spend the rest of the afternoon taking a quiet scenic drive into Greenbrier Cove, a gravel back road just north of Gatlinburg leading into one of the national park's little-traveled areas. This is also the region of the Smokies where Dolly Parton's ancestors once lived.

Day 2

On the second day, you'll take an overnight hike to the summit of Mount LeConte. You can backpack if you want, but for a truly unique experience, consider making reservations at the hike-in only LeConte Lodge. While there are more than half a dozen trails you can take to reach LeConte's summit (6,593 ft.), the most scenic is the

trail shelter on Mount LeConte

stream along the Alum Cave Bluffs Trail

you a hearty hiker's dinner. Just make sure to make reservations first.

Day 3

Most of your third day will be spent hiking down Mount LeConte and, if you've arranged for a hiker's shuttle, you can take a different route on the way down. Consider the Rainbow Falls Trail or Trillium Gap Trail, both of which lead down into Roaring Fork. Rainbow Falls is an incredibly steep downhill trek with a lot of loose rock, but it will take you past the cascade of Rainbow Falls. For a little bit easier but longer hike, take Trillium Gap. This is also the trail used by the llamas who supply LeConte Lodge, and you might meet them on your way down. The trail will also take you under (yes, I said under) Grotto Falls. No doubt about it, when you reach the bottom you'll be bone tired. Take the auto tour around the Roaring Fork Motor Nature Trail, and then hit the hay!

Day 4

You'll probably be pretty tired on the final day of this adventure, so we've saved the most relaxing for last. Sleep in if you like, and then sign up for a trail ride at Smoky Mountain Riding Stables just north of Gatlinburg. Saddle up your horse and join other riders on a tour of the national park around Greenbrier Cove. A two-hour journey will take you up some steep mountain terrain (but at least *you're* not doing the hiking this time!), through mountain streams, and past some beautiful forest scenery before you have to head home again.

Alum Cave Bluffs Trail. This is a steep 5.5-mile hike that will take you through the strange natural tunnel of Arch Rock, past some incredible views from the heath balds of Inspiration Point, and then to the bizarre feature of Alum Cave Bluffs, where it, quite literally, never rains. The last leg of the hike will be a continual uphill rewarded by regular long-distance mountain views and will involve some scrambling along rock ledges with steel cables to help you keep your balance. When you arrive at the summit, you can spend the night in a rustic cabin (no electricity or running water) at LeConte Lodge. They'll also fix

▶ THE PEOPLE BEFORE THE PARK

One thing that's easy to overlook in the Smokies, if you're just speeding through on a quick scenic driving tour, is the human history. Long before the Great Smoky Mountains National Park was established, thousands of people, both Native and European American, called these mountains home. If you'd like to learn some of the history of the Smokies, here's your itinerary.

Day 1

Start your journey in Cherokee, where you'll spend a full day learning about the Native American culture of the Smokies. Start your tour at the Museum of the Cherokee Indian to learn about the native people who have lived in these mountains for at least 11,000 years, and then browse through some of the Cherokee's locally made river-cane and white-oak baskets, pottery, beadwork, and woodcarving at the Qualla Arts and Crafts Mutual. Then head up to the Oconaluftee Indian Village to see Cherokee craftspeople working their trades. Close the day with an evening viewing of the outdoor drama *Unto These Hills,* which deals with the history of the Cherokee and the Trail of Tears.

Day 2

On your second day, head north to the Cataloochee Valley, which was once the most populous area of what is now the Great Smoky Mountains National Park. Here you will see a quiet valley of long-abandoned houses, a school, a church, and several barns. You may also get the extra treat of seeing some of the park's elk. When you've completed your tour of the valley, head over to the Tennessee side of the park to tour the Roaring Fork Motor Nature Trail, which will take you on a short loop tour of a small community that existed above present-day Gatlinburg (originally known as White Oak Flats).

Day 3

On your final day, get up at dawn and head into Cades Cove, in the southwestern corner of the park, and rent a bicycle at the Cades Cove Campground store. (Try to hit Cades Cove on a Wednesday or Saturday, when the cove is closed to automobiles until 10 A.M.) Spend the morning on a leisurely bike ride through the largest collection of preserved Appalachian farm structures in the park, and see some mill demonstrations at Cable Mill. If you get out there early enough you'll likely spot some black bears hanging out in the apple trees, too—quite a memory to take home with you that afternoon.

mill race at Cable Mill in Cades Cove

NORTH CAROLINA HIGH COUNTRY

The High Country occupies the northwest corner of North Carolina and has the highest average land elevation of any region in the eastern United States. Even its towns are high, with the village of Blowing Rock situated at an elevation of 4,000 feet. Blowing Rock is an upscale destination with a Main Street of trendy boutiques, chocolatiers, and fine dining. Its inns and bed-and-breakfasts all have a luxurious edge, some featuring gas log-burning fireplaces in the master bathrooms. On the other side of the Parkway, Boone is more laid-back. It is home to Appalachian State University, and the youth culture is evident. Main Street houses perennial tourist favorites like the Mast General Store but also some funky gift shops selling books on Eastern religion and philosophy as well as vintage clothing. Restaurants in

Boone are mostly casual and rife with college students during the school season, but they serve up some first-rate, filling victuals like "Hunka Mozzarella" appetizers.

Once the summer resort destination of well-to-do lowlanders, the High Country today is a major tourist destination, bisected as it is by the Blue Ridge Parkway and home to such famous landmarks as Grandfather Mountain. The region is also rich with industry, ranking as the second-biggest producer of Christmas trees in the nation and also serving as a major mining district. This makes the High Country a fun place to purchase unique gemstones and also a popular winter destination with its ski resorts, pick-your-own Christmas tree farms, and quaint Main Street towns. For outdoors enthusiasts, fishing,

© DEBORAH HUSO

HIGH COUNTRY

HIGHLIGHTS

◖ **Bluff Mountain Trail:** The center-piece of the Blue Ridge Parkway's 6,000-acre Doughton Park tract, this scenic ridge trail alternates between wildflower meadows and rugged rock outcroppings while paralleling the Parkway for 7.5 miles (page 50).

◖ **Todd General Store:** Located in the middle of nowhere, the Todd General Store is worth a winding road trip, as it offers first-rate bluegrass jams provided by local musicians (page 57).

◖ **Original Mast General Store:** This rural country store in Valle Crucis has been almost continually operational since its opening at the end of the 19th century. Today it is the original of a famous franchise (page 68).

◖ **Moses H. Cone Memorial Park:** Once the home of Denim King Moses H. Cone, the park now houses the Southern Highland Craft Guild and offers miles of scenic carriage trails (page 75).

◖ **Linn Cove Viaduct:** The final section of the Parkway to be completed in 1987, and an engineering wonder in its own right, the viaduct is the most photographed structure on the Parkway after Mabry Mill in Virginia (page 84).

◖ **Grandfather Mountain:** Known for its rugged profile, this peak is one of the highest along the Parkway and is home to the famous Mile-High Swinging Bridge (page 86).

◖ **Linville Falls Erwin's View Trail:** Located at the mouth of one of the deepest gorges in the Blue Ridge, the trail to these falls is among the most popular on the Parkway (page 91).

◖ **Orchard at Altapass:** An excellent music venue, the orchard hosts regular musical entertainment from regional performers as well as some fine two-stepping (page 95).

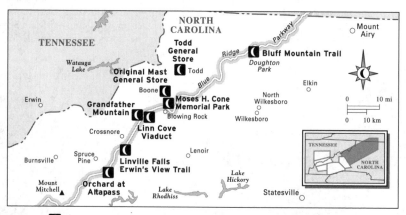

LOOK FOR ◖ TO FIND RECOMMENDED SIGHTS, ACTIVITIES, DINING, AND LODGING.

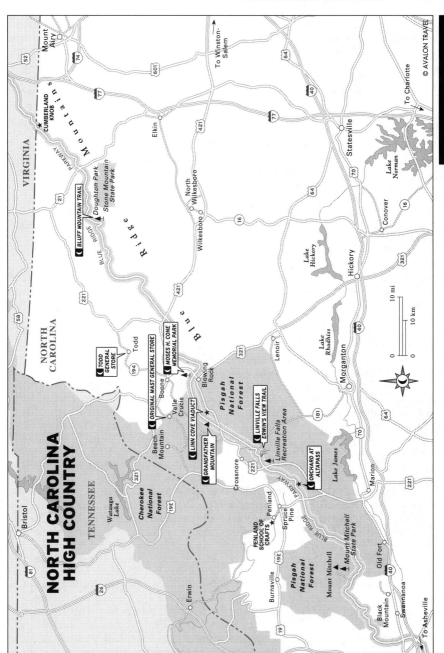

© AVALON TRAVEL

horseback riding, and even rock climbing opportunities abound, and the area boasts some of the most challenging hikes in the southern Appalachians, including the Grandfather Trail, which requires climbing rope ladders and crawling through rock crevices.

HISTORY

It is easy to get lost in the scenic beauty of the Blue Ridge Parkway as it skirts the crest of the Blue Ridge. The road itself is a history lesson, having been initiated as a Public Works Project during the Great Depression and built largely by the hands of the young men who served in the Civilian Conservation Corps in the 1930s. But the High Country that surrounds the Parkway from the North Carolina state line down to the Black Mountains above Asheville has a history far older than that of America's best-loved scenic byway.

The first inhabitants of the Blue Ridge were, of course, Native Americans. The Cherokee, Monacan, Saponi, and Tutelo nations all called this region either home or hunting ground long before the Europeans that drifted here from the mid- to late 18th century. Evidence of their existence is difficult to trace, though many of the mountain and river names here (like Watauga, Yadkin, and Chestoa) attest to the historic influence of native tribes on the landscape and history of the region.

Europeans, most of them pioneer farmers, began moving into the High Country as early as the latter half of the 18th century. Some structures from this era remain, like the Brinegar Cabin (Milepost 238.5) and the Caudill Cabin (visible from Bluff Mountain at Milepost 241), but unfortunately when the Parkway was being built emphasis was placed on the natural landscape, not the historic, and many remnants of early Appalachian settlement were torn down.

As you travel the peaceful mountain ridgelines today you may be surprised to know that throughout the 19th century and into the early 20th, the High Country was thriving with industry. Narrow-gauge railroads crisscrossed the mountains, providing access to vast stands of virgin timber, and mining and quarrying operations became the centerpieces of small towns like Spruce Pine and Mount Airy. Much of the industry of the 1800s and early 1900s continues to thrive here, though on a less impactful scale. Mount Airy is still home to the largest granite quarry in the nation, and the 25-mile-long by 10-mile-wide Spruce Pine Mining District still churns out deposits of mica, feldspar, and quartz.

But even as industry boomed here, the High Country also served as a getaway for well-to-do residents of North Carolina's coast and Piedmont areas for much of the latter half of the 19th century and early 20th. Towns like Blowing Rock, Linville, and Little Switzerland became summertime havens, supporting resorts and the second-home "cottages" of the wealthy, many of which still stand today along tree-lined streets in the area's numerous small towns. They were the region's earliest "tourists" and, no doubt, paved the way for the High Country's modern tourism industry.

PLANNING YOUR TIME

While most Blue Ridge Parkway visitors typically spend just a couple of days exploring the High Country region, I recommend devoting at least five days to the area if you have the time. Mount Airy, which is about a 20-minute drive from the Parkway if you exit at Fancy Gap in Virginia, and its environs are worthy of at least a day's exploration. Model for the fictional Mayberry, Mount Airy has several attractions Andy Griffith fans will appreciate, like the mounds of memorabilia at the Andy Griffith Playhouse, and the Main Oak Emporium on Main Street is worth at least an hour or two of browsing and shopping. The surrounding Yadkin Valley has become a destination for wine enthusiasts and has almost two dozen vineyards, while Pilot Mountain (Mount Pilot in *The Andy Griffith Show*) offers opportunities for hiking, fishing, and boating.

This northern stretch of the Parkway in North Carolina between the state line and Blowing Rock is among the loneliest, boasting long stretches with no sign of civilization.

If you're coming to enjoy the roadside show of blooming rhododendron, mountain laurel, and azalea, the best time to visit is usually mid-June through early July. Fall color season, which can vary from one year to the next from late September to the end of October, is the busiest season. Good times to visit to avoid the crowds but still enjoy pleasant weather are early spring and September.

The Boone/Blowing Rock area is the busiest part of the High Country, with several of the Parkway's most popular attractions, including the Parkway Craft Center at Moses H. Cone Memorial Park, the International Biosphere Reserve of Grandfather Mountain, the Linn Cove Viaduct, and Linville Falls. All of these are must-see sights worthy of your time, but be prepared for crowded hiking trails and even traffic jams in the neighboring towns of Boone and Blowing Rock. A winter trip is always an option for those anxious to avoid the crowds, and the Mile-High Swinging Bridge on Grandfather Mountain is quite stunning encrusted in snow and ice, but you may find the Parkway closed if the weather is particularly poor. It is hard to cover all the worthwhile attractions in this area in less than two days. Grandfather Mountain alone is a half-day excursion, and that's if you only hit the highlights.

As far as services and accommodations go, Boone offers a wide array of lodging options to fit any budget and a variety of restaurants, ranging from popular chains to funky downtown eateries populated by the students of Appalachian State University. Those with kids or grandkids in tow should make time for at least a half-day visit to Tweetsie Railroad in Blowing Rock, an amusement park geared toward toddlers and young elementary-age kids. If you're looking for a slower pace and more upscale atmosphere, Blowing Rock is the place to go, as it has several fine bed-and-breakfasts and a number of white-linen-tablecloth dining options. Keep in mind, however, that this region is still largely rural, and the streets typically roll up the carpets about 5 P.M. Restaurants, too, often only serve until 9 P.M., though you will find a few open later when college is in session.

The southern end of the High Country is a bit more peaceful and leaves what we know as the Blue Ridge, heading into the Black Mountains (the highest mountain range east of the Mississippi). Mount Mitchell, at 6,684 feet, is the highlight of this section of the Parkway. It is the highest peak east of the Mississippi River. Even if you only have an hour, head into Mount Mitchell State Park and take the short summit trail to the 360-degree view.

Mount Airy

The model for Mayberry on *The Andy Griffith Show,* this small town is the idyllic American Main Street, with an afternoon's worth of fun shopping and restaurants as well as a number of nearby outdoor recreational opportunities and a wine trail. Mount Airy is Andy Griffith's hometown, a fact on which just about every local business capitalizes. Andy and Barney fans will enjoy the Old City Jail on City Hall Street, a re-creation of the Mayberry courthouse, and visitors can also take a tour of Mount Airy in a 1962 vintage police car.

Mount Airy has another claim to fame,

however. It is home to NC Granite, the world's largest open-face granite quarry, covering some 90 acres. It's so big, in fact, that astronauts can see it from outer space. The granite quarry has been in operation for more than 100 years, and geologists believe it can be worked for another 500, so limitless is its supply of granite. If you pay attention, you may notice that many of Mount Airy's buildings are made of the local white granite speckled in black.

The region around Mount Airy was originally settled by Saura Indians, a tribe of the southern branch of the Sioux. They were here

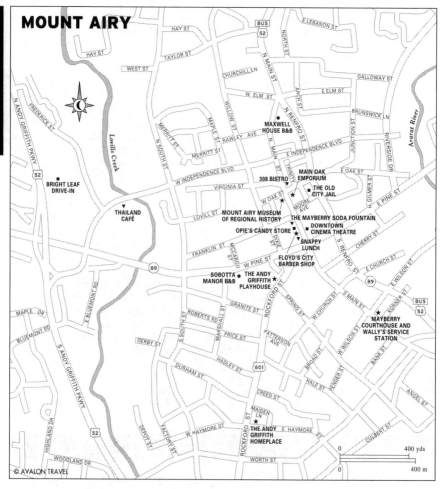

when white explorers and settlers first came to the region but had disappeared as an independent tribe by the end of the 18th century. Joshua Frye and Peter Jefferson, father of Thomas Jefferson, surveyed the region around Mount Airy in 1747. Early settlers called this place "The Hollows" because the valley here is actually a vast circular depression surrounded by mountains, including the Blue Ridge, Pilot Mountain (the model for Mount Pilot in *The Andy Griffith Show*), and the Sauratowns. Even though the town is best known today for its

connection to the fictional Mayberry, it was the coming of the railroad in 1888, and the subsequent spur line to the granite quarry three years later, that first put Mount Airy on the map.

SIGHTS
Mount Airy Museum of Regional History

If you're planning on spending more than a couple of hours in Mount Airy, it's a good idea to visit the Mount Airy Museum of Regional

History (301 N. Main St., 336/786-4478, www.northcarolinamuseum.org, Apr.–Oct. Tues.–Sat. 10 A.M.–4 P.M., Nov.–Mar. Tues.–Fri. 10 A.M.–4 P.M., Sat. 10 A.M.–2 P.M., adults $4, seniors $3, students $2, groups of 10 or more $3). The museum provides an overview of the region's history from the days of the Saura Indians to its modern-day celebrities like Andy Griffith and old-time country music legend Tommy Jarrell, another Mount Airy native son. There are also exhibits on the region's unique topography, the local granite industry, and the Yadkin River that flows through town. Some of the more interesting exhibits here include a replica settler's cabin, 150-year-old barnyard loom, a replica country store, and a model railroad reflecting the communities of the North Carolina Piedmont. Kids will love the antique fire truck exhibit in the museum's basement. It includes Mount Airy's very first fire truck, purchased by the town in 1917.

The museum also contains an exhibit on country songstress and Mount Airy native Donna Fargo as well as a fascinating display on the original Siamese twins, Eng and Chang Bunker, who lived in Surry County from 1837 until their deaths in 1874. The twins married sisters, had 21 children between them, and were both successful farmers and businessmen. They also toured both nationally and internationally and regularly sought medical intervention to separate them, to no avail.

You will find this museum surprisingly crisp and well organized for a small-town history center. Its excellent organization makes it easy to understand the region's history, growth, and development. While here, be sure to climb to the top of the museum's brick clock tower for views of the entire town as well as the surrounding countryside. The museum also has a gift shop, which sells regional books and music as well as some handicrafts and Christmas ornaments.

Floyd's City Barber Shop

Floyd's City Barber Shop (129 N. Main St., 336/786-2346, Mon.–Wed. 7 A.M.–5 P.M., Sat. 7 A.M.–3 P.M., free, unless, of course, you

© FRENCH C. GRIMES

Floyd's City Barber Shop

want a haircut) has a "Wall of Fame," which includes more than 18,000 photographs of tourists, passersby, locals, and even a few celebrities like Oprah Winfrey, all of whom barber Russell Hiatt has coaxed into one of his barber chairs for a picture.

Mayberry Courthouse and Wally's Service Station

The Mayberry Courthouse (625 S. Main St., 336/786-6066, www.wallysserviceatmayberry.com, Mon.–Fri. 9 A.M.–4:30 P.M., Sat. 10 A.M.–3 P.M., free) is a re-creation of the courthouse on *The Andy Griffith Show* and is a popular photo spot in town. Believe it or not, many people hold their weddings here every year. Next door is Wally's Service Station, an original 1937 gas station that served both as a Gulf and Esso station. In addition to being the starting point for squad-car tours of Mount Airy, the station carries candy, sodas, snacks, and gift baskets.

Squad-Car Tours

Die-hard Andy Griffith fans can enjoy a tour of the town in Barney's squad car. The narrated tour begins at Wally's Service Station (625 S. Main St., 336/789-6743, www.tourmayberry.com, Mon.–Fri. 9 A.M.–4:30 P.M., Sat. 10 A.M.–3 P.M., $30 for a "carload" of 5 people) and takes about 20 to 30 minutes, hitting all the highlights of the town, including Andy's Homeplace, Floyd's Barber Shop, the Old City Jail, and the Andy Griffith Playhouse.

The Old City Jail

A re-creation of the courthouse set used in many episodes of *The Andy Griffith Show,* the Old City Jail (215 City Hall St., 800/948-0949, Mon.–Fri. 8 A.M.–4:30 P.M., free) served as Mount Airy's real jail for many years. Today it is the site of the Mayberry Days Proclamation delivered annually by Mount Airy's mayor.

World's Largest Open-Face Granite Quarry

While the "world's largest open-face granite quarry," owned by North Carolina Granite Corporation (Hwy. 103, 336/786-5141, www.ncgranite.com, daily 8 A.M.–5 P.M., free), is not

Wally's Service Station

© FRENCH C. GRIMES

open to the public for tours, you can view the 90-acre quarry from an observation deck. The current quarry is one mile long and one-third mile wide, though the entire granite mass is estimated to be seven by four miles in size.

ENTERTAINMENT AND EVENTS

A typical American small town, Mount Airy tends to close up after dark, with the exception of a few restaurants and local theaters. But that's part of the charm. When the sun goes down, you can take a stroll to the Downtown Cinema for an after-dinner movie for only $3 or see first-run movies at the Bright Leaf Drive-In just outside town. There is plenty of local and live music to be heard around town, particularly in the summer. You will find yourself amazed by the talent of local "pickers" who show up for free jam sessions weekly at both the Andy Griffith Playhouse and the Downtown Cinema.

Music is a major part of Mount Airy's festival scene as well and is the centerpiece of the town's annual Bluegrass and Old-Time Fiddlers Convention, which draws talent from around the Blue Ridge region but particularly from the talent-heavy areas of southwest Virginia (where bluegrass legends like Ralph Stanley and the Carter family got their starts) and northwest North Carolina. Music also plays a central role in Mount Airy's fall Mayberry Days, where the repertoire expands to include Carolina beach music as well as blues and country.

The Andy Griffith Playhouse

The Andy Griffith Playhouse (218 Rockford St., 336/786-7998, www.surryarts.org, Mon.–Fri. 8 A.M.–5 P.M., Sat. 11 A.M.–4 P.M., Sun. 1:30–4:30 P.M., adults $3, children 12 and under free) is a must-see, regardless of whether you're a fan of the *The Andy Griffith Show*. In the basement of the playhouse is the Andy Griffith Museum, where the walls are covered, nearly floor to ceiling, with memorabilia from *The Andy Griffith Show* as well as *Matlock*. The playhouse has the largest collection of Andy Griffith memorabilia in the

world. It was originally started by Griffith's childhood friend Emmett Forrest, who still lives in Mount Airy. In front of the playhouse is a statue of Andy Griffith and co-star Ron Howard, who played Opie.

Also home to the Surry Arts Council, the playhouse hosts local community theater productions and concerts. Every Thursday night at 7 P.M. the playhouse holds bluegrass, gospel, folk, country, and blues jam sessions that are free and open to the public. In summer the Blackmon Amphitheatre across the street holds outdoor concerts and plays on Friday and Saturday nights with entertainment ranging from Carolina beach music with shag and line dancing to the local history drama *Wedding of the Siamese Twins*. On Tuesdays the amphitheater holds a Living Storybook Series for families with small children.

Movie Theaters

The **Downtown Cinema Theatre** (142 N. Main St., 336/786-2222, www.surryarts.org, Wed.–Mon., movies $3) only has one 450-seat theater, but it shows new movies weekly with showtimes on Friday and Saturday at 7 P.M. and 9 P.M., Sunday at 2 P.M. and 7 P.M., Monday at 7 P.M., and Wednesday at 7 P.M. Tourists (and locals, too) flock here on Saturday mornings at 9 A.M. to enjoy free bluegrass jam sessions by local pickers. There's more of the same on Thursday nights at 7 P.M. on the lawn. After the jamming is over on Saturdays, you can linger to enjoy a live airing from the theater of Mount Airy radio WPAQ-AM's *Merry-Go-Round* from 11 A.M. to 1:30 P.M. One of the longest-running live radio programs in the United States, the show features old-time music and bluegrass performed on-stage by local musicians. You can call in advance to find out what is showing from week to week at the theater and also to learn about any upcoming Surry Arts Council concerts.

Located on Highway 52 one mile north of town, the **Bright Leaf Drive-In** (150 N. Andy Griffith Pkwy., 336/786-5494, www.bright-leafdrivein.biz, Fri.–Sun., movies begin at dark, adults $6, children 4–10 $3, 3 years and under free) has been in operation since 1955, and is one of only about 500 drive-in movie theaters left in the United States. Though the theater is open year-round, in warm weather moviegoers tend to gather outside their cars on blankets and lawn chairs and watch movies under the stars. The theater shows first-run double features.

Festivals and Events
BLUEGRASS AND OLD-TIME FIDDLERS CONVENTION
Held annually on the first weekend in June, Mount Airy's Annual Bluegrass and Old-Time Fiddlers Convention (691 W. Lebanon St., 336/345-7388, www.mtairyfiddlersconvention. com, adults $5 per day, children 6 and under free) is actually a contest open to bands and individuals performing old-time and bluegrass music and consists of two days of musicians on fiddles, banjos, mandolins, autoharps, dobros, and other traditional instruments duking it out for prize money while spectators enjoy the show. About 150 bands compete each year. Bring your lawn chairs and picnic blankets for two days of outdoor entertainment. The best part of the convention, however, isn't the formal contests but the individual impromptu jam sessions you'll find in the festival campground at Veteran's Memorial Park.

MAYBERRY DAYS
Occurring annually across four days at the end of September, Mayberry Days (336/786-7998, www.mayberrydays.org) celebrates Mount Airy as the hometown of Andy Griffith and the inspiration for Mayberry. Check out the website or call ahead for specific showtimes and admission to individual concerts and dramas. While events and activities take place all over town, the Andy Griffith Playhouse and Blackmon Amphitheatre host most of the musical and dramatic entertainment, including Carolina beach music and dancing and bluegrass, as well as comedy and old-time country by the VW Boys. The Andy Griffith Playhouse is the best place to spot tribute artists Allan Newsome and David Browning,

who interpret Floyd the barber and Barney, the Mayberry deputy.

Visitors can also participate in a variety of contests, including a checkers tournament, apple-peeling contest, pie-eating competition, and a pork-chop-sandwich-eating competition. There is also a barbecue cook-off, and a variety of vendors and craftspeople set up on the streets around town.

SHOPPING
Mount Airy's downtown isn't as prosperous as you might expect from a town that served as the model for Mayberry and continues to draw Andy Griffith fans, but there are a handful of specialty shops along Main Street as well as the highly popular Main Oak Emporium that will offer at least a couple of hours worth of browsing. You have a fairly small window to do business, however, as most places open late morning and close late afternoon.

Well worth an hour or two of browsing is the three-story **Main Oak Emporium** (245 City Hall St., 336/789-2404, www.mainoakemporium.com, Mon.–Sat. 10 A.M.–5:30 P.M., Sun. 1–5 P.M.), which houses 30,000 square feet of shops carrying toys, handmade gifts, jewelry, kids' clothes, interior decor items, and candy from over 100 vendors. If you want to stock up for outdoor adventures on your Blue Ridge Parkway trip, check out Good Life Outfitters for outdoors gear, clothes, and camping supplies. On the Main Street level is a replica Mayberry Courthouse and Jail. On the 3rd floor is a well-stocked toy and baby section, which carries an extensive menagerie of plush toys, high-end infant clothes, and all the nostalgic toys of yesteryear. The basement level carries cookware; Paula Deen sauces, mixes, and cookbooks; and local wine and chocolates. Free Wi-Fi available.

Barrel candy galore is available for purchase by the pound at **Opie's Candy Store** (135 N. Main St., 336/786-1960, Mon.–Thurs. 10 A.M.–5 P.M., Fri.–Sat. 10 A.M.–6 P.M., Sun. 11 A.M.–4:30 P.M.). You can fill up your basket here for $5.50 a pound with everything from tootsie rolls to gummy cola bottles. The shop also has hand-dipped ice cream, fudge, and glass-bottled sodas as well as regionally produced honey, jams, and jellies for sale.

If you're looking for some Andy Griffith memorabilia to take home as a souvenir, **Specialty Gifts** (140 N. Main St., 800/551-7970, www.mayberrygifts.com, Mon.–Sat. 9 A.M.–5 P.M.) is the place to go. In addition to *The Andy Griffith Show* T-shirts, mugs, DVDs, and books, the store also carries Department 56, Jim Shore, Boyds Bears, and Yankee Candle items.

This is not the kind of store you would expect to find on a "Mayberry" street, but **Froo Froo Pet Boutique** (171 N. Main St., 336/719-6818, www.froofroopetboutique.com, Tues.–Sat. 10 A.M.–6 P.M.) is one of only a few stores in downtown Mount Airy that will let you bring your pooch inside. The store carries gourmet dog snacks, pet clothing for small dogs, chew toys, pet strollers, and even spa-grade grooming products.

The **Meadows of Dan Trading Company** (192 N. Main St., 336/789-5899, Mon.–Sat. 10 A.M.–6 P.M., Sun. noon–5 P.M.) is almost as fun as the Main Oak Emporium, only smaller. This upscale outdoors store carries outdoors clothing for men and women, as well as natural fiber clothing, hiking shoes, Burt's Bees skin care items, sterling silver and gemstone jewelry, and a wide array of rustic home decor items, including unfinished cedar furniture like tables and headboards.

Whether you have kids or not, the **Mount Airy Tractor Company and Toy Land** (195 N. Main St., 336/783-9505, www.mayberrytoyland.com, Mon.–Fri. 9 A.M.–5 P.M., Sat. 9 A.M.–1 P.M.) is worth a visit. Here you'll find all the toys you probably enjoyed as a kid, including a full array of John Deere tractors and farm sets.

A full-service store for toy train collectors, **Dry Bridge Station** (236 N. Main St., 336/786-9811, www.drybridgestation.com, Mon.–Fri. 10 A.M.–6 P.M., Sat. 9 A.M.–5 P.M.) has a working toy steam engine on display that will delight the kids as well as Thomas the Train toys and accessories. The store carries plenty of

gear for adult collectors, too, including trains, tracks, and accessories for all models.

If you enjoy antiquing, there isn't a lot to be had in Mount Airy. One exception is the **Surrey Emporium** (220 N. Main St., 336/786-4398, Mon.–Sat. 10 A.M.–5 P.M.), which carries a wide array of relatively inexpensive antiques and collectibles, including furniture and glassware. The store also carries some local handicrafts.

ACCOMMODATIONS

Mount Airy has a surprisingly wide array of offerings for overnight accommodations, including all the typical chain hotels. But to experience the full flavor of "Mayberry," consider staying in one of the local bed-and-breakfasts. There are also a handful of vacation rentals in the countryside outside town.

Hotels and Motels

Mount Airy has a full array of standard chain hotels, including Best Western, Quality Inn, Hampton Inn, and Microtel Inn and Suites. If you're seeking a lower-budget option with some Mayberry-like 1950s atmosphere, you might consider **The Mayberry Motor Inn** (501 N. Andy Griffith Pkwy., 336/786-4109, www.mayberrymotorinn.com, $55–99), which has a fairly peaceful setting on 10 landscaped acres with 27 simple guest rooms. A 1963 Ford squad car and Emmet's fix-it truck are both parked in the driveway. The motel has free continental breakfast, a swimming pool, and Wi-Fi available to guests. While you're here, check out Aunt Bee's Room, a room decorated in memory of Frances Bavier, who played Aunt Bee on *The Andy Griffith Show*. Loaded with items collected at Bavier's estate sale in 1990, the room is available for viewing by appointment and includes many of the actress's personal items, including a dress, gloves, and eyeglasses.

Bed-and-Breakfasts

The Maxwell House Bed & Breakfast (618 N. Main St., 336/786-2174, www.maxwellhousebb.com, $129–169) is a Queen

Anne–style Victorian home conveniently located on Mount Airy's Main Street. Built in 1901, the home has four rooms, one of them pet friendly. Guests can enjoy afternoon tea, lemonade served on the front porch in summer, evening snacks, and a full breakfast each morning. Some rooms have whirlpool tubs available as well.

Also close to the downtown shopping and dining district is the **Sobotta Manor Bed & Breakfast** (347 W. Pine St., 336/786-2777, www.sobottamanor.com, $139–149). The 1932 Tudor Revival mansion has four guest rooms, including one pet-friendly room, and has several beautiful interior features, including an Italian marble fireplace, 10-foot ceilings throughout the 1st floor, and hand-carved black walnut walls surrounding a curving staircase. Rooms are mostly decorated in Victorian style with heavy walnut and mahogany furniture, plush velvety textiles, and deeply colored wallpaper and rugs. In some rooms you may feel like you're in a cave, so if you prefer a light and sunny space choose Room Two, which faces the street. A shaded side patio offers tables and chairs for relaxing in the evening while overlooking the inn's extensive gardens, first established in 1919. Sobotta Manor has an evening social hour, a very filling gourmet breakfast that might include frittata with garlic cheese bread and even chocolate cake, and free Wi-Fi access. It is also within walking distance of downtown.

Vacation Rentals and Cabins
The Andy Griffith Homeplace (711 E. Haymore St., 336/789-5999, $175) is the place to stay for the die-hard Andy Griffith fan. This small neat home, less than a mile from downtown Mount Airy, was Andy Griffith's childhood home. It is owned and operated by the Mount Airy Hampton Inn. It is decorated in 1930s and '40s style, features many antiques, and has two bedrooms and one bath. Overnight guests can use the Hampton Inn's pool and exercise room.

Large families traveling together might like the **Arnolds Oak Mayberry House** (2412 Wards Gap Rd., 336/786-2223, www.

mayberryvacations.com, $120–155), which has five bedrooms and two full baths. A 1920s Arts and Crafts–style residence, the home has been fully modernized, and one bath features a whirlpool tub. A full kitchen is also available for those who want to cook rather than eat out. Situated on a half-acre lot, the home offers a fair amount of privacy and is only a few minutes' drive from downtown Mount Airy.

Camping
Mayberry Campground (114 Bunker Rd., 336/789-6199, campsite $25, tent site $15) has Wi-Fi and electric, cable, and water and sewer hookups, as well as a bathhouse. There is a 24-by-26-foot picnic shelter with community fire pit, and the campground also has two catch-and-release fishing ponds. The campground also happens to be located at the homeplace of the descendants of the original Siamese twins, Eng and Chang Bunker.

Beech Nut Campground (315 Beech Nut La., 336/320-3802, RV site $40, tent site $30, primitive tent site $25) offers 11 RV sites, 14 tent sites, and 10 primitive tent sites; there's a $25 fee for reservations, with a three-day minimum stay on holiday weekends. Using the campground's three pools, which are open from Memorial to Labor Day, requires an additional charge (children 2 and under free, 3–5 years $4, 6 and up $7). The campground is open with full services from April through October. There are three fishing ponds as well as a volleyball court. Water and electric hookups are available. No alcohol is allowed on-site.

Veterans Memorial Park (691 Lebanon St., 336/786-2236, campsite $20, tent site $5) is not only a campground but an event space. Each June the Annual Fiddlers Convention is held here, and the park is also home to the Surry County Fair in September. Rates may change during special events.

FOOD
Dining in Mount Airy is completely casual. There are no fancy restaurants here, so you can feel comfortable going out in casual clothes. If you're in town on a Monday or Tuesday,

however, you might have a little trouble finding restaurants open for dinner, and almost no place stays open later than 9 P.M.

308 Bistro (308 N. Main St. 336/786-8600, www.308bistro.com, Mon.–Wed. 11 A.M.–3 P.M., Thurs.–Sat. 11 A.M.–3 P.M. and 5–9 P.M., $8–17) serves up mostly pasta, steak, and seafood entrées. My personal favorite is the chicken cacciatore, which is served over spaghetti with mushrooms, green peppers, and onions. For lunch try the Spicy Southwestern Scorcher, which consists of turkey, banana peppers, and pepper jack cheese on a Kaiser roll and topped off with chipotle aioli. Free Wi-Fi available.

Elliott's Main Street Eatery (245 City Hall St., 336/786-2761, www.mainoakemporium.com/elliotts, Mon.–Wed. 11 A.M.–3 P.M., Thurs.–Sat. 11 A.M.–9 P.M., Sun. noon–5 P.M., $2–22) is located on the bottom level of the Main Oak Emporium and has a broad selection of ribs, steaks, burgers, sandwiches, and seafood. There is a decidedly southern streak to the menu, which features fried pickles, fried green beans, and shrimp and grits. If you'd like to try something a little different for an appetizer, order the beer-battered mushrooms.

A local favorite, ◖ **Snappy Lunch** (125 N. Main St., 336/786-4931, www.thesnappylunch.com, Mon.–Wed. and Fri. 6 A.M.–1:45 P.M., Thurs. and Sat. 6 A.M.–1:15 P.M., $1–4) serves tasty pork-chop sandwiches and burgers in minutes (hence the name). Owner Charles Dowell, who manned the grill and cash register at Snappy Lunch for over 50 years, pops in every now and again for a visit. Mr. Dowell was worthy enough to earn mention in an early episode of *The Andy Griffith Show,* and Snappy Lunch was featured on the show on a number of occasions.

The Mayberry Soda Fountain (175 N. Main St., 336/786-4006, www.mayberrysodafountain.com, Mon.–Thurs. 10 A.M.–5 P.M., Fri.–Sat. 10 A.M.–7 P.M., Sun. 1–5 P.M., $2–4) has everything you would expect of an old-time soda fountain, including malts, milkshakes, floats, banana splits, hot-fudge cakes, and, of course, hand-dipped ice cream cones. The

building formerly housed the local drugstore, which was in operation from 1925 to 1990. After it closed, the Mayberry Soda Fountain opened and still uses the drugstore's original 1940s soda fountain.

Outside the downtown area is the reliably good standby **Goobers 52** (458 N. Andy Griffith Pkwy., 336/786-1845, www.goobers52.com, Mon.–Thurs. 11 A.M.–10 P.M., Fri.–Sat. 11 A.M.–11 P.M., Sun. noon–8 P.M., $6–17). You'll know it by the spray-painted VW bus and painted limo out front. For an appetizer, try the Crispy Pickle Chips. One of the best dinner entrées is undoubtedly the Black and Blue: a seven-ounce beef tenderloin covered with caramelized onions and blue cheese. Another good one is the pulled-pork barbecue, which comes with coleslaw, fries, and buttered toast. The restaurant has a colorful atmosphere with blue tiled tables and vinyl booths in yellow, aqua, and blue. The servers here are sprightly, even if the restaurant's floor could use a good scrubbing. The tables are perhaps the cleanest you'll find, as the servers wipe them down with glass cleaner and paper towels instead of the damp dirty rag used at most casual places.

Toward the outskirts of town is **Thailand Café** (647 W. Independence Blvd., 336/786-8480, $8–14). A local favorite, particularly for lunch, the café has an extensive menu of traditional Thai food. Apart from the usual fare like rice, curry, and stir fry, the chef's specialties include mussels with basil, carrots, onions, and peppers, as well as Chicken in a Nest served in an egg-noodle basket with mushrooms, bell peppers, zucchini, cashews, and onions.

INFORMATION AND SERVICES
Information
The **Mount Airy Visitors Center** (200 N. Main St., 800/948-0949, www.visitmayberry.com, Mon.–Fri. 8:30 A.M.–5 P.M., Sat. 10 A.M.–4 P.M., Sun. 1–4 P.M.) is located inside the Chamber of Commerce building in the historic district, appropriately made of locally quarried granite. You can pick up brochures and maps on Mount Airy and the Yadkin

Valley here, and the staff is extremely helpful and eager to answer questions.

Emergency Services

The **Northern Hospital of Surry County** (830 Rockford St., 336/719-7000, www.northernhospital.com) is the only hospital in Mount Airy proper, but it is a full-service facility with 24-hour emergency care.

For non-emergency services, contact the **Mount Airy Police Department** (150 Rockford St., 336/786-3535, www.mountairy.org).

Post Office and Internet Access

Mount Airy has a post office (111 S. Main St., 336/786-2805, Mon.–Fri. 9 A.M.–4:30 P.M.) conveniently located in the downtown historic district.

While most of the hotels in Mount Airy offer free Wi-Fi to guests, you can also gain access to the Internet at the **Mount Airy Public Library** (145 Rockford St., 336/789-5108, www.nwrl.org, Mon.–Thurs. 8:30 A.M.–8 P.M., Fri. 8:30 A.M.–5 P.M., Sat. 10 A.M.–1 P.M.).

GETTING THERE
Air

The closest airport to Mount Airy is **Piedmont Triad International Airport** (GSO, 6415 Bryan Blvd., 336/721-0088, www.flyfrompti.com) in Greensboro, about 60 miles southeast on Route 52 and I-40. The airport is served by Allegiant (www.allegiantair.com), American Eagle (www.aa.com), Continental (www.continental.com), Delta (www.delta.com), United (www.united.com), and US Airways (www.usairways.com).

Another option is the **Roanoke Regional Airport** (ROA, 5202 Aviation Dr. NW, 540/362-1999, www.roanokeairport.com), which is about 105 miles away in Virginia, accessible by taking Route 52 north to I-77 and then I-81. The airport is served by Allegiant (www.allegiantair.com), US Airways (www.usairways.com), United (www.united.com), Northwest (www.nwa.com), and Delta (www.delta.com).

Car

There are a variety of routes into Mount Airy. If you're traveling the Blue Ridge Parkway and plan to take a side trip to Andy Griffith's hometown, then the best option is to exit the Parkway in Virginia at Fancy Gap (Milepost 200) and come into Mount Airy on Route 52 south, which will drop you right into the center of downtown.

If you fly into Roanoke, then the best route is taking I-81 south to where it intersects with I-77 just north of Wytheville. You can then take I-77 to Exit 8, which will put you on Route 52 at Fancy Gap, Virginia, for a drive through scenic countryside to Mount Airy. From Greensboro/Winston-Salem, take I-40 west to its intersection with Route 52 north, and stay on 52 all the way to Mount Airy.

GETTING AROUND
Car Rentals

Piedmont Triad International Airport has car rentals available from Alamo/National (336/665-2542), Avis/Budget (336/665-5700), Enterprise (336/662-0188), Hertz (336/668-7961), and Dollar/Thrift (336/668-3488).

Roanoke Regional Airport has car rentals available from Avis (540/336-2436), Budget (540/265-7328), Enterprise (540/563-8055), Hertz (540/336-3421), and Alamo/National (540/563-5065 or 540/563-5050).

Parking

There are many free public parking lots in Mount Airy, including on the corner of South Main and Cherry Streets next to the post office, the corner of Willow and Franklin Streets behind the Mayberry Soda Fountain and Opie's Candy Store, next to the Old City Jail on the corner of Moore Avenue and City Hall Street, and next to the Old North State Winery on Main Street. There is also a public parking lot located on the outskirts of town at Riverside Park. There is no metered parking in Mount Airy; parking is entirely free!

Yadkin Valley

The Yadkin Valley that surrounds Mount Airy has gained fame in recent years as a wine enthusiast's destination and is actually North Carolina's first federally recognized American Viticultural Area. There are nearly two dozen wineries in the valley, which you can explore as part of the Yadkin Valley Wine Trail. The region, which is subdivided by the lazy Yadkin River, reputed to be one of the world's oldest rivers, is also a great weekend escape for outdoors enthusiasts and is home to several well-maintained and beautiful state parks, including Pilot Mountain State Park, the summit of which was the inspiration for Mount Pilot on *The Andy Griffith Show*.

The Yadkin Valley is actually the western edge of the North Carolina Piedmont, its key feature being rolling farmland bordered by mountains, some of them, like Pilot Mountain and Stone Mountain, standing strangely out of place on an open plain. This was also once a thriving tobacco region, and you'll still see some farms sporting row upon row of the big green curling leaves, but the literally dozens of abandoned often century-old tobacco barns you'll see along the roadside are a reminder that this agricultural industry is not as common and prosperous as it once was.

While Mount Airy is the largest town in the region, the Yadkin Valley has several smaller towns that provide lodging and dining options for visitors touring the local wineries. Among them are Dobson, near Shelton Vineyards, just south of Mount Airy off I-77, and Elkin, which is a little south of Dobson and also accessible directly off the interstate. Both villages are easily accessible from Pilot Mountain via Highway 268.

PILOT MOUNTAIN STATE PARK

Native Americans called Pilot Mountain "Jomeokee," which meant "great guide" or "pilot," and it is easy for visitors to Surry County, which rests on the state line northeast of Winston-Salem, to understand why. Standing like a lonesome sentinel in the relatively flat plain of the North Carolina

© FRENCH C. GRIMES

Pilot Mountain

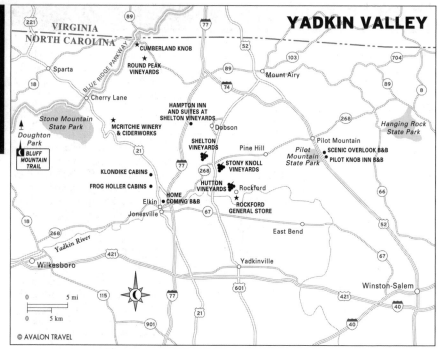

Map: YADKIN VALLEY

© AVALON TRAVEL

Piedmont, Pilot Mountain is indeed an oddity, visible for miles around. Formed of quartzite monadnock that has withstood the weathering of millions of years while surrounding mountains have eroded away into rolling plain, Pilot Mountain is recognizable by its two rock pinnacles jutting skyward out of a lonely forested mountain.

Pilot Mountain State Park (1792 Pilot Knob Park Rd., Pinnacle, 336/325-2355, www.nc-parks.gov, free) is accessible off Highway 52 (soon to become I-74) south of Mount Airy, and the exit for the park is clearly marked. The park covers more than 3,700 acres and consists of two sections, the Mountain Section and the River Section. The two are connected by a 6.6-mile corridor of bridle and hiking trails.

From the exit off Highway 52, a circling road carries visitors into the Mountain Section (Nov.–Feb. daily 8 A.M.–6 P.M., Mar.–Apr. daily 8 A.M.–8 P.M., May–Aug. daily 8 A.M.–9 P.M., Sept.–Oct. daily 8 A.M.–8 P.M., closed Christmas Day) through a low canopy of maples to a high parking area just below the two feature pinnacles. Here you can take a short trek through the woods to the top of Little Pinnacle and enjoy a sweeping view of the Piedmont and distant Hanging Rock, as well as an up-close look at Big Pinnacle, which rises 200 feet from its forested base to a total elevation of 2,421 feet. You will likely see hawks soaring around the knob. In fall, bird-watchers visit to see the park's 13 species of raptors, the most common of which is the broad-winged hawk.

If you're interested in rock climbing at the park, you can download a Pilot Mountain climbing guide from the Carolina Climbers Coalition website (www.carolinaclimbers.org), but you must register at the park office before doing any rappelling.

To reach the River Section (north side:

Nov.–Feb. daily 8:30 A.M.–5 P.M., Mar.–May daily 8:30 A.M.–7 P.M., June–Aug. daily 8:30 A.M.–8 P.M., Sept.–Oct. daily 8:30 A.M.–7 P.M.; south side: Nov.–Feb. daily 8:30 A.M.–4:30 P.M., Mar.–May daily 8:30 A.M.–6:30 P.M., June–Aug. daily 8:30 A.M.–7:30 P.M., Sept.–Oct. daily 8:30 A.M.–6:30 P.M.) by automobile, take the Pinnacle exit off Highway 52 and follow the signs to Horne Creek Living Historical Farm. The entrance to the Yadkin River section of the park is a quarter mile past the farm. Be advised that the road into the River Section is dirt and will require you to ford streams. If you plan on horseback riding in this section of the park, parking for horse trailers is one-tenth of a mile past the River Section park entrance.

Both sections have facilities, including picnic areas and restrooms, though the River Section restrooms are primitive. There is no running water.

Hiking
JOMEOKEE TRAIL

- Distance: 0.8 mile round-trip

- Duration: 45 minutes

- Elevation gain: None

- Difficulty: Easy

- Trailhead: Accessible off the Little Pinnacle overlook trail

Just off the Little Pinnacle overlook trail, you can continue your trek on the Jomeokee Trail, a level hike that circles the base of Big Pinnacle. The trail crosses the gap between Little and Big Pinnacle, then loops around the base of Big Pinnacle's knob. The trail puts you within touching distance of this odd stone spire, which bears the lava-like ripples and crevices of stone cut by countless generations of water and wear. You might even get a glimpse of a rock climber or two making their way up the vertical surface of the spire. If you're hiking in late spring, you'll likely see Catawba rhododendron and mountain laurel in bloom along the trail. The loop circles the entire base of the pinnacle, then returns to the Little Pinnacle via the same trail.

Boating
To the south of the pinnacles is the state park's southern section, known as River Section North. Here the Yadkin River Trail offers a peaceful hike, just below the railroad tracks, along the wide and lazy Yadkin, which many visitors enjoy for boating and fishing. Dogwoods, hickories, and beech trees line the river, and if you're lucky you might spot a bald eagle fishing the river, as well as loads of bright-winged butterflies, and blue-tailed skinks in summer and early fall.

Slow-moving and peaceful, the Yadkin is a great spot for canoeing if you're looking for a leisurely float, and Pilot Mountain State Park holds two miles of the 165-mile Yadkin River Canoe Trail. You'll have to bring your own boat or seek the assistance of a local outfitter if you'd like to paddle the river, however, as there are no canoe rentals available at the park. **Yadkin River Adventures** (104 Old Rockford Rd., Rockford, 336/374-5318, www.yadkinriveradventures.com), based in Rockford, offers half- and full-day trips on the river in kayak or canoe with shuttle service. They also provide shuttle service to paddlers with their own boats. The larger of two islands in the river located within park boundaries offers primitive campsites.

STONE MOUNTAIN STATE PARK
Named for the 600-foot granite dome that dominates the park, Stone Mountain State Park (3042 Frank Pkwy., Roaring Gap, 336/957-8185, www.ncparks.gov, May–Aug. daily 8 A.M.–9 P.M., Mar.–Apr. and Sept.–Oct. daily 8 A.M.–8 P.M., Nov.–Feb. daily 8 A.M.–6 P.M., closed Christmas Day, free) is another of the Yadkin Valley's many geological oddities. While the granite dome is not visible from the park entrance, it is visible from various points along the Blue Ridge Parkway. The Parkway really offers the best vantage point, but Stone Mountain State Park is still worth a visit if you're making

© FRENCH C. GRIMES

Garden Creek Baptist Church in Stone Mountain State Park

a leisurely trip. Covering over 14,000 acres, the park has more than 18 miles of hiking trails and over 20 miles of designated trout waters, making it a perfect afternoon stopover for avid anglers. As at Pilot Mountain, rock climbers are welcome here but must register with the park office before rappelling.

If you only have an hour or so, stop by the park visitors center, which is to the right as you enter the park. The visitors center has exhibits on local Appalachian culture and history, including both a handmade loom and a confiscated still. Through much of the 20th century, Wilkes County was known as the "moonshine capital of the world." But whiskey's history in the area is far longer. Farmers began making it more than 200 years ago because it was more portable than the corn from which it is made and, thus, more easy to transport to market. Many people don't realize that stock car racing actually grew out of the illegal moonshine industry when young men would "run moonshine" up and down the mountain roads. Wilkes County native Junior Johnson started his racing career as a moonshine hauler.

After leaving the visitors center, where there are also public restrooms and vending machines, take the park's loop road, which curls around the base of Stone Mountain, offering some occasional but limited views of the granite dome. There are several good fishing streams easily accessible from the loop road, and keep an eye out for some of the park's historic structures as well like the 1837 Garden Creek Baptist Church.

YADKIN VALLEY WINE TRAIL

The region around Mount Airy has become a popular destination for wine connoisseurs. In fact, the Yadkin Valley is home to 32 wineries, all of which are part of the Yadkin Valley Wine Trail (336/325-0918, www.yvwt.com). The Wine Trail traverses six counties extending from the North Carolina state line, west to the Parkway, east to Winston-Salem, and south to Yadkinville. The landscape is rolling and the soil rocky—unsurprisingly, much like the environment of southern Europe.

Round Peak Vineyards

Round Peak Vineyards (765 Round Peak Church Rd., Mount Airy, 336/352-5595, www.roundpeak.com, Sun.–Fri. 8 A.M.–5 P.M., Sat. 11 A.M.–6 P.M., wine tasting $5) is located southwest of Mount Airy and is the closest vineyard to the Blue Ridge Parkway. You can access it directly from the Parkway at the exit for Route 89 just south of Low Gap; go 1.4 miles east. Round Peak has 12 acres of vineyard producing chardonnay, merlot, cabernet franc, cabernet sauvignon, nebbiolo, and sangiovese grapes. Round Peak's wines are all made from locally produced grapes. If you happen to hit the vineyard at the right time, you might get an extra treat—the winery often hosts craft exhibits in the tasting room, and local musicians often play live music for patrons. There is regular musical entertainment on Saturday evenings in the summer.

McRitchie Winery & Ciderworks

Another winery that's easily accessible off the Blue Ridge Parkway is McRitchie Winery

& Ciderworks (315 Thurmond PO Rd., Thurmond, 336/874-3003, www.mcritchiewine. com, Thurs.–Sun. noon–5 P.M., wine tasting $5). To get here, take Route 21 south off the Parkway at Roaring Gap and go six miles. The winery is just 10 minutes from Stone Mountain State Park, so you might want to visit the park as well while you're in the area. Operated by three generations of the same family, McRitchie not only offers wine but also hard cider from locally grown apples. McRitchie is the only North Carolina winery that does a hard cider from mountain apples. The winery also has walking paths and a picnic facility.

Stony Knoll Vineyards

Near Dobson, Stony Knoll Vineyards (1143 Stony Knoll Rd., Dobson, 336/374-5752, www.stonyknollvineyards.com, Jan.–Feb. Fri. noon–5 P.M., Sat. 10 A.M.–6 P.M., Mar.–Dec. Thurs.–Sat. and Mon. 10 A.M.–6 P.M., wine tasting $5) is located on a farm that has been in the Coe family since 1896. The farm's staple crop through most of its history has been

tobacco. The Coe family harvested its first grapes in 2002, and currently grows chardonnay, syrah, cabernet sauvignon, and cabernet franc grapes.

Hutton Vineyards

If you've decided to visit Rockford, then you might as well take a quick jaunt to Hutton Vineyards (176 Hutton Vineyards La., Dobson, 336/374-2621, www.huttonwinery.com, open by appointment, red *or* white wine tasting $6, red *and* white tasting $8) while you're in the area, as it's only 1.5 miles from the historic village off Rockford Road. This winery, which is one of the newest in the Yadkin Valley wine region, has 45 acres of grapes and 30 acres of pasture and offers five red wines and five white wines. Be sure to call ahead of time, as the winery is open only by appointment.

Shelton Vineyards

If you visit no other winery in the Yadkin Valley, be sure to visit Shelton Vineyards (286 Cabernet La., Dobson, 336/366-4724,

© FRENCH C. GRIMES

Shelton Vineyards

www.sheltonvineyards.com, Mon.–Sat. 10 A.M.–6 P.M., Sun. 1–6 P.M., tour and tasting $5). Easily accessible off I-77 north of Dobson, it is North Carolina's largest family-owned estate winery and is a destination unto itself. Winery tours depart every half hour and provide an overview of the Sheltons' 33,000-square-foot winery as well as a tasting of five wines. Make sure to ask to take the tour, as the staff doesn't always advise visitors that the tasting includes a tour. Be sure to try the Yadkin Valley Riesling, fruity and crisp (and one of my favorite North Carolina wines) with just a hint of sparkle. During the summer, the winery holds monthly evening concerts on its outdoor stage, with musical styles ranging from beach to swing. Check the website for concert dates and ticket prices. The vineyard also has a series of walking trails, picnic areas (with picnic supplies available in the wine store), and a lovely lake. In October, Shelton Vineyards hosts a Harvest Festival, offering free tours and tastings, arts and crafts vendors, live music, and an antique tractor show. The winery also has its own restaurant, the Harvest Grill, and a Hampton Inn and Suites (with a wine bar) on-site.

ROCKFORD GENERAL STORE AND VILLAGE

Worth a quick side trip is the Rockford General Store and Village (5417 Rockford Rd., Rockford, 336/374-5317, Mon. 10 A.M.–5 P.M., Wed.–Fri.10 A.M.–5 P.M., Sat. 10 A.M.–6 P.M., Sun. 1–6 P.M.), which is located about 20 miles south of Mount Airy. (From Highway 602 in Dobson, turn west onto Rockford Road, and go 3.5 miles to the light at Route 268. Go straight across 268, and drive 0.7 mile. Just across the Fisher River Bridge, turn right. You are still traveling on Rockford Road. Go 5.6 miles, and you will see Rockford General Store on the right.) This almost-deserted former railroad town was the county seat of Surry County from 1789 to 1853. Today not much of the village remains, but the town's signature general store is still operational. It has been open since about 1890. Among the goodies here are loads of barrel candy, Christmas ornaments, an assortment of antiques, and roasted peanuts. This old-time store with its sloping front porch, tin overhang, and white clapboard siding also serves hand-dipped ice cream and oozing delicious fried apple pies. The store has public restrooms with sinks made to look like hand pumps and tin wash basins.

Across the street in Rockford Park are the ruins of the old **Grant Burrus Hotel,** built in 1796. Local legend holds that Andrew Johnson once slept here. And just down the street at the **Rockford Methodist Church** is a fresco of Christ behind the altar. The church can be toured by appointment only (336/374-3825). If you're in town on a weekend, you can also visit the **Rockford Mercantile** (5160 Rockford Rd., Rockford, 336/374-2255, www.rockfordmercantile.com, Sat. 10 A.M.–5 P.M., Sun. 1–5 P.M.), which has a photo gallery of historic images of the town as well as a store with books on regional history, games, puzzles, and Christmas ornaments.

ENTERTAINMENT AND EVENTS
Yadkin Valley Wine Festival

The Yadkin Valley Wine Festival (Hwy. 268, Elkin, 336/526-1111, www.yvwf.com, 11 A.M.–6 P.M., $16 in advance, $20 at the gate) is a one-day event held on the third Saturday in May at the Elkin Municipal Park. In addition to tastings of area wines, the event also features area craft vendors and live musicians as well as a grape stomp for guests. Food and non-wine beverages are available for purchase. Attendees are welcome to bring a blanket for seating to enjoy the outdoor concerts. Pets are not permitted.

Fourth Fridays

During the summer months, historic downtown Elkin hosts Fourth Fridays (Main St., Elkin, 336/835-9800, June–Sept., fourth Fri. of each month 5–10 P.M.) with live music from local bands, extended hours at downtown shops, and children's activities. The event takes

© FRENCH C. GRIMES

Rockford General Store in Rockford

place between Wachovia bank and the Reeves Theater on Main Street.

ACCOMMODATIONS
Hotels, Inns, and Bed-and-Breakfasts
PILOT MOUNTAIN

If you want to enjoy the finest views around of Pilot Mountain, then spend the night at **Scenic Overlook Bed and Breakfast** (271 Scenic Overlook La., Pinnacle, 336/368-9591, www.scenicoverlook.com, $149–169) adjoining Pilot Mountain State Park. Situated next to a large pond on which guests are welcome to paddle, Scenic Overlook is appropriately named, offering breathtaking sunrise views of Pilot Knob that turn the forest-tufted quartzite pinnacle to colors of marshmallow pink. Scenic Overlook also offers some of the best southern hospitality you'll find on this trip, even though the longtime innkeepers are actually natives of Long Island. Rooms here are sumptuous, decorated with Tiffany lamps, reproduction antiques, and, best of all, private tables for in-room breakfasts, robes and slippers required.

Additional luxuries include whirlpool tubs and bedside chocolates.

To truly experience the culture of North Carolina's Yadkin Valley, consider staying the night in a restored tobacco barn similar to the many you will pass, long abandoned and often leaning close to earth, in the golden fields of Surry County. The **Pilot Knob Inn Bed and Breakfast** (361 New Pilot Knob La., Pilot Mountain, 336/325-2502, www.pilot-knobinn.com, suites $129–249, tobacco barn cabins $129–199) has five traditional rooms as well as seven restored tobacco barns, all of them original, that have been converted into private, rustic sleeping quarters. Some of them have fireplaces and whirlpool baths, and there is nothing quite like nestling under quilts in the loft bedrooms with rain tapping against old tin roofs and a fire crackling in the living room below.

DOBSON

The **Hampton Inn and Suites at Shelton Vineyards** (150 Charlestowne Dr., 336/353-9400, www.dobsonsuites.hamptoninn.com,

$104–164) is unique among chain hotels due to its affiliation with Shelton Vineyards. The hotel has a wine bar operated by the winery, and its 102 rooms are easily accessible off I-77 at Exit 93. It was recently ranked as the second-best Hampton Inn and Suites hotel in the world. The hotel has whirlpool suites, a heated pool, and exercise facilities. All rooms feature microwaves, refrigerators, and pillow-top mattresses. Breakfast and high-speed Internet access are free. If you're in a rush, the hotel even offers breakfast to go Monday through Friday.

ELKIN
Home Coming Bed and Breakfast (608 N. Bridge St., 336/526-7770, www.homecominghouse.com, $109–129) is located right in town and has three Victorian-style suites available. On arrival, guests can enjoy a lovely afternoon spread in the dining room, including fresh fruit, bottled water, soft drinks, coffee, snacks, and candies. Guests also enjoy a full breakfast and free Wi-Fi access.

Cabins
If you're seeking seclusion while visiting the Yadkin Valley wine country, then **Frog Holler Cabins** (564 E. Walker Rd., 336/526-2661 or 336/835-2578, www.froghollercabins.com, $95–125) outside of Elkin is the place to go. About 15 minutes from Stone Mountain State Park, Frog Holler has three cabins available, all of them situated in the woods and two of them overlooking Big Elkin Creek. The cabins all feature private decks with hot tubs as well as gas log fireplaces available in the colder months. Each cabin has one bedroom, though they each feature a sleeper sofa as well so they can accommodate up to four people. Though they're listed as having fully equipped kitchens so you can do your own cooking, the selection of kitchen tools is pretty slim, so don't count on doing much more than throwing a frozen pizza in the oven. All of the rentals have clean, comfortable accommodations, however, and are ideal for romantic getaways. Bathrooms have showers, no tubs.

Klondike Cabins (Chatham Lodge La. off Klondike Rd., 336/835-4230, www.grassycreekvineyard.com, The Playhouse $150–200, Hanes Cottage $200–250, Main Log Cabin $600–700, total Klondike Cabins complex $1,000–1,200) offers three cabins at the Grassy Creek Vineyard on 100 peaceful acres, just outside Elkin. The cabins date to the 1920s and earlier, when John Hanes of Hanes hosiery bought a small cabin and 1,000 acres of land. Today you can stay in these well-appointed cabins and still see antiques, artwork, and other memorabilia that transport you back to the early part of the 20th century.

Camping
Pilot Mountain State Park (1792 Pilot Knob Rd., Pinnacle, 336/325-2355, www.ncparks.gov, Mar. 15–Nov. 30, $18, senior rate $13) has 49 campsites available for tents or trailers and also hosts a variety of evening educational programs for campers. The park always has campsites available but recommends that visitors reserve campsites by calling 877/722-6762 or make reservations online at www.nc.reserveworld.com. There are two bathhouses available as well as spigots for drinking water staggered every four to five sites. There are no hookups for water or electrical, and there is no dump station. Firewood is available from the campground host for a fee.

Jomeokee Campground (1140 Pace's Pl., 336/325-2296, www.jomeokee.net, Apr.–Nov., $20) is located in Pinnacle at the foot of Pilot Mountain and has tent camping as well as 75 RV hookups, water, electric, and dump sites. There are fire pits, a bathhouse, a pond for fishing, and places for bike riding. The campground also has LP gas for sale.

FOOD
Pilot Mountain
It can be difficult to find a restaurant open for dinner, other than the standard fast-food chains, in Pilot Mountain on a weeknight. One exception, however, is **Aunt Bea's** (642 S. Key St., 336/368-2300, daily 6 A.M.–10 P.M., $5–6), one of only a handful of sit-

down restaurants open seven days a week. In addition to their signature barbecue, which you can get with a hickory smoked sauce or a hot-and-tangy sauce, they have burgers and chicken sandwiches. You can also get some pretty good barbecue sandwiches at **Smokin' D's Grill** (711 Old Hwy. 52 Bypass, 336/368-3293, Mon.–Fri. 5:30 A.M.–8:30 P.M., Sat. 6:30 A.M.–8:30 P.M., $2–12) as well as cheeseburgers, some deadly-but-delicious deep-fried homemade chips, buffalo wings, club sandwiches, hamburger steak, and a variety of ice cream desserts.

Dobson Area

The **Harvest Grill at Shelton Vineyards** (230 Cabernet La., 336/366-3590, www.sheltonvineyards.com, Mon.–Thurs. 11 A.M.–9 P.M., Fri.–Sat. 11 A.M.–10 P.M., Sun. 11 A.M.–6 P.M., $18–36) is located right next door to the winery and serves upscale southern comfort food based around local ingredients, many of them straight from the kitchen garden adjacent to the restaurant. Try the brown sugar–brined grilled pork chops, served with a blackberry demi-glace and white-cheddar grits on the side. Dessert is a new experience for the palate, too, with choices like balsamic-marinated strawberries with blackberry cabernet sorbet. The restaurant offers an afternoon tasting menu Monday–Saturday from 3 to 5 P.M. Seating options include an outdoor patio with fireplace overlooking the vineyard and kitchen garden.

Elkin

Twenty-One and Main Restaurant & Wine Bar (102 E. Main St., 336/835-6246, www.twentyoneandmain.com, Tues.–Sat. 5:30–9 or 10 P.M., $11–25) is easily the best place to eat in town. With its intimate brick-walled dining room, Twenty-One and Main has a laid-back elegance. The dinner menu is small but southern. Try the shrimp and grits, which are served with smoked bacon and caramelized onion and flavored with garlic and tomato. Another good option is the maple-glazed pork loin, equal parts salty, sweet, and tangy. The restaurant's

wine list is what really makes it special. The wine bar has an incredible selection of wines from around the world as well as a fine sampling of local wines from the Yadkin Valley.

Diana's Bookstore and Coffee Shop (127 W. Main St., 336/835-3142, Mon.–Fri. 9:30 A.M.–5:30 P.M., Sat. 10 A.M.–4 P.M.) is a great place to pick up a cup of coffee and a good book, prices ranging from $1.50 to $50. Smoothies and biscotti are also served and Wi-Fi is available for customers.

Royall's Soda Shoppe (128 W. Main St., 336/835-3412, www.royallssodashoppe.com, Mon.–Fri. 9 A.M.–5 P.M., Sat. 9 A.M.–3 P.M., $2–8) is a good place to stop for lunch, particularly if you're a hot dog lover. For $1.75 you can get a hot dog loaded with mustard, coleslaw, chili, and onions, plus your choice of cheese. In addition to hot dogs, they also have a delicious homemade chicken salad and a classic southern favorite, chicken and egg salad with pimento cheese. You can also get hand-dipped ice cream cones and creamy old-time milkshakes.

Mazzini's (1521 N. Bridge St., 336/526-7400, Mon.–Thurs. 10 A.M.–9 P.M., Fri.–Sun. 10 A.M.–10 P.M., $5–11) is located outside the downtown area and serves up typical Italian fare like pizza and pasta but also traditional entrées like chopped steak. Portions are massive, and two can easily eat from one plate. If you're not worried about your cholesterol, be sure to order a plate of their Pizza Fries smothered in bacon, cheese, and ranch dressing.

INFORMATION AND SERVICES

The **Yadkin Valley Visitors Center** (116 E. Market St., Elkin, 877/728-6798, www.visit-theyadkinvalley.com, Mon.–Fri. 9 A.M.–5 P.M.) is easily accessible off I-77, Exit 82, or off Highway 21, which intersects the Blue Ridge Parkway at Roaring Gap near Milepost 229. The **Jonesville Welcome Center** (1503 NC 67, 336/835-2000, Mon.–Sat. 8:30 A.M.–8 P.M., Sun. 1–8 P.M.) is situated right next door to Elkin in the town of Jonesville, also readily accessible from I-77 via Exit 82.

GETTING THERE AND AROUND

The Yadkin Valley is spread across six counties, but if you're interested in touring the area directly adjacent to the Parkway you'll likely stick to Surry and Wilkes Counties. Both counties are most easily reached via I-77, which runs right through the middle of the region and provides simple access from both Charlotte, about 100 miles to the south, and the I-81 corridor in Virginia, about 40 miles to the north.

If you're already in Mount Airy, the best route for touring the Yadkin Valley is to take Highway 601 south toward Dobson. If you want to exit the Blue Ridge Parkway to reach the valley, then the best routes off the Parkway are Highway 21 south (Milepost 229) or Highway 421 east (Milepost 276.4), both of which will take you to the I-77 corridor that bisects the region.

Cumberland Knob to Deep Gap

The northern section of the Blue Ridge Parkway in North Carolina has a splendidly lonesome feel. Between Cumberland Knob (at Milepost 217.5) and Doughton Park (at Milepost 241.1), you'll start climbing into the taller mountains of western North Carolina, quite a contrast from the Parkway in southwestern Virginia. Here high-elevation meadows offer rolling blue vistas on either side of the Parkway.

The communities along this stretch are small and sparse, making for long-distance views uninterrupted by marks of civilization. There are a number of short hikes along this stretch that provide access to nice views as well as several longer treks for experienced hikers. Surrounding towns are small but rich with character, hosting everything from Friday-night bluegrass jamborees to stunning religious frescoes.

CUMBERLAND KNOB

Cumberland Knob (Milepost 217.5) was the first recreational area constructed on the Blue Ridge Parkway by the Civilian Conservation Corps (CCC) and was completed in 1937. The Cumberland Knob visitors center is no longer open, but there is still a nice picnic area as well as a large grassy area where families often gather to play baseball and Frisbee on summer weekends.

Hiking
CUMBERLAND KNOB TRAIL

- Distance: 0.6 mile round-trip
- Duration: 20 minutes
- Elevation gain: 100 feet
- Difficulty: Easy
- Trailhead: Located adjacent to the picnic area, the trail uses a portion of the Gully Creek Trail.

If all you want is a leg stretcher, this is the perfect hike. The trail begins in the woods near the picnic area and passes through a tunnel of flame azalea and rhododendron, which you'll see in full bloom if traveling in late spring or early summer. By late summer, you may see wild blueberries along the trail. After walking about a third of a mile, you'll come to a shelter. There was once a view here, but trees have grown up over the years, making it little more than a clearing where you might enjoy a quiet picnic. Bear left off the Gully Creek Trail and continue on the Cumberland Knob Trail to make a loop back to the picnic area.

FOX HUNTER'S PARADISE TRAIL

- Distance: 0.2 mile round-trip
- Duration: 10 minutes
- Elevation gain: None

- Difficulty: Easy
- Trailhead: Marked at the Cumberland Knob Picnic Area

This shady leg-stretcher follows a paved path suitable for wheelchairs and strollers. It heads through the forest to a walled overlook where you can enjoy long-distance views of the Blue Ridge foothills. Legend has it that this spur ridge (the very ridge on which you'll be walking) once hosted fox hunters who waited here, listening for their hounds.

DOUGHTON PARK

The 6,000-acre Doughton Park area is one of the best wildlife-viewing places along the Parkway, with its high-elevation meadows that draw white-tailed deer by the dozens in early morning and just before sunset. It is not uncommon to catch a passing glimpse of a red fox or even a bobcat on this open ridgeline dominated by the summit of Bluff Mountain (3,792 ft.).

The park is named after Alleghany County native Robert Lee Doughton, a longtime advocate of the establishment of the Blue Ridge Parkway and a member of the U.S. House of Representatives from 1911 through 1953. He was also chairman of the House Ways and Means Committee for 18 of those years.

The landscape of Doughton Park is reminiscent of the European American settlers who once called this region home. The National Park Service continues to maintain open meadow and grazing land on the slopes of Bluff Mountain, creating an environment not so far removed from the cleared land of mountain farmers at the turn of the 20th century. Houses are beginning to pop up on the ridgelines to the northwest, spoiling some of the scenery here, but the views to the south and east, where the Park Service owns land down to the valley floor, remain long and lovely. As you pause to take in the views from the numerous scenic overlooks, watch for the naked round face of Stone Mountain to the east.

Brinegar Cabin

Among the remnants of human habitation along the Parkway is the Brinegar Cabin, at Milepost 238.5, an early-20th-century Appalachian farmstead. Peek in the cabin window for a look at Caroline Brinegar's century-old loom, and then take a walk down the hill to the springhouse where the Brinegars' spring is still active. While the cabin itself stands in

© FRENCH C. GRIMES

views of the North Carolina Piedmont from the Parkway south of Cumberland Knob

shadow most of the day, protected by forest and slope from winter winds, the overlook adjacent to the cabin provides long-distance views of the Blue Ridge Mountains to the north as well as the North Carolina Piedmont, including the smooth granite face of Stone Mountain.

The cabin was once part of a 125-acre farm purchased by Martin Brinegar in 1876 for $200. Two years later he married Caroline, who was sixteen. The two had four children together. Besides farming, Martin also made shoes, served as justice of the peace, and offered services as a notary public. He died of pneumonia in 1925. His widow sold the farm to the state of North Carolina for incorporation into the Blue Ridge Parkway in 1935. Caroline was given lifetime rights to the property, but she moved away shortly after the park's establishment, claiming the place had become too "noisy."

In peak season on Friday, Saturday, and Sunday from 10 A.M. to 4 P.M., there is an interpretive park ranger at the Brinegar Cabin, who offers presentations on the farm garden where buckwheat, cabbage, corn, and flax grow. Volunteers also demonstrate weaving. The first weekend in August, the cabin site hosts Brinegar Days with cultural demonstrations of quilting, blacksmithing, open-hearth cooking, weaving, natural dyeing, and woodworking as well as shaped-note singing. For more information, call the Doughton Park office at 336/372-1947. The office is seasonal, open May–October.

Hiking
C BLUFF MOUNTAIN TRAIL

- Distance: 7.5 miles one-way

- Duration: 4–5 hours (with a car shuttle from one end to the other)

- Elevation gain: 320 feet

- Difficulty: Moderate

- Trailhead: There are several places to access the trail, including the overlook at Brinegar Cabin (Milepost 238.5); the Doughton Park picnic area, campground, and coffee shop

garden at Brinegar Cabin in Doughton Park

© FRENCH C. GRIMES

(Milepost 241); and the Basin Cove Overlook (Milepost 244.7).

The parking area at Brinegar Cabin is a good place to access the Bluff Mountain Trail, which parallels the Parkway and offers almost constant open-meadow views of the surrounding mountains. From Brinegar Cabin, the trail passes through dense pine forest, so impenetrable that it blocks the sound of passing cars and dampens the forest with silence. The hike itself is mostly level and, since it is accessible from several overlooks and parking areas in the Doughton Park area, you don't have to hike the entire length to enjoy the views.

After about half a mile the trail opens into a meadow, where you'll cross your first fence stile before passing through the campground (where water and restrooms are available). After you leave the campground area, you'll cross the Parkway after roughly two miles of walking. This is one of the lovelier stretches along the trail as you gain your first view of mountain summits stretching as endlessly as the waves of the ocean. You'll walk through an open meadow scattered with boulders, paralleling a fence line, cross over another overlook parking area, and then descend toward the Doughton Park Coffee Shop (Milepost 241), offering a chance for refreshment and restrooms.

As you leave the coffee shop area watch closely, as the trail is not as clearly marked as it ascends into beautiful woods loaded with rhododendron (which in June and early July are likely to be laden with white and pink blossoms). When you reach the picnic area, bear to the right and follow the trail up above the picnic tables toward the summit of Bluff Mountain. Here the trail is wide and sunny, crossing a broad meadow, which, in early summer, will likely be alive with wildflowers. At the summit, roughly 3.5 miles into your trek, you'll enjoy more long-distance views across the Blue Ridge and down into the cove of Grassy Gap.

If you choose to continue beyond the summit, you'll enjoy ever-increasing views as you ascend a rough cliff overlooking the steep walls of Cove Creek Valley and then descend through wooded switchbacks. As you near the last half mile of the trail and approach the meadows above Basin Cove, you'll continue to experience stunning vistas, with the final one coming at the Basin Cove Overlook (Milepost 244.7), which provides a view of the barren granite face of Stone Mountain.

WILDCAT ROCKS OVERLOOK

- Distance: 0.1 mile round-trip
- Duration: 5 minutes
- Elevation gain: None
- Difficulty: Easy
- Trailhead: Far end of Bluffs Lodge upper parking area

A quick leg-stretcher loop, this walk will take you to an overlook where you can see the deep hollow of Basin Creek Cove and the tiny one-room Caudill Cabin, where Martin and Jamie Caudill raised 14 children, 1,500 feet below. Martin's father, Harrison Caudill, was pretty prolific with regard to offspring as well, having fathered 22 children. He lived one mile downstream from Martin, though his house is no longer standing.

FODDER STACK TRAIL

- Distance: 2 miles round-trip
- Duration: 45 minutes
- Elevation gain: None
- Difficulty: Moderate
- Trailhead: Far end of Bluffs Lodge upper parking area

If you're an early riser, this is a perfect just-before-dawn hike, as there are numerous benches along the way and occasional open views to the east. Just to the left of Wildcat Rocks overlook, you can access the Fodder Stack Trail, which starts out paved but begins to descend steeply along a poorly maintained path as it follows the edge of Bluff Cliffs. The trail levels out in a cave of arching rhododendron, then descends again into a forest of hardwoods and ferns. If you look to your right you'll notice a near-vertical slope of lush green lady fern in spring and summer. The trail offers frequent glimpses of wildflowers in spring.

After you've hiked just over a quarter mile, the trail will curl around a boulder mass to the right and then open for a lovely view of Basin Creek Cove and Bluffs Cliffs to your right. The trail then climbs again, this time through thick spruce forest, which deadens the sounds of vehicle traffic from the nearby Parkway. You'll follow some natural stone steps through woods of stunted fir trees, take a quick switchback, and come out on a knoll with views in two directions—one to the mowed meadows of Bluff Mountain on the right and the other of Wildcat Rocks in front of you.

The trail will descend slightly before curling around Fodder Stack, where you can pause on a bench to rest and perhaps pick a few blueberries (if you're here in late July) before making a brief rock scramble to loop back to the trail on which you started, returning to the parking area on the same trail.

BASIN CREEK TRAIL

- Distance: 3.3 miles one-way (though it requires a 1.7-mile hike along Grassy Gap Fire Road to reach the trailhead, making it a 10-mile round-trip hike)

- Duration: 6 hours

- Elevation gain: 700 feet

- Difficulty: Strenuous

- Trailhead: Accessible via the primitive campsite on the Grassy Gap Fire Road, reached by taking Route 18 off the Parkway just past Milepost 245 toward North Wilkesboro for 6.2 miles, then a left onto Route 1728 (Longbottom Rd.), which you will follow for seven miles. After crossing a bridge, the trail parking area will be to your right, and the trailheads for the Doughton Park backcountry are across the road. There are three trail-

Basin Creek along the Basin Creek Trail in Doughton Park

© FRENCH C. GRIMES

heads here, so be sure to stay on the Grassy Gap Fire Road all the way to the Basin Creek trailhead.

The Basin Creek Trail is a bit of a trial to reach, but it's well worth the effort. A lightly traveled trail, it leads into the backcountry beneath the Parkway and also provides seldom seen glimpses into Appalachian life before the creation of this great American roadway. While the hike offers a gradual uphill climb, it involves more than 30 stream crossings, which can make it challenging for the less-than-sure-footed.

The hike begins along the Grassy Gap Fire Road, a wide path open to horseback riders, that is likely to be muddy even on a dry day. The fire road parallels the course of a creek for most of its 1.7 miles to the Basin Creek Trail, and there are a number of pleasant pools here that anglers enjoy. (Single-hook artificial flies are permitted here with a size limit of seven inches and a creel limit of four fish.) You'll also enjoy pretty views of small cascades and rills of water coursing around boulders in the stream. Just before you reach the primitive campsite at Basin Cove, where the Basin Creek Trail joins the fire road, you'll encounter your first stream crossing. This is one of the few that offers a log bridge. Most of the others will require you to pick your way across rocks or wade.

Just past the campsite you'll see the trail-head for Basin Creek. The trail will begin to climb a little more steeply than the fire road, and off to your right you'll enjoy the tumbling cascades of Basin Creek as well as occasional clear pools, where you might like to pause to cool off on a hot summer day. As you hike, watch carefully for signs of the former Basin Creek Cove community that existed here at the turn of the 20th century. Shortly after passing a large hollowed-out log on your right, look to the left to see a still-standing chimney and house foundation. A little further up the trail on the right lies an old millstone next to a deep pool.

After you've been on the Basin Creek Trail for less than a mile, off to your right you'll see the first of two waterfalls on this hike; after your seventh stream crossing, watch for another crumbling chimney stack. Following stream crossing #11, you'll see another old chimney with most of its foundation intact as well as a couple of rotted sills. Take note of the heavy mantel stone over the fireplace.

At the turn of the 20th century, there were a number of families living in Basin Creek Cove, despite the fact that the nearest settlement was eight miles away in an era of no automobiles. The residents of the Caudill Cabin, which you'll see at the end of this hike, had to make four miles of that trek by footpath and the rest by rough mountain road. In 1916, a flood washed away the Basin Creek Cove community, leaving three people dead. The Caudill Cabin was the only structure to survive.

At about 2.5 miles (4.2 if you include the hike along Grassy Gap Fire Road), you'll have the chance for a view of a 30-foot waterfall off to your left. The waterfall swirls into a little cave at its base before dropping again to a deep pool farther below.

For the last half mile or so you'll experience a steep ascent through former grazing land to a small clearing where the weathered Caudill Cabin stands. It rests precariously on stone piers in an overgrown meadow. This log home with wood shingled roof was the home of Martin and Jamie Caudill, who raised 14 children in this small house. About 1,500 feet above you are the cliffs of Bluff Ridge, Fodder Stack, and Wildcat Rocks. Return via the same route.

Accommodations
LODGE
Bluffs Lodge (Milepost 241, 336/372-4499, www.blueridgeresort.com, May–Nov., $85–95) is the only close-by lodging facility available along this stretch of the Blue Ridge Parkway. Situated on Bluff Mountain, the lodge consists of two buildings overlooking mountain pastureland and has 24 rooms available. Though most of the rooms are small,

© DEBORAH HUSO

view from Bluffs Lodge at Doughton Park

dated, and rustic, it's a good idea to make advance reservations, as the setting alone makes this a popular overnight spot. The next closest options are in Laurel Springs or Sparta, a 20-to-30-minute drive. The best room here is 203A, which is a larger corner room with king-size bed and the best views. Don't fret if you end up staying on the parking-lot side of the buildings, however, as a large stone patio between the two lodge structures has chairs and tables offering mountain sunset views to everyone plus a wood-burning outdoor fireplace. The Bluffs Lodge office has candy bars and chips for sale as well as books and games to borrow.

CAMPING
The **Doughton Park Campground** (Milepost 238.5, 877/444-6777, www.recreation.gov) has 25 RV sites and 95 tent sites. Like all National Park Service campgrounds on the Blue Ridge Parkway, it is open May through October, and rates range $16 to $19 per site depending on whether you make reservations beforehand. The campground has an RV dump station available. Reservations are a good idea if you plan to camp on weekends or holidays when the campground will fill up quickly. You can pick up firewood, ice, batteries, and even S'mores kits at the camp store next to the Doughton Park Coffee Shop at Milepost 241. Backcountry camping is available with a permit at the primitive campsite in Basin Creek Cove; call 336/372-8568 for more information.

Food
The only concessionaire and dining option along this stretch of the Parkway is the **Doughton Park Coffee Shop** (Milepost 241, 336/372-4744, daily 7:30 A.M.–7:30 P.M., $6–13), which serves breakfast, lunch, and early dinner. The food is down-home in style and, for the most part, leaves a bit to be desired with regard to flavor. Menu items include fried chicken, mountain trout, and hamburgers. I recommend the Bluffs Country ham biscuits with a side of spiced apples. It's only $5, and is probably the tastiest meal in the house. Keep in mind, however, that the biscuits here are "army style"—not the light and fluffy kind you might expect. Service is a little on the negligent side, though the water servers are excellent and will help you when the other waitstaff doesn't.

If the weather is nice, opt for a picnic. There is a beautiful picnic area adjacent to the summit of Bluff Mountain just south of Bluff Lodge. You can access the picnic area at the lodge entrance road directly across from the coffee shop; turn right and follow the signs. There are two sets of restrooms available at the picnic area.

GLENDALE SPRINGS AND WEST JEFFERSON AREA
North Carolina's northwest corner is home to a number of very small and sparsely populated communities, and its character remains largely rural with agriculture continuing to serve as the major economic driver, just as it did when Ashe County was formally established in 1799. Today, however, agriculture here is dominated by Fraser firs, which support North Carolina's

barn quilt near West Jefferson

© FRENCH C. GRIMES

CHRISTMAS TREE FARMS IN NORTHWEST NORTH CAROLINA

North Carolina is the nation's second-largest producer of Christmas trees (after Oregon), and more than 90 percent of the Christmas trees harvested in the state are Fraser firs, a North Carolina native that grows best at elevations of 3,000 to 6,500 feet.

The industry is concentrated in the northwestern corner of the state, where Fraser fir farms abound. As you cruise the Blue Ridge Parkway here, you'll be able to see many of the farms from the Parkway overlooks as they fill the mountainsides with row upon row of dark-green sculpted giants and seedlings. But these slopes haven't always looked this way. When compared to other agricultural industries, Christmas tree farming is relatively new in North Carolina and didn't really start taking off until the 1950s. Yet today there are more than 1,600 Fraser fir growers in North Carolina's fast-growing $110 million Christmas tree industry, which has become a major agricultural economic base for the state.

But it's no easy thing, starting a Christmas tree farm. One first has to purchase seedlings, which stay in transplant beds for about three to five years. Then they go into the ground for harvesting. It takes at least seven years to grow a Fraser fir from seedling stage, and approximately 12 years to grow a Fraser fir of 6–7 feet in height. The average retail cost of such a tree is around $40 if purchased on a Christmas tree farm.

The Fraser fir has soft dark-green needles, strong needle retention, a long-lasting, fresh aroma, and strong yet pliable branches, making it the best-selling Christmas tree in North America. If left to grow naturally, a Fraser fir will reach a maximum height of about 80 feet and will have a 1.5-foot-diameter trunk. The only place the Fraser fir grows naturally is in the southern Appalachians at elevations over 3,000 feet.

Many of the state's Christmas tree farmers are choose-and-cut growers who allow private individuals to come onto their land during the holiday season to select and cut their own trees. Often this process is accompanied by hayrides, refreshments, children's activities, and music.

If you'd like to visit one of North Carolina's many choose-and-cut farms, contact the North Carolina Christmas Tree Association (800/562-8789, www.ncchristmastrees.com) to find a location in the state's northwest corner.

---

burgeoning Christmas tree industry. North Carolina is, in fact, the second-largest producer of Christmas trees in the United States and the industry brings more than $100 million in annual revenue into the pockets of area growers.

This alternately rolling and mountainous countryside is also where the New River starts, formed by the confluence of the South Fork and the North Fork. North America's oldest river and the second-oldest in the world after the Nile, the New flows 320 miles northward through Virginia and into West Virginia (where it has gained fame as a white-water-rafting destination).

If you have the time to journey off the Parkway here, you'll be amply rewarded,

particularly if you travel the winding and beautiful Route 194 on the High Country Back Roads Tour. This slow but scenic byway will draw you around green hillocks, into quiet coves, alongside acres and acres of Fraser firs aligned with military precision, and past more than a few classic red barns, some with mounted quilt-block paintings adding to the rural decor, courtesy of a recent project by the Ashe County Arts Council to paint the countryside with "barn quilts." There are more than 130 quilt blocks on barns throughout the High Country (www.quilttrailswnc.org).

Many of the towns here are little more than village crossroads, but each holds small and special charms, like Glendale Springs with its

Churches of the Frescoes, and West Jefferson, which is home to the only cheese manufacturing facility in North Carolina as well as about a dozen art galleries.

Northwest Trading Post

The Northwest Trading Post (Milepost 259, 336/982-2543, May–Oct. daily 9:30 A.M.–5:30 P.M.) is worth a leg-stretcher stop. This old-time country store right on the Parkway has a wide array of local handicrafts and food items, including baskets, brooms, quilts, woodcrafts, jams, and fudge, and has been in operation for more than 50 years.

Churches of the Frescoes

The Churches of the Frescoes (The Parish of the Holy Communion, 336/982-3076, www.churchofthefrescoes.com, daily 24 hours, free) are an unusual attraction worth a quick jaunt off the Parkway at Glendale Springs. Here artist Ben Long and some of his students began painting frescoes, first at **St. Mary's Episcopal Church** (400 Beaver Creek School

Rd.) in West Jefferson and then later at the **Holy Trinity Church** (120 Glendale School Rd.) in Glendale Springs. Paintings include a moving portrait of John the Baptist and a scene of The Last Supper, for which Long and his students used local residents as models. Long is a native North Carolinian, though he gained his mastery of fresco and oil painting while studying in Italy. Thousands of visitors come to view the frescoes each year, and both churches are open 24 hours a day to the public for viewing of the frescoes, though not during church services.

Ashe County Cheese Company

The Ashe County Cheese Company (106 E. Main St., West Jefferson, 800/445-1378, www.ashecountycheese.com, Mon.–Sat. 8:30 A.M.–5 P.M.) has been in operation since 1930, when it was started by the Kraft Corporation. Kraft operated the facility until 1975. Today it is run by two natives of Wisconsin who have turned the Cheese Company into one of the region's most popular

Ben Long fresco at Holy Trinity Church in Glendale Springs

tourist destinations. The main attraction, of course, is watching cheese being made, though the schedule changes from week to week, so it's good to call ahead if you want to be sure to arrive when cheesemaking is in process. The factory continues to make the standby old-style cheddar daisy wheels, but it has also expanded its offerings to include mild Scandinavian cheeses and its own signature Sienna cheese. Across the street at the factory store you can purchase the locally made cheeses as well as old-fashioned salted butter.

Mount Jefferson State Natural Area

The Mount Jefferson State Natural Area (1481 Mount Jefferson State Park Rd., Jefferson, 336/246-9653, www.ncparks.gov, Nov.–Feb. daily 9 A.M.–5 P.M., Mar.–Apr. daily 9 A.M.–7 P.M., May–Aug. daily 9 A.M.–8 P.M., Sept.–Oct. daily 9 A.M.–7 P.M., closed Christmas Day) is worth a quick side trip. Located just outside town off the 221 bypass (turn onto Mount Jefferson State Park Road at Lowe's Foods), the park takes you up a winding road with several scenic overlooks to the summit of Mount Jefferson (elevation 4,683 ft.), a square-shaped mountain standing by itself just west of the Blue Ridge Parkway. Just past the park entrance gate is a small information center, and there is a scenic picnic area with covered shelter, large grill, and restrooms at the summit. Note that reaching the restrooms requires a steep hike uphill through the picnic area. Several trails on the mountaintop provide views of the Blue Ridge skyline as well as Ashe County's ubiquitous tree farms. During the winter months, it is a good idea to check the park's website before visiting to get status reports on park roads.

Todd

Todd is not an easy place to reach, but if you have the time this little mountain village is worth the drive—especially if you can plan your visit to coincide with the town's regular music and storytelling sessions. You need to have an adventurous spirit to take this side trip,

as it will take you on winding, narrow back roads, but the beautiful rural scenery makes it well worth the trip.

The easiest way to reach Todd is to exit the Blue Ridge Parkway at Milepost 276.4 at Deep Gap onto Highway 421 toward Boone. Shortly after exiting the Parkway, take 221 north 1.9 miles, and then take a left onto Cranberry Springs Road about one mile after you cross into Ashe County. Along the way, look for Ashe County's ubiquitous barn quilts on the sides of outbuildings. Next you'll take a jog to the right on Railroad Grade Road all the way to Todd. You can also reach Todd via Route 194 from West Jefferson. The road is curling and narrow but offers a gorgeous drive through the Ashe County countryside. Expect to go 40 mph or slower most of the way. To the east, you'll enjoy lovely views of the Blue Ridge skyline.

◖ TODD GENERAL STORE

The main reason people go to Todd is to check out the Todd General Store (3866 Railroad Grade Rd., 336/877-1067, www.toddgeneralstore.tripod.com, Mar. Mon.–Sat. 10 A.M.–4 P.M., Sun. noon–4 P.M., Apr. Mon. 10 A.M.–5 P.M., Tues. 10 A.M.–7 P.M., Wed.–Sat. 10 A.M.–5 P.M., Sun. noon–4 P.M., May–Oct. Mon. 10 A.M.–5 P.M., Tues. 10 A.M.–7 P.M., Wed.–Thurs. 10 A.M.–5 P.M., Fri. 10 A.M.–10 P.M., Sat. 10 A.M.–5 P.M., Sun. noon–4 P.M., Nov.–Dec. Mon.–Thurs. 10 A.M.–4 P.M., Fri. 10 A.M.–10 P.M., Sat. 10 A.M.–4 P.M., Sun. noon–4 P.M., closed Jan. 1–Mar. 15). Today the endearingly rundown store's inventory includes two levels of gourmet foods, crafts, toys, furniture, and antiques. Among the gems spread around the creaking floors are bird cages, old Coca-Cola signs, Blue Willow china, apple peelers, and rolling pins. The store also has a deli open for breakfast and lunch, and they serve hand-dipped ice cream and old-time glass-bottled sodas as well.

The Todd General Store is also famous for its Friday-night bluegrass music, Tuesday-evening storytelling, and Saturday's Authors and Artisans, where local artists and craftspeople conduct book signings and craft

© FRENCH C. GRIMES

Todd General Store in Todd

demonstrations. The storytelling has become so popular that it's not unusual to have 100 people in attendance. Tourists and locals alike come out again on Friday evenings for old-time Appalachian music and bluegrass played by artists from around the region such as The Neighbors, Back Porch Bluegrass, Creekside Grass, Roan Mountain Moonshiners, and the Sweetbrier Jam. Anywhere from a handful to a couple dozen musicians will show up to delight onlookers with the sounds of fiddles, hammered dulcimers, and guitars.

On Friday dinner is served at 6 P.M., and bluegrass bands start playing at 7 P.M. On Tuesday storytelling starts at 5:45 P.M., and dinner is also served. Storytelling on Tuesday and Authors and Artisans on Saturday run from April through October, while the Friday bluegrass jams are featured from May through December.

You can also enjoy the Todd Summer Music Series in the community park across the street right on the New River. June through July, music generally begins on select Saturdays at 2 P.M. Check out the Todd Community Preservation Organization website (www.toddnc.org) for concert days, times, and performers.

New River

The North and South Forks of the New River are accessible from various points in the northwest corner of North Carolina, including several that fall within the boundaries of New River State Park (358 U.S. 221, Laurel Springs, 336/982-2587, www.ncparks.gov, Nov.–Feb. daily 8 A.M.–6 P.M., Mar.–Apr. daily 8 A.M.–8 P.M., May–Aug. daily 8 A.M.–9 P.M., Sept.–Oct. daily 8 A.M.–8 P.M., closed Christmas Day), which has riverside locations in both Alleghany and Ashe Counties. If you'd like to make a stop at the park visitors center, it is located about nine miles north of West Jefferson off Highway 221. Here you can pick up a park map that will show you the various river access points as well as places for canoe-in camping. If you don't have your own canoe, you'll need to touch base with a local river outfitter, as the park does not offer boat rentals. It's always a good idea to make reservations in advance if you'd like to rent a canoe, as many outfitters book up quickly on weekends and in the summer months.

There are a number of river outfitters throughout Ashe and Alleghany Counties. Among them is **New River Outfitters** (10725 Hwy. 221 N., Jefferson, 800/982-9190, www.canoethenew.com, Apr.–Oct. daily 8:30 A.M.–6 P.M.), located nine miles north of Jefferson in the New River General Store. They offer a variety of canoe trips, from short two-hour paddles to overnight excursions, on the South Fork of the New River and are the only outfitter located within the National Scenic River area. New River Outfitters also has tube rentals and shuttle service.

Zaloo's Canoes (3874 Hwy. 16 S., Jefferson, 800/535-4027, www.zaloos.com, departure hours June–Aug. daily 9 A.M.–2 P.M., Apr.–May and Sept.–Oct. 9 A.M.–noon, inner tubes $12, 5-mile canoe trip $39 per canoe, 10-mile canoe trip $45 per canoe, 16-mile canoe trip

$49, 2-day overnight canoe trip $75 per canoe) is the oldest canoe rental service in the area and rents canoes, kayaks, and inner tubes for exploring the South Fork of the New River. Launch the vessel of your choice from the outfitters for a 5- or 10-mile float trip; at the end their shuttle will be waiting to pick you up (shuttle included in the rental price).

Located in the old Elkland Station next door to the post office in Todd, **River Girl Fishing Company** (4041 Todd Railroad Grade Rd., 336/877-3099, www.rivergirlfishing.com, daily 10 A.M.–5 P.M., $15 and up) also offers watercraft rentals, including kayaks, canoes, and tubes. Shuttle service is included in the rental price. You can also rent bikes and purchase fishing supplies. In addition, the store sells hunting and fishing licenses and also carries locally handmade crafts. Fly-fishing lessons and guided fly-fishing trips are also available.

Entertainment and Events

Something of a rural mountain take on the traditional dinner theater, **Mountain Music Jamboree** (9331 Hwy. 16, Glendale Springs, 336/977-1374, www.mountainmusicjamboree.com, Sat. 6–10:30 P.M., dinner and music $21, music only $8) in Glendale Springs offers an extensive country buffet on Saturday night from 6 to 7:30 P.M. followed by a live music show. Bands from around the region perform, usually country, bluegrass, and southern rock, with a different band each weekend. The buffet is served May through October, but the concerts are year-round.

On the second Friday of every month from June through October, you have the opportunity to explore West Jefferson's art galleries as the sun goes down. The West Jefferson **Gallery Crawl** (West Jefferson, 336/846-2787, www.ashecountyarts.org, June–Oct. second Fri. of each month 5–8 P.M.) covers seven galleries and shops on Jefferson Avenue as well as five more on the side streets. Many of the galleries offer refreshments or have local musicians performing. Be sure to pick up a map of the crawl at one of the galleries or at the Ashe County

Arts Council (303 School Ave.) so you don't miss any.

Friday Nights on the Backstreet (Backstreet Park, Back St., West Jefferson, 866/607-0093, www.visitwestjefferson.com) are held June through September every fourth Friday 5:30–7:30 P.M. and feature regional musicians from a variety of genres, including bluegrass, rock-and-roll, folk, and old-time music. Call ahead or check the website for information on performers.

Shopping

Like most of the small mountain towns in this region, West Jefferson tends to roll up the streets early, and the town is all but closed on Sundays. However, the village is home to about a dozen art galleries, making it well worth a visit. While you're here, note West Jefferson's many murals, depicting everything from a Norfolk & Western steam engine to a zoo train, and the town's gaily decorated fire hydrants. There are 12 murals total, all of them created by local and regional artists. You can learn more about the mural project at the **Ashe County Arts Council** (303 School Ave., 336/846-2787, www.ashecountyarts.org, Mon.–Fri. 9 A.M.–4 P.M., Sat. 10 A.M.–4 P.M.), which has a gallery of changing exhibits by area artisans. You can also purchase the work of local artists and crafters at the gallery shop.

Among the many private downtown galleries is **Broomfields Gallery** (414 E. 2nd St., 336/846-4141, www.broomfieldsgallery.com, Jan.–Apr. Sat. 11 A.M.–5 P.M., May–Dec. Tues.–Sat. 11 A.M.–5 P.M.), which carries both fine art and antiques. The shop carries 18th- and 19th-century farm tools, 19th-century American furniture, flower frogs, and fine porcelain and glassware. The gallery hosts regular changing exhibitions of area artists' work; check the website for updated information on artist showcases.

Bohemia Gallery (106 N. Jefferson Ave., 336/846-1498, www.bohemianc.com, Mon.–Fri. 7 A.M.–6 P.M., Sat. 8 A.M.–6 P.M.) carries the work of local and regional artists but is also a coffee shop; it also holds a tasting room for the New River Winery.

R. T. Morgan Art Gallery (120 N. Jefferson Ave., 336/246-3328, www.rtmorganartgallery.com, Mar.–Dec. Mon.–Tues. 11 A.M.–5 P.M., Thurs.–Sat. 11 A.M.–5 P.M.) has a beautiful gallery of artwork from all over the world, including paintings, sculpture, and handmade jewelry. The works of gallery co-owner R. T. Morgan are also on display, including vibrant oil and acrylic landscapes and an eclectic array of sculpture in stone, bronze, and even stainless steel. The gallery also showcases the work of Camille Morgan, who focuses on stained glass, garden art, and metal wall sculpture.

Smart Gallery (109 N. Jefferson Ave., 336/246-7399, www.smartgallerync.com, Tues.–Sat. 10 A.M.–5 P.M.) features a wide array of artwork in many different mediums, including fine art, pottery, glass, photography, woodwork, painted silk, furniture, and jewelry.

Originals Only (3-B N. Jefferson Ave., 336/846-1636, www.originalsonlygallery.com, Tues.–Sat. 10 A.M.–5 P.M., Wed. 9 A.M.–4 P.M.) features original works of art by local artists Joan Bell and Lenore De Pree. There's also wood furniture and pottery by several local artists.

Mountain Outfitters (102 S. Jefferson Ave., 336/246-9133, Jan.–Mar. Mon.–Thurs. 10 A.M.–5:30 P.M., Fri.–Sat. 10 A.M.–6 P.M., Apr.–Dec. Mon.–Thurs. 10 A.M.–5:30 P.M., Fri.–Sat. 10 A.M.–6 P.M., Sun. 12:30–4 P.M.) carries outdoors gear, including all the major brands like Merrell, The North Face, and Columbia. In addition to clothing and footwear, they also have camping and hiking supplies.

Sally Mae's Emporium (10 S. Jefferson Ave., 336/846-9069, www.sallymaesemporium.com, Jan.–Sept. Mon.–Sat. 10 A.M.–5 P.M., Oct.–Dec. Mon.–Sat. 10 A.M.–5 P.M., Sun. noon–4 P.M.) is a fun place to browse, as this large store has a little bit of everything, including antiques, gifts, and works by local artists. The store carries Vera Bradley handbags, Middleton dolls, gourmet food items, home decor items, jewelry, and even furniture.

Backstreet Beads (1A West Ashe St.,

336/877-7686, www.backstreetbeads.com, Mon. 10:30 A.M.–5 P.M., Thurs.–Fri. 10:30 A.M.–5 P.M., Sat. hours vary) is operated by local jewelry designer Michelle Fisher-Hanson. The shop not only sells Fisher-Hanson's handmade creations but also a variety of beads made from semi-precious stones, wood, bone, Czech glass, shells, and freshwater pearls. The shop offers classes on jewelry making.

The **Acorn Gallery** (103 Long St., 336/246-3388, www.acorngallery.com, Tues.–Fri. 11 A.M.–5 P.M., Sat. 11 A.M.–2 P.M.) is located off the main drag in West Jefferson on a side street on the eastern edge of town. You'll recognize it easily, as the house is light blue with flowers painted on the siding and is surrounded by a purple picket fence. The gallery features the work of artist and owner Raney Rogers, who specializes in impressionistic landscapes, many of them inspired by the surrounding Blue Ridge Mountains. She also works in *plein air.* Raney offers workshops throughout the year; check the website for details on upcoming offerings.

Accommodations
HOTELS AND INNS

The **Hampton Inn** (203 Hampton Place Ct., West Jefferson, 800/426-7866, www.hamptonwj.com) is the newest kid on the block in West Jefferson and is the only chain hotel in town apart from a Best Western that is starting to show some wear. The Hampton Inn has an exercise room, business center, high-speed Internet access, and complimentary breakfast.

The **Rocking Chair Inn Bed and Breakfast** (1115 Hwy. 16 S., Jefferson, 336/246-9833, www.rockingchairinnbb.com, May–Oct., $85–125) is probably the nicest place to stay in the West Jefferson area. This circa-1860 home is located a few miles east of West Jefferson on Highway 16. Its loveliest feature, not surprisingly, is the large breeze-catching front porch with rocking chairs. The inn is decorated with family antiques and heirlooms and has five bedrooms, three with private baths and two with a

© DEBORAH HUSO

Rocking Chair Inn Bed and Breakfast near West Jefferson

shared bath. The house has an interesting history: It was once a stop on the Underground Railroad, and a tunnel used by escaped slaves still runs under Highway 16, coming out in the Rocking Chair's backyard where the carriage house once stood. The owners of the Rocking Chair also provide fishing guide service.

Buffalo Tavern Bed and Breakfast (958 W. Buffalo Rd., West Jefferson, 877/615-9678, www.buffalotavern.com, $89–159) is situated in a scenic valley outside West Jefferson and surrounded by Bluff, Three Top, and Buck Mountains. On offer are three rooms and one suite with tastefully decorated accommodations, some with claw-foot soaking tubs and electric fireplaces. You can enjoy a view of Bluff Mountain from the wide and shady front porch loaded with rocking chairs. A full breakfast is served each morning. Built in the 1870s, this gracious home served as a tavern from the late 19th century well into the 20th century.

VACATION RENTALS

€ **The Tower House** (427 Peregrine's Pl., 336/246-9833, $115) is probably among the most unusual lodgings in which I've ever stayed. Originally constructed by early enthusiasts of the green movement, this three-story cottage is a small metal-sided structure situated in the midst of acres and acres of tree farms. While the cottage has three bedrooms, one on each floor, the top two floors are only accessible by ladder. The bathroom is small, but has a "commode with a view" with a large sunny window overlooking the rolling landscape below. The cottage also has a mini-fridge and coffee maker, and guests can go to the Rocking Chair Inn for breakfast if they choose. All around the Tower House are mowed paths through meadows and a successional forest landscape loaded with blackberry brambles, milkweed, sumac, and locust saplings. Behind the cottage a path leads to a lovely view of the Blue Ridge, and the house is backed by a dense dark forest of pines. The best activity here is to pull the chairs off the cottage's small front porch, settle in amidst the birdhouses and vegetable gardens, and listen to the evening birdsongs and watch resident rabbits nibble on the grass. The Tower House is located off Highway 16 South southeast of

West Jefferson and is only a few miles from the Blue Ridge Parkway.

A variety of vacation rental options are available at **4 Seasons Vacation Rentals and Sales** (370 S. Main St., West Jefferson, 866/207-4837, www.4seasonsvacations.com, $99–275), from riverfront cottages to villas with long-range mountain views. Amenities include hot tubs, game tables, and Wi-Fi access. **Carolina Mountain Properties & Rentals** (8 N. Jefferson Ave., West Jefferson, 336/246-2803, www.carolinamtn.com, $125–250) also has a variety of vacation rentals available—over 100, in fact. Homes are available for rent by the day, week, or month.

Located south of West Jefferson near Deep Gap, **Fall Creek Cabins** (Fall Creek Rd., 336/877-3131, www.fallcreekcabins.com, $145–250) offer eight two-story cedar log cabins on a private 78-acre property with a trout stream running through its center. All cabins have two bedrooms, fully equipped kitchens, washer and dryer, fireplace, hot tubs, gas grills, and porch swings.

Food
GLENDALE SPRINGS
Blue Ridge Bakery Café (246 J w Luke Rd., 336/982-4811, Tues.–Thurs. 11 A.M.–4:30 P.M., Fri. 11 A.M.–7 P.M., Sat. 8 A.M.–7 P.M., Sun. 8 A.M.–4:30 P.M., $6–17), easily accessible right off the Blue Ridge Parkway via Route 16 at Milepost 258.6, is a fun place to eat. The restaurant specializes in Cajun dishes, though one can also order burgers and sandwiches. It is located next door to the Greenhouse Crafts Shop and across the street from the Churches of the Frescoes.

WEST JEFFERSON
Fraser's Restaurant and Pub (108 S. Jefferson Ave., 336/246-5222, www.frasersrestaurant.com, Mon.–Wed. 11:30 A.M.–2:30 P.M. and 5–8 P.M., Fri.–Sat. 11:30 A.M.–2:30 P.M. and 5–9 P.M., Sun. 11:30 A.M.–2:30 P.M., $5–25) serves traditional steak, seafood, and pasta fare. Try the North Carolina Pecan Trout, which features pan-sautéed local trout

marinated in a nut-flavored butter and topped with chopped pecans. If you're in for lunch, Fraser's has a full lineup of hamburgers topped with everything from blue cheese and bacon to roasted pepper and mozzarella.

Black Jack's Pub & Grill and Club 21 (18 N. Jefferson Ave., 336/246-3295, www.blackjackspubandgrill.com, Mon. 11:30 A.M.–10 P.M., Wed.–Thurs. 11:30 A.M.–10 P.M., Fri.–Sat. 11:30 A.M.–2 A.M., Sun. noon–9 P.M., $2–10) is best known for its hot wings, which you can order in amounts from 6 to 30. Their best sandwich is the Philly Jack. Black Jack's is mostly a sandwich place, though they also have a salad bar. The bar features draft and bottled beer, wine, and cocktails, and they offer nightly drink specials. This isn't the place to come for a quiet meal, as there are seven televisions running all at the same time as well as live music, karaoke, and featured DJs on select weekend nights. Club 21 is open on Friday and Saturday night and serves drinks only.

Brick Stone Pizza & Pasta (3 W. Main St., 336/846-1716, www.brick-stonepizza.com, Tues.–Thurs. 11:30 A.M.–2 P.M. and 4:30–8 P.M., Fri. 11:30 A.M.–2 P.M. and 4:30–9 P.M., Sat. noon–9 P.M., Sun. noon–8 P.M., $4–20) is one block off Main Street with an outdoor dining area facing Back Street. They offer a full array of Italian-inspired offerings. Try their five-cheese pizza, which is loaded with Monterey Jack, cheddar, provolone, Romano, and mozzarella cheese. And for an appetizer be sure to order the garlic knots—they're basically balls of dough drenched in olive oil and sprinkled with garlic and Romano cheese. If you're eating here in summer it's best to dine alfresco, as the restaurant does not have air-conditioning and the restaurant's interior is almost as hot as the pizza ovens. Brick Stone also has a full bar.

Good Ole Days Ice Cream, Candies & More (2 S. Jefferson St., 336/846-2353, Mon.–Sat. 10 A.M.–10 P.M., Sun. noon–8 P.M., $2–7) is a good place to stop in if you just want to grab a sandwich and go. Try the Pork BBQ sandwich, which you can get with potato salad and baked beans. The restaurant's specialty,

HIGH COUNTRY

of course, is ice cream. They have milkshakes, floats, banana splits, strawberry shortcake parfait, and, my personal favorite, Moon Pie Over West Jefferson, which consists of a double-decker Moon Pie heated to oozing with ice cream served over the top.

West Jefferson Coffee House (119-A 2nd St., 336/846-3873, www.westjeffersoncoffeehouse.com, Mon.–Fri. 8 A.M.–5 P.M., Sat. 8 A.M.–3 P.M., $4–12) is located on the corner of Back and 2nd Streets and has a homey atmosphere with chairs, tables, and sofas tucked into comfy nooks. The coffeehouse serves up coffee, tea, fruit smoothies, and sweet treats from breakfast until mid-afternoon and also has free Wi-Fi available.

The **Ashe County Farmer's Market** (108 Back St., 336/877-4141, www.ashefarmersmarket.com, Apr.–June Sat. 8 A.M.–1 P.M., July–Oct. Wed. and Sat. 8 A.M.–1 P.M., Nov.–Dec. Sat. 8 A.M.–1 P.M.) is a good place to pick up fresh produce in season as well as crafts, homemade soaps, jewelry, wood products, quilts, baked goods, and ornamental plants. A holiday market, held on the second and third Saturday in November and the first and second Saturday in December, features craft vendors, trees, wreaths, and other holiday goodies.

E. B. JEFFRIES PARK

E.B. Jeffries Park is a 600-acre recreation area located at Milepost 272. Named after the chairman of the North Carolina State Highway Commission in 1933, the park features a lovely shaded picnic area, restroom facilities, and access to hiking trails.

Hiking
CASCADES TRAIL

- Distance: 0.9 mile round-trip

- Duration: 45 minutes

- Elevation gain: 170 feet

- Difficulty: Moderate

- Trailhead: Next to restrooms at E. B. Jeffries Park picnic area

© DEBORAH HUSO

Cascades Trail at E. B. Jeffries Park

The Cascades Trail is a great hike for anyone wanting to see one of the many waterfalls located off the Parkway without too strenuous a climb. The trail also has a lot of interpretive signs along the way providing information on the area's flora. Bear to the right to make this loop hike. The first section of the trail is mostly level, passing through a hardwood forest dominated by tulip trees, the tallest broadleaf trees in North America. Gradually the trail descends through thickets of mountain laurel and rhododendron, and you'll begin to hear the first sounds of the cascade.

If you're traversing this trail in mid-May through early June, be on the lookout for the brilliant orange flowers of flame azalea. In July, you may see ripe blueberries along the trail. Watch also for the thick and sturdy trunks of tall chestnut oaks, which often obstruct the path.

After descending slowly, you'll cross a plank and log bridge over the small tumbling cascades of Falls Creek, which winds through rhododendron and the pointy-leafed vines of doghobble. At the first viewing platform to your right, pause and watch the creek take its first tumble over the cliff and listen to the tremendous roar.

Next you can take a series of stone steps to the bottom viewing platform and watch the creek drop over glistening black rocks. The spraying sound of the falls is accompanied by a deep whoosh as it hits the natural rock staircase.

You'll retrace your steps to return to the top of the falls, then veer to the right at the trail junction to take the second loop of the hike as it parallels the amber-colored waters of Falls Creek through a forest of birch and hemlock. You'll see more little cascades along the creek as you ascend back to the parking area.

TOMPKINS KNOB TRAIL

- Distance: 0.6 mile one-way

- Duration: 30 minutes

- Elevation gain: None

- Difficulty: Easy

- Trailhead: Southern end of E. B. Jeffries Park picnic area parking lot

This short and easy trail passes through hardwood forest for the first half mile and then opens into a clearing where you can view a number of historic Appalachian structures. Among them is the Cool Springs Baptist Church, which is actually more shelter than church, having been used for circuit-riding preachers to give sermons. To the right of the church is the Jesse Brown cabin, which was built in the late 1800s and moved to this site at the turn of the 20th century. Though largely reconstructed, the cabin offers some insight into the lives of mountain settlers. Walk inside and see the rough stone fireplace and consider the close quarters in which mountain families lived.

Jesse Brown cabin along the Tompkins Knob Trail

© FRENCH C. GRIMES

INFORMATION AND SERVICES

There are a handful of local tourism information offices in northwest North Carolina. The **Alleghany County Chamber of Commerce** (58 S. Main St., Sparta, 800/372-5473, www.sparta-nc.com, year-round Mon.–Fri. 8:30 A.M.–5 P.M., June–Oct. Sat. 10 A.M.–3:30 P.M.) has a visitors center in Sparta about seven miles off the Parkway via Route 21 (exit at Milepost 229.6), and the **Ashe County Chamber and Visitors Center** (01 N. Jefferson Ave., Ste. C, 888/343-2743, www.ashechamber. com, Jan.–Mar. Mon.–Fri. 9 A.M.–5 P.M., Apr.–Dec. Mon.–Sat. 9 A.M.–5 P.M.) is in West Jefferson; it can be reached by exiting the Parkway at the Northwest Trading Post (Milepost 259) and taking Route 16 toward Glendale Springs.

Boone to Linn Cove Viaduct

This is the most popular stretch of the Blue Ridge Parkway in North Carolina, and for good reason. The most photographed Parkway scene—the Linn Cove Viaduct—is here, along with the famous International Biosphere Reserve of Grandfather Mountain. Boone and Blowing Rock are both fun small towns; the former is home to Appalachian State University. Excellent restaurants abound in both towns, and Blowing Rock has some downright sumptuous lodgings.

BOONE

Home to Appalachian State University, one of the top 15 public universities in the south, Boone benefits not only from its proximity to the Blue Ridge Parkway but to its almost year-round student population of some 11,000 students.

Boone is your typical college town and, when combined with the tourist traffic from the Blue Ridge Parkway, it becomes something of a nightmare for drivers. Even though the town is small, expect it take you at least 20 minutes to cross town by car on any given day.

Horn in the West

Horn in the West (591 Horn in the West Dr., 828/264-2120, www.horninthewest.com, June–Aug. Tues.–Sun. 8 P.M. showtime, adults $18, children $9) is a summer outdoor drama series in Boone that details the story of the Revolutionary War in western North Carolina. The third-oldest outdoor historical drama in the United States, it began in 1952 and has been running continuously ever since. It has a cast of more than 50 characters who perform at the Daniel Boone Amphitheatre. If you arrive early you can check out the on-site Hickory Ridge Living History Museum, which features demonstrations of 18th-century crafts including weaving, candle making, and blacksmithing. The museum begins demonstrations each show night at 5 P.M.; admission is included with a ticket to *Horn in the West*.

Shopping

Green Mother Goods (116 W. King St., 828/262-3525, www.greenmothergoods.com, Mon.–Sat. 10 A.M.–6 P.M., Sun. 1–5 P.M.) is exactly what it sounds like—a shop devoted to the green lifestyle. In keeping with the general artsy and liberal feel of the college town in which it's located, Green Mother Goods carries organic cotton clothing, fair-trade items, body-care products, natural toys, and local art.

The Mast General Store (630 W. King St., 828/262-0000, www.mastgeneralstore.com, Mon.–Fri. 10 A.M.–6 P.M., Sun. noon–6 P.M.) in Boone was the second location of this popular country store to open in the High Country, following the successful reopening of the original Mast in nearby Valle Crucis in 1980. In the late 1980s, the town of Boone approached the Mast General Store owners in Valle Crucis about opening another branch of the store in the closed Hunt's Department Store on Main Street; it opened in 1988. If you do no other shopping in Boone, at least stop here. As in country stores of old, you'll find oak and glass display cabinets, hardwood floors, and lots of items ranging from useful (crockery and camping equipment) to just plain fun (barrel candy and nostalgic toys).

Doe Ridge Pottery (585 W. King St., 828/264-1127, www.doeridgepottery.com, daily 10 A.M.–6 P.M.) is located in a below-street-level gallery. It is one of only a very few places in Boone where you will likely see an artist at work. Bob Meier can often be found in his studio behind the shop, plying away at his potter's wheel. His specialty is stoneware, always functional, though he also works on commission.

Dancing Moon Earthway Bookstore (553 W. King St., 828/264-7242, www.thedancing-moon.com, Mon.–Sat. 10 A.M.–6 P.M., Sun. noon–6 P.M.) is one among many local shops oriented toward the local college scene, but it's a great specialty bookstore if you're interested in religion, philosophy, and revisionist history. Dancing Moon has an especially good selection of books on the history and philosophy of Buddhism and also carries greeting cards, jewelry, and incense. The store also hosts free guided meditation every Wednesday at 5:30 P.M.

Hands Gallery (543 W. King St., 828/262-1970, www.handsgallery.org, daily 10 A.M.–6 P.M.) is a cooperative gallery of local crafters. Be sure to look for the work of member Phil Hull, a master woodturner who makes items such as wooden sinks of laminated walnut. Another fun stop is **Grateful Grounds** (585 W. King St., 828/265-2315, www.bead-boxboone.com, daily 10 A.M.–7 P.M.), which is a coffee shop and bead store where you can make your own necklaces and bracelets.

Artwalk (611 W. King St., 828/264-9998, www.artwalkboone.com, Mon.–Sat. 10 A.M.–6 P.M., Sun. noon–5 P.M.) is an unusual craft store with three floors of funky handmade art and gifts.

Appalachian Antiques (631 W. King St., 828/268-9988, May–Oct. Mon.–Sat. 10 A.M.–6 P.M., Sun. 11 A.M.–6 P.M., Nov.–Apr. Mon.–Sat. 10 A.M.–5 P.M., Sun. noon–5 P.M.) tends to carry more in the way of junktiques than antiques, but it's worth a browse. With three floors of shops, it holds an unbelievable array of old stuff from the Corningware you remember from your mother's kitchen to hand-stitched handkerchiefs. Don't walk through too fast or you might miss something, like deviled-egg plates, lots of fun costume jewelry, Fostoria glassware, bike horns, old phonographs, and hundreds of copies of old *Life* magazines.

Ten miles south of Boone is a place you must check out if you're an art lover or collector. The **Carlton Gallery** (10360 Hwy. 105 S., 828/963-4288, www.carltonartgallery.com, Tues.–Sat. 10 A.M.–5 P.M., Sun. 11 A.M.–5 P.M.) features fine art as well as crafts by artists from around the world, though the gallery also has a nice selection of works from local artisans. You'll be surprised to find such an extensive collection of art in this small community. Longtime gallery owner and High Country native Toni Carlton features the works of some 300 artists and also has an outdoor sculpture garden.

Entertainment and Events

An Appalachian Summer Festival (733 Rivers St., 800/841-2787, www.appsummer.org) takes place every June through July on the campus of Appalachian State University and includes a month's worth of performing-arts events, featuring music, dance, theater, visual arts, and even film. Among the regulars who perform here are the Charlotte Symphony Orchestra and the Broyhill Chamber Ensemble, though the festival hosts acts from around the country in all genres, from jazz and blues groups to modern dance troupes.

The **Downtown Boone Art Crawl** occurs the first Friday of every month from 5 to 9 P.M. The Crawl, which is centered on Boone's Main Street, features live music, and most shops and galleries stay open late for the festivities, with some serving refreshments.

Accommodations

HOTELS AND INNS

Boone is loaded with all the major chain hotels, including Best Western, Fairfield Inn & Suites, Country Inn & Suites, Hampton Inn, Sleep Inn, Super 8, and La Quinta, but there are a few private offerings here, too, including the **Broyhill Inn and Conference Center** (775 Bodenheimer Dr., 800/951-6048, www.broyhillinn.com, standard rooms $69–99, suites $104–198), situated on a mountaintop at 3,535 feet overlooking Boone. It has 83 guest rooms, free Wi-Fi is available, and the hotel's Jackson Dining Room is well known for its grand Sunday brunch as well as its 25-mile views. Spa services are also available. If you decide to stay here keep in mind that the Broyhill is owned by Appalachian State University and used as a teaching facility for coaching students in business and customer service.

The **High Country Inn** (1785 Hwy. 105, 800/334-5605, www.highcountryinn.com, rooms $49–109, suites $95–175, cabins $175–250) has 120 clean renovated comfortably furnished guest rooms, some with fireplaces and whirlpool tubs. They also have cabins available. The inn has an indoor/outdoor pool (which is especially neat because the outdoor section connects right into the indoor section), hot tub, sauna, and fitness room, as well as an on-site restaurant.

The **Lovill House Inn Bed & Breakfast** (404 Old Bristol Rd., 800/849-9466, www.lovillhouseinn.com, $169–219) is located on 11 wooded acres in a historic farmhouse only a mile outside downtown Boone. The inn has six rooms, each with private bath, some with fireplaces, and Wi-Fi access. Rooms are comfortably furnished to make you feel like you're at grandmother's house, and each morning the innkeepers serve a full breakfast with menu choices.

VACATION RENTALS

There are vacation rental companies galore in the High Country, particularly in the area around Boone. Among the best is **Foscoe Rentals** (133 Echota Pkwy., 800/723-7341, www.foscoerentals.com, condos at Hawks Peak $150–185, condos at Echota Woods $180–295, condos at Echota on the Ridge $245–350), which offers 135 single-family residences and condos in a variety of settings from wooded lots overlooking ponds and streams to high-elevation sites with incredible views of Grandfather Mountain. Rentals are available in a variety of resort communities around Boone, and guests staying at Echota Woods or Echota on the Ridge enjoy access to resort amenities during their stay. The best thing about Foscoe Rentals, however, is the staff's attention to customer service. It's hard to find a friendlier and more accommodating group of rental staff in the High Country.

Boone Cabin Rentals (1460 Snaggy Mountain Blvd., 800/282-2507, www.boonecabins.com, $150–225) are located two miles from town in a wooded setting at 4,400 feet. They offer six luxury vacation rentals with hot tubs, fireplaces, pool tables, and long-distance mountain views (and plenty of rocking chairs and porch swings for enjoying them).

Jenkins Rentals (452 Sunset Dr., 800/438-7803, www.jenkinsrentals.com) offers a wide selection of rental properties, ranging from cottages and cabins to chalets and condominiums. Their main office is located in Blowing Rock, but they offer rentals in both Boone and Blowing Rock. Settings are wide ranging and include properties in resort communities as well as private homes with long-distance views. Prices are wide ranging as well: $150–425 a night, $605–3,000 a week, and $750–4,000 a month.

CAMPING

Grandfather Campground (125 Riverside Dr., 800/788-2582, www.grandfatherrv.com, tent and RV sites $20–33, cabins $50–140) offers a scenic location south of Boone. Located on 142 acres on a slope of Grandfather Mountain, the campground borders the Watauga River. The campground has an on-site trading post, laundry, and hot showers available. Full hookups for RVs are available, as is cable TV. The campground also rents rustic cabins. Service here, however, is a bit lackluster.

Honey Bear Campground (229 Honey Bear Campground Rd., 828/963-4586, www. honeybearcampground.com, primitive tent sites $20–25, tent and RV sites $30–39, 4-person cabin $85, 6-person cabin $125) has 75 wooded campsites, many of them fronting a stream, and offers full RV hookups, including cable TV. On-site are a camp store, game room, hot showers, fishing pond, dump station, and hiking trails. The campground also has complimentary Wi-Fi. Rustic cabins are also available.

Food

Red Onion Café (227 Hardin St., 828/264-5470, www.theredonioncafe.com, Mon.–Thurs. 11 A.M.–9 P.M., Fri.–Sat. 11 A.M.–10 P.M., $12–20) is a local favorite a bit removed from the downtown tourist area. A casual bistro, Red Onion has a varied menu with everything from Cajun chicken fettuccini to Chinese chicken salad.

Dan'l Boone Inn Restaurant (130 Hardin St., 828/264-8657, www.danl-booneinn.com, Jan.–May Mon.–Thurs. 5–8 P.M., Fri. 5–9 P.M., Sat. 8 A.M.–9 P.M., Sun. 8 A.M.–8 P.M., June–Oct. Mon.–Fri. 11:30 A.M.–9 P.M., Sat.–Sun. 8 A.M.–9 P.M., Nov.–Dec. Mon.–Thurs. 11:30 A.M.–2 P.M. and 5–8 P.M., Fri. 11:30 A.M.–2 P.M. and 5–9 P.M., Sat. 8 A.M.–9 P.M., Sun. 8 A.M.–8 P.M., $5–16) has a family-style set menu offering fried chicken, country-style steak, country ham biscuit, mashed potatoes and gravy, corn, green beans, stewed apples, coleslaw, and biscuits with a choice of desserts.

Boone Drug (202 W. King St., 828/264-8929, www.boonedrug.com, Mon.–Fri. 9 A.M.–5 P.M., Sat. 9 A.M.–3 P.M., $3–7) is an old-time soda fountain that has been operational since 1919 and is a good place to pick up a sandwich or ice cream treat midday.

Cha Da Thai (173 Howard St., 828/268-0434, www.chadathai-nc.com, Mon.–Thurs. 11 A.M.–3 P.M. and 5–10 P.M., Fri. 11 A.M.–3 P.M. and 5–11 P.M., Sat. 5–11 P.M., Sun. noon–10 P.M., $6–15) is one of several restaurants on the back side of Main Street.

With both alfresco and indoor seating featuring woven red tablecloths with gold stitched elephants and slick varnished wood decor, this is a true Thai restaurant. Waitresses serve you in traditional garb, and there are Old Country crafts for sale in the back of the restaurant. Dishes are traditional Thai—noodles and sticky rice served with marinated meats in peanut sauces and curries. The restaurant also has a full wine list as well as sake.

If you're camping or picnicking and need to do some grocery shopping while in the area, check out **Earth Fare: The Healthy Supermarket** (178 W. King St., 828/263-8138, www.earthfare.com, Mon.–Sat. 8 A.M.–10 P.M., Sun. 9 A.M.–9 P.M.), which carries local, organic, and bulk foods. None of the store's products contain high-fructose corn syrup, artificial substances, or animal by-products.

VALLE CRUCIS

Located in a narrow verdant valley on Route 194 via a circuitous route west of Boone, Valle Crucis ("Valley of the Cross") was North Carolina's first rural historic district. The valley was named in 1842 by an Episcopal bishop who helped run a monastery and boarding school in the valley.

Once a thriving country village, Valle Crucis is probably less busy today than it was 100 years ago, though tourists still flock to this isolated spot of earth to visit the original Mast General Store and experience a brief taste of yesteryear in a landscape that has remained virtually unchanged since the turn of the 20th century.

◖ Original Mast General Store

The Mast General Store (Hwy. 194, 828/963-6511, www.mastgeneralstore.com, Mon.–Sat. 7 A.M.–6:30 P.M., Sun. noon–6 P.M.) was once the Wal-Mart of yesteryear. When it opened in the late 19th century as the Taylor Store, it proclaimed to carry everything from cradles to caskets—and it did. Like all country stores, it offered farm equipment, clothes, dry goods, seed, food items—anything one could possibly need or want to survive in the mountains of western North Carolina at the turn of the 20th century. But like so many community stores, it eventually fell on hard times, succumbing to the automobile age and the convenience of large supermarkets and shopping malls. The Mast family had maintained full ownership of the store since 1913, but eventually sold it in the 1970s. The store passed through owner after owner and became less and less profitable, finally closing its doors in 1977.

That could have been the end of Mast's story, but it wasn't. Former Floridians John and Faye Cooper purchased Mast General Store in 1979 and reopened it in 1980, adding an annex in 1982 because they were growing so fast. While they carry traditional country-store goods like seed and farm clothes, they also carry outdoors clothes, camping equipment, mountain souvenirs, toys, and barrel candy.

Today the Mast General Store has locations in Boone, Waynesville, Hendersonville, Asheville, Greenville (South Carolina), and Knoxville (Tennessee).

Festivals and Events

The **Valle Country Fair** (Valle Crucis Conference Center, Hwy. 194, 828/963-4609, www.vallecountryfair.org, free, parking $5) is always held on the third Saturday in October during the peak of fall color. A country church bazaar gone wild, the fair is sponsored by the Holy Cross Episcopal Church and features over 100 arts and crafts booths, freshly made apple cider, homemade jams and jellies, chili, barbecue, and Brunswick stew. Entertainment includes bluegrass, country, and traditional mountain music as well as clogging and square dancing.

Accommodations

There are a surprising number of lodging options in this isolated valley, including the popular **Mast Farm Inn** (2543 Broadstone Rd., 888/963-5857, www.mastfarminn.com, rooms $99–269, cottages and cabins $149–459), which has seven rooms and seven cottages available and also operates a restaurant.

Just down the road is **Valle Crucis Bed & Breakfast** (2171 Broadstone Rd., 828/963-

2525, www.vallecrucisbandb.com, $139–199), which has some of the most elegantly decorated rooms in the valley.

The **Taylor House Inn** (4584 Hwy. 194 S., 828/963-5581, www.taylorhouseinn.com, rooms $84–159, suites $149–199) has seven guest rooms and two suites decorated in simple, crisp country style. Amenities include afternoon tea, coffee, and sweets, a two-course gourmet breakfast, and Wi-Fi.

The Mountainside Lodge Bed & Breakfast (1709 Broadstone Rd., 877/687-4333, www.mountainsidelodgebb.com, $120–180) is a great place for sportsmen to hang their hats, as the bed-and-breakfast offers hunting and fishing trips in the surrounding mountains.

For more lodging options in areas surrounding Valle Crucis, visit www.vallecrucis.com.

Food

The Mast Farm Inn Restaurant (2543 Broadstone Rd., 888/963-5857, www.mastfarminn.com, $38) is the only option in town. And since the restaurant has a set four-course meal each day, the options are especially slim. This is not to say, however, that Mast Farm doesn't serve up fine food. They do, and they've been repeatedly recognized for it, too. The restaurant's focus is on local, fresh, and organic food with an ever-changing menu. Entrées you might encounter include local pork and Ashe County cheese in a blanket, marinated beef with wedged potatoes, or barbecue turkey wraps. The dinner menus are especially fun, as they include descriptions of exactly where every ingredient came from. Reservations are required.

BANNER ELK

About a 30-minute drive from Boone and most easily accessible via Routes 105 and 184 south of Boone, Banner Elk is a prosperous small village offering an alternative to the bustle of Boone and Blowing Rock (except during the winter ski season when it can get quite busy here). The major industry in this area, situated at an elevation of 3,739 feet and surrounded by the peaks of the Blue Ridge, is Christmas trees (which you'll notice as you drive through the rolling countryside). With three ski resorts, cool summers, and colorful autumns, Banner Elk enjoys an almost year-round influx of tourists and vacation home–owners.

The population of Banner Elk is just under 1,000, and that includes the resident students of Lees-McRae College, a small private four-year college affiliated with the Presbyterian Church. The Performing Arts Department of the college offers summer theater performances to residents and visitors.

Banner Elk, like much of the High Country, owes a lot of its tourism-based prosperity to the local Robbins family. Now-deceased brothers Grover and Harry Robbins were responsible for the development of the beloved amusement park Tweetsie Railroad in Blowing Rock in the 1950s; the brothers also built the theme park Goldrush Junction in Pigeon Forge, which eventually became Dollywood.

In 1962, the two brothers began the first of their mountain resort communities, the Hounds Ears Club outside Boone. They also developed the resort at Beech Mountain, and youngest brother Spencer joined in the creation of the Elk River Club, a high-end residential resort community just outside Banner Elk that sports its own jetport. Harry and Spencer, along with Grandfather Mountain founder Hugh Morton, also helped establish High Country Host, the regional tourism organization that helps promote attractions in northwest North Carolina.

Skiing

Banner Elk and adjacent Beech Mountain receive the bulk of their visitors in winter when the three ski resorts are all in full swing. **Hawksnest** (2058 Skyland Dr., 800/822-4295, www.skihawk.com) has the largest snow-tubing operation in the East with 20 snow-tubing lanes, some of them up to 1,000 feet long. Snow tubing is offered November–March Monday–Friday 10 A.M.–4 P.M. ($22), Saturday 10 A.M.–8 P.M. ($30), and Sunday 10 A.M.–4 P.M. ($30). There's no need to trek uphill with your tube, either, as the resort has

two moving-carpet lifts available. Hawksnest also offers a zip line year-round (daily 10 A.M.–6 P.M., $65 for a tour of 10 cables).

Ski Beech (1007 Beech Mountain Pkwy., 828/387-2011, www.skibeech.com, Nov.–Mar. daily 8 A.M.–10 P.M., day or twilight adults $28–38, juniors/seniors $20–30; weekend adults $45–60, juniors/seniors $35–40; Sunday twilight adults $50, juniors/seniors $35) has the highest elevation skiing on the East Coast with a peak elevation of 5,506 feet and a base elevation of 4,675 feet. The resort has 14 slopes with nine lifts and also offers night skiing and ice skating.

Sugar Mountain Resort (1009 Sugar Mountain Dr., 800/784-2768, www.skisugar.com, Nov.–Mar. daily 9 A.M.–10 P.M., half or full day adults $22–64, children 5–11 $14–43; twilight adults $29–64, children 5–11 $23–43; night adults $17–30, children 5–11 $14–22) has 20 slopes for a range of skiing abilities on 115 acres. Ski and snowboarding instruction are available for all ages. The resort also has a 10,000-square-foot outdoor ice rink.

Horseback Riding

Horse owners flock to the trails at Moses H. Cone Memorial Park, but if you don't have your own steed and still want to enjoy some riding in the High Country, there are a handful of local outfitters who can set you up. Among them is **Dutch Creek Trails** (3287 Hwy. 194 S., 828/297-7117, www.dutchcreektrails.com, Mon.–Sat. 8 A.M.–4 P.M., $40), which offers one-hour trail rides into the mountains around Valle Crucis.

Banner Elk Stables (Shoemaker Rd., 828/898-5424, www.bannerelkstables.com, $30) takes beginners as well as experienced riders on one-hour guided trail rides along Beech Mountain.

Banner Elk Winery

The first commercial winery in the area, Banner Elk Winery (135 Deer Run La., 828/260-1790, www.bannerelkwinery.com, summer daily noon–6 P.M., winter daily noon–5 P.M., wine tasting $5) is located on a producing blueberry farm a mile and a half north of Banner Elk just off Highway 194. The winery's offerings include a sweet blueberry wine made from the berries grown on the estate as well as High Country Rose. All grapes are locally grown in the High Country. The winery offers complimentary tours, picnic grounds, and live music on Sunday afternoons.

Entertainment and Events

Lees-McRae College (191 Main St., 828/898-8709, www.lmc.edu or www.lmst.lmc.edu, adults $26, students and children $15) hosts summer-evening theater productions June through August. Professional dancers, singers, and actors are chosen through a local audition process; auditions are also held in New York and Memphis. The theater's repertoire has included popular musical hits like *Cats* and *Guys and Dolls*. Call for current performances and showtimes.

The **Woolly Worm Festival** (185 Azalea Cir., 828/898-5605, www.wollyworm.com, adults $5, children $2, children under 5 free), which started as a festivity to celebrate the coming of winter snows, has been held in Banner Elk each October since 1978. Locals and visitors alike can enter their own woolly worms in a number of races and heats (worm registration $5). The judges will determine the severity of winter weather based on the color of the winning worm's 13 segments.

Accommodations

INNS AND BED-AND-BREAKFASTS

The **Blueberry Villa** (60 Deer Run La., 828/260-1790, www.blueberryvilla.com, $189–289) is located on the grounds of the Banner Elk Winery. The villa has eight suites, each with private bathroom and whirlpool tub. Some suites also have gas log fireplaces. The entire villa can also be rented for events or large family gatherings. The price of accommodations includes a complimentary wine tasting, full breakfast, and Wi-Fi.

Azalea Inn Bed & Breakfast (149 Azalea Cir., 828/898-8195, www.azalea-inn.com, rooms $99, suites $129, cottages $165–190)

has 11 rooms, suites, and cottages, some with fireplaces, whirlpool baths, and kitchens. The inn has a convenient in-town location within walking distance of many shops and restaurants and has carefully landscaped grounds surrounded by a white picket fence. Guests can arrange in advance for an afternoon English tea for $20 per person. Full breakfast is served each morning.

The **Banner Elk Inn Bed & Breakfast and Cottages** (407 E. Main St., 828/898-6223, www.bannerelkinn.com, rooms $95–125, suites $140–180, cottages $150–185, barkhouse cabin $185–250, rental cabins $175–250) offers a wide array of lodging options, including five guest rooms in the main inn, three cottages, a barkhouse cabin, and vacation rentals in the surrounding area. The cottages and barkhouse cabin (sided in rustic poplar bark siding) offer an alternative to the conventional, impersonal vacation rental with cheerfully decorated rooms rich in texture, color, and personality. Full breakfasts are served on weekends and holidays, with continental breakfast being the norm on weekdays. Tea, coffee, and treats are available throughout the day.

RESORTS

Both of the ski resorts of Banner Elk and adjacent Beech Mountain offer overnight and weekly rentals. **Sugar Mountain Resort** (3390 Tynecastle Hwy., 828/898-9746, www.staysugarmountain.com) has log cabins, condominiums, and single-family residents available for rent year-round, and **Beech Mountain Chalet Rentals** (405 Beech Mountain Pkwy., 828/387-4231, www.gobeech.com, 1-bedroom $100, 2-bedroom $125, 3-bedroom $150, 4-bedroom $175, 5-bedroom $200, 7-bedroom $275) has homes and townhomes available. Guests have access to the facilities of the private Beech Mountain Club, which include golf, tennis, and a swimming pool.

Food

Despite its seemingly isolated location, Banner Elk has some nice restaurants serving up rather unusual fare for a small town. Among them is

Louisiana Purchase Food and Spirits (397 Shawneehaw Ave., 828/963-5087 or 828/898-5656, www.louisianapurchasefoodandspirits.com, Tues.–Sun. 5:30–9 or 10 P.M., $18–32), which offers Creole and Cajun cooking. They have a seasonal menu that changes every six weeks. Reservations are preferred but not necessary.

Zuzda Tapas Restaurant and Bar (502 Main St. W., 828/898-4166, www.zuzda.com, Mon.–Thurs. 5–10 P.M., Fri.–Sat. 3–11 P.M., $5–13) has over 100 menu items available in small tapas-style servings, providing a good excuse to try more than one. Despite the tapas theme, however, the menu is not restricted to Spanish fare. While you can get a traditional Spanish paella, you can easily follow it with steak *au poivre,* tuna sashimi, or lobster bisque. Sweet-potato fries are always a good bet for comfort food.

BLOWING ROCK

The first thing you'll notice when you drive into Blowing Rock is how perfect it is. Everywhere are trim and well-maintained historic homes, carefully manicured lawns and gardens, streets laden with hanging baskets of flowers, and summer blooms by the armfuls. The architecture here is largely Arts and Crafts, reflecting the town's roots as a popular resort area for well-heeled lowlanders at the turn of the 20th century.

Though Blowing Rock had been drawing visitors to its cooler summer climate since the mid-1800s with guesthouses and hotels springing up everywhere, the town was not officially incorporated until 1889—and even then Blowing Rock's year-round population remained pretty small.

Tourism, however, was Blowing Rock's destiny, and by the 1930s the town's namesake rock formation put the mountain village on the map. It was in 1933 that Blowing Rock's mayor, Grover Robbins Sr., opened The Blowing Rock as a tourist attraction. The rock was a hit. *Ripley's Believe It Or Not* called Blowing Rock "the only place in the world where the snow falls upside-down."

More success would soon follow, including the opening of North Carolina's first family theme park, Tweetsie Railroad, which was operated by Robbins' eldest son, Grover Robbins Jr. The theme park's steam locomotive, once owned by the East Tennessee & Western North Carolina Railroad Company and affectionately known as "Tweetsie," had left its native North Carolina after being bought by Gene Autry. But Grover Robbins Jr. brought the engine back home and built an amusement park around it that still draws families by the thousands.

Over the years, Grover Robbins Sr.'s three sons have held a good share of the responsibility for making Blowing Rock the tourism hub it is today, all of them having been involved in developing resort communities and attractions throughout the High Country and even in Pigeon Forge, Tennessee. The brothers even started the theme park known then as Goldrush Junction that would ultimately become Dollywood.

Today, Blowing Rock's permanent population rests at around 1,500, but in the busy summer months the town often balloons to 10,000 or more residents, most of whom still come from the lowlands of the Carolinas to their own or rental summer cottages here.

Tweetsie Railroad

Tweetsie Railroad (300 Tweetsie Railroad La., 800/526-5740, www.tweetsie.com, May Fri.–Sun. 9 A.M.–6 P.M., June–Aug. daily 9 A.M.–6 P.M., Sept.–Nov. Fri.–Sun. 9 A.M.–6 P.M., adults $30, children 3–12 $22, 2 and under free) is worth at least a half day if you have kids or grandkids in tow. Despite all the cowboys and Indians running around, this is more than a typical amusement park. The park's central attraction is its train and, more specifically, old Engine No. 12. Built by Baldwin Locomotive Works of Philadelphia in 1917, No. 12 was among the 13 locomotives that served the East Tennessee & Western North Carolina Railroad from 1881 until its closing in 1950, on a line stretching 34 miles from Johnson City, Tennessee, to Cranberry,

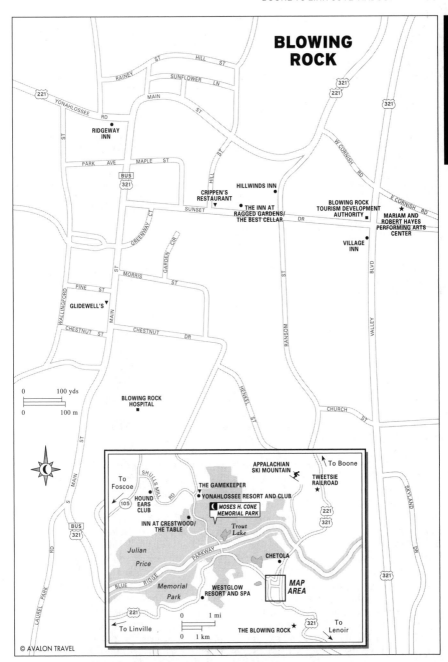

© AVALON TRAVEL

BIRD-WATCHING IN THE BLUE RIDGE

They come to us with names that sing across our tongues like the lovely colors of their wings – scarlet tanager, indigo bunting, belted kingfisher, cerulean warbler, and northern flicker. They are the birds of the North Carolina High Country – the year-round residents, the seasonal migrants, the sparsely spotted interlopers that have been driven here by odd weather and confusion. Their numbers and varieties in the southern mountains are at first astonishing, but what makes the High Country a bird-watcher's paradise is the region's varied ecosystems, from its long sloping valleys to its tallest ridgelines stretching nearly 6,000 feet above sea level.

Because of the high elevation of much of the region, the High Country plays host to many northern species who reach the southernmost limit of their range in these mountains. And the lower elevations represent a haven for birds more common to the Southeast, making for a lovely mix of song and sightings for both backyard and avid bird-watchers.

Bird-watching is becoming a more popular pastime among outdoor enthusiasts, and it's easy to understand why: It's an inexpensive hobby that allows you to get close to nature.

If you've never done it and would like to get started, the first step is purchasing a good field guide and a pair of binoculars. Then consider joining a local bird club.

The High Country is an excellent place to get started bird-watching because of the multitude of parks and forests where one can wander hundreds of miles of hiking paths. Bring along a bird-watching checklist (many parks and visitors centers have them), and record your sightings in a notebook. To identify birds, pay attention to colors and markings, size, and silhouette, as well as habitats and behavior. As you become more skilled, you will be able to identify birds by their songs. Early to mid-morning is the ideal time for viewing birds, and you're most likely to see them along the edges of woods or fields and alongside streams and lakes.

Top local bird-watching spots include Grandfather Mountain, Beech Mountain, Moses H. Cone Memorial Park, Julian Price Park, and Linville Gorge. You might consider joining a bird-watching trip or workshop with the High Country Audubon Society; call 828/733-4326 for more information. You can also download a Blue Ridge Parkway bird list at www.nps.gov/blri.

North Carolina, through rough, mountainous terrain. After the railroad closed, the engine made its way through various owners, including actor Gene Autry, until it finally came back to North Carolina in 1956 and became the centerpiece of the Tweetsie Railroad theme park.

Today rail enthusiasts and kids interested in being at the center of a train robbery or shoot-out can ride the train around a three-mile track. But the most intriguing part of Tweetsie is something most visitors never see—the Tweetsie train shop. One of only a handful of shops in the country that can reconstruct old steam engines, the train shop maintains a busy schedule, not just maintaining No. 12 and her back-up counterpart No. 190, but restoring and rebuilding steam engines from all over the country. Some years ago

the shop rebuilt all four of Disney World's engines, which are Baldwin locomotives like No. 12 and No. 190.

In addition to the train, the park features various other amusement park rides including the Free Fall, Tornado, Round Up, and Tweetsie Twister, as well as a petting zoo. There are live shows available throughout the day, including a saloon performance with cancan girls. Kids and adults alike can ride a chair to Miner's Mountain and pan for gold. Tweetsie holds special events and shows throughout the year, including Thomas the Train rides, a show by Riders in the Sky, and an October Ghost Train Halloween Festival.

Keep in mind that this is not an amusement park for teenagers, but toddlers and young elementary school–age kids will love it.

The Blowing Rock

The Blowing Rock (Hwy. 321 S., 828/295-7111, www.theblowingrock.com, Jan.–Feb. Sat.–Sun. 9 A.M.–5 P.M., Mar.–May daily 9 A.M.–5 P.M., Memorial Day weekend–Labor Day daily 8:30 A.M.–7 P.M., Sept.–Oct. Sun.–Thurs. 9 A.M.–6 P.M., Fri.–Sat. 9 A.M.–7 P.M., Nov.–Dec. daily 9 A.M.–5 P.M., adults $6, seniors 60 and over $5, children 4–11 $1, 3 and under free) has been a High Country tourist attraction since 1933. Apart from the opportunity to view this odd-shaped attraction that catches the wind and blows it back to where it came from, the observation tower at the Blowing Rock offers views of Table Rock, Grandfather Mountain, and Hawksbill as well. The park has lovely gardens, a nature trail, and a gift shop on-site. The Blowing Rock is situated at about 4,000 feet and protrudes above the Johns River Gorge. The strange phenomenon here that sometimes makes snow blow upside-down is caused by the steep walls of the gorge below, which create a flume that, when it catches the wind from the northwest, can return lightweight objects thrown over the cliff.

◖ Moses H. Cone Memorial Park

Moses H. Cone Memorial Park and Visitor Center (Milepost 294, 828/295-7938, Mar.–Nov. daily 9 A.M.–5 P.M. daily, free) is a 3,600-acre park and wildlife preserve originally developed by textile magnate Moses Cone, a turn-of-the-20th-century environmentalist. Flat Top Manor, Cone's mountaintop mansion, today houses the art and craftwork of the Southern Highland Craft Guild.

Moses Cone was known as the Denim King because of the denim his textile factories produced. Cone and his wife, Bertha, came to the North Carolina mountains in the 1890s seeking to relieve his poor health with the moderate climate, fresh air, and natural spring water. In 1899, they began construction on the 20-room Flat Top Manor overlooking their orchard of some 32,000 apple trees and Bass Lake. The Cones also constructed 25 miles of carriage trails through their park, all of which are still open to horseback riders and hikers today. Moses Cone died of heart disease in 1908, and Bertha then assumed management of their mountain estate, continuing to harvest apples and raise sheep and cattle.

© DEBORAH HUSO

Flat Top Manor at Moses H. Cone Memorial Park

In 1935 Bertha Cone found herself in a battle with the National Park Service to keep the proposed Blue Ridge Parkway from crossing her property, but the issue was not decided in her lifetime. She died in 1947, and two years later, Cone heirs donated the estate to the Park Service.

The Parkway Craft Center is located in the former Cone mansion. It is the retail home of the Southern Highland Craft Guild, and one of the guild members is usually demonstrating his or her art on the front porch. Rocking chairs on the front veranda offer views of Bass Lake, Blowing Rock, and the mountains to the north. Inside are multiple galleries with displays of handmade jewelry, quilts, watercolors, baskets, woodcarvings, blown glass, coverlets, hats, and pottery, all of which are for sale.

The Craft Center also has a small National Park Service bookstore (828/295-3782), and tours of the mansion's upstairs are available on Saturday and Sunday at 10 and 11 A.M. and 2, 3, and 4 P.M. The tours are free, but you must sign up at the information desk on the front porch.

After the Craft Center, the best-loved feature of the Moses H. Cone Memorial Park is its 25 miles of carriage trails, which visitors enjoy for both hiking and horseback riding. Bicycles are not allowed on the trails. There are no outfitters nearby offering trail rides, so if you want to enjoy the carriage trails of Moses Cone on horseback, you'll need to bring your own mount. If you require boarding for your house, the **Blowing Rock Equestrian Preserve** (1500 Laurel La., 828/295-4700, www.blowingrockequestrian.com) offers overnight boarding and is located adjacent to Moses Cone.

Many visitors also come to Moses H. Cone Memorial Park to fish. The park has two lakes, **Bass Lake** and **Trout Lake,** both of which are accessible either via carriage trail from the manor house or via separate entry from Blowing Rock. Bass Lake can be reached from Highway 221 on the eastern side of the Parkway, while Trout Lake can be accessed from Shulls Mill Road on the western side of

the Parkway. Exit at Milepost 294.6 for either option. Most equestrian owners park their horse trailers and mount at the Bass Lake parking area. Bass Lake also has a nice loop trail of about a mile, which follows the perimeter of the lake and is suitable for wheelchairs and strollers. The trail provides some lovely views of Flat Top Manor from below. Also along the trail are water lilies, countless rhododendron, beaver dams, and some surprisingly friendly Canadian geese. If you'd like to fish in the lake, you'll likely find bass, bream, and bluegill.

Julian Price Memorial Park

A bit less crowded than its northern neighbor, the Moses H. Cone Memorial Park, Julian Price Memorial Park (Mileposts 296–297) has one of the most beautiful rhododendron displays along the Parkway in early to mid-July. On either side of the drive are walls and walls of pale pink and white blooms, and more of these tangled blossoms can be viewed along the perimeter of Price Lake, which is visible right from the Parkway. The park encompasses 4,200 acres. The park's picnic area (Milepost 296.4) is easily the Parkway's most popular, offering picnic sites alongside a stream. It is a popular weekend destination for area families, and you might find every table occupied in summer months. Many families come here, claim a table, and stay the day, playing volleyball, croquet, or just lounging. There are restroom facilities.

BOATING

The most popular activities at Price Lake are boating and fishing, and it's no wonder. The lake is a particular gem, situated as it is under the distant shadow of Grandfather Mountain and rimmed with a forest of rhododendron and mountain laurel. It is well known for its good trout fishing. There is a boat ramp at the lake, so you can bring your own non-powered boat. From Memorial Day weekend through Labor Day weekend you can also rent a canoe or rowboat and life jackets from the boat rental facility; weekend rentals are available through

October. The first hour is $12, and each additional hour is $10. The boat ramp, boat rental facility, and amphitheater are all accessible from the Price Lake Overlook parking area at Milepost 296.7. One can also purchase snacks, drinks, and firewood at the boat rental facility. All boats must be returned by 6 P.M.

PRICE LAKE TRAIL

- Distance: 2.5 miles round-trip
- Duration: 1.5 hours
- Elevation gain: None
- Difficulty: Easy
- Trailhead: Price Lake Overlook parking area to the right of the boat rental facility

The Price Lake Trail is one of the best trails along the Parkway that is accessible to people of all abilities. The first portion of the trail is even accessible for wheelchairs and strollers. The trail follows the entire perimeter of Price Lake, is mostly level, and has numerous benches along the way for resting. This is a good trail for walking your dog if you have one, as leashed pets are allowed and the walking is pretty easy.

The first part of the trail courses through a forest loaded with rhododendron and has several small bridges that cross amber-colored streams feeding into the lake. There are occasional openings in the trees that reveal views of the placid glass-like surface of the water. After just under a mile, the trail veers away from the lake through a dark rhododendron thicket, then descends into a bog that can be pretty sloppy after recent rain. This is a popular trail, so expect traffic jams wherever there is lots of mud!

As you come about halfway around the lake, you'll start to see leftover signs of beavers, including some abandoned dams and half-gnawed tree trunks. You'll briefly leave the lakeshore again, entering another rhododendron thicket that is so dark it turns a sunlit day into dusk. Then the trail opens again, paralleling the lake and offering ongoing views

© DEBORAH HUSO

view of Grandfather Mountain from Price Lake

of the water with Grandfather Mountain in the distance.

The last leg of the trail parallels the Parkway through another gorgeous forest of rhododendron with a spongy pine-needled path beneath your feet. Just before you reach the parking lot again you'll have a brief stretch of hike through the Julian Price Park Campground (with the trail passing right next to a restroom facility).

Entertainment and Events

Mariam and Robert Hayes Performing Arts Center (152 Jamie Fort Rd., 828/295-9627, www.brcac.org) is not only the home stage for the Blowing Rock Stage Company but also hosts the Appalachian State University opera, orchestra, and other music programs, including guest performing artists in a variety of genres and film festivals. Check the website for upcoming programs and ticket information.

Blowing Rock WinterFest (7738 Valley Blvd., 877/295-7801, www.blowingrockwinterfest.com) is one way that the locals try to sustain tourism into the winter, draw people into town from the ski resorts, and bring some fun to an otherwise dreary season. Occurring annually in January, this festival has no general admission charge, though some activities come with a fee. Available for free are the polar plunge (if you're brave enough to participate, that is), kids' activities, bonfires, pet show, and hayrides. Festivalgoers can warm up at the chili cook-off or the wine tasting and auction. The festival also features musical concerts and a Winterfeast. Check the website for admission fees to various shows and activities.

Art in the Park (Park Ave. and Wallingford St., 828/295-7851 or 800/295-7851, www.blowingrock.com/artinthepark, free) occurs one Saturday a month from May through October; the juried art and craft show takes place in downtown Blowing Rock. Artists from all over the eastern United States participate, and you'll likely see exhibits in watercolor, oil painting, metal, fiber, wood, basketry, jewelry, clay, and glass. The price range is wide, allowing you to purchase everything from a small souvenir to a stunning piece of original art for the home. Free shuttle service is available from the Tanger Shoppes or Food Lion on Highway 321. Check the website for dates.

Each year during the last weekend in July, Blowing Rock hosts the **Art & Antique Show** (Blowing Rock Elementary School, 828/295-9099, www.blowingrockmuseum.org, $10), which features a wide array of English, American, and European furniture as well as oriental rugs, estate jewelry, china, crystal, clocks, and linens.

Shopping

Blowing Rock's Main Street as well as Sunset Drive are loaded with antiques shops, art galleries, and specialty shops, almost all of them high-end and geared toward the town's demographic of decidedly well-to-do vacationers. If you're planning on exploring the Parkway during the day and doing your shopping at night, think again: The streets of Blowing Rock roll up early. The only thing you can buy after 5 P.M. (6 P.M. on weekends) is wine, beer, and ice cream. Most shoppers walk to the

downtown shopping district from their lodgings, but there is also on-street parking with a two-hour limit between 9 A.M. and 5 P.M. Public restrooms are available in the park on Main Street.

The **Bob Timberlake Gallery** (946 Main St., 828/295-4855, www.bobtimberlake.com/gallery, Mon.–Thurs. 10 A.M.–5 P.M., Fri.–Sat. 10 A.M.–6 P.M., Sun. noon–5 P.M.) is one of the most popular stores on Main Street. In addition to selling Timberlake's artwork, the store also carries his signature furniture line, home decor items, and clothing. The most striking thing about the gallery, whether you're a Timberlake fan or not, is its architecture. Inside is a striking cathedral ceiling with exposed beams with canoes hanging from them.

The **Main Street Gallery** (960 Main St., 828/295-7839, www.blowingrockfinecrafts.com, daily 10 A.M.–6 P.M.) is a cooperative gallery featuring the works of regional crafters. Some of the wares include handmade walnut and curly maple tables, pottery, fine-art photography, baskets, and wooden bowls.

Around the corner is **Last Straw** (978 N. Main St., 828/295-3030, www.thelaststrawinc.com, Mon.–Sat. 10 A.M.–5 P.M., Sun. 1–5 P.M.), a sprawling shop with beautifully landscaped grounds. They carry a wide array of silk flower arrangements and wreaths as well as fountains, birdfeeders, garden trellises, wind chimes, and decorative garden pots. Kitty-corner across the street is **Follow Your Dream** (1009 Main St., 828/295-6026, www.followyourdreamshop.com), a fun little store in a tiny purple building on the corner, which has an eclectic mix of baby gifts, jewelry, aprons, and home decor items.

Blowing Rock Market and Wine Shop (990 Main St., 828/295-7373, www.blowingrockmarket.com) is the only store in town open into the evening, and this is, in part, because it's also a gas station. However, this will rank among the nicest gas stations you've ever visited—the well-organized market is not one's typical convenience store. Mostly, the market sells wine (both local and international), cheese, crackers, beer, and ice cream. It's a good place to stock up for the evening, which you will likely spend rocking on the porch at your inn. You can indulge in daily wine tastings by taking a quick side trip down Sunset Drive, kitty-corner across the street, to **Christopher's Wine and Cheese** (110 Sunset Dr., 828/414-9111, www.christopherswineandcheese.com, Mon.–Sat. 11 A.M.–6 P.M., Sun. 1–6 P.M.), which carries both regional and international wines and a small selection of artisan cheeses. Next door is **Gregory Alan's** (110 Sunset Dr., 828/414-9091, www.gregoryalans.com), which carries a wide array of beautiful home decor and furniture items.

There are a handful of high-end antiques stores in Blowing Rock. Among them is **Carriage Trade Antiques** (1079 Main St., 828/295-3110, Mon.–Thurs. 10 A.M.–5 P.M., Fri.–Sat. 10 A.M.–5:30 P.M., Sun. 11 A.M.–5 P.M.), which carries 19th-century English, French, and American antique furniture, silver, and porcelain. More high-end antiques can be found at **Finley House Antiques** (1121 Main St., 828/295-6373, Mon.–Thurs. 10 A.M.–5 P.M., Fri.–Sat. 10 A.M.–5:30 P.M., Sun. 11 A.M.–5 P.M.), which carries French and English antiques, estate and silver jewelry, and majolica and oil paintings.

If you're looking for a less pricey gift to take home, check out **Mrs. Brumble's** (1107 Main St., 828/295-9191), a fun shop of glitz and glam, carrying everything from beaded purses and sparkling costume jewelry to dazzling hair accessories and home decor items.

The Dulcimer Shop (1098 Main St., 828/295-3616, www.thedulcimershop.com) sells dulcimers as well as kits for building one's own dulcimer. The shop also carries CDs of dulcimer music, books on dulcimers, and gifts for music lovers.

A small bookstore, **Tucker's on Main** (1116 S. Main St., 828/295-4231, www.tuckersonmain.com, Mon.–Thurs. 9 A.M.–6 P.M., Fri.–Sat. 9 A.M.–7 P.M., Sun. 9 A.M.–6 P.M.) is located in the courtyard of the historic Martin House and offers fresh coffee as well as Internet access ($3 for 15 minutes, $6 for an hour, free Wi-Fi) and a large collection of books by local authors, including the Mitford series by Jan Karon.

On the outskirts of town, those looking for a bargain can check out the **Tanger Outlets** (828/295-4444, www.tangeroutlet.com), located only a half-mile from the Blue Ridge Parkway. The outlet mall has over 40 brand-name retailers, including Banana Republic, Liz Claiborne, J. Crew, Nautica, Bass, and Gap.

Sports and Recreation

Appalachian Ski Mountain (940 Ski Mountain Rd., 800/322-2373, www.appskimtn.com), while not the only ski resort in the High Country, is the only one in Blowing Rock. It has 10 slopes, offering terrain for skiers from beginning to accomplished levels, as well as two terrain parks, an ice-skating rink, and ski and snowboarding lessons for all ages. Seven nights a week the skating rink has a rinkside bonfire for warming up. The ski resort's lodge has guest rooms as well as a 200-foot observation deck, a restaurant, ski shop, and gift shop. The resort is open from mid-November through late March, but the lodge offers rooms year-round. The resort also has 22 campsites with RV hookups available year-round for $20 per night.

Accommodations
INNS AND BED-AND-BREAKFASTS
◖ **The Village Inns of Blowing Rock** (315 Sunset Dr., 800/821-4908, www.thevillageinnsofblowingrock.com) is actually a family of three inns, all of them located in or within walking distance of the downtown shopping and dining district. My favorite is the **Village Inn** (7876 Valley Blvd., 828/295-3380, $69–249), which is located on the outskirts of the downtown area. The 22-room inn has beautifully landscaped grounds abutting a small stream, and you're likely to see ducks floating on the inn's fountain pond. The rooms and suites here feature private covered porches overlooking the stream that flows behind the inn, and the atmosphere is secluded and peaceful enough that it's easy to forget you're right in town. Many suites feature hot tubs on the

porches, and most rooms have king-size beds, hardwood floors, small refrigerators, microwaves, coffee makers, and Wi-Fi access. The interior decor is warm and stylish with patterned rugs and cushioned lounge chairs. Bathrooms feature cultured stone showers. The only drawback is the inn's continental breakfast, which is sparse to say the least, with coffee, tea, bagels, muffins, and cereal. The other Village Inns of Blowing Rock are **Hillwinds Inn** (315 Sunset Dr., 828/295-7660, $69–169), which is less than a block from Main Street and has 20 guest rooms, and **Ridgeway Inn** (131 Yonahlossee Rd., 828/295-7321, $69–249), which was actually Blowing Rock's first inn and has 21 guest rooms available. Also close to Main Street, it is right behind the Bob Timberlake Gallery. All three inns offer additional accommodations in private cottages.

    The Inn at Ragged Gardens (203 Sunset Dr., 877/972-4433, www.ragged-gardens.com, $145–325) is in one of the sprawling "summer cottages" of many thousands of square feet that was once used to escape the heat and humidity of the coast and Piedmont. Of course, this inn isn't like any "cottage" you've ever seen, at least not in the modern sense of the word. The Inn at Ragged Gardens has, in fact, served as a boardinghouse or inn off and on since 1903. The home's original chestnut shakes have since been replaced with poplar bark siding, but still intact are its heavy wormy chestnut doors and a century-old rock wall that lines the inn's namesake gardens. All of the inn's 11 guest rooms are decadently luxurious. One of the most sumptuous is the Tree House Suite on the 3rd floor. A fantasy room with bark shingles for wall paneling and rough unfinished logs for ceiling beams, the Tree House Suite achieves its purpose—making guests feel they are spending the night in the boughs of the treetops. With a king-size bed positioned under skylights that peer into the leaves of overhanging tree limbs outside and a warm inglenook fireplace that can be viewed from both the bedroom and the spacious bath, this room spells escape from floor to ceiling.

    The **Inn at Crestwood** (3236 Shulls Mill Rd., 877/836-5046, www.crestwoodnc.com, $90–465) is actually located outside Blowing Rock and is a nice place to stay if you're looking to get away from town but still have easy access to area attractions. Available for overnight or weekly accommodations, the rooms, suites, and villas here are furnished like those of a typical nice hotel, with nothing particularly outstanding about them. But the views from the rooms' private porches are what you're really paying for. The inn is situated to afford lovely pink sunset views over the profile of Grandfather Mountain. (For one of the best views, request Room 12 on the 3rd floor.) Some rooms have fireplaces and jetted bathtubs. All inn guests have access to the spa with lap pool, steam bath, dry sauna, and exercise room; spa services require an additional fee. The inn has Wi-Fi available in common areas, though you may also be able to pick up a connection in your room, depending on its location. Between 4 and 5 P.M. the inn serves complimentary wine and cheese. Complimentary continental breakfast is served each morning in the inn's library, a quaint room with a stone fireplace and windows overlooking the landscaped grounds. But breakfast itself is lackluster—expect cereal, muffins, and danishes—and the service isn't great either. The inn has two restaurants on-site: The Table, which offers fine gourmet dining, and the Dawg Star Bar and Grille, which serves up burgers and sandwiches. To reach the inn, follow Highway 221 north out of town and take a right on Shulls Mill Road immediately before the Blue Ridge Parkway entrance. Shulls Mill Road is winding and narrow. Use caution, as drivers often drift over the center line.

RESORTS

Chetola (17 N. Main St., 800/243-8652, www.chetola.com, Chetola Lodge $145–322, Chetola Condominiums $164–680, Bob Timberlake Inn $209–369) is a resort community at the edge of town offering accommodations at the popular Bob Timberlake Inn as well as in a variety of condominium vacation rentals. At the center of the 87-acre resort is a scenic pond loaded with ducks and geese, where guests and owners can enjoy paddleboat rides. The Bob Timberlake Inn has warm and comfortably decorated guest rooms, all with fireplaces, whirlpool tubs, and signature Bob Timberlake furnishings. Chetola Lodge has 42 guest rooms and suites, and all lakefront rooms have private balconies. Guests can enjoy breakfast each morning at the Manor House Restaurant on-site or have breakfast delivered to their rooms. The Manor House also offers lunch and dinner. The quality of vacation rentals available at Chetola varies, as all are independently owned. If you want accommodations with full kitchens, two or more bedrooms, and plenty of space for large family get-togethers, the condos probably offer the better option. Whirlpool tubs, private porches, and Internet access are pretty standard amenities. Both inn and condominium guests enjoy access to all Chetola resort amenities, including the Highlands Sports and Recreation Center with its indoor pool, whirlpool, sauna, and fitness center. Guests can also arrange for horseback rides, boating, and massage services. Chetola has an interesting history. The estate was established in 1926 by J. Luther Snyder, who came to operate 10 Coca-Cola bottling plants in the Charlotte area, earning him the nickname the Coca-Cola King of the Carolinas. The property remained in the family until 1972, and became a resort in the 1980s.

Yonahlossee Resort and Club (Shulls Mill Rd., 828/963-6400, www.yonahlossee. com, $119–654) is just down the road from the Inn at Crestwood and offers cottages, townhomes, and single-family residences for rent. The resort is located at the original site of Camp Yonahlossee, a girls' camp developed here in the 1920s that thrived for nearly 60 years. The Gamekeeper Restaurant on-site is housed in the home of the camp's founders, Dr. and Mrs. A. P. Kephart. Today's guests can enjoy use of the resort's pool, tennis courts, and fitness center.

The **Hound Ears Club** (328 Shulls Mill Rd., 828/963-4301, www.houndears.com, $235–325) is one of the resort communities founded by the local Robbins clan; it offers lodge rooms and suites in the resort's Swiss-style clubhouse, some of them overlooking the club's 18-hole golf course, which guests can play if they are renting an accommodation that comes with club membership. There are also several single-family residences available for rent by the week, with rates starting at $1,400.

Located south of town off Highway 221, the **Westglow Resort and Spa** (224 Westglow Cir., 800/562-0807, www.westglowresortand-spa.com, $350–525) has six rooms available for overnight accommodations in its 1917 mansion house and three rooms available in its cedar lodge across the street. If you want to enjoy a sunny room with both sunrise and sunset views, request Room 12. Most guests who stay here purchase a spa package (one-night packages $576–849, two-night packages $1,137–1,588) that keeps them on-site all day, with meals included in the sunny dining room and enclosed porch of Rowland's Restaurant. The restaurant is only open to the general public for dinner. The grounds of Westglow are carefully manicured and offer long blue vistas to both the east and west, as the spa is situated on a narrow ridgeline. One can even see the famous Blowing Rock from here. Guests can choose to participate in a 9 A.M. guided hike of three to six miles each morning. Most, however, gravitate toward the Life Enrichment Center, which has a large fitness room with state-of-the-art exercise and weight-lifting equipment as well as an indoor pool, two hot tubs, steam room, and two dry saunas. A small poolside café offers refreshments throughout the day as well as lunch (all entrées are under 500 calories). The spa offers all the treatments you would expect—Swedish massage, facials, pedicures, wraps, and hair styling. The treatment rooms are especially posh, some with gas log fireplaces. While at the spa, guests enjoy free use of spa products (which are also available for sale) in the women's and men's baths. The best location at the spa is the Relaxation Lounge, which features comfy chaise lounges

Westglow Resort and Spa near Blowing Rock

facing a wall of windows overlooking the John's River Gorge.

CAMPING

The **Julian Price Park Campground** (Milepost 297, 828/963-5911, May–Oct., $16) offers a mix of sunny and shady campsites with several along a creek. The campground has 129 tent sites and 68 RV sites as well as a dump station. The campground is very popular on summer weekends, and you may find it full if you arrive late on a Friday.

Food

Crippen's Restaurant (239 Sunset Dr., 877/295-3487, www.crippens.com, $20–45), with its daily changing menu offerings, might just be the best spot for dinner in Blowing Rock. Among the specialty entrées you might encounter here are banana leaf–wrapped Florida swordfish, honey-glazed salmon, or chili-rubbed rib-eye steak. They're most famous for their chocolate steak, but unfortunately since the menu changes nightly you can't always get it! Be sure to try the chili fried

onion rings if they're available, and be sure to order the molten lava cake for dessert, with at least two forks—you probably won't want to eat it alone. The restaurant has a full bar, and reservations are recommended.

The Best Cellar (203 Sunset Dr., 828/295-3466, www.ragged-gardens.com, $10–42), located at the Inn at Ragged Gardens, is also popular. If you don't make a reservation beforehand, expect to wait up to an hour to be seated. The atmosphere is decidedly rustic, masculine, and a little bland, so it really does remind one of a wine cellar, especially in the basement seating area, where you can dine in a dim stone-walled room or the restaurant's actual wine cellar. If you're claustrophobic, opt for the main-floor dining room, which is located in a glassed-in porch. Due to the restaurant's popularity late diners will often find the most popular menu items unavailable; the Vidalia onion dip appetizer and zucchini casserole side dish are common victims. I recommend the rib-eye steak with blue cheese crumbles presented over a rich cheese sauce. Be wary, as the chef here seems

The Table restaurant at the Inn at Crestwood near Blowing Rock

to favor lemon on the heavy side; if a menu item indicates lemon as an ingredient expect the dish to be extremely tart, whether it's chicken or cheesecake. The restaurant also has a full wine list.

Glidewell's (1182 Main St., 828/295-9683) offers Blowing Rock's most scenic alfresco dining option, with a spacious stone terrace dining area overlooking Main Street. The fare here can probably best be described as global comfort food, with entrées ranging from conch fritters and jerk chicken to gumbo and crab cakes. The restaurant offers nightly specials based on what one might find in the chosen international city of the evening. The restaurant also offers live music.

While there are plenty of dining options downtown, you may want to check out the restaurants on the outskirts of Blowing Rock, many of which draw as many locals as tourists. Among them is **Canyons** (8960 Valley Blvd., 828/295-7661, www.canyonsbr.com, $7–18), which is a great spot to watch the sun set over Linville Gorge and Grandfather Mountain. The restaurant may look a little dilapidated

from the outside, but you'll know it's good just from the number of cars in the parking lot. Canyons has an extensive menu serving everything from North Carolina mountain trout to beef tenderloin, and it's a great place to hang out once the sun has gone down, too. Thursday to Sunday, beginning at 9 or 10 P.M., the restaurant has live music, ranging from blues and jazz to classic rock. Every Sunday, Canyons hosts a Jazz Brunch at 11 A.M., featuring Todd Wright and Friends.

The Gamekeeper (3005 Shulls Mill Rd., 828/963-7400, www.gamekeeper-nc.com) is located almost next door to the Inn at Crestwood on Shulls Mill Road. As its name suggests, the Gamekeeper serves buffalo, ostrich, and pheasant, as well as some tamer meat offerings. Many entrées are flavored with ramp pesto and blackberry barbecue sauce, giving them a unique kick.

The Inn at Crestwood has its own restaurant, too—**The Table** (3236 Shulls Mill Rd., 828/963-1417, www.crestwoodnc.com, $25). The setting is lovely, and the dining room has a cathedral ceiling, two-story stacked rock fireplace, and a wall of windows facing the outline of the Blue Ridge. Make reservations in advance, especially if you plan to dine on the weekend. Entrées include chocolate-ginger duck and teriyaki-glazed salmon. Be sure to try the sweet-potato spring rolls, too. One can get three courses here for only $25. For dessert, be sure to try the Cheerwine Ice Cream Napoleon.

INFORMATION AND SERVICES
Information
The main tourism office for the High Country, **North Carolina's High Country Host** (1700 Blowing Rock Rd., 800/438-7500, www.mountainsofnc.com), is located in Blowing Rock next door to KFC. However, there are visitors centers in just about every town in this part of the High Country. Among them are the **Blowing Rock Tourism Development Authority** (7738 Valley Blvd., 877/750-4636, www.blowingrock.com), which offers information on area attractions and businesses,

and the **Boone Area Chamber/Convention and Visitors Bureau** (208 Howard St., 800/852-9506, www.visitboonenc.com). You can also visit the **Watauga County Tourism Development Authority** (814 W. King St., 828/266-1345, www.exploreboonearea.com) in Boone.

The town of Banner Elk has a visitors bureau as well. The **Avery/Banner Elk Chamber** (800/972-2183, www.averycounty.com) is located in the Tynecastle Shopping Center (4501 Tynecastle Hwy., Unit #2). The **Beech Mountain Area Chamber of Commerce** (403-A Beech Mountain Pkwy., 828/387-9283, www.beechmtn.com) has information and brochures available for the East's highest town as well as surrounding communities.

Emergency Services
The **Watauga Medical Center** (336 Deerfield Rd., 828/262-4100, www.apprhs.org) is located right off Highway 321 in Boone on Deerfield Road.

South from Linville to Crabtree Meadows

█ LINN COVE VIADUCT
Construction of the Blue Ridge Parkway began in 1935, in the midst of the Great Depression, as one of President Franklin D. Roosevelt's many public works projects. What many people don't realize, however, is that the Parkway was not actually finished until 1987 with the completion of the Linn Cove Viaduct, a double-S-curve elevated bridge that clings to the side of Grandfather Mountain at Milepost 304.6.

The Linn Cove Viaduct is the poster child of the Parkway—it's likely you've seen pictures of it in countless brochures and guidebooks. The viaduct is something of an engineering marvel even by today's standards. Designed to avoid disturbing Grandfather Mountain's rare ecosystem with the vagaries of road construction, the viaduct is an elevated roadway composed of 153 concrete segments, only one of which

is straight. Each segment weighs 50 tons, and they are joined together by epoxy and massive steel tendons, the entire weight of the structure supported by seven concrete piers.

The viaduct is 1,243 feet long and 35 feet wide and is located at an elevation of 4,100 feet. The unusual construction process involved progressive placement of the roadway sections, in which each section was built upon the next to avoid setting up equipment and scaffolding on the mountainside. All of the bridge sections were cast indoors near the construction site. The total cost of the project was $10 million.

Linn Cove Viaduct Visitor Center
The Linn Cove Viaduct Visitor Center (Milepost 304.8, 828/733-1354, May–Oct. daily 9 A.M.–5 P.M.) is worth a quick stop, as it provides an explanation of the bridge's

© FRENCH C. GRIMES

bridge on the Tanawha Trail

construction and displays many historic photographs of the process. There is an information desk here with maps and brochures as well as a small gift shop and restrooms.

Tanawha Trail, Rough Ridge to Wilson Creek

- Distance: 1.45 miles one-way
- Duration: 2 hours
- Elevation gain: 480 feet
- Difficulty: Moderate
- Trailhead: At the Rough Ridge parking area, Milepost 302.4

While the entire length of the Tanawha Trail is more than 13 miles, most travelers only hike small sections of the trail. One of the best parts is from the Rough Ridge parking area to the Wilson Creek Overlook; it offers several viewpoints of the Linn Cove Viaduct. From the parking area you'll climb up a series of log steps through rhododendron and past a gnarled birch tree to a fork. Take the left fork of the trail, and cross a pedestrian bridge over a stream that courses over the long face of a rock under the bowing limbs of rhododendron and hemlock. Like the other trails that skirt around Grandfather Mountain, the path is laden with small boulders, making the going slow.

The trail ascends steeply for a short distance, then levels out as it curls around the mountain. Gradually, the tree cover lessens, and you move into a more open landscape of mountain laurel and rhododendron thickets. The path will diverge onto a boardwalk, designed to keep hikers from damaging the mountainside's fragile flora, and you'll experience mountain views in all directions plus a nice photo opportunity of the Linn Cove Viaduct to the south. Above you is Grandfather Mountain, likely encircled in a ring of white clouds. To the east is the rolling North Carolina Piedmont. All around you are chunky rock outcroppings slowly being overtaken by creeping blueberries, moss, grass, lichen, and sandmyrtle. To the south, you can see the open face of Beacon Heights, the endpoint of the Tanawha Trail were you to hike it from one end to the other.

Be sure to obey the signs and stay on the boardwalk. If you look around you'll see gray and dying vegetation, the result of damage inflicted by hikers who strayed from the designated trail. If you happen to visit in fall, look for the bright orange-red berries of the Mountain Ash.

Once you leave the boardwalk, you'll ascend through a tunnel of short dense trees. Keep an eye out for the razor-like leaves of small chestnut trees—none of them will grow to mature height, as they eventually succumb to blight. Eventually, the trail opens up again to a series of small rock outcroppings offering more views and a closer look at the viaduct. The trail becomes progressively steeper, climbing over boulders and curling up the mountain. Pause and sit on one of the boulders. Take in the view for a time, and listen to the multitude of birds skipping among the branches of the low-growing trees and shrubs searching for berries.

As the trail starts to descend again you might want to turn around and hike back to your car, or, if you set up a car shuttle, you can continue to the Wilson Creek Overlook parking area.

◖ GRANDFATHER MOUNTAIN

I can just barely remember my first visit to Grandfather Mountain (2050 Blowing Rock Hwy., 800/468-7325, www.grandfather.com, daily spring 8 A.M.–6 P.M., summer 8 A.M.–7 P.M., fall 8 A.M.–6 P.M., winter 9 A.M.–5 P.M., adults $15, 60 and over $13, children 4–12 $7). It was 1978 and I was three years old. Those were the days of Mildred the Bear, the since-departed mascot of Grandfather Mountain. Mildred made an impression. This black bear that Grandfather Mountain park founder Hugh Morton purchased in 1968, hoping to return her to the wild on the rocky mountainside he inherited from his maternal grandfather, followed me all my days and prompted a lifelong fascination with bears. Even though Mildred is long gone, having died in 1993, her descendants aren't, and they remain one of the primary attractions at this vastly beautiful nature park that today is listed as an International Biosphere Reserve.

Grandfather Mountain is only one mile from the Parkway; exit at Highway 221 south toward Linville at Milepost 305. Approaching the entrance during summer or fall, you'll see a gentleman to your left selling shelves of homemade preserves. He has been there as far back as I can remember and will likely be there when you visit, too! Keep in mind as you prepare to visit this rugged mountain that Grandfather has its own weather. It might be sunny and warm on the Parkway, but on the summit of Grandfather the fog might be so dense you can feel the dampness of it, and, more likely than not, it will also be chilly, no matter the time of year. If you're brave enough to visit in winter, expect high winds at the summit but also an incredible and otherworldly display of rime ice. The highest recorded wind speed at Grandfather was 196 mph on April 18, 1997.

With an elevation of 5,946 feet, Grandfather Mountain gets more than its fair share of exposure to pollutants, including 100 pounds of sulfates per acre per year in acid rainfall, which has led, over the years, to the decline of the mountain's spruce-fir forest at the summit. However, if you've visited the mountain in the past, you will be pleased to see some recovery of the high-elevation forest, due in part to increasing regulations against the release of harmful emissions by automobiles, power plants, and factories.

An International Biosphere Reserve, Grandfather Mountain has its own ecosystem and some 70 varieties of endangered flora and fauna. Among the rare and endangered species who call this mountain home are the Northern Flying Squirrel and the peregrine falcon, which was first reintroduced here in 1984.

Picnic areas are scattered throughout the park, and there are restroom facilities at both the Nature Museum and the Top Shop. There is also a restaurant and gift shop adjacent to the Nature Museum.

Nature Museum

The Nature Museum is the best place to start your tour of Grandfather Mountain, as it will provide you with some background on the

© FRENCH C. GRIMES

black bear at Grandfather Mountain's Wildlife Habitat

mountain's ecology as well as information on the critters you'll see in the Wildlife Habitat. Be sure to get your picture taken with the bronze statue of Mildred the Bear and her cubs! The museum also has a continually running film in the theater. The film's subject matter varies depending on the season, but you'll likely see a video by either the late Hugh Morton or his son Jim Morton, celebrating the scenic beauty and beloved wildlife of Grandfather Mountain. If you have children in tow, be sure to pick up a Grandfather Mountain Junior Ranger brochure at the museum to help make the visit more fun for the little ones.

Wildlife Habitat

Grandfather Mountain has an expansive Wildlife Habitat where black bears roam in company with injured bald and golden eagles, mountain lions, and playful river otters. After the Mile-High Swinging Bridge, the wildlife habitat is Grandfather's biggest attraction. The entrance to the habitat area is to the left of the Nature Museum. A paved trail descends here through a lush forest of rhododendron, spruce,

firs, and hemlocks. If you have pets traveling with you, leave them at your vehicle, as no pets are allowed in the Wildlife Habitat.

The first habitat you'll encounter is that of the bald and golden eagles. All of the birds were injured by gunshot wounds and are no longer able to fly. Though they'll likely not spread their wings for you, these birds have wing spans of six to eight feet. For nearly four decades, the bald eagle was an endangered species in the continental United States, his declining population due in large part to the widespread use of DDT as a pesticide after World War II and a general lack of public education on the fragility of the national bird and his sensitivity to human activity and changes in habitat. Today, however, the bald eagle has made an amazing recovery; in 2006 it was delisted as an endangered species by the U.S. Fish and Wildlife Service.

The black bear habitat is, not surprisingly, the most popular. And the bears know they're stars, too. There is one who, every time I have visited, can be found sitting on his haunches, paws in his lap, looking mournfully up at human onlookers in hopes of getting a treat. Staff sell treats to feed the bears during certain periods of the day; this might be one of the few opportunities you have while visiting the mountains to legally feed the wildlife. Keep in mind that the bears at Grandfather Mountain, though endearingly rotund, are not anything like the average black bear you might encounter in the woods. Wild black bears are much leaner, weighing in at anywhere from 100 to 600 pounds and measuring about four to six feet in length. While we tend to look on them as carnivores, black bears eat mostly vegetative matter like nuts and berries. They also like insects. There are about 4,000 black bears in the mountains of western North Carolina, and their population is steadily growing.

The Wildlife Habitat is also home to an Eastern Cougar, a species that is almost extinct in the eastern United States. There are no known mating pairs in North Carolina, the panther having been nearly extinguished by hunting. If you're amazed by the number of white-tailed deer you see in the Blue Ridge Mountains, keep in mind that their only major predator (apart from man, whose

hunting is regulated) is the now nearly extinct Eastern Cougar.

The river otter habitat is also very popular, especially with kids, who enjoy watching the antics of these limber swimmers. As a species, the North American river otter can live almost anywhere, from high-elevation mountains to lowland coastal areas. Their numbers in the wild are diminishing, however, because they are extremely sensitive to pollution. The use of pesticides, in particular, which contaminates the waters they inhabit as well as the fish they eat, is a major cause of their decline.

Rangers hold programs at the various wildlife habitats throughout the day. Check for times on signage at each habitat.

Mile-High Swinging Bridge

The major draw of Grandfather Mountain is no doubt the Mile-High Swinging Bridge, which is exactly what its name indicates, a swinging bridge just below the 5,890-foot summit of Grandfather Mountain. You'll have to climb several steps to reach the bridge, and if it's windy, you might find a walk across the bridge a jolting experience! Even on a calm day,

Mile-High Swinging Bridge at Grandfather Mountain

however, the bridge will move some with your motion and the motion of other visitors. The swinging bridge crosses a forested ravine to a rock outcropping that provides 360-degree views of the surrounding mountains and High Country communities of Linville and Banner Elk. You can get the best photographs of the swinging bridge by climbing up onto the rocks beyond the observation platform, but be careful—and keep a tight rein on your children.

The trade-off for a calm day up here is the likelihood that you'll also be fogged in. But even if you end up visiting the mountain on such a day, take advantage of the opportunities the fog provides for you to focus on what is near instead of what is far away. Observe the mountain's high-elevation vegetation— the low-growing spruce, mosses clinging to boulders, trees with branches and needles all growing on the side against the prevailing winds. Consider the marvel of flora carving out a life on this desolate, rocky mountainside. In late summer, you'll notice ripe blueberries everywhere.

Hiking

To truly experience Grandfather Mountain (and to escape the swarms of people you'll likely find here in mid-summer and fall), take time to hike some of the mountain's trails. Grandfather Mountain is loaded with trails on which most visitors never set foot, including the five-mile round-trip Grandfather Trail, a steep and strenuous journey from the Black Rock parking area that traverses the mountain's jagged ridgeline. Ladders and cables occasionally provide aid to the intrepid hiker on this trail, but far less strenuous yet equally overlooked hikes also beckon here.

BRIDGE TRAIL

- Distance: 0.4 mile one-way
- Duration: 45 minutes
- Elevation gain: 400 feet
- Difficulty: Moderate

- Trailhead: Accessible across the road from the Black Rock parking area as well as from a trailhead to the right of the Top Shop at the Mile-High Swinging Bridge

This is a popular trail because of its close access to the Swinging Bridge, and is a good hike to take if you have kids and want something short but fun (children will love the little bit of rock scramble required here). If you start this hike from the Mile-High Swinging Bridge parking area, you'll get a unique look at the swinging bridge from below, including a peek at its massive spring-loaded anchors. After passing under the bridge, the trail descends quickly through dense vegetation. The path is rugged (like all trails on Grandfather), requiring you to scramble a bit over rocks and watch your footing. The trail provides a quick look at the flora of Grandfather Mountain as well as the incredible ruggedness of the landscape. If you prefer to be hiking downhill on your way back, then hike up from the Black Rock parking area rather than starting at the Swinging Bridge.

BLACK ROCK TRAIL

- Distance: 0.8 mile one-way
- Duration: 1.5 hours
- Elevation gain: 400 feet
- Difficulty: Moderate
- Trailhead: At the end of the Black Rock parking area

The Black Rock Trail is a self-guided nature trail that leads all the way to an overlook for Grandmother Mountain. Along the way, trail signs identify the surrounding flora. This is an excellent trail for observing the plant life of Grandfather Mountain and also a good place for getting away from the crowds. The trail first passes through a forest of American Mountain Ash and rhododendron, then moves into a dense spruce forest. Watch your footing as you go; there are a lot of exposed tree roots and rocks to scramble over. If you happen to be traversing this trail in mid-summer, watch for the white spiky blooms of galax, which can also be identified by its heart-shaped waxy green leaves.

The farther you progress from the parking lot, the more narrow and less traveled the trail becomes, passing through the entwined limbs of rhododendron and mountain laurel and under the dense shade of ash and spruce trees. This is a very peaceful trail. Pause occasionally and listen for birds skittering through the branches and for the dropping sounds of condensing fog and leftover dew.

At interpretive sign 10, you'll have the opportunity to pause at a tiny trilling brook. Note the sumptuous forest carpet of lady fern, and shortly after this brook crossing you'll see a red spruce and yellow spruce growing together in what looks like a single tree. Stop for a while, sit quietly on a rock, and let the forest come alive around you. This is the purpose of this trail, after all. If you are observant, you might see a shrew scamper across an old rotted tree trunk, or you can trace the sinuous striped roots of a birch tree as it nuzzles among the rocks for a soil foothold.

As you continue on your trek, the views will open gradually to reveal views of the Swinging Bridge as well as lovely views of Grandmother Mountain, Beacon Heights, and the Blue Ridge Parkway far below. Return to the parking lot via the same route.

GRANDFATHER MOUNTAIN STATE PARK

Grandfather Mountain State Park (828/297-7261, www.ncparks.gov) is a recent addition to North Carolina's State Park system, having been carved out of Grandfather Mountain's backcountry in 2008. Most of the 12 miles of trails in the park are extremely challenging, following the mountain ridgeline and cresting Calloway Peak. Use of ladders and cables is necessary on many trails, and you should allow a full day to complete any of the hikes here.

HIGHLAND GAMES

The Highland Games (828/733-1333, www.gmhg.org) at Grandfather Mountain are the super bowl of Highland games on the East Coast. Held each year in July (usually on the second weekend), the games draw thousands of people to MacRae Meadows. Activities include live traditional Celtic music, Highland dancing, Scottish track and field events, sheep-herding demonstrations, piping, and drumming. If you're not coming to Grandfather Mountain for the games, it's best to completely avoid the mountain that weekend, as it will be swarming with people.

BEACON HEIGHTS

Outside the nature park of Grandfather Mountain and almost directly across the Parkway from its profile is the Beacon Heights Trail at Milepost 305.1, one of my favorite short hikes on the Parkway. Less than a mile one-way, this moderate hike opens onto a wide, flat, open quartzite ledge with some of the best views around of Grandfather Mountain as well as Table Rock and Hawksbill.

LINVILLE FALLS WILDERNESS AREA
Linville Falls Visitors Center

Most travelers access the trails of the Linville Falls Wilderness Area at the Blue Ridge Parkway's Linville Falls Visitors Center (Milepost 316.4, 828/765-1045, May–Oct. daily 9 A.M.–5 P.M.), which has a small gift shop, an information desk where you can pick up trail maps and other Parkway brochures, and restrooms. Unless you're desperate, however, skip the restrooms here: They are small and not designed to accommodate the stream of visitors this section of the Parkway receives so are, as a result, not very well maintained. You can avoid some of the visitor traffic (and enjoy slightly easier hikes to the falls) by entering the Wilderness Area from the Forest Service entry point at Wiseman's View. Exit the Parkway at Milepost 317.5 and get on 221 south, then take an immediate left onto Wiseman's View Road.

Parking for the Linville Falls trailhead will be on your left.

◖ Linville Falls Erwin's View Trail

- Distance: 1.6 miles round-trip

- Duration: 1.5 hours

- Elevation gain: 300 feet

- Difficulty: Moderate

- Trailhead: Directly behind the Linville Falls Visitors Center

Whether you begin your journey at the Linville Falls Visitors Center or at the Forest Service entrance at Wiseman's View, you'll find the first part of your hike an easy one along a wide (and heavily traveled) trail loaded with stands of rhododendron on either side. If you're lucky enough to be here in July, the Rosebay rhododendron will be in full bloom, creating a wall of pale pink and white flowers on either side of you. The trees here are mostly hardwoods—oaks, maples, hickories, and poplars.

After less than half a mile, you'll reach the intersection of the Parkway and Forest Service trails, and from here the hike is the same for everyone. There are various overlook points along the way that will provide different views of the falls and the Linville Gorge. You can make your hike as short or as long as you want, but if you have the time, it's worth exploring them all.

The trail to Chimney View and Erwin's View is wide but a continual uphill climb. Chimney View has two overlooks accessible via a series of steps. The upper Chimney View provides a full portrait of the upper falls and a limited look at the lower. You may notice, if you visit in spring or summer, the masses of dead and dying hemlocks scaling the walls of the gorge, all of them victims of the hemlock woolly adelgid. The Forest Service is making efforts to treat trailside hemlocks. If you look carefully while walking the trails, you'll see some healthy hemlock trees marked with blue

Linville Falls

© FRENCH C. GRIMES

dots, which indicate they're receiving treatment against this invasive pest.

The lower Chimney View provides a panorama of the plunge basin where the Linville River curls through a tunnel of limestone, swirling into white foam, before dropping again at the lower falls.

As you approach Erwin's View, veer to the right for a Gorge View overlook, which will provide you a glimpse of the Linville River Gorge and, again, the ghostly effects of the hemlock woolly adelgid. The left fork of the trail takes you to Erwin's View on a gradual uphill walk to a full panorama of the falls.

To return, retrace your steps to the parking area.

Dugger's Creek Loop

- Distance: 0.25 mile

- Duration: 20 minutes

- Elevation gain: Minimal

- Difficulty: Easy
- Trailhead: Accessible to the left of the Linville Falls Visitors Center

This easy walk through the woods is an overlooked gem of the Linville Falls area and not very heavily traveled either. Make sure you take a few minutes for this one, which I like to describe as a walking poem. The trail begins through a tunnel of Rosebay rhododendron along a spongy, pine-needled path. There are a few signs along the way carrying the quotations of conservationists like John Muir. Shortly after the trail veers away from the Linville Falls parking area, it crosses a small bridge over a cascading stream with a tiny (yet remarkably loud) waterfall spilling into a dark pool below.

After crossing the bridge, you'll climb a series of stone steps up around a large boulder wreathed in mountain laurel. You'll notice carpets of shiny galax on either side of the trail as you descend again and enter another tunnel of rhododendron branches. The trail then follows the stream again, which you'll cross on stepping stones below a gentle cascade. Pause for a moment at this crossing and note the view of more dribbling stream cascades as well as the rhododendron climbing around the trees and then bending low to kiss the water.

Linville Falls Picnic Area

If you happen to hit the Linville Falls area at lunchtime, consider having a picnic at the Linville Falls picnic area, which is directly across the Parkway from the visitors center and trailheads. The picnic area is large and situated alongside the Linville River. Rhododendron is everywhere, including along the river, where its branches dip delicately into the amber-colored water. If you can, get a table along the river. The picnic area has a nice covered shelter for large groups that is available on a first-come, first-served basis, and most of the picnic tables have grills nearby. There are also restrooms available.

LINVILLE AND LINVILLE FALLS AREA

Because of these two villages' proximity to the popular attractions of Grandfather Mountain and Linville Falls, they can be very busy places. As much as possible, travel the Parkway through these areas rather than getting on congested Highway 221 between Linville and Linville Falls.

Linville River Mercantile and Bakery

Worth a quick stop if you're on your way to The Crossnore School, the Linville River Mercantile and Bakery (5650 Hwy. 221, Crossnore, 828/719-9510) carries homemade apple butter, peach and blueberry preserves, and desserts made by baker-owner Jennifer King. The store also sells fresh-squeezed lemonade and carries a small inventory of costume jewelry, pottery, and gifts.

E. H. Sloop Chapel at The Crossnore School

E. H. Sloop Chapel (100 DAR Dr., Crossnore, 828/733-4305, daily 8:30 A.M.–5 P.M., except when chapel is in session) at The Crossnore School is part of the Churches of the Frescoes Trail (www.churchofthefrescoes.com) and houses another of Ben Long's frescoes, *Suffer the Little Children*. The Crossnore School can be a little tricky to find. The easiest way from the Parkway is to exit onto Highway 221 north at Milepost 317. You'll travel about five miles. Watch for a small sign on your right, directing you to turn left to reach The Crossnore School (the road is not otherwise marked). Next you'll take a right onto Miracle Hills Drive, and then just follow the signs for the E. H. Sloop Chapel and Frescoes.

Crossnore Weavers and Gallery

Just below the E. H. Sloop Chapel is the Crossnore Weavers and Gallery (DAR Dr., Crossnore, 800/374-4660, www.crossnore-weavers.org, free), a working museum that gives you the opportunity to watch loom weavers at

© DEBORAH HUSO

Linville River Mercantile and Bakery near Crossnore

work. An on-site store has textiles, wearables, and crafts by local artisans for sale. All proceeds from the gallery store go to benefit The Crossnore School, which serves abused, abandoned, and neglected children from all over North Carolina.

Linville Caverns

Linville Caverns (19929 U.S. 221 N., Marion, 800/419-0540, www.linvillecaverns.com, Mar. and Nov. daily 9 A.M.–4:30 P.M., Apr.–May and Sept.–Oct. daily 9 A.M.–5 P.M., June–Aug. daily 9 A.M.–6 P.M., Dec.–Feb. Sat.–Sun. 9 A.M.–4:30 P.M., adults $7, seniors $5.50, children 5–12 $5, under 5 free) is the only show cave in North Carolina and perhaps, for that reason alone, worth a visit. Tours only take about 45 minutes, and the caverns are pretty easy to access. Exit the Parkway at Milepost 317, and take Highway 221 south toward Marion. The cavern entrance is on the right after four miles and is well marked.

The caverns are popular and busy, which is one reason tours run every five minutes.

You may still have to wait a bit to get in, however. The caverns stretch 1,200 feet inside Humpback Mountain (which you'll drive across on the Parkway), though visitors are only allowed inside the first 600 feet of the cave. As you enter the cave along a tiny stream that feeds out of it, you'll notice speckled trout swimming in and out of the entrance, and you might spot a few salamanders and crawdads as well.

If you've ever visited some of the more popular eastern show caves like Luray Caverns in Virginia, you might be disappointed with Linville. The cavern passages are narrow, and often it's like walking through a tunnel. The highest room stretches 23 feet from floor to ceiling, and one section of the cave will require you to make your way down a passage so narrow that you'll have to shimmy and stoop between walls while walking over a metal bridge over what seems like a depthless pool below. (Note that the tour guide will let you stand this section out if you want!)

The caverns are made up mostly of dolomite

and limestone, and the shiny green coloring you'll see on many of the rocks is actually the result of algae and the cave's electric lights. The purple and blue colors are from cobalt deposits. Be warned that, like so many show cave tours, this one does involve a stage where the guide will turn out the lights and leave you standing for a few minutes in total darkness. If that gives you the willies, you might want to skip this tour.

Remember to wear a sweater or jacket into the cave, even in summer. The caverns remain at a consistent temperature of 52 degrees. Do not touch the surfaces of the walls, stalagmites, or stalactites while on tour. The oil in your hands can ruin the colors and stunt the growth of formations over time. Cameras are allowed but no tripods.

Chestoa View

The Chestoa View Overlook (Milepost 321) is a good place to stop and stretch your legs. There are picnic tables and trash cans here but also an easy 0.8-mile loop trail from the parking lot to a viewpoint from Humpback Mountain that overlooks the Catawba River Valley and the Linville Gorge Wilderness. This is an ideal spot for hawk-watching as well, and chances are you'll see them soaring over the valley from the various viewpoints along the path.

Accommodations
LODGING
While there are a number of accommodations in the Linville and Linville Falls area, most are motor inns and not particularly inviting. One exception is **Eseeola Lodge** (175 Linville Ave., Linville, 800/742-6717, www.eseeola.com, deluxe room $400–475, suites $500–575, cottage $700 for two people, $1,050 for four people), which has 24 luxuriously appointed rooms and one guest cottage available. The lodge is located at the Linville Falls Golf Club. Guests can take advantage of the bar, fitness center, spa, and, of course, the golf course. All rooms have Wi-Fi. The lodge is only open May through October.

Another option that's not as pricey is **Linville Falls Lodge and Cottages** (8730 NC 183, Linville Falls, 828/765-2658, www. linvillefallslodge.com), which has prettily landscaped grounds and gardens that surround the simple yet neat gray board-and-batten one-story lodge.

CAMPING
The **Linville Falls Campground** (Milepost 316.3, 828/765-7818, $16) is accessible via a spur road off the Parkway, the same road that leads to the Linville Falls Visitors Center. This is a very scenic campground with many campsites on the river, though there are a number of sites standing out in full sun as well, making them a bit less pleasant. There are 50 tent sites and 20 RV sites as well as a dump station. Arrive early if you want to claim a site in the shade.

Linville Falls Campground and Trailer Lodge (717 Gurney Franklin Rd., 828/765-2681, www.linvillefalls.com, Apr.–Nov., tent sites $20, RV sites $32–35, cabins $60–150) has 35 full hookup sites as well as primitive tent sites and tent sites with water and electric. Bathhouses are available, and there is a playground on-site. Cabins are available year-round.

Bear Den Campground (600 Bear Den Mountain Rd., 877/308-2888, www.bearden.com, Mar.–Nov., tent and RV sites $35–105, cabins and cottages $65–230) is located directly off the Parkway. Exit at Milepost 324.8 onto Bear Den Mountain Road (due to Parkway regulations, there are no signs for the campground on the Parkway). The campground has both tent and RV sites with electric, water, and sewer hookups as well as fire rings and picnic tables. Bathhouses are available, as are laundry facilities. Campers can purchase firewood, ice, drinks, groceries, and LP gas at the campground trading post. There are also playgrounds, shuffleboard, and a game room with table tennis, pool tables, and video games. The campground has a small lake with a sand beach. Bear Den has camping cabins, creekside cabins, and RV rentals available as well.

Food
The Tartan Restaurant (1 Hemingway St., 828/733-0799, Mon.–Wed. 7 A.M.–2 P.M.,

Thurs.–Sat. 7 A.M.–2 P.M. and 5:30–9 P.M.,
$7–19) is my first pick for breakfast, lunch,
or dinner when in Linville. The fare here is
consistently good, no matter what you order,
and the restaurant has an excellent fresh salad
bar that includes in-season fruits with yogurt
for dipping, fresh bread, soup, and a variety
of cheeses. You can get just about anything
here from prime rib to popcorn shrimp, or
you can easily get a full meal out of the salad
bar for $9.95. Their homemade soups are di-
vine. The vegetable beef soup is so loaded
with ingredients that there is barely room for
the broth. The Scottish-themed atmosphere
is decidedly green and a bit 1950s, and the
Tartan serves a very local and senior crowd.
If you arrive before opening time at breakfast or dinner, expect a line outside the door.
Not readily apparent from Highway 221,
the Tartan Restaurant is located behind the
Highland Games headquarters building on
Hemingway Street.

SPRUCE PINE

The mountains along this stretch of the
Parkway and the surrounding communities
are part of the Spruce Pine Mining District,
which is home to large deposits of feldspar,
mica, and quartz, all of which can be viewed
at the Museum of North Carolina Minerals.
714 mines are on record in the district, most of
them now defunct. North Carolina is home to
North America's only emerald crystal deposits,
including ruby, sapphire, garnet, aquamarine,
tourmaline, and even a handful of diamonds.
Some of these gemstones, like sky-blue hyanite
and emerald-green hiddenite, are found here in
the Spruce Pine Mining District and almost
nowhere else in the world.

Mining was going on in these mountains
long before European Americans began formal
mining operations here in the 19th century.
The earliest people who lived here during the
Woodland period 2,000 years ago mined for
mica, which they used as grave decoration and
for wampum or money. Supposedly Spanish
explorer Hernando De Soto explored the area
around 1540 hoping to find gold and silver,

though all he managed to uncover was the silver mica we know today as muscovite mica.

In the 1700s, the Cherokee mined feldspar
and kaolin and traded it with settlers, who ultimately sent it off to England where it became
an ingredient in English ceramics. Mining of
mica and feldspar in what would later become
known as the Spruce Pine Mining District continued on and off into the early 20th century.
Some of that mining was fueled by the need for
sheet mica as an electrical insulator for Thomas
Edison's newly developed electric motor.

In the early 20th century, mining operations
began to take off more rapidly in the Spruce
Pine area with the formation of the Carolina
Minerals Company of Penland, which mined
feldspar for ceramic plants as far away as New
Jersey and Ohio. In 1914, the Clinchfield
Mineral and Mining Company built feldspar-
grinding plants in nearby Erwin, Tennessee,
and by 1917, North Carolina was the largest
producer of feldspar in the United States, a
claim it still holds to this day.

The primary minerals off the Spruce
Pine Mining District are feldspar, mica, and
quartz. Feldspar is an essential ingredient in
many types of glass, including the glass used
in electric lightbulbs and vehicle windshields.
It continues to be a major ingredient in manufacturing ceramic products, too. Muscovite, a
variety of mica, is a major component of dry-
wall joint compound, while quartz is used in
concrete and concrete mortar.

◖ Orchard at Altapass

The Orchard at Altapass (Milepost 328,
Altapass, 888/765-9531, www.altapassor-
chard.com, Nov.–Apr. Mon. and Wed.–Sat.
10 A.M.–6 P.M., May–Oct. Mon. and Wed.–
Sat. 10 A.M.–6 P.M., Sun. noon–6 P.M., free)
has been in almost continuous operation in one
form or another since the early 1900s when
it was created by the Chesapeake & Ohio
Railroad. CSX still runs coal trains through
13 miles of switchbacks near the orchard, but
the railroad sold the orchard in 1925. Since
then the orchard has had half a dozen owners,
the most recent ones having turned it into a

© DEBORAH HUSO

the Orchard at Altapass

nonprofit organization dedicated not only to growing nearly infinite varieties of apples but also to promoting local Appalachian culture and music.

Today the orchard consists of 135 acres, 60 of them in apple trees. Some of the orchard's varieties include Red Delicious, York Imperial, and Grimes Golden. In all, the orchard produces 40 varieties of apples from 3,000 trees. The largest harvest the current orchard owners have ever produced was 7,000 bushels of apples. In its heyday, the orchard produced 125,000 bushels. But the biggest harvest today is the orchard's visitors—60,000 a year, in fact.

In addition to growing, harvesting, and selling apples to the public, the orchard has also become a center of western North Carolina culture and history, drawing locals and tourists alike to its many special events from May through October. In the summer, local musicians play country and bluegrass music at the orchard every Saturday and Sunday afternoon, drawing two-steppers out onto the orchard store's nine-sheet dance floor. Among the regulars who play at Altapass are Terry McKinney, Jann Welch, and Alan Tinney. The Orchard at Altapass also hosts craft demonstrations by local artisans, book signings and lectures,

butterfly tagging, and local storytelling. The orchard also has herb and butterfly gardens. An on-site country store sells apples and apple products, fudge, books, crafts, and gifts as well as CDs of some of the musicians they host.

The Orchard at Altapass also happens to be located on a portion of the Overmountain Victory Trail, the route that 1,000 patriots from the mountain backcountry followed in 1780 on their way to join forces with patriots in the Piedmont in an effort to drive the British out of the mountains. The effort ultimately succeeded in doing just that. The push east resulted in the Battle of Kings Mountain on October 7, 1780, which pushed the British out of North Carolina, making a decisive impact on the outcome of the American Revolution. To learn more about the Overmountain Victory National Historic Trail, visit www. nps.gov/ovvi.

Museum of North Carolina Minerals

The Museum of North Carolina Minerals (Milepost 330.9, 828/765-2761, daily 9 A.M.–5 P.M., free) shares a building with the Mitchell County Chamber of Commerce just off the Parkway at the Spruce Pine exit. While a museum on gemstones and minerals doesn't sound that exciting, this place is worth a stop because it provides some fascinating insights into the local mining culture and history.

This area was mined long before European Americans began scouring the mountainsides for gemstones; 3,000 years ago Native Americans mined soapstone here and used it for carving bowls and household implements. Among the other fun facts you'll learn while touring the museum is that the ultrapure quartz used to form the crucibles for growing the silicon found in our computer chips comes exclusively from Spruce Pine.

The museum is kid friendly with many interactive exhibits on small-person level, and there are displays of some of North Carolina's more than 300 minerals in the rough. Among the exhibits here are oral histories of local miners, a black light display that causes certain minerals to fluoresce or "glow," and a video showing a high-speed re-creation of the grand collision that created the Appalachian Mountains.

Penland School of Crafts

About a 20-minute drive from Spruce Pine and accessible only via a winding narrow mountain road that climbs and climbs into the woods, the Penland School of Crafts (67 Doras Tr., 828/765-2359, www.penland.org) is one of many craft and folk schools in the southern Appalachians, most of them born out of the Great Depression and efforts to bring self-sufficiency and additional income sources to the working poor. The Penland School was founded by western North Carolina native Lucy Morgan, who came to the community of Penland to teach in 1920 when she was 30 years old. Discovering the local and nearly dead art of handweaving among her new mountain neighbors, Morgan decided to dedicate her life to reviving handweaving and other native crafts. She founded the Penland Weavers, a group of local female handweavers, in 1923, and that initially small group would be the genesis of the craft school.

In 1929, Morgan, who had helped with the founding of the Southern Highland Craft Guild the year before, decided it was time to found a school, and that was the first year Penland hosted weaving students from outside the local community. Students paid $1 per day for room, board, and tuition.

Penland garnered national attention when the weavers demonstrated at the World's Fair in Chicago in 1933, and by the 1940s and '50s the Penland School was enrolling students from all over the world. It began to add other handicrafts, including metalwork and pottery making. Morgan retired from the school in 1962, but it is still operational today and consists of a rustic campus of 40 log and frame buildings where students of all ages from all walks of life spend anywhere from one to several weeks learning the old-time crafts of the southern mountains.

The school offers 98 one- to two-week classes in a variety of handicrafts, including textiles, clay, painting, drawing, metalwork, wood, glass, and printmaking. Eight-week sessions are available in the spring and fall. Today the Penland campus encompasses nearly 400 acres, and 1,200 students attend classes at the school each year. The school also has a residency program for established artists who can stay at the school and concentrate on their work for up to three years.

Taking a class here is a worthwhile experience, but if you don't have a week to devote to learning a new skill you should at least pay a visit to the **Penland Gallery** (31315 Conley Ridge Rd., Mar.–Dec. Tues.–Sat. 10 A.M.–5 P.M., Sun. noon–5 P.M., free), which showcases and sells the work of resident artists and students.

Penland is about five miles northwest of Spruce Pine off U.S. 19E.

Entertainment and Events

It should come as no surprise that special events in the Spruce Pine area often center around gems and minerals. One of the most popular annual festivals is the **North Carolina Mineral, Gem & Jewelry Festival** (800/227-3912, www.ncgemfest.com, $3) during the last weekend in July. The four-day event takes place at the Pinebridge Coliseum (207 Pinebridge Ave.) and features gem, jewelry, and mineral dealers from all over the country. You can purchase anything here from fine jewelry to raw minerals and crystals. The festival also offers the opportunity for tours to area mines.

An outdoor festival of similar description, the **Grassy Creek Mineral & Gem Show** (828/765-2177, free) occurs annually in July. Here gem and mineral dealers from around the world set up shop for a week in the field next to the Parkway Fire and Rescue (12966 Hwy. 226 S.) in Spruce Pine.

Shopping

There isn't a great deal in the way of shopping in Spruce Pine, as this is more working town than tourist town, but the downtown district (about six miles from the Parkway) does have a few stores worth checking out if you have some time to wander. Note, however, that the small downtown area is split by two streets, Oak Avenue and Locust Avenue (which borders the railroad tracks). Your best bet when entering the downtown is to veer to the right onto Locust Avenue first, and then loop around to Oak Avenue on the way out. Most of the shops are on Oak Avenue, though there are a few cafés on Locust.

Home of the Perfect Christmas Tree (262 Oak Ave., 828/765-0571, www.homeoftheperfectchristmastree.org, Mon.–Sat. 10 A.M.–5 P.M.) is not your usual Christmas shop. The store takes as its theme the award-winning children's book *The Year of the Perfect Christmas Tree* by local author Gloria Houston and features over 300 handcrafted items from artisans in the surrounding counties of Mitchell, Yancey, McDowell, Avery, and Buncombe, all of them licensed as part of the Home of the Perfect Christmas Tree collection. All of the products have some relationship to the children's story and range from tree ornaments and hand-blown glass trees to hand-crafted dolls and dried flowers.

River's Edge Outfitters (280 Oak Ave., 828/765-3474, www.riversedgeoutfittersnc. com, Mon.–Sat. 9 A.M.–6 P.M.) is the place

to stop if you're looking for gear for your mountain fishing trip. The store has an extensive collection of flies as well as fly-tying materials and fishing equipment. In addition, they offer guided fly-fishing trips and fishing-trip packages that include overnight accommodations.

Though not located in downtown Spruce Pine, **The Blue Ridge Soap Shed** (179 Meadow View Rd., 828/765-6001, www. soapshed.com, May–Oct. Mon.–Sat. 10 A.M.–6 P.M., Sun. 1–5 P.M.) is worth a visit and easy to check out even if you don't plan on visiting the town of Spruce Pine. Located only half a mile off the Parkway at Milepost 331, the Blue Ridge Soap Shed offers soap-making demonstrations daily at 11 A.M. and 2 P.M. The soap is made from all-natural materials like oils, goat milk, herbs, and vegetable butters, and the company specializes in soaps for unique needs like customers suffering from eczema or psoriasis. Soaps are available for sale and range from flowery scented bath soaps to soaps designed to soothe poison ivy and sunburn. The shop also sells lotions, creams, and salves.

Accommodations
INNS AND HOTELS

The **Richmond Inn Bed and Breakfast** (51 Pine Ave., 828/765-6993, www.richmondinn. us, $85 and up) has eight guest rooms, all with private bathrooms. There is a butler's pantry, gathering room, and drink and ice machine available around the clock, and a full breakfast is served each morning. The inn is also pet friendly.

The **Pine Bridge Inn** (207 Pinebridge Ave., 800/356-5059, www.pinebridgeinn.com, $55–140) occupies a 1920s school building that was made into an inn in 1983. The inn offers 44 spacious school-themed rooms and suites and also provides free continental breakfast. There is nothing particularly fancy about the Pine Bridge, but it's clean and comfortable and a good overnight choice if you're traveling with kids. Families staying at the Pine Bridge can get overnight accommodations and a seven-foot Fraser fir from Sugar Plum Farm for $130 during the holiday season.

CAMPING

Spruce Pine Tent and Trailer Campground (260 Spruce Pine Campground Rd., 828/765-7007, www.sprucepinecampground.com, $15–40) is open May through October and offers electric, water, and sewer hookups as well as cable TV. There is a bathhouse and grills and tables.

Armstrong Creek RV Park (Stockton Rd., 828/756-4494, $32) is an RV-only campground. They do not allow tent campers. They offer electric, water, and sewer hookups as well as access to two private lakes and a nearby public trout fishing stream.

Food

D.T.'s Blue Ridge Java Coffee Shop and Café (169 Locust St., 828/766-8008, Mon.–Fri. 7 A.M.–8 P.M., Sat. 8 A.M.–5 P.M., $3–7) has a create-your-own sandwich, wrap, and bagel menu with offerings that range from turkey clubs to egg salad as well as a selection of soups and salads and vegetarian meals. Even if you're not a vegan, you might find it worth chowing down on the Veggie Guacamole Heaven, which consists of cheddar cheese, guacamole, tomato, cucumbers, and sprouts on toasted whole-wheat bread.

Upper Street Café (198 Oak Ave., 828/765-0622, Wed.–Thurs. 11 A.M.–3 P.M., Fri.–Sat. 11 A.M.–8 P.M., $4.50–9) serves lunch and dinner but is best known for its bakery fare, which includes homemade buttermilk pie as well as a wide array of cakes and cookies.

Information and Services

The Mitchell County Chamber of Commerce (Milepost 330.9, 800/227-3912, www.mitchell-county.com, daily 9 A.M.–5 P.M.) has an office in the Museum of North Carolina Minerals right off the Parkway. In addition to having a wall of brochures available on area attractions, dining, and lodging, the office also has a public computer available with free Internet access.

LITTLE SWITZERLAND AREA

The village of Little Switzerland is the only developed area on the Blue Ridge Parkway, which runs right through it at Milepost 334. One can also reach this tiny mountaintop town by way of a weaving, winding trip up Route 226A north of Marion. Like Blowing Rock, it came into existence as a summer resort in the 1800s. The Switzerland Land Company of Charlotte discovered this spot on Grassy Mountain at an elevation of 4,000 feet and purchased the original 600 acres that would become Little Switzerland to open as a resort area to visitors wanting to escape the summer heat of North Carolina's cities.

Though you probably won't find too many Swiss in Little Switzerland (its name comes from the sweeping mountain views), you will find a town that emulates the look of an Alpine village with brightly decorated craft, jewelry, and food shops.

It's worth a quick divergence from the Parkway to travel Route 226A, which parallels the Parkway between Little Switzerland and Gillespie Gap to the north (where the Museum of North Carolina Minerals is located). While there are a number of dining establishments and lodgings along this precarious curling route, the real fun comes from observing the homes that cling desperately to the steep mountainsides on either side of the road.

Emerald Village

While there are a number of places where one can engage in gem mining around Spruce Pine, many of them are little more than tourist traps designed to draw you in to spend money in their gift shops. One exception, however, is Emerald Village (331 McKinney Mine Rd., 828/765-6463, www.emeraldvillage.com, Apr. daily 9 A.M.–4 P.M., May daily 9 A.M.–5 P.M., Memorial Day weekend–Labor Day weekend daily 9 A.M.–6 P.M., Sept.–Oct. daily 9 A.M.–5 P.M., Nov. Sat.–Sun. 10 A.M.–4 P.M., adults $6, seniors $5.50, students grades 1–12 $5), where underground mines are open to visitors. Emerald Village preserves loads of mining memorabilia, from Bon Ami cleansers made from feldspar to old steam engines. Visitors can also prospect for their own treasures at the Emerald Village gemstone mine and can keep any precious stones they find. On Friday and Saturday nights from May through October, Emerald Village hosts a black-light display in the Bon Ami Mine, which makes minerals on the mine walls glow in oddly fluorescent colors. Admission for the night show is $15 for adults and $10 for students and seniors.

Crabtree Meadows
CRABTREE FALLS

- Distance: 2.5-mile loop trail

- Duration: 2–3 hours

- Elevation gain: 500 feet

- Difficulty: Strenuous

- Trailhead: Well marked at Milepost 339.5 at the Crabtree Meadows Campground

This shady loop hike to Crabtree Falls passes under an arbor of mature rhododendron, descending gradually along a boulder-strewn path past a spring-fed stream. Early summer hikers will enjoy trailside displays of iris, yellow lady slippers, and buttercups. Mountain laurel bows into the path, as the sound of rushing water grows from faint to uproarious as you approach the falls. At just under a mile, hikers will arrive at the base of the falls. At full throttle, Crabtree Falls cascades 60 feet to a small pool and over gray boulders and fallen trees underneath a moss-covered walking bridge, where one can stand and feel the spray of the falls.

A steep trail of switchbacks leads back to the campground. Along the way, hikers will cross several small streams and have the opportunity for more appreciation of the local flora, including the cup-like stems of jack-in-the-pulpits and fields of snowy white trillium. The steep mile-long ascent to the campground, thankfully, offers several benches along the way for resting. The trail's last half mile takes hikers through the campground and back to the parking area.

CAMPING
The **Crabtree Meadows Campground** (Milepost 339.5, 828/675-5444, $16) is open May through October and has 70 tent sites and 20 RV sites. There are no hookups. Cold running water is available in the campground's three comfort stations, and each campground loop has one water spigot available.

FOOD
The Crabtree Meadows area has a small **snack bar and gift shop** (Milepost 339, 828/675-4236, May–Oct. daily 10 A.M.–6 P.M.) located directly off the Parkway. Here one can purchase drinks, snacks, hot dogs, and barbecue as well as camping supplies (including firewood) and gifts such as books, local crafts, and T-shirts.

The **Crabtree Meadows Picnic Area** is located across the road from the snack bar and gift shop and has picnic tables situated in grassy areas surrounded by rhododendrons. There are grills, water fountains, and restrooms.

Shopping
The Swiss Shops at Little Switzerland (86 High Ridge Rd., www.switzerlandinn.com/shops, May–Oct. daily 9 A.M.–5 P.M.) are located adjacent to the Switzerland Inn and are, for the most part, seasonal operations. Hours for individual shops may vary, as some stay open later if they have a steady flow of customers. My favorite is **The Trillium Gallery** (www.trilliumgalleryonline.com), which features crafts by local artists such as functional pottery, terra-cotta reliefs, and handcrafted Christmas ornaments.

Next door is **Village Gems**, which is owned by Emerald Village, the gemstone mine one can visit on the other side of the Parkway. The shop carries gemstones and jewelry of all descriptions, some of it made from locally acquired stones. The shop sells loose stones and will help you design your own jewelry. **The Swiss Shoppe** is the best place to stop after a long day of hiking. They have hand-dipped ice cream, fudge, chocolates, coffee, and smoothies as well as a small outdoor patio.

Simple Pleasures is a rather off-the-wall shop, carrying a variety of unusual gifts with no particular theme, such as antique-looking glass Christmas ornaments and purses, outdoors gear and Peruvian-made sweaters. Right next door is **Hearthside Handmades** with a variety of outdoors items, including a few gardening implements as well as birdfeeders. One of their most popular items is pottery made by locals Keith and Darlene Fletcher, who press wildflowers into the clay before firing. The shop also carries soaps, moisturizers, children's books, and books on local flora, fauna, and outdoors recreation.

If you turn left out of the Switzerland Inn and proceed down the hill on 226A, you'll find another shop worth visiting if you'd like to pick up some local wine and cheese to enjoy on the balcony of your room at the inn. **The Switzerland General Store** (9441 Hwy. 226A, 828/765-5289, Apr.–Oct. daily 10 A.M.–6 P.M., Nov. Sat.–Sun. 10 A.M.–6 P.M.), in operation since 1927, opens onto the Switzerland Café next door. The store carries a variety of regional wines, some foodstuffs, and locally made crafts as well as typical gifts like T-shirts.

Accommodations

The centerpiece structure in Little Switzerland is **The Switzerland Inn** (86 High Ridge Rd., 800/654-4026, www.switzerlandinn.com, Apr.–Oct., $110–180) with its green-roofed lodge buildings, green-shuttered windows, and short balconies overlooking long blue hazy mountain ridges to the east. Reportedly 80 percent of the guests here are repeats, and it's a good idea to make reservations well in advance. The inn is especially popular among motorcyclists and even offers special accommodations for bikers with bike-washing stations. Some of the accommodations at the Old World inn are starting to show their age, but rooms and suites are, by and large, spacious and sunny, and most offer stunning views to the east. If you stay in the main lodge, request a mountain-view room, otherwise your view will be of the parking lot. The scenery here is the best available in Little Switzerland, but the walls of the rooms and suites are thin. If you have noisy neighbors, you *will* hear them. The Switzerland Inn sports a well-manicured and expansive mountaintop lawn where guests can lounge, play shuffleboard and tennis, or relax

© DEBORAH HUSO

The Switzerland Inn in Little Switzerland

in the heated mountain-view pool with two hot tubs. The inn's expansive lobby features comfortable overstuffed couches and easy chairs as well as checkers and board games and a guest computer. Wi-Fi is available throughout the inn as well.

Just around the corner from the sprawling Switzerland Inn is the understated **Alpine Inn** (8576 NC 226A, 828/765-5380, www.alpineinnnc.com, $80–95), a 1929 restored motor lodge. Situated precariously alongside Route 226A (look carefully before you back out of the parking lot!), this motel is perfect if you're looking for reasonably priced accommodations, and are satisfied with the basics but still want to enjoy incredible views. Most of the inn's 12 rooms have private balconies overlooking what is arguably the most expansive skyline in this high-elevation community. The Alpine Inn also offers a Mountain Suite for $150 per night. Early breakfast on the balcony of the common room offers amber and pink sunrises over Table Rock and some stunning photo opportunities.

Big Lynn Lodge (Hwy. 226A, 828/765-4257, www.biglynnlodge.com, Apr.–Oct., $117–177) offers comfortable rooms just off the Blue Ridge Parkway, and rates include dinner and breakfast for two. The dining room and many of the rooms offer panoramic mountain views.

Food

The Chalet Restaurant at the Switzerland (86 High Ridge Rd., 828/765-2153 or 800/654-4026, www.switzerlandinn.com, Sun.–Thurs. 7:30–10:30 A.M., 11:30 A.M.–2:30 P.M., and 5:30–9 P.M., Fri.–Sat. 7:30–10:30 A.M., 11:30 A.M.–2:30 P.M., and 5:30–9:30 P.M., $5–28) is the most picturesque place to eat in the village. A glass-enclosed dining room offers views across manicured gardens to the hazy mountains

beyond. There's a prime rib and seafood buffet on Fridays, and a children's menu.

The best sandwiches, salads, and desserts in Little Switzerland can be found at (**The Switzerland Café** (9440 Hwy. 226A, 828/765-5289, www.switzerlandcafe.com, May–Oct. Sun.–Thurs. 11 A.M.–4 P.M., Fri.–Sat. 11 A.M.–9 P.M., $6–10), across the street from the Little Switzerland post office. They have wonderful fresh sandwiches and salads, but my personal favorite here is the bread, cheese, and fruit board, which comes with a small loaf of fresh-made bread, havarti cheese, and seasonal fruit. It's easily enough for a meal for one. The café has a small wine list as well as both domestic and imported beers available. On Friday and Saturday evenings May through October, the café hosts live music from area artists, mostly rock, blues, and Americana.

The best views are available at the (**Mountain View Restaurant** (Hwy. 226 S., 828/766-9670, www.mountainviewrest.com, Tues.–Thurs. 11 A.M.–8 P.M., Fri.–Sat. 11 A.M.–8:30 P.M., Sun. 11 A.M.–2 P.M., $15–23), which offers long-range vistas to the north and east. Don't be deterred by the restaurant's hole-in-the-wall exterior. It's backed up behind a budget motel, but there's a reason the parking lot here is always jammed with cars, many of them local, which is surely a sign the food is good. If the weather is nice, eat on the deck. The casual atmosphere belies the tasty victuals you'll find, which range from filet mignon to kielbasa and kraut. All entrées come with bread, salad, and linguine in olive oil or garlic mashed potatoes. For appetizers, order either the buffalo wings or the house specialty of sweet-potato fries, which are addictively sweet and salty at the same time. A no-risk tasty entrée option is the Mediterranean chicken, which has a just-tangy-enough flair to its sauce loaded with tomatoes, peppers, and herbs.

ASHEVILLE AREA

With the Blue Ridge Parkway curling around it on the east and the blue haze of the Smoky Mountains bordering it on the west, Asheville is the consummate eastern mountain city. Here is the headquarters of the 469-mile-long Parkway, the eastern gateway to the Smokies, the largest private residence in North America, and one of the grandest gatherings of art deco architecture in the nation. Once the playground of America's northern industrialists, including the Vanderbilts, Fords, and Firestones, Asheville today is little changed in its architecture or in the magnetic draw it has to those seeking communion with nature. And everywhere the remnants of the city's gilded era mingle with the beauty of its mountain landscape.

Not only is Asheville surrounded by some of the East's tallest mountains, it also has some equally striking buildings, with more art deco architecture in the downtown district than any other southeastern city besides Miami. Most visitors readily recognize the art deco features of the popular Grove Arcade, but there are dozens of other structures built in this modern style at the turn of the 20th century. They include Asheville's city hall and the First Baptist Church, both designed by Douglas Ellington, who popularized the art deco style in Asheville after studying it in Paris. These historic structures, many of them revitalized to their 1920s and '30s heyday appearance, form an upscale urban backdrop to the city's many cultural offerings.

North of Asheville are the looming peaks of the Black Mountains, with 10 peaks topping out at over 6,000 feet, forming a rugged area

© DEBORAH HUSO

HIGHLIGHTS

◖ Mount Mitchell State Park: The highest mountain east of the Mississippi at 6,684 feet, Mount Mitchell is also home to North Carolina's first state park (page 106).

◖ Folk Art Center: Home to the Southern Highland Craft Guild, this gallery and store features both traditional and contemporary crafts from Appalachian artisans (page 109).

◖ Pack Place: Situated on busy Pack Square in downtown Asheville, this education, arts, and science center houses the Asheville Art Museum, Colburn Earth Science Museum, The Health Adventure, and Diana Wortham Theatre (page 114).

◖ Biltmore Estate: The centerpiece of this 8,000-acre estate is the Vanderbilt mansion, the largest private home in the United States with 250 rooms (page 115).

◖ Grove Arcade: Built as a public market in 1929, the Grove Arcade is one of Asheville's finest examples of art deco architecture (page 117).

◖ Chimney Rock Park: The film location for *The Last of the Mohicans*, this park is known for its unusual rock formations jutting out of Hickory Nut Gorge (page 140).

◖ Boating on Lake Lure: Declared one of the nation's most beautiful lakes, Lake Lure is a crucifix-shaped reservoir at the base of Hickory Nut Gorge (page 140).

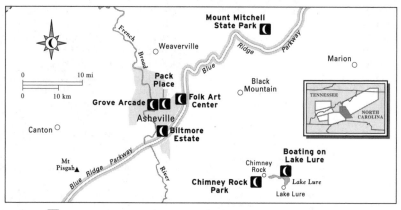

LOOK FOR ◖ TO FIND RECOMMENDED SIGHTS, ACTIVITIES, DINING, AND LODGING.

of beautiful wilderness within easy reach of the city. And just to the southeast of Asheville is Lake Lure, which *National Geographic* has described as one of America's most beautiful man-made lakes.

PLANNING YOUR TIME

If you want to experience Asheville fully, you should probably allow several days, especially if your travels are going to include some of the Blue Ridge Parkway and the area around Lake Lure to the east. Avoid the area in October unless you absolutely must see fall color, as it will be overwhelmed with visitors doing just the same. Consider an early- to mid-summer visit to enjoy the Parkway areas around Asheville in full bloom with mountain laurel, flame azalea, or rhododendron. If you want to enjoy mild weather but completely avoid the crowds, consider an April or September visit.

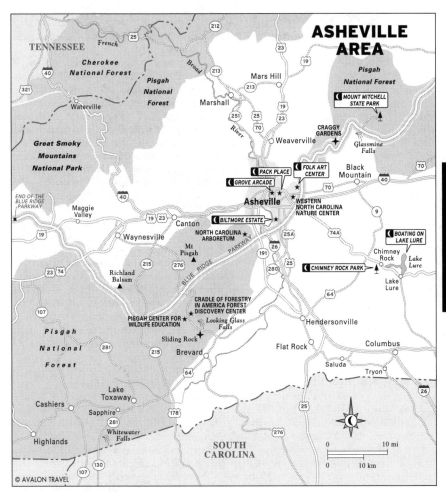

Asheville can be a little tricky to navigate at times, but most of the attractions, shopping, and restaurants are in the 60-block downtown historic area just south of I-240. The best plan is to park and walk or use the trolley system, as driving around, with all of the city's one-way streets, will likely just get you lost and frustrated.

If you're going to visit just Asheville, allow at least two days, particularly if the Biltmore Estate is part of your itinerary. That gives you one day for Biltmore and one for the downtown area. Add another day for the Lake Lure area, and a fourth if you want to get up on the Parkway around Asheville and explore.

Black Mountains

The Black Mountains make up what is probably the most lonesome section of the Parkway, and understandably so. The drive is bounded by the Pisgah National Forest on all sides, making for long-distance views rarely obstructed by the trappings of civilization. The Black Mountain range, which is dominated by the spruce and fir that give the range its "black" appearance, has 10 peaks rising over 6,000 feet. Mount Mitchell, the highest peak east of the Mississippi, is one of these.

SIGHTS
Glassmine Falls

One of the only waterfalls visible from the Parkway, Glassmine Falls (Milepost 361.4) drops 800 feet and can be viewed from an overlook just a few steps away from the Glassmine Falls overlook parking area. Bring your zoom lens or binoculars, however, as the falls is almost a mile away from the overlook and sometimes difficult to spot. In dry seasons, in fact, you might not be able to see it at all.

◖ Mount Mitchell State Park

The first designated state park in North Carolina, Mount Mitchell State Park (Milepost 355, 828/675-4611, www.ncsparks.net/momi.htm, Nov.–Feb. daily 8 A.M.–6 P.M., Mar. and Oct. daily 8 A.M.–7 P.M., Apr. and Sept. daily 8 A.M.–8 P.M., May–Aug. daily 8 A.M.–8 P.M., free) is located just off the Parkway on Highway 128. Mount Mitchell State Park, which earned its designation as a state park in 1915 to protect it from the logging that was ravaging much of the rest of the Black Mountain range, covers just under 2,000 acres. Mount Mitchell is the highest peak east of the Mississippi River, rising 6,684 feet above sea level. Its summit is about five miles from the state park entrance.

Mount Mitchell's original owner was Jesse Stepp, a Black Mountain farmer who also operated a guide service on the mountain in the 1800s. The mountain's most famous explorer, Dr. Elisha Mitchell, a professor from the University of North Carolina, was one of Stepp's clients. In 1857, Dr. Mitchell, for whom the summit is named, fell to his death while on a mission to prove Mount Mitchell to be the highest peak. For a time, both Grandfather Mountain and Clingmans Dome (in the Great Smoky Mountains National Park) were believed higher. Shortly after Mitchell's death, Stepp began selling off his land, save for five acres at the summit, which he saved as the burial place for Dr. Mitchell, whose grave is still there today.

As you enter the state park, the park office (828/675-4611, daily 8 A.M.–5 P.M.) is to your right. You can obtain a park map here as well as access restrooms and vending machines. Two miles further is the summit parking area, where there are picnic tables and shelters as well as a snack bar (May–Oct. daily 10 A.M.–6 P.M.). Be prepared for a significant drop in temperature as you approach Mount Mitchell's summit. Even in summer, daytime highs are often only in the upper 50s.

MOUNT MITCHELL MUSEUM

At the summit parking area, the Mount Mitchell Museum (828/675-0799, May–Oct. daily 10 A.M.–6 P.M., free) provides an overview of the mountain's ecological and human history, and there are a number of hands-on exhibits for children. Of particular interest is the museum's coverage of forest decline on Mount Mitchell. You may notice the spruce and fir die-off near the summit. Much of this decline is due to air pollution as well as to invasive pests like the balsam woolly adelgid. Summer clouds on Mount Mitchell are 100 times more acidic than normal rainwater. This acid deposition as well as ozone can damage tree needles and also interfere with photosynthesis. Combine that with the slow growth rate of the mountain's spruce-fir forest, impacted in large part by the summit's severe and windy weather, and forest recovery is difficult. The balsam woolly adelgid has had its role in the forest die-off here as well. First discovered on the mountain in 1955, the pest has since contributed to the death of more than 80 percent of this region's native Fraser firs.

Interestingly enough, the summit of Mount Mitchell, like much of the rest of the Black Mountain range, has not been the victim of extensive logging. The mountain was logged extensively at the turn of the 20th century but only to within a mile of the summit.

Next door to the museum is the Balsam Shop, which carries books and souvenirs.

SUMMIT TRAIL

- Distance: 0.25 mile one-way

- Duration: 15 minutes

- Elevation gain: 144 feet

- Difficulty: Moderate, uphill hiking but the distance is short

- Trailhead: Directly adjacent to the Mount Mitchell Museum at the summit parking area at the end of the main park road

The favorite activity of visitors to Mount Mitchell State Park, not surprisingly, is taking in the panorama from the summit of Mount Mitchell, which is relatively easy to do these days. This short but steep paved walk leads to a newly constructed, supposedly wheelchair-accessible observation platform. (I would not recommend, however, attempting to push a wheelchair up this steep trail.)

In 2006, the old observation tower was torn down with the rather feather-brained idea that the views should be accessible to everyone (i.e., ADA compliant). Hence, the stone tower of the old days was pulled down, since the top of it was accessible by stairs only. If you hit Mount Mitchell on a clear day, which is hard to do at this elevation, the summit offers 85-mile views. You can see as far as the Smokies from Mount Mitchell's summit, and the competing peak of Grandfather Mountain is also visible. At the summit is a stone marker covering the grave of Dr. Elisha Mitchell.

If cloud cover is thick when you visit, you can still take in the unique forest landscape that surrounds you—a spruce-fir-dominated woodland similar to what you would find in Canada.

ACCOMMODATIONS

The Mount Mitchell Campground ($18) is, surprisingly, open year-round, though it has only nine sites and full facilities are open May through October only. There is no running water available in winter, only pit toilets. Modern restrooms are available in warm weather, but there are no showers or hot water. The campground accommodates tents only.

FOOD

The Mount Mitchell State Park Restaurant (828/675-1024, May–Oct. daily 10 A.M.–8 P.M., $2–16) is located just below the summit parking area and offers standard down-home southern fare like grilled mountain trout, barbecue, peach cobbler, and pecan pound cake. It's the only restaurant for miles around, and if you hit Mount Mitchell near lunch or dinner time, this is likely where you'll have to eat. While there is a picnic area near the summit, rare is the day it is warm enough to eat outside. There is also a snack bar at the summit, open May through October daily 10 A.M. to 6 P.M., but it only serves sodas, coffee, hot chocolate, candy bars, and chips.

Craggy Gardens
CRAGGY GARDENS VISITOR CENTER

Craggy Gardens is a striking region of the Black Mountains just north of Asheville consisting of heath balds dominated by low-growing shrubs like mountain, laurel rhododendron, and stunted spruce trees. The Craggy Gardens Visitor Center (Milepost 364.5, 828/775-0976, May–Oct. daily 9 A.M.–5 P.M., free) is a good place to stop before exploring the area, as it provides a brief overview on the ecology of the surrounding mountains. The visitors center also has a small gift shop and restrooms. Several rocking chairs are lined up against the visitors center's west wall facing views of the Black Mountains and providing a nice spot to warm up next to the visitors center's wood-burning fireplace (which is usually going strong even in mid-summer at this elevation over 5,000 feet).

From the visitors center, you can see both Craggy Dome and Craggy Pinnacle, both of which feature stunted flora. Trees here rarely grow very tall because of the high winds that regularly scrape the mountaintops, and if you hike the trails in the area you'll get an up-close view of wind-gnarled trees, many with vegetation growing on the side opposite that of the prevailing winds. The Craggies are a special area for anyone interested in unique species of plants and creatures. They are home to some 20 endangered, threatened, or rare plants and are also the summer nesting place of a variety of warblers.

CRAGGY PINNACLE TRAIL

- Distance: 0.7 mile one-way

- Duration: 45 minutes

- Elevation gain: 252 feet

- Difficulty: Moderate

- Trailhead: At the Craggy Pinnacle parking area just north of the Craggy Gardens Visitor Center at Milepost 364

Hikers in the know seek this trail out in late May through June to see the trail's tremendous lavender displays of Catawba rhododendron, which tends to grow best at elevations over 3,000 feet. The first portion of the trail, in fact, passes through a tunnel of rhododendron, the forest floor beneath the twisting branches loaded with delicate green ferns. The hike is uphill but gradual, and along the way you'll enjoy opportunities to see the gnarled and twisted trees of this wind-battered mountainside.

Once you reach the summit of Craggy Pinnacle (5,892 ft.), you'll be treated to 360-degree views of the surrounding mountains as well as some good photographic opportunities of the Parkway both south and north. In August, you may see ripe blueberries at the summit as well as sprays of blackberry

© DEBORAH HUSO

view from Craggy Pinnacle

TWO SISTERS SAVE THE PARKWAY'S WILDFLOWERS

In May 1996, O. Norris Smith of Greensboro, North Carolina, wrote a simple letter to Blue Ridge Parkway headquarters in Asheville offering up a collection of more than 3,000 wildflower slides and dozens of notebooks collected over the course of 25 years documenting the flora and fauna along the Parkway milepost by milepost. The photographs and notebooks had belonged to his sisters, Helen and Julia Smith, former residents of the Presbyterian Home of High Point, who had dedicated a fair portion of their lives to saving the wildflowers of the Blue Ridge from the cutting blades of park maintenance personnel.

"During spring-summer-fall," Smith wrote later to Parkway curator Jackie Holt, "they kept close watch on the flowers along the parkway, and could direct you to the best display of certain flowers in relation to the mileage markers, and knew the parkway police by name." Smith was offering his sisters' archives to the Park Service only two weeks after Helen's death at age 97.

The Parkway accepted the gift, acknowledging the sisters' contribution to the Parkway, not just in their photographs and notes, but in the way they changed the Park Service's and the public's perception of what is beautiful. After 15 years of lobbying park personnel to stop cutting wildflowers along the roadway, by the early 1980s the sisters won their battle to change the Parkway's policy of carefully manicured roadways in favor of a more natural appearance that not only benefited the public with gorgeous wildflower displays but provided more wildlife food and habitat as well. The park's current mowing policy, and the wildflowers you'll enjoy while driving the Parkway, are largely the result of the Smith sisters' lobbying efforts.

An exhibit on the Smith sisters' contribution to the protection of the Parkway's flora is on display at the Peaks of Otter Visitor Center in Virginia.

brambles. You can easily imagine the mountaintop as a summer buffet for birds and black bears. Just below the summit, a trail veers off to the right, taking you on a short walk to a second and lower overlook where you'll have an open view of the mountainside above you, coated in mountain laurel, azalea, rhododendron, and low-growing grasses.

CRAGGY GARDENS PICNIC AREA

Located 3.6 miles south of the Craggy Gardens Visitor Center and accessible via its own winding and scenic side road, the Craggy Gardens Picnic Area is a great place to stop for lunch. With picnic tables covering the hillside in both shade and sun, the area is loaded with rhododendron and summer wildflowers like Turks-cap lily. Restrooms are available here as well, and a nearby 0.8-mile walking trail leads from the picnic area back to the visitors center.

◖ Folk Art Center

One of the most popular stops along the Blue Ridge Parkway, the Folk Art Center (Milepost 382, 828/298-0495, Jan.–Mar. daily 9 A.M.–5 P.M., Apr.–Dec. daily 9 A.M.–6 P.M., free) is the home of the Southern Highland Craft Guild, which was established in 1930 to serve the craftspeople of the Appalachians in nine southeastern states. The Folk Art Center has displayed and sold guild members' wares for more than 20 years and consists of some 30,000 feet of exhibit space, including three galleries, an auditorium, craft library, the Allanstand Craft Shop, and a small Blue Ridge Parkway information center.

The Folk Art Center's permanent collection contains over 2,400 works of art and artifacts spanning the last century and a half and is focused mainly on the decorative arts of the southern Appalachians. Among the permanent displays here are a double bow knot coverlet of wool and cotton made by a guild member from Pisgah Forest, North Carolina, and an intricate pine needle and raffia tray that resembles delicate lacy needlework created by another guild member from Arden, North Carolina. All crafts in the gallery have been made using natural materials, most of them locally produced, such as benches carved from mountain laurel branches and the wood of the hickory tree. As you explore the gallery you will likely marvel at the crafts, both useful and decorative, that can be created from simple materials like seeds, bark, and pinecones.

Every day one or more Southern Highland Craft Guild members will be demonstrating his or her skills at the entrance to the Folk Art Center, and those demonstrations may involve anything from spinning wool into yarn to weaving on a loom. You can purchase the crafts of guild members in the Allanstand Craft Shop, which sells everything from pottery and basketry to beautiful kitchen linens and handmade jewelry.

Just outside the Folk Art Center's front doors, you may notice signs for the Mountains-to-Sea Trail, which passes right through the center's grounds. The Mountains-to-Sea Trail spans 1,000 miles from Clingmans Dome in the Great Smoky Mountains National Park to Jockey's Ridge on the Outer Banks of North Carolina. There are more than 500 miles of footpath, with temporary connectors on back roads and state bike routes. For more information, visit www.ncmst.org.

Blue Ridge Parkway Visitor Center

Located adjacent to the Blue Ridge Parkway headquarters outside Asheville, the Blue Ridge Parkway Visitor Center (Milepost 384, 828/298-5330, daily 9 A.M.–5 P.M., free) provides visitors a broad overview of the history and natural heritage of the Blue Ridge Parkway as well as an introductory high-definition film to exploring this most-visited unit of the National Park Service. The building is especially noteworthy for receiving Leadership in Energy Efficient Design (LEED) certification at the Gold level from the U.S. Green Building Council in 2008. Among the destination center's sustainable features is its green roof planted in sedum. The center also has a gift shop with books for sale on Parkway travel, hikes, and flora and fauna, as well as T-shirts, hats, and toys. The information desk carries brochures on Parkway as well as Asheville area attractions, and one especially nifty feature of the destination center is an I-Wall interactive Parkway map with moveable road trip monitor that highlights top attractions along the Parkway as you move the monitor over each section of the drive. For information on special programs at the visitors center, call 828/298-5330, ext. 301.

Asheville

Today, Asheville is a city in the midst of revitalization. It has attracted many artisans and artists, many of them musical, and a stroll downtown on Friday nights will bring one in contact with the weekly drum circle at Pritchard Park, while oozing jazz ballads and soul-wrenching bluegrass pour out of the city's clubs. Some 4,000 artists call Asheville and surrounding areas home, and dozens of galleries, studios, and shops in Asheville's downtown feature their work.

The atmosphere is decidedly alternative, and while the city sports its share of arts-oriented college students from the campus of the University of North Carolina–Asheville, not all the hippie types here are students. Downtown Asheville, on any given summer evening, is loaded with street performers, from dreadlocked young men playing mandolins to middle-aged bald matrons reading Tarot cards. The city's intellectual and artistic atmosphere is palpable, and from dusk till well after

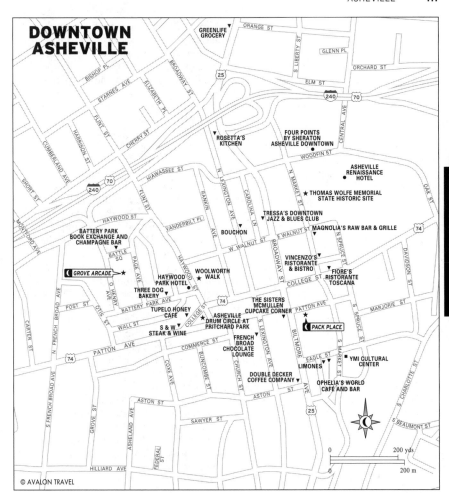

DOWNTOWN ASHEVILLE

© AVALON TRAVEL

nightfall in the summer the downtown restaurants, cafés, coffee shops, and bookstores (one of which even serves wine and cheese) have patrons spilling into the streets.

HISTORY

The land that the city of Asheville now occupies was first settled in the 1780s, and the first town lots here sold for $2.50 each in 1793. Four years later the city was incorporated and named after then North Carolina governor Samuel Ashe. Through much of the 19th century, Asheville remained a relatively small town—its population in 1840 was only 500. But with the arrival of the railroad in the 1880s, Asheville began to experience the beginnings of its boom.

It was New York native George Vanderbilt's love for the western North Carolina mountains that was largely responsible for Asheville's sudden growth. When the youngest child of this powerful New York family first visited the area in 1888, he fell in love and decided to build a country home here. He purchased 125,000 acres of land and then set out to build what would become known as the largest private residence in North America—a mansion modeled on French Renaissance–era châteaux.

On the heels of the Vanderbilts came a whole wave of wealthy and powerful visitors who sojourned in these mountains, seeking the cool summers, fresh air, and wealth of outdoor recreation. Among them were Edwin Wiley Grove, who built another of Asheville's landmarks, the Grove Park Inn. His mountainside hotel drew a distinguished roster of guests, including Henry Ford, Thomas Edison, F. Scott Fitzgerald, Calvin Coolidge, and even Will Rogers.

During this boom phase at the turn of the 20th century, Asheville grew by leaps and bounds as building after building rose out of the hillsides, earning the city its current distinction of having the second-largest collection of art deco architecture in the southeastern United States. Much of that architecture is still visible in Asheville's thriving downtown centered around the museums of Pack Place, the shopping and dining venues of the Grove Arcade, and the galleries and clubs of Patton Avenue, Broadway, and Lexington.

Asheville's early-20th-century heyday was short-lived, however. With the stock market crash of 1929, the city nearly came to ruin. The Central Bank and Trust Company, which held most of surrounding Buncombe County's funds, failed and closed its doors in November 1930, pitching the city of Asheville and surrounding county into massive debt. The city's governing council, however, vowed to pay back all of its creditors, a move which crippled Asheville's growth for decades but also saved much of its historic architecture from the wrecking ball. The city debt was not paid off until 1977.

SIGHTS
Western North Carolina Nature Center
The Western North Carolina Nature Center (75 Gashes Creek Rd., 828/298-5600, daily 10 A.M.–5 P.M., adults $8, seniors $7, children 3–15 $4, 2 and under free) is located on the northeast edge of Asheville. The easiest way to reach it is to take Exit 8 off I-240 and follow the signs. The Nature Center offers a good introduction to the flora and fauna of western North Carolina, particularly for those with children in tow, as the museum exhibits are kid friendly, allowing children to touch everything from sweetgum seeds to rattlesnake skins. It's likely parents will learn a few things here, too, like the fact that North Carolina has scorpions—non-poisonous ones, of course. Kids will also enjoy the center's numerous displays of live snakes, including king snakes, corn snakes, timber rattlesnakes, and copperheads, as well as the exceedingly playful Least Weasel, North Carolina's smallest living carnivore.

The Nature Center's outdoor exhibits include a variety of animal habitats with black bears, coyotes, bobcats, gray and red wolves, and eagles on display. Most of the animals living at the Nature Center are injured wildlife that have been rehabilitated or are no longer releasable. Some, like the red wolves, are part of recovery programs in which the Nature Center participates. The center also has an educational farm, where kids can pet goats, alpacas, and sheep. There are special programs available throughout the day, including craft workshops for children and presentations on the center's resident river otters. When you arrive at the visitors center, be sure to check the event signboard for any activities going on that day.

Asheville Urban Trail
One unique way to explore downtown Asheville is on the Asheville Urban Trail (2 Pack Sq., 828/259-5800, www.ashevillearts. com/trail), which is a walking tour exploring 30 metal sculptures that depict the city's history, architecture, and famous residents. The 1.7-mile trail covers five distinct periods of the city's history from 1784 to modern times. If you tour the trail in its entirety, allow at least two hours. You can pick up trail maps for a self-guided tour at a number

of city locations, including Pack Place, the Asheville Area Arts Council, the Thomas Wolfe Visitor Center, and the Chamber of Commerce Visitor Center. Downloadable iPod tours are also available at www.ashevillenc.gov/parks.

Thomas Wolfe Memorial State Historic Site

The Thomas Wolfe Memorial State Historic Site (52 N. Market St., 828/253-8304, www.wolfememorial.com, Tues.–Sun. 9 A.M.–5 P.M., Sun. 1–5 P.M., adults $1, children $0.50) is the Queen Anne Victorian boardinghouse that served as the boyhood home of Thomas Wolfe, author of *Look Homeward, Angel.* The autobiographical novel, published in 1929, is based largely on Wolfe's childhood growing up in the boardinghouse his mother owned in Asheville. The victim of a house fire in 1998, the old boardinghouse has since been restored and reopened and is furnished and decorated to reflect its appearance in 1916 when Wolfe was a teenager.

Wolfe was six years old when he and his mother, Julia, moved to the boardinghouse; Wolfe's siblings and alcoholic father remained at the family home just down the street. The boardinghouse was entirely Julia Wolfe's investment. Progressive for her time, she believed in maintaining her own business interests, and the Old Kentucky Home, as the boardinghouse was known, provided her a steady stream of income. Wolfe's *Look Homeward, Angel* hit home so hard with the citizens of Asheville that it was banned from the local public library for seven years following its initial publication.

The rambling boardinghouse has 29 rooms, 17 of which are bedrooms. When Julia Wolfe ran the boardinghouse, it could sleep 30 people. Julia charged $1 a day for a bed and two meals. Regardless of whether or not you're a Thomas Wolfe fan, the site is worth a visit if for no other reason than to see what an early-20th-century boardinghouse would have looked like. Adjacent to the house is a visitors center with museum exhibits on Thomas Wolfe's life as well as an introductory film and bookstore.

Thomas Wolfe Memorial State Historic Site

(Pack Place

Pack Place Education, Arts, and Science Center (2 S. Pack Sq., 828/257-4500, www.packplace. org) is a centerpiece of the cultural scene in downtown Asheville, housing three of the city's best museums. The center is located at the newly expanded Pack Place Park that features outdoor art by regional artists, an interactive water fountain, and a large amphitheater for live performances. The park is also a good place to observe some of the city's art deco architecture, including the Buncombe County Courthouse and City Hall.

The **Asheville Art Museum** (2 S. Pack Sq., 828/253-3227, www.ashevilleart.org, Tues.–Sat. 10 A.M.–5 P.M., Sun. 1–5 P.M., adults $6, students and seniors $5) has a surprisingly large and diverse collection of 20th- and 21st-century art given its location in a small southern city. Its permanent collection consists of more than 2,000 works of art. Among them are some of the photographs of George Masa, the Japanese photographer who documented the Smoky Mountains on film and helped lobby

Asheville City Hall viewed from Pack Place

for creation of the Great Smoky Mountains National Park, as well as the photography of Carrie Mae Weems, who documents the experience of African Americans with stunning black-and-white portraiture. If you don't consider yourself a fan of modern art, the Asheville Art Museum may surprise you with its collection of works both realistic and interpretive. The museum also carries the work of local Cherokee artists and the works of members of the Southern Arts Federation. The museum gift shop is open during museum hours and has some fine art available for sale as well as cards, art books, and posters.

The **Colburn Earth Science Museum** (2 S. Pack Sq., 828/254-7162, www.colburnmuseum.org, Tues.–Sat. 10 A.M.–5 P.M., Sun. 1–5 P.M., adults $4, children and seniors $3) is an interactive museum focusing on earth science in general but with a heavy emphasis on the geology of western North Carolina. The museum has examples of the more than 350 minerals found in North Carolina, many of which have been and continue to be mined such as quartz, mica, and feldspar. Among the museum's most noteworthy exhibits are a 376-pound aquamarine from Brazil and the teeth of a mastodon and a woolly mammoth.

The **Health Adventure** (2 S. Pack Sq., 828/254-6373, www.thehealthadventure. org, Mon.–Sat. 10 A.M.–5 P.M., Sun. 1–5 P.M., adults $8.50, students 12 and over $7.50, children 2–11 $6, children under 2 free) was founded in 1968 by the Buncombe County Medical Society Auxiliary and was among the first health education centers of its kind in the United States. While The Health Adventure gets much of its visitation from school groups, families often visit here as well, as the center has exhibits on everything from substance abuse and DNA to cholesterol and arthritis. The Health Adventure hosts different traveling exhibits throughout the year, and, as an interactive space, is best for families with children.

Diana Wortham Theatre (2 S. Pack Sq., 828/257-4530, www.dwtheatre.com) is an intimate 500-seat theater featuring live productions

© FRENCH C. GRIMES

of opera, theater, and dance by both local companies and touring theater groups and musical groups. The theater also holds author readings and shows for children. You'll be amazed by the extensive list of offerings. The Asheville Lyric Opera, Asheville Contemporary Dance Theatre, and Asheville Ballet all use the Diana Wortham Theatre as their home stage. Call or check the website for showtimes and tickets.

YMI Cultural Center
The YMI Cultural Center (39 South Market St., 828/252-4614, www.ymicc.org, Tues.–Fri. 10 A.M.–5 P.M., adults $6, students and seniors $3) was founded in 1892 by local African-American businessmen, with the assistance of George Vanderbilt, for the hundreds of African-American craftsmen who helped construct Biltmore. The Tudor building began its life as the Young Men's Institute, offering a gymnasium, kindergarten classes, space for congregations without churches to meet, and bathing facilities. It is the oldest African-American community center in the United States. By the mid-1920s, YMI had become a centerpiece of Asheville's African-American scene with its own drugstore, medical center, and funeral parlor. In 1980, YMI took on its current incarnation as a repository of the cultural heritage of Asheville's African-American experience and an educational center. Among the YMI Cultural Center's permanent exhibits are drawings by African-American social-realist artist Charles W. White and an exhibit on the historic ties between YMI and Biltmore. The center also regularly holds Arts-in-Education workshops featuring local African-American artists and is the host site for Goombay! Festival, a local celebration of African and Caribbean culture. Check the website for details.

North Carolina Arboretum
On the southern edge of Asheville and easily accessible off the Blue Ridge Parkway at Milepost 393 or Highway 191/Brevard Road, the North Carolina Arboretum (100 Frederick Law Olmsted Way, 828/665-2492, www.

ncarboretum.org, Apr.–Oct. 8 A.M.–9 P.M., Nov.–Mar. 8 A.M.–7 P.M., free, parking $6, free on Tues.) is worth a quick side trip. Part of the University of North Carolina, the arboretum covers 434 acres with 65 acres of cultivated gardens, including a quilt and a stream garden, a bonsai garden (with a model of Mount Mitchell made using dwarf spruce, creeping thyme, blue stone creeper, and creeping loosestrife), and a shady native plants garden complete with rocking chairs and benches for quiet meditation and relaxation. The arboretum also has 10 miles of biking and hiking trails.

If you're a bird-watcher, ask for a copy of the *Birds of the North Carolina Arboretum* brochure, so you can check off those you see while touring the grounds.

The Baker Exhibit Center (Mon.–Sat. 9 A.M.–5 P.M., Sun. noon–5 P.M.) has a small gift shop selling regionally made handicrafts and arts, a temporary exhibit space often featuring local artists, and science and nature exhibits all with a basis in plants. This is also the place to sign up for daily hosted garden tours and trail walks. The arboretum's Education Center, which is located adjacent to the native plants garden, has another gift shop selling gardening items, books, and toys as well as a café serving wraps, sandwiches, and soups. Evening is probably the best time to visit the arboretum if you wish to avoid the crowds that can often be found here in bloom season and if you're willing to forgo entry to the Education Center. Call for gift shop and café hours.

◖ Biltmore Estate
The 8,000-acre Biltmore Estate (1 Approach Rd., 828/225-1333, www.biltmore.com, daily 9 A.M.–7 P.M., admission to estate and standard house and grounds tour $60, children $30, 9 and under free, specialty tours $10–19, premium house tour $150) on Asheville's southern edge was built as a family retreat by George Vanderbilt at the end of the 19th century. It took six years to build the 175,000-square-foot mansion, and today it is a showcase of priceless artwork and antiques. The centerpiece attraction is, of course, the 250-room mansion, the

largest private home in the United States. The home occupies four acres, has 199 bedrooms, 65 fireplaces, 43 bathrooms, and a three-mile-long approach road. Built just before the turn of the 20th century, Biltmore was modeled on a 16th-century French château, and it certainly looks like something that would be more at home in the Loire Valley. Among its most breathtaking interior features are a 100,000-volume library and a collection of massive 16th-century tapestries. You may note as well that some rooms sport 70-foot ceilings, and gilded rooms are standard here. Walking through Biltmore is almost like visiting a museum of art and material culture. There are works of art by some of the finest artists in the world, including Renoir and Boldini, and furniture designed by Sheraton and Chippendale.

Reservations are required for tours of Biltmore. You can order tickets online or purchase them by phone. When you arrive on the estate, go to the Welcome Center, which will be on your left shortly after passing through the entrance gates, for orientation and ticket pickup. Allow yourself a full day at Biltmore if you want to take full advantage of your tour, including a house tour, time to stroll the gardens, a visit to the winery, and exploration of River Bend Farm.

BILTMORE HOUSE
Unless you're into over-the-top decorating, you might find the Biltmore mansion a bit disappointing. Like the castle it was designed to be, it is dark and dreary and overloaded with gilding, tapestries, and heavy, ornate furniture. There are some truly unique features, however, including the Sistine Chapel–like ceiling in the library and the Grand Staircase with its four-story iron chandelier weighing in at around two tons, according to Biltmore curators. I prefer the more understated rooms, among them the Damask Room on the 2nd floor, a corner turret room with large windows—it is one of the few light-filled rooms in the mansion and features reproduction wallpaper that is an exact replica of the original damask fabric–looking wallpaper that once covered its walls. If you've

visited the house previously, there are several new rooms open as part of the tour. They include the Louis XV room, where George and Edith Vanderbilt's daughter Cornelia was born, and where Cornelia also delivered her two sons.

Keep in mind that the main house tour is provided as an audio tour and does not give you the opportunity to interact with a trained guide. Another option is the Rooftop Tour, which will put you in company with a guide who takes you on a private tour of some of the home's undecorated and unrestored rooms as well as provides access to views from the roof of the mansion. Consider as you survey the grounds from the rooftop of Biltmore that Vanderbilt once owned all the land as far as your eye can see to the east, south, and west. Standing on the roof of Biltmore provides you an opportunity to truly feel the scale of this residence, which is built out of more than one million tons of limestone shipped in from Indiana and steel from the Carnegie mills in Pittsburgh. Vanderbilt designed the home to be entirely fireproof. Over 1,000 workers were involved in the construction of Biltmore. The project was overseen by Vanderbilt's friend and architect Richard Morris Hunt.

George Vanderbilt was an avid collector, with some of his favorite items being mirrors, pictures, mantelpieces, and fireplaces. On the Rooftop Tour, you'll get to see some of these stored collections, including Vanderbilt's collection of monogrammed chamber pots, as well as some unrestored rooms with original wallpaper still on the walls. This insider view of the mansion is worth checking out, particularly since you'll get up-close access to some of the home's "modern" bathrooms, many of which had 600-pound bathtubs shipped from England as well as flush toilets, a completely uncommon feature in the American south at the turn of the 20th century.

BILTMORE'S GROUNDS
The Biltmore estate originally encompassed 125,000 acres, purchased by Vanderbilt for as little as 25 cents to $1 per acre. Today, the

gardens and manicured grounds of the estate cover about 75 acres and include formal English gardens such as the Walled Garden, a conservatory, azalea garden, woods, fishing ponds, and even a small man-made waterfall. You may at first find the gardens here unimpressive. But they were designed, for the most part, to look natural, with plantings enhancing the already existing landscape. The grounds are largely the work of landscape architect Frederick Law Olmsted, who also designed New York City's Central Park. Biltmore's grounds were Olmsted's last project.

THE BILTMORE WINERY
The Biltmore Winery (1 Approach Rd., 877/245-8667, daily noon–7 P.M., admission included in Biltmore ticket) is the nation's most-visited winery and offers complimentary tastings with visitor tours. If you're pressed for time, however, you might to skip it. The tours are crowded, you'll likely have to wait in line to take a tour, and the tastings, which take place in a room that once housed the Vanderbilts' 80 Jersey dairy cows, are run in cattle chute–like fashion. The tasting room is large, overcrowded, and noisy, not the intimate experience you'd expect of a winery, and the tasting staff is trained to get you in and out as quickly as possible—there is not even an option of rinsing your glass between tastings. If you want to take a bottle of Biltmore wine home with you, you can easily do so without even setting foot in the winery, as they are offered for sale in many of the estate's gift shops as well.

RIVER BEND FARM
Also included with a standard Biltmore tour is River Bend Farm, the estate's rural living-history area. The farm puts visitors in touch with the estate's rural heritage by allowing them to interact with working blacksmiths and woodworkers as well as a meet-the-farmyard petting area where kids will likely enjoy petting lambs and calves. You can visit Biltmore's original Horse Barn, designed in 1900, which today houses crafting displays as well as exhibits of antique farm equipment. The farm also has

its own kitchen garden, which actually supplies many of the estate's restaurants with fresh ingredients. While you're here you can shop for old-time country-store merchandise at the Mercantile or pick up a hand-dipped ice cream cone at the Creamery.

SHOPPING AND RECREATION
On-site at Biltmore, guests can take carriage rides through manicured forests; sign up for fly-fishing school; go horseback riding, bike riding, or rafting; stroll the gardens; even shop, sleep, and dine without ever leaving the estate. Biltmore is something of a world unto itself. In addition to its several days' worth of activities and sightseeing, the estate also has five restaurants, its own inn, and a number of gift shops on-site. Among the best gift shops is the Garden Place Gift Shop, which is located below the conservatory and carries live plants, gardening supplies, and home decor items in addition to offering daily how-to workshops on everything from floral arranging to wreath decorating. The Carriage House Shop, directly adjacent to the mansion, is another good place to browse, as it has an extensive collection of jewelry, home decor gifts, and estate-produced wines.

The estate's skeet shooting and Land Rover driving school are worth checking out if you have the time and extra cash to spend, but if you're interested in outdoor activities like biking and boating, there's no need to do them at Biltmore. You can enjoy the same activities and better scenery in the nearby Pisgah and Nantahala National Forests or sign on with a local outfitter in Asheville for much the same experience at a better price.

SHOPPING
€ Grove Arcade
The Grove Arcade (1 Page Ave., 828/252-7799, www.grovearcade.com, Mon.–Sat. 10 A.M.–6 P.M., Sun. hours vary by store) was built in 1929 by self-made millionaire Edwin Wiley Grove (who also built the Grove Park Inn) as a public market. The Arcade thrived through the end of World War II. After the

© DEBORAH HUSO

ASHEVILLE AREA

Grove Arcade

entertheearth.com, Mon.–Sat. 10 A.M.–6 P.M., Sun. 11 A.M.–5 P.M.) has a collection of gemstones, minerals, and fossils from all over the globe as well as a selection of gemstone jewelry. **Mountain Made** (828/350-0307, www.mtnmade.com, Mon.–Sat. 10 A.M.–6 P.M., Sun. noon–5 P.M.) carries regionally made handicrafts, including beautiful turned wood bowls in walnut, rosewood, maple, and cherry as well as hand-carved chairs, jewelry, pottery, and framed art. **Tic-n-Time** (828/257-2281, www.ticntime.com, Mon.–Sat. 10 A.M.–6 P.M., Sun. by appt.) is probably not the place to pick up a souvenir that will fit in the trunk, but it's fun to browse. The store carries a full array of grandfather, floor, wall, and mantel clocks, including the Biltmore Collection, which features clocks inspired by those found in the Vanderbilt home.

If you're looking to restock your picnic basket, there are some good opportunities to do so at the Arcade, like **The Big Cheese** (828/350-8044, www.msfmarket.com, Mon.–Sat. 10 A.M.–6 P.M., Sun. 10 A.M.–5 P.M.), which carries a large selection of cheese spreads, deli meats, block cheese, spices, crackers, bulk candy, and Amish butter cheese. **The Fresh Quarter** (828/252-0023, Mon.–Sat. 10 A.M.–6 P.M., Sun. noon–5 P.M.) is a small farmers market with fresh fruits and vegetables, mostly local.

Downtown Asheville

Part of the fun of shopping in downtown Asheville is the sheer diversity of the experience. The extensive historic district is loaded with repurposed art deco buildings turned into artists' studios and cooperatives, funky gift shops selling everything from fair-trade merchandise to incense, and shops selling wigs and lingerie. The city is a magnet for aspiring artists and artisans of all stripes, and you can see some of their works at **Woolworth Walk** (25 Haywood St., 828/254-9234, www.woolworthwalk.com, Mon.–Thurs. 11 A.M.–6 P.M., Fri.–Sat. 11 A.M.–7 P.M., Sun. 11 A.M.–5 P.M.), which, as you might have guessed, is located in the city's old F. W. Woolworth 5 and 10

war, the Arcade became the headquarters for the National Climatic Data Center. In 1995, the city of Asheville acquired the building. Renovated in late 2002 and reopened to the public, this stunning art deco structure, which occupies a block unto itself on Page Avenue, houses more than a dozen high-end galleries of jewelry, porcelain, cigars, lighting, and home accessories. The interior of the Arcade is worth checking out with its marble walls, curling staircases, carved columns, and glass ceiling. More than half a dozen restaurants offer alfresco dining along the sidewalks of the Arcade, making it a popular destination for locals and visitors alike even once the shops inside have closed for the day.

Given Asheville's status as a showplace of art deco and Arts and Crafts style, it is appropriate that the Arcade is home to **Mission at the Grove** (828/350-9669, Mon.–Sat. 10 A.M.–6 P.M., Sun. 11 A.M.–5 P.M.), a gallery of Mission-style furniture, mainly dining sets, Tiffany lamps, and bric-a-brac of all sorts. **Enter the Earth** (828/350-9222, www.

building, replete with working soda fountain where you can buy milkshakes and malts just like in the good old days. The gallery portion of the building covers three floors and a full array of artistic genres, including blown glass, photography, jewelry, and oil painting as well as some decidedly alternative art forms like beer-carton books and dog portraits from over 170 area artists and craftspeople. Anything goes in Asheville, and the same is true for what galleries define as art. Expect to see an eclectic mixture of the fine and downright weird. Among some of the more interesting items here are the sculptures of Heather Knight, who builds stark yet realistic models in clay of barnacles, fungi, and urchins, everything carrying a mythic quality of the sea. You'll also find here the wispy watercolors of Pamela Haddock, who makes her hometown in nearby Sylva and paints richly colored landscapes and farm scenes inspired by the Great Smoky Mountains.

Less than a block from Woolworth Walk is the **Vadim Bora Gallery & Studio** (30.5 Battery Park Ave., 828/254-7959, www.vadimborastudio.com, Tues.–Sat. 11 A.M.–6 P.M.), featuring the work of Russian-born artist Vadim Bora, who moved to Asheville in 1993 from the Caucasus Mountains and opened his studio here five years later. The range of his work is impressive. Bora works in graphite, charcoal, oil, and ink, and is also an accomplished sculptor. My favorites are his impressionistic, almost Van Gogh–style landscapes in vibrant swirling colors. His gallery also showcases artwork from other regional and international artists.

Behind Battery Park Avenue on Wall Street is the unique **Overström Studio** (35 Wall St., 828/258-1761, www.overstrom.com, Wed.–Sun. noon–5 P.M., and by appt.), a gallery of modern jewelry that reflects the clean and modern designs of Swedish-American artist Michael Overström. The gallery has a stunning collection of engagement and wedding rings in sleek designs you will not find replicated anywhere else. My favorites are his Australian opals, where the gemstones take center stage

in simplistic settings that draw the eye to the jewel's inherent colorful complexity.

If you're a serious art collector, **16 Patton** (16 Patton Ave., 828/236-2889, www.16patton.com, May–Oct. Tues.–Sat. 11 A.M.–6 P.M., Sun. 1–6 P.M., Nov.–Apr. Tues.–Sat. 11 A.M.–6 P.M.) is probably among the best galleries to explore. The fine-art gallery on the corner of Patton and Lexington features the work of southeastern artists working in oil, watercolor, stone, and glass and holds regular receptions and book signings; check the website for dates and times.

Kress Emporium (19 Patton Ave., 828/281-2252, www.thekressemporium.com, Mon.–Thurs. 11 A.M.–6 P.M., Fri.–Sat. 11 A.M.–7 P.M., Sun. noon–5 P.M.) is located in the old Kress and Co. 5 and 10. This 1928 art deco building today houses the works of more than 80 regional artisans. Among the items available for purchase are hand-thrown pottery, stained glass, paintings, metal wall art, and handmade jewelry. Not everything here is local, however: The gallery also carries art from developing nations.

Kress Emporium

Chevron Trading Post & Bead Company (40 N. Lexington Ave., 800/881-2323, www.chevronbeads.com, May–Dec. Mon.–Sat. 10 A.M.–6 P.M., Sun. 1–5 P.M.) is probably one of the largest bead stores in the world, with some 4,000 square feet of beads. If you're interested in starting a new hobby in jewelry making, this is the place to go.

Blue Spiral 1 (38 Biltmore Ave., 828/251-0202, www.bluespiral1.com, Jan.–Mar. Mon.–Sat. 10 A.M.–6 P.M., Apr.–Dec. Mon.–Sat. 10 A.M.–6 P.M., Sun. noon–5 P.M.) is a three-story gallery of southeastern fine art and crafts. The gallery holds artist exhibitions throughout the year and maintains a permanent gallery devoted to 20th-century modernist painter Will Henry Stevens. This spacious, light-filled gallery with its exposed ceilings and steel stairwells is a pleasure to browse, even if you're not in the market for art. There are works here in all genres, from elaborate basketry to glass wall sculptures.

The Chocolate Fetish (36 Haywood St., 828/258-2353, www.chocolatefetish.com, Mon.–Thurs. 11 A.M.–6 P.M., Fri.–Sat. 11 A.M.–9 P.M., Sun. noon–6 P.M.) is a must-visit if you're a chocolate fiend. They offer truffles and chocolates of all descriptions.

River Arts District

The recently revitalized River Arts District (122 Riverside Dr., 828/252-9122, www.riverartsdistrict.com) is home to over 100 artists and crafters. You can visit the area anytime, but if you want to be sure to catch the artists at work, check out the Studio Stroll, which is held the second weekend of June and the second weekend of November. Most of the artists will be in residence, demonstrating their crafts. Otherwise, the best day is Friday, as that's when the most artists will likely be on-site.

Among the studios and galleries in the district are **The Fine Arts League of the Carolinas** (362 Depot St., 828/252-5050, www.fineartsleague.org, Mon.–Fri. 10 A.M.–5 P.M.), which features portraits, landscapes, and still lifes from the school of classical realism; **Jonas Gerard Fine Art**

(240 Clingman Ave., 828/350-7711, www.jonasgerard.com, Mon.–Sat. 10 A.M.–6 P.M., Sun. 1–6 P.M.), showing the work of nationally recognized painter Jonas Gerard; and **The Potter's Mark** (122 Riverside Dr., Studio A, 828/252-9122, www.pottersmark.com, Mon.–Sat. 10 A.M.–4 P.M.), which specializes in hand-crafted functional stoneware pottery, including dinnerware and serving pieces.

Biltmore Village

Located adjacent to the main entrance of the Biltmore estate, Biltmore Village (828/274-8788, www.biltmorevillage.com, Mon.–Sat. 10 A.M.–5 P.M., Sun. 11 A.M.–5 P.M.) was once a part of the Vanderbilt holdings. Built in the 1890s, the village was designed to replicate an English community with streets laid out like the ribs of a fan. Biltmore Estate architect Richard Hunt and landscape architect Frederick Law Olmsted co-designed the village to consist of residences with a school, post office, and infirmary. Many of Vanderbilt's employees lived in the village, which provided the Vanderbilts with rental income and a quaint village entrance to their estate. On the first weekend each December, the village holds a **Dickens Festival** with period historic interpreters and carolers on-site as well as horse-drawn carriage rides.

Today the village is its own distinct shopping destination, with many locally owned galleries and shops located in the former homes of Biltmore estate workers. There are also a number of high-end chain boutiques here, including Talbot's Jos. A. Bank, White House Black Market, Chico's, and Coldwater Creek, and chain gift stores and galleries like Williams-Sonoma and **Thomas Kinkade at Biltmore Village** (10 Biltmore Plaza on Boston Way, 828/277-0850, www.thomaskinkadeasheville.com, Mon.–Sat. 10 A.M.–5:30 P.M., Sun. noon–4 P.M.).

Biltmore Village Company (1 Kitchin Pl., 828/274-5570, www.thebiltmorevillagecompany.com, Mon.–Sat. 9:30 A.M.–6 P.M., Sun. 1–5 P.M.) is one of my favorite shops in the village. It has an extensive collection of Tiffany lamps as well as leather furniture, wall fountains, framed art, clocks, and even model airplanes for sale. The **Olde World Christmas Shoppe** (5 Boston Way, 828/274-4819, www.oldeworldchristmasshoppe.com, Mon.–Sat. 10 A.M.–5:30 P.M., Sun. noon–5 P.M.) carries a wide array of Christmas ornaments, Hummel figurines, Boyds bears, and Steinbeck nutcrackers, as well as homemade fudge.

If you have small children to shop for, **William and Grace** (4 Swan St., 828/277-8991, www.williamandgrace.com, Mon.–Sat. 10 A.M.–6 P.M., Sun. noon–5 P.M.) is a high-end clothing and accessories shop for infants and kids with a selection of darling if pricey outfits and toys. **Yarn Paradise** (6 All Souls Crescent, 828/274-4213, www.yarnparadise.com, Mon.–Sat. 10 A.M.–6 P.M., Sun. noon–4 P.M.) offers all the accoutrements you can think of for knitters as well as a small selection of handmade items, from sweaters to scarves.

For fishing and hiking supplies, check out **Curtis Wright Outfitters** (5 All Souls Crescent, 828/274-3471, www.curtiswrightoutfitters.com, Mon.–Sat. 10 A.M.–6 P.M.), which has a fair selection of outdoors gear, including clothing, hiking shoes, and fly-fishing supplies. The store also offers fly-fishing and fly-tying classes as well as guide services.

The ultimate in personal indulgence is available at the luxurious bath and home store **Porter and Prince, Ltd.** (2 Hendersonville Rd., 828/236-2337, www.porterandprince.com, Mon.–Sat. 11 A.M.–5 P.M.) with its luxury linens from thick bamboo towels to organic bath oils and soaps. The shop has a darling collection of baby items, too, including booties, plush toys, blankets, and designer crib sets.

ENTERTAINMENT AND EVENTS
Performing Arts
The **Asheville Lyric Opera** (2 S. Pack Sq., 828/236-0670, www.ashevillelyric.org, Mon.–Fri. 10 A.M.–5 P.M., $28–49) is the city's professional opera company, which performs three fully staged productions each year at the Diana Wortham Theatre in Pack Place. The opera's repertoire is extensive, and you might see anything from *The Marriage of Figaro* to *Madame Butterfly* performed here. Call or check the website for showtimes and tickets.

The **Asheville Symphony Orchestra** (87 Haywood St., 828/254-7046, www.ashevillesymphony.org, box office Mon.–Fri. 9 A.M.–5 P.M., $19–50) performs regularly at the Thomas Wolfe Auditorium at the Asheville Civic Center, offering seven full orchestra concerts a year featuring the music of classical greats like Beethoven and Mozart as well as more contemporary composers like Gershwin and Copland. Each concert includes a performance by a guest artist. Call or check the website for concert times and tickets.

Nightlife
The **Asheville Drum Circle at Pritchard Park** (corner of Haywood and Patton, Fri. 7 P.M.) is not a formal event by any means, though it can be counted on to happen just about every Friday evening in fair weather. Local drummers gather here weekly to show off their skills and entertain the public. All you have to do is show up.

The Orange Peel (101 Biltmore Ave., 828/225-5851, www.theorangepeel.net, call for showtimes and ticket prices) is probably Asheville's best-known nightclub. In 2008, *Rolling Stone* magazine named it one of the top five rock venues in the United States. The club features top-name bands like the Smashing Pumpkins, the Avett Brothers, and the Beastie Boys.

Tressa's Downtown Jazz and Blues Club (28 Broadway St., 828/254-7072, www.tressasdowntownjazzandblues.com, Sat., Mon., and Tues. 7 P.M.–2 A.M., Wed.–Fri. 4 P.M.–2 A.M.) is another hot spot for music. The cover charge varies depending on what band is playing. Music ranges include local jazz, karaoke, dance music, and blues.

Asheville Brews Cruise (828/545-5181, www.ashevillebrewscruise.com, $35–40) provides tours of three of the city's microbreweries. Depending on which tour you select, you can visit the Pisgah Brewing Company, Green Man

Ales, Highland Brewing Company, French Broad Brewing Company, and Asheville Pizza and Brewing Company. At each stop you'll get to sample the company's brews in addition to seeing how the local ale is made. You can take the tour by van or by walking tour. Advance reservations are required.

Festivals

The Annual Arts and Crafts Conference at Grove Park Inn (290 Macon Ave., 828/628-1915, www.arts-craftsconference.com, admission to craft shows $10, conference events pass $145) is a three-day event that any lover of Arts and Crafts style will love. Occurring annually in February, the event features Arts and Crafts antiques shows and sales, seminars on the Arts and Crafts style in history and in its modern revival, silent auctions, walking tours of the historic Grove Park Inn, and various other activities.

The **Festival of Flowers** (Biltmore, 1 Approach Rd., 877/245-8667, www.biltmore. com/visit/calendar/spring.asp, Apr.–mid-May daily 9 A.M.–7 P.M., admission included in Biltmore Estate ticket—$45 and up) at Biltmore takes place during the prime spring blooming season and features ongoing daily events that include classical music in various garden locations, gardening seminars, dance demonstrations, art shows, and workshops.

The **Montford Park Players** (1 Gay St., 828/254-5146, www.montfordparkplayers. org, May–Oct. Fri.–Sun. 7:30 P.M., free) offer North Carolina's longest-running Shakespeare Festival with free theater in the park throughout the summer. Their repertoire includes well-known plays like *The Taming of the Shrew* as well as less-performed works like *Cymbeline*. Shows take place at the Hazel Robinson Amphitheatre in the Montford Community Complex, which can be reached from I-240 by taking Exit 4C and following Montford Avenue to West Chestnut Avenue, where you will see signs for the amphitheater.

Occurring during the last weekend in July each year, the **Mountain Dance & Folk Festival** (Diana Wortham Theatre, 828/257-4530, www.folkheritage.org, $20) is the nation's longest-running folk festival, having been in existence for more than 80 years. The festival features performers from all over the southern mountains who specialize in the song and dance of the region's Scotch-Irish, English, Cherokee, and African heritage.

Then on summer Saturdays from July through early September, Asheville hosts **Shindig on the Green** (Martin Luther King Jr. Park, 828/258-6101, ext. 345, www. folkheritage.org, 7:30 P.M., free), which features traditional mountain music and dance performances on the stage with informal jam sessions occurring on park grounds. This is an informal event, so bring your lawn chairs and blankets.

The Craft Fair of the Southern Highlands (87 Haywood St., 828/298-7928, www.craft-guild.org, adults $7, children under 12 free) has been going on since 1948, and occurs twice a year in July and October at the Asheville Civic Center. It features the works of members of the Southern Highland Craft Guild, a 900-member organization of artisans from all over the mountain South. Some 200 exhibitors generally participate, offering demonstrations of their work and the opportunity to purchase their handmade wares. Live regional music is another hallmark of the fair.

The fourth weekend of August, the YMI Cultural Center sponsors **Goombay! Festival** (39 S. Market St., 828/252-4614, www. ymicc.org, free), a celebration of African and Caribbean culture named after the Caribbean Goombay dance form in which participants wear traditional masks, play drums, and wear colorful costuming. If you've ever been to Jamaica or the Bahamas, you have likely seen this dance style. The Asheville festival features steel drum players, dancers, gospel and rhythm bands, handicrafts and art, as well as Caribbean food.

SPORTS AND RECREATION
French Broad River

Curling around downtown Asheville, the French Broad River is calm and wide and provides an excellent opportunity for family-friendly float trips. Its rapids range from Class II to IV, depending on where you are on the river, making it suitable for both families and experienced rafters and kayakers. Skip the overpriced river trips at Biltmore and opt instead for a local outfitter. What many people don't realize is that you can paddle right through the Biltmore Estate on the placid waters of the French Broad. One of the best sections of the river in Asheville is the seven miles between Bent Creek River Park and the Asheville Outdoor Center River Park. The **Asheville Outdoor Center** (521 Amboy Rd., 828/232-1970 or 800/849-1970, www.paddle-withus.com, Apr.–May trips at 10 A.M., 11 A.M., and 1 P.M., June–Aug. trips at 9 A.M., 10 A.M., 11 A.M., 1 P.M., and 2 P.M., Sept.–Oct. trips at 10 A.M., 11 A.M., and 1 P.M.) offers a variety of river trip options, plus canoe, kayak, raft, and bike rentals as well as shuttle service. If you have your own canoe or kayak, visit www.riverlink.org/riverguide.pdf for French Broad access points. For fishing guide service, contact **Curtis Wright Outfitters** (5 All Souls Crescent, 828/274-3471, www.curtiswright-outfitters.com, Mon.–Sat. 10 A.M.–6 P.M.).

Land Rover Experience and Driving School at Biltmore

While most of the outdoor activities offered at Biltmore can be had just as easily anywhere else in the mountains around Asheville, the Land Rover Experience and Driving School (1 Approach Rd., 877/245-0656, www.biltmore.com/visit/activities/land_rover.asp, daily 9 A.M.–5 P.M., Land Rover Ride-Along Expedition $20, Kids' Land Rover Adventure Course $49, Land Rover Experience & Driving School 1 hour $225, up to 6 hours $850, prices do not include estate admission) is one exception. The school starts with instruction in off-road driving on an obstacle course, and then you and your instructor will graduate to some rough trails where you'll climb steep hills, make careening descents, and perhaps even drive sideways on an off-road tour of Biltmore Estate. If you're not up for doing the off-road

RIVERLINK PRESERVES THE FRENCH BROAD

The French Broad River that flows through downtown Asheville and bisects the Biltmore Estate hasn't always been the recreational gem it is today. The newfound health of the river owes a lot to local conservation organization RiverLink (170 Lyman St., 828/252-8474, www.riverlink.org). Founded more than two decades ago by a group of Asheville area volunteers interested in protecting the health of the French Broad River both as a water supply and as a recreational venue, this nonprofit organization bills itself as devoted to making the river "a place to live, work, and play."

Slowly and steadily, RiverLink has done just that. Among the group's achievements have been the creation of Asheville's first greenway, the French Broad River Park, and the first adaptive reuse of a historic structure – the Warehouse Studios (170 Lyman St., www.riverdistrictartists.com/artists/warehouse_studios) on Asheville's waterfront that serve as work and retail space for dozens of local artists.

RiverLink has been central to the revitalization of Asheville, having bought the old Asheville Speedway and turned it into Carrier Park, the most-used recreational park in the city system. Adaptive reuse of the kind made real at Carrier Park has become a signature of RiverLink, which has become well known for revitalizing "junk" property quite literally. The nonprofit group has ensured more than 200 acres of land bordering the French Broad is in conservation easement.

RiverLink has also expanded its Riverkeepers program from the headwaters of the French Broad all the way to Knoxville. RiverLink has trained more than 40 volunteers to visit construction sites along the river to check for appropriate erosion and sediment control practices and report violations. The group has more than 300 active volunteers.

driving yourself, however, you can elect to have your instructor drive for you while you hang on in the passenger seat. You can sign up for experiences ranging from one hour to two full days. There is also a Kids' Land Rover Adventure Course available using quarter-scale vehicles.

Hot Air Balloon Rides

Asheville Hot Air Balloons (828/667-9943, www.ashevillehotairballoons.com, Apr. 1– Jan. 1, general seating flight $200 per person, private flight $600 per couple) offers one-hour flights along the Pisgah National Forest boundary and over Hominy Valley west of Asheville. The flight includes complimentary champagne. Call ahead to make reservations. Balloons fly regularly, weather permitting.

ACCOMMODATIONS
Hotels

The Grove Park Inn Resort and Spa (290 Macon Ave., 800/438-5800, www.groveparkinn.com, value rooms $250, property view and mountain view rooms $300–400, club-level rooms $750) is one of Asheville's signature features. Rising majestically above the city skyline, the Grove Park Inn was built in 1913 of granite mined from nearby Sunset Mountain. The vision of St. Louis millionaire E. W. Grove, the grand hotel was designed by his son-in-law Fred Seely, who later became the resort's general manager. The luxurious resort played a central role in Asheville's golden age, hosting the likes of the Vanderbilts, Henry Ford, and Thomas Edison. The inn houses one of the world's largest collections of Arts and Crafts furniture and accessories, much of it from the Grove Park's original Roycroft collection. This stone palace above Asheville is so revered for its Arts and Crafts decor that it hosts an Arts and Crafts Conference each February, drawing architects, designers, furniture aficionados, and ordinary bungalow owners from across the country. The inn has 512 rooms, including themed suites and a club floor, and eight restaurants and lounges on-site. Among the guest amenities, apart from the well-known world-class spa, are a 100-year-old

Donald Ross–designed golf course, outdoor pool, fitness center, tennis, and on-site shopping. The Grove Park's spa is relatively new, having opened in 2001, with more than 40,000 square feet of treatment space and sumptuous escapist surroundings. Part of what makes the Grove Park's spa so unique is that it is located almost entirely underground, with sculpted tunnels of granite leading from room to room. The most spectacular feature is the spa pool, where stone walls, dual waterfalls, and sublime golden and rose light displays make the water glisten a cerulean blue. The treatments here mimic the elements of earth and complement the spa's natural subterranean design. The spa also offers special romance packages for couples. Eastern healing treatments like Reiki, Shiatsu, and reflexology are also available as well as hot stone therapy and cool stone facials. Keep in mind that this is an adults-only spa. The Grove Park Inn Resort and Spa also offers a Summer Day Camp for children visiting with their families. Through this program children can learn tennis, golf, and swimming. Camp opportunities run from May through September at a cost of $50 per child per day.

Most of the city's chain hotels are located along Tunnel Road a good distance from downtown, but if you want easy access to the historic area choose the **Asheville Renaissance Hotel** (31 Woodfin St., 828/252-8211, www.ashevillerenaissance.com, guest rooms and 1-bedroom suites $109–279, presidential suite $449–479), which will put you within walking distance of galleries, restaurants, and shops. The hotel, which is operated by Marriott, has 282 guest rooms, an indoor lap pool, fitness center, and complimentary Wi-Fi in the lobby. Just down the street is **Four Points by Sheraton Asheville Downtown** (22 Woodfin St., 828/253-1851, www.starwoodhotels.com/fourpoints, $84–144), which has 150 rooms, fitness center, pool, and complimentary high-speed Internet access in the hotel's business center. The hotel is pet-friendly and also has an on-site steakhouse, The Chop House.

Also downtown is the **Haywood Park Hotel** (1 Battery Park Ave., 800/228-2522, www.haywoodpark.com, master rooms $170–215, superior rooms $190–235, grand suites $275–370), which has 30 rooms and three suites, all with complimentary Wi-Fi, evening turndown service, wet bar, and plush bathrobes. The hotel features a promenade inside its atrium with two restaurants, a spa, and a couple of specialty boutiques and is directly adjacent to the Grove Arcade.

The Grand Bohemian Hotel Asheville (11 Boston Way, 828/505-2949, www.bohemianasheville.com, superior rooms $169–199, junior suites $259–299, 1-bedroom suites $309–349) is a fun Tudor-style boutique hotel in historic Biltmore Village directly across from the entrance to the Biltmore Estate. Operated by the Kessler Collection, the hotel has 104 rooms, all of them luxuriously and individually furnished. Guests have access to an on-site fitness center, spa, and valet parking and can dine on-site as well at the Red Stag Grill. The hotel also has its own art gallery, featuring the works of over 100 local and regional artists.

Another option close to Biltmore is **Doubletree Hotel Biltmore** (115 Hendersonville Rd., 828/274-1800, www.biltmoreasheville.doubletree.com, $169–380), which is only one block from the estate entrance and within walking distance of Biltmore Village. With 197 rooms, the hotel has a fitness room and pool, free Wi-Fi, and the usual Doubletree warm chocolate chip cookie on arrival.

The Inn on Biltmore Estate (1 Antler Hill Rd., 800/858-4130, www.biltmore.com, deluxe double and king rooms $199–628, estate suites $700, junior suites $900, mountain suites $1,500, grand luxury suite $2,000) is, as the name suggests, located right on the Biltmore Estate, overlooking the Blue Ridge Mountains and the Biltmore Winery. Designed to complement the French château style of Biltmore House, the inn is a sprawling hilltop structure with 213 guest rooms, many with private terraces and balconies. The inn has a rimless pool, hot tub, and high-speed Internet access. With all the amenities of a four-star hotel, including evening turndown service, concierge services, complimentary slippers and bathrobes,

and 24-hour room service, the Inn on Biltmore is a convenient accommodation for visitors who intend to spend more than one day at the Biltmore Estate. The inn has its own dining room serving breakfast, lunch, and dinner as well as traditional afternoon tea in the library. Rates for deluxe and king rooms vary widely throughout the year, making it a much better deal in the off-season (early Jan.–mid-Mar.).

Bed-and-Breakfasts

Asheville has a host of privately owned bed-and-breakfasts, many of them offering accommodations convenient to downtown. For a full listing of options, contact the **Asheville Bed & Breakfast Association** (877/262-6867, www.ashevillebba.com/avg). Among my favorites is **Cumberland Falls Bed and Breakfast** (254 Cumberland Ave., 828/253-4085 or 888/743-2557, www.cumberlandfalls.com, $160–260), which is located in Asheville's historic Montford District, home to a number of historic bed-and-breakfasts. Built in 1903, the home is decorated with beautiful original maple woodwork in the living room and foyer. Here you can sleep in a 100-year-old bed and enjoy the popping and snapping of a real wood-burning fire or read a book in the private garden with a softly bubbling waterfall, fountain, pond full of koi fish, delicate weeping willow, lilies, and a host of lounging chairs and swings. Amenities include evening turndown service with chocolates on the pillows, homemade cookies and pastries throughout the day, soft music playing throughout the house and gardens, and modern whirlpool baths or antique claw-foot tubs in most of the rooms.

◖ **The Black Walnut Bed and Breakfast** (288 Montford Ave., 800/381-3878, www.blackwalnut.com, $180–320) is something of a standout among Montford accommodations for its food. And I don't just mean breakfast. Be sure to arrive in time for afternoon tea, which runs from 5:30 to 6:30 P.M. The innkeepers serve up enough treats here to keep you full until you venture out for a fashionably late dinner downtown. Among the offerings you might find spread before you on arrival are

GEORGE MASA: THE ANSEL ADAMS OF THE SMOKIES

In July 1915, a small, wiry Japanese man with close-cropped hair came to Asheville, North Carolina, to work at the posh Grove Park Inn, which at the time was frequented by the likes of Henry Ford, Thomas Edison, Harvey Firestone, and the Vanderbilts. He claimed to have come from Osaka, Japan, and said he had studied mining engineering, though no one has ever found any records of his origins as Masahara Izuka. Where he came from and why is a mystery.

Less mysterious, perhaps, is why the self-named George Masa stayed in Asheville, why he came to love the Smoky Mountains just to the west of the city, and how he dedicated the latter portion of his life to their exploration and preservation only to fade into obscurity, his incredible photographs credited to others (if credited at all).

Before Masa came to Asheville he had wandered around the United States, keeping a diary written in the form of a report and a careful record of all his expenses. The reports abruptly stopped sometime after his arrival in Asheville. At one point his employer, Fred Seely, manager of the Grove Park Inn, suspected Masa might be involved in espionage, given the circumstances of World War I, and reported his presence to the U.S. Department of Justice. Nothing ever came of it, and over time Masa became one of Seely's most beloved employees, starting in the hotel's laundry and later becoming a valet, which is how he first became acquainted with the inn's wealthy visitors, including the Vanderbilt family.

Masa loved his new surroundings and wrote in his diary, "Nothing could be better now unless I make a lot of money." Masa was a darling of the Grove Park's most distinguished visitors, especially after becoming head porter, sometimes accompanying them on fashionable treks into the mountains and always entertaining them with his lively personality, sense of humor, and his own uniqueness at the time as an Asian in America.

The ambitious Masa soon decided to make his fortune elsewhere, however, and went into business with Asheville photographer Herbert Pelton in February 1919, though the relationship didn't last long. By the end of the year Masa had started his own business, Plateau Studios, and he was thriving as a photographer in the city's golden age. Home to some 30,000 people, Asheville, with its grand art deco architecture and well-to-do summer visitors, seemed the ideal place for a talented photographer like Masa to make a living. Where he learned his skills – skills that have since earned him the moniker "Ansel Adams of the Appalachian Mountains" – is as much a mystery as his origins.

While Masa demonstrated a fair amount of financial success as a photographer after starting Plateau Studios, covering news events and selling prints and colored postcards of his photographs of Asheville and the Smokies, he gradually began spending more and more time in the mountains and less in the studio. He began financing his own projects, including a showcase of Mount Mitchell called The Mt. Mitchell Motor Road. Part of his inspiration must have been his relationship with the well-known writer, naturalist, and activist Horace Kephart, who wrote the still-acclaimed account of southern Appalachian life Our Southern Highlanders.

By the 1920s there was a concerted effort to create a national park in the Appalachians on the scale of the West's great parks. Kephart was a major player in that effort, having lived in what is now the Great Smoky Mountains National Park and gotten to know the local Appalachian people. He was concerned about industrial-scale logging and the long-term preservation of the Smokies. He recorded his thoughts through writing and maps, which eventually were accompanied by Masa's photographs.

Even before the creation of the Great Smoky Mountains National Park became a major topic of discussion, Masa had already become a familiar figure in the Smokies, walking around with his camera and a bicycle wheel he had converted into an odometer for measuring distances. As the public in North Carolina and Tennessee rallied support for the park, Masa and Kephart became major figures in its promotion through their joint efforts at mapping, writing, and photography. In 1926, president Calvin Coolidge signed a bill into law allowing for a park in the Smokies, but the two states had to raise the money to purchase the land – no easy feat.

In 1927, however, John D. Rockefeller made a $5 million donation toward purchase of land for the park after seeing some of Masa's photographs of the mountains. Masa had also sent photographs to Coolidge.

Masa and Kephart were among several who volunteered to help map the park and record the names of mountains, creeks, coves, rivers, and valleys. The two men recorded the Cherokee names of many of the geographic features in honor of the local tribe that both men studied.

Masa was so involved in the park promotion effort that he was spending very little time in his Asheville studio, which he eventually sold in 1925 to Yurit Ball along with a catalog of his pictures. But along with the sale of his studio went a major source of

income, and while Masa continued to photograph for money, including taking photos to promote the Biltmore estate as a tourist attraction, his financial situation grew more troublesome as his time in the mountains increased. That trouble was compounded by the Great Depression.

Masa lost much of his inspiration when, in 1931, his dear friend Kephart was killed in a drunk driving accident. "I don't know what to say about the death of Kephart," Masa wrote. "It shocked me to pieces." Masa never recovered from the loss and continued to be devastated by the suicides of friends and acquaintances who had lost everything in the Great Depression. Masa himself was nearly penniless and wrote, "Local people think I have plenty of money." Of course, he did not. He had invested everything in hiking, mapping, and photographing his beloved adopted mountains.

When he died of tuberculosis in 1933, one year before the Great Smoky Mountains National Park was officially created, Masa left almost nothing behind. Within a couple of years he was largely forgotten, except among the members of the North Carolina Trail Club, who eventually lobbied to have a peak in the Smokies named after him in 1961 – Masa Knob (elevation 5,685 ft.), directly adjacent to the earlier named Mount Kephart.

The Ball family, which bought Plateau Studios from Masa, became owners of much of the Japanese photographer's work. In recent years, Masa's significance as a photographer and park promoter has been revitalized due in large part to the 2002 PBS documentary *The Mystery of George Masa* by Bonesteel Films and more recently to Ken Burns' series *America's Best Idea: Our National Parks*, which aired in 2009.

quiche, cheesecake, and crackers and cheese, as well as a selection of wines, all of it complimentary. The inn also has complimentary beverages 24 hours a day, including coffee, tea, hot cocoa, sodas, and water. Like most of the houses in Montford, Black Walnut is built in the Arts and Crafts style. It was built about 1899 by Richard Sharp-Smith, the supervising architect of Biltmore, and was, in fact, his first residential project. The rooms, of which there are eight, are all beautifully furnished and range from cozy to spacious. There are two pet-friendly rooms available. If you want room to spread out, choose the Walnut Room, which has a dark walnut king-sized sleigh bed facing an antique coal-burning fireplace with sofa and two upholstered chairs available for additional lounging space. Morning breakfast is every bit as decadent as afternoon tea and is generally served in three filling courses, and could easily power you through a whole day without lunch. You'll find your breakfast served on antique china collected over the years by the innkeepers.

If you have kids in tow but still want to enjoy the atmosphere of a bed-and-breakfast, the **Oakland Cottage Bed and Breakfast** (74 Oakland Rd., 866/858-0863, www.vacationinasheville.com, $80–150) is a family-friendly option about a five-minute drive from Asheville's downtown historic district. Oakland Cottage has five rooms, three of them two-bedroom suites, and welcomes children of all ages and even has a collection of toys and games for the little ones in its common area. A 1910 Arts and Crafts bungalow, Oakland Cottage is more sprawling than it looks from the street, and rooms, suites, and bathrooms are spacious. The one drawback is that the place shows some wear and the decor is lackluster. If you're looking for atmosphere, stick to the Montford District. The kids, however, will enjoy the place (and its offerings of afternoon cookies), and the innkeepers also have a number of handy amenities for traveling families, including a washer and dryer that is available for guest usage and a guest refrigerator where you can store your picnic supplies overnight.

Don't forget the passcode for the front door, however. Oakland Cottage, like many bed-and-breakfasts in city limits, keeps its doors locked at all times.

Richmond Hill Inn (87 Richmond Hill Dr., 800/545-9238, www.richmondhillinn. com, garden pavilion rooms $270–445, cottage rooms $275–360, Seven Oaks suite $380–480, Thomas Pearson suite $435–535, Ambassador's suite $515–615, Emily's family cabin $380–480, William's family cabin $515–615) was at one time the premier luxury inn in Asheville, but in the spring of 2009 the mansion house burned to the ground, leaving only the inn's 16 garden pavilion rooms and suites and nine croquet cottage rooms. The inn's beautiful formal gardens with man-made waterfall remain, however, just below the site of the old mansion house and directly adjacent to the suites, many of which have private patios looking onto the gardens. The suites all have wood-burning fireplaces and CD players with a couple of instrumental CDs, and all guests are treated to a decadent afternoon tea with crackers, an assortment of cheeses, fruit, sandwiches, and chocolate truffles. The garden pavilion rooms are roomy and comfortable, decorated and outfitted on the order of an upscale hotel but starting to show some wear around the edges. The best activity here is to go into the gardens after dark, settle onto a bench near the waterfall with a glass of wine, and listen to the trickling water.

The ☙ **Sourwood Inn** (810 Elk Mountain Scenic Hwy., 828/255-0690, www.sourwood-inn.com, $160–195), while not particularly convenient to the downtown historic area, is nevertheless one of my favorite lodging options in the city. Located about a 25-minute drive north of downtown, the last few miles on a curling mountain road, the Sourwood Inn offers the most peaceful accommodations in the city. Situated on 100 acres at 3,200 feet with long mountain views from many of the rooms, the inn has 12 guest rooms, all of them with spacious tiled bathrooms with deep soaking tubs under a wall of windows. The inn is Arts and Crafts in style with open-beamed ceilings in the common living room and a center stone fireplace surrounded by comfortable Mission-style furniture. If you can, select a corner room, as they offer more windows and greater privacy. All rooms have small private balconies overlooking the woods and distant mountains. At night, you can sit outside and hear nothing but the chirps of tree frogs. There are two miles of hiking trails on-site. The inn offers dinner Thursday to Sunday with advance reservations, and the resident chef will make it worth your while to eat in rather than making the inconvenient trek back into downtown Asheville. Guests can dine indoors or on a lovely outdoor patio with fountain and fireplace. The dinner menu changes daily; you can see what's offered from one night to the next on the inn's website. Dinner is $30 and includes a salad, entrée, and dessert. If you wish to have wine with dinner you will need to bring your own, as they do not sell alcohol on-site. To reach Sourwood Inn, take I-240 from Asheville and exit onto Merrimon Avenue. Follow Merrimon north 2.1 miles, and then turn right onto Beaverdam Road. Stay on Beaverdam for 0.6 miles, and then turn left onto Elk Mountain Scenic Highway. Stay on Elk Mountain Scenic Highway for 5.5 miles. The entrance to Sourwood is on the left.

Camping

Asheville East KOA (2708 Hwy. 70 E., 800/562-5907, www.ashevilleeastkoa.com, open year-round, $32–116) is actually located in the nearby community of Swannanoa about seven miles from Asheville. The campground has 60 tent and 125 RV sites with full hookups as well as 17 cabins and three rental units. There are two fishing lakes, a swimming pool, playground, camp store, LP gas available, paddleboat and bike rental, and free Wi-Fi and cable TV.

Campfire Lodgings (116 Appalachian Village Rd., 828/658-8012, www.campfirelodgings.com, open year-round, $30–50) is situated seven miles from downtown Asheville on 100 acres, providing the opportunity to sleep

under the stars while still being close to all of the city's attractions and amenities. There are 12 tent and 19 RV sites with water and electric hookups. The campground also offers very popular yurt rentals for $135 (yurts sleep two people).

Lake Powhatan National Forest Recreation Area (375 Wesley Branch Rd., 828/670-5627, www.cradleofforestry.org/camping, Apr.–Oct., $20–28) is a U.S. Forest Service campground with 97 sites located nine miles from downtown Asheville. There are 14 sites with water and sewer hookups and five full hookup sites. The campground has shower facilities and a swimming beach. From Asheville, take I-26 east to Exit 33, and turn left on NC 191 south. Go four miles and turn right on Bent Creek Ranch Road; go 3.5 miles. The campground entrance is on the left.

Another U.S. Forest Service campground, **North Mills River Campground** (5289 N. Mills River Rd., 828/890-3284, www.cradleofforestry.org/camping, Apr.–Oct., $13–26) has 32 sites available 22 miles from downtown Asheville. Camping is primitive with no shower facilities, electric or water hookups, or dump station. From Asheville, take I-26 east to Exit 40, and turn right on 280 west. Go four miles, and turn right on SR 1345. The campground is in five miles.

FOOD

While Asheville proper has all the expected restaurant chains like Olive Garden and Sagebrush Steakhouse, the downtown area has its own thriving food scene with dozens of locally owned restaurants and cafés. The Buncombe County Tourism Development Authority has launched the Foodtopian Society website (www.foodtopiansociety.com) to allow Asheville residents and visitors to easily connect with local growers and farmers markets and find restaurants that serve fresh local fare. The website not only promotes farm-to-table restaurants that support local agriculture but also works to get more consumers involved in the environmentally sound concept of buying local.

Downtown Asheville
CASUAL FINE DINING

There really is no such thing in Asheville as "fine dining" with regard to atmosphere. The city is very casual, and it is rare to see anyone dress up for dinner. That being said, the city has more than its fair share of first-rate food. More than a few fine chefs have relocated here and opened restaurants, so it's relatively easy to find a good meal. The sheer number of offerings can be a bit overwhelming, however. I wish I could say I've tried them all, but I do have some top picks.

If you're looking for Italian food like you'd find in Italy, then **Vincenzo's Ristorante & Bistro** (10 N. Market St., 828/254-4698, www.vincenzos.com, Mon.–Thurs. 5–10 P.M., Sat. 5–11 P.M., Sun. 5–9 P.M., $11–32) is the place. Don't let the crisp and contemporary dining room fool you—this is northern Italian fare at its best. If you love cheese like I do, start your meal off with the Formaggi al Forno, which blends provolone, parmesan, and romano into a baked puff pastry with Pomodoro sauce on the side. For Italian comfort food, you might try the Gnocchi al Emelia-Romagna, which is basically potato dumplings tossed together with prosciutto ham and onions in zesty Gorgonzola cream. If you've got a big appetite, then by all means try to chow down on one of Vincenzo's numerous veal offerings like Cotoletta alla Valdosta, a classic breaded veal chop topped with prosciutto ham and Fontina, and drizzled in a rosemary demi-glace. The restaurant hosts live music nightly, usually jazz, piano, or folk music.

It's hard for me to pin down a favorite downtown, but one restaurant that serves consistently tasty eats is 【 **Bouchon** (62 N. Lexington Ave., 828/350-1140, www.asheville-bouchon.com, Mon.–Thurs. 5–9:30 P.M., Fri.–Sat. 5–10:30 P.M., $6–20), a tiny little French restaurant with a tiny little outdoor bar where you can nab some drinks while waiting for a table (which you most likely will have to do). This place is popular and seating is limited, tables are crammed close together, and the atmosphere is one of a continuous low din that discourages much intimate conversation. Don't be deterred, however: The food is worth the slightly uncomfortable surroundings. Bouchon is best known for two things—its mussels and its french fries. You can get all you can eat of both on Monday, Tuesday, and Wednesday. You've never had mussels like these before—they're steamed in Pabst Blue Ribbon beer, butter, and Dijon mustard. If you're not into mussels, however, I recommend Le Croque Monsieur Frites, a knife-and-fork ham-and-cheese sandwich oozing with melted cheese and served with the restaurant's famous herbed fries, which are crispy, sweet, and salty all at once and served with a mayonnaise-based sauce that you will find hard to get enough of. Bouchon has lots of other options, including a beef shoulder tenderloin steak, lamb, and, of course, french onion soup. There is a full bar and patio dining is available as well.

If you're vegetarian or vegan, you will probably want to check out **Rosetta's Kitchen** (111 Broadway, 828/232-0738, www.rosettaskitchen.com, Mon.–Thurs. 11 A.M.–11 P.M., Fri.–Sat. 11 A.M.–3 A.M., Sun. 11 A.M.–3 P.M., $2–10), which has some darn good vegetarian chili-cheese fries and lots of other creative options.

Magnolia's Raw Bar & Grille (26 E. Walnut St., 828/251-5211, www.magnoliasasheville.com, Mon.–Sat. 11:30 A.M.–2 P.M. and 5–10 P.M., $10–47) has a spacious covered outdoor dining area. The restaurant serves mostly seafood, including Maine lobster tail, Alaska king crab, trout, and salmon. They have a large oyster menu and also serve prime rib. With a full bar, the restaurant also has live shows Friday and Saturday nights from 10 P.M. to 2 A.M., featuring a variety of music from the house band, A Social Function.

Tupelo Honey Café (12 College St., 828/255-4863, www.tupelohoneycafe.com, Tues.–Thurs. 9 A.M.–3 P.M. and 5:30–10 P.M., Fri.–Sat. 9 A.M.–3 P.M. and 5:30–11 P.M., Sun. 9 A.M.–3 P.M., $5–23) is unique in that the restaurant has its own farm, Sunshot Organics, which provides a continuous supply of fresh, local, pesticide-free ingredients. The menu here is decidedly southern, so make sure you crave that south-of-the-Mason-Dixon-line mix of sweet and salty before settling in to dine here. You'll find comfort food with a kick if you order the Kobe hamburger steak with its mushroom and sweet onion gravy and mashed sweet potatoes. (Sweet potatoes, by the way, come with just about everything here. If by some twist of fate you don't get sweet potatoes with your meal, order the sweet and salty sweet-potato fries.) Come for breakfast and try the sweet-potato pancake, a buttermilk pancake spiked with cinnamon and sweet potato and loaded with peach butter and spiced pecans. Skip the soda and iced tea and instead order the house-made rosemary peach lemonade.

S&W Steak & Wine (56 Patton Ave., 828/505-3362, www.swsteakandwine.com, Sun.–Thurs. 5:30–9:30 P.M., Fri.–Sat. 5:30–10 P.M., bar service begins daily at 4:30 P.M., $14–47) is worth checking out if for no other reason than because it's located in the whimsical Art Deco S & W Cafeteria Building. The atmosphere is first-rate, with a mezzanine bar overlooking the crisp dining room below. While hardly anyone ever dresses up to dine in Asheville, if you really want to, this might be the place to do it. Steak & Wine specializes in seafood and steak, including prime rib and center-cut sirloin steak as well as salmon, tuna, shrimp, and scallops. The emphasis here is on letting the natural flavor of the food shine through. The bar offers a menu of tempting martinis, too, including a Chocolate Kiss and a Cucumber Rose.

The best item on the menu at **Tomato Cocina Latina** (1455 Patton Ave., 828/254-5046, www.tomatocl.com, Mon.–Thurs. 11 A.M.–9 P.M., Fri.–Sat. 11 A.M.–9:30 P.M., $2–15) is the grilled skirt steak served on the restaurant's signature *bandeja paisa* plate, simply but effectively seasoned in oil and pepper.

Limones (13 Eagle St., 828/252-2327, www.limonesrestaurant.com, daily 5–10 P.M., Sunday brunch 10:30 A.M.–2:30 P.M., $7–32) is one of many examples of Asheville's thriving chef-owner restaurant scene. It is owned by Mexico City native Hugo Ramirez and his

© FRENCH C. GRIMES

S & W Cafeteria Building, where S&W Steak & Wine is located

wife, Amy Cavanaugh, who have made it their mission to provide diners with a whole new experience of Mexican and Californian cuisine made with fresh, local, and seasonal ingredients. If you're not familiar with Asheville you might find yourself a little reluctant to dine in a restaurant located on less-than-prosperous-looking Eagle Street. But once inside Limones, which has a relatively small but intimately decorated dining room with cushioned window seats, tin ceiling, and walls filled with Mexican art, you'll know you've come to the right place if for no other reason than to enjoy the staff's attentiveness to your happiness. It's nearly impossible to order anything here that won't satisfy and likely excite your palate. If it's on the menu when you're in town, try the chicken *tinga sopes* (marinated shredded chicken wrapped in a light pastry and topped with goat cheese and guacamole). Other possible menu options include lamb and goat cheese enchiladas, *ceviche del mercado* (the fish of the day marinated in a citrus and vegetable sauce), or a spicy cowboy steak. For dessert, indulge in cinnamon and brown sugar churros with hot caramel and chocolate sauce. Limones is also well known for its pricey but fun selection of margaritas; for a tongue-biting treat, try the Blood Orange. At the end of your meal your check will come with a dark chocolate truffle just in case you've decided to skip dessert.

Next door to Limones is **Ophelia's World Café and Bar** (15 Eagle St., 828/255-8154, www.opheliasworldcafe.info, Tues. 5–10 P.M., Wed.–Sat. 11 A.M.–3 P.M. and 5–10 P.M., Sun. 10 A.M.–3 P.M. and 5–9 P.M., $10–23), which has a very eclectic menu, carrying everything from vegetarian entrées to rabbit. Try the tempeh and goat cheese buckwheat crepes, or, if you're seeking vegan fare, the restaurant offers a raw food plate with sunflower garden burger. Ophelia's carries some traditional southern favorites, too, like shrimp and grits.

Fiore's Ristorante Toscana (122 College St., 828/281-0710, www.fioresasheville.com, Mon.–Thurs. 11 A.M.–3:30 P.M. and 4:30–9:30 P.M., Fri.–Sat. 11 A.M.–3:30 P.M. and 4:30–10 P.M., $5–22) is another of Asheville's restaurants specializing in fresh and local food, only Fiore's does it with a Tuscan flair. The menu changes seasonally, but some of the good offerings you might find here include shrimp simmered in white wine sauce, extra virgin olive oil, garlic, roasted peppers, and lemon over angel hair pasta, or locally raised breaded pork chops topped with bruschetta and lemon. The restaurant also offers gluten-free pasta upon request and some truly unique pizzas, including a vegetable pizza and a three-cheese white pizza.

Nine Mile (233 Montford Ave., 828/505-3121, www.ninemileasheville.com, daily 11:30 A.M.–10 P.M., $3–15) is actually just outside the traditional downtown area in the adjacent Montford neighborhood and is a good choice if you happen to be staying in one of the district's nearby bed-and-breakfasts. Its specialty is Caribbean pasta. The best dish in the house is the Concrete Jungle, a mix of shellfish, squash, and fire-roasted tomatoes served over linguine and coated in garlic butter. The restaurant has a full bar selling many local beers, and you can't beat the pick-me-up atmosphere. Reggae is the background music of choice.

If you find yourself in need of a greasy New York pizza, look no farther than **Circle in the Square** (640 Merrimon Ave., 828/254-5442, www.circleinthesquarepizza.com, Mon.–Thurs. 11:30 A.M.–8 P.M., Fri. noon–9 P.M., Sat. noon–8 P.M., Sun. noon–8 P.M., $3–9). The restaurant draws some northeastern transplants, but that's only because the pizza really is that good. You can order one with all the toppings if you like, but my preference is the unadulterated cheese pizza, which carries enough oozing yellow goodness to satisfy the most discerning pizza palate.

QUICK BITES

Across from the Grove Arcade on Battle Square, the **Battery Park Book Exchange and Champagne Bar** (1 Battle Sq., 828/252-0020, Mon.–Sat. 11 A.M.–11 P.M., Sun. 2–11 P.M., $4–20) is a decidedly different take on mega-bookstores like Barnes & Noble that offer books and café latte. A sprawling used bookstore with leather arm chairs and Mission-style sofas, the Battery Park Book Exchange has a full wine list and cheese boards available to enjoy while perusing books on topics ranging from the American Civil War and Americana to interior design and wine. The atmosphere is decadent—red walls, a low tin ceiling, and black-clad waiters zigzagging between the shelves. Dogs are welcome here, too, and the staff keeps filled water bowls on hand just outside the front door. There is also an outdoor "dining" area and more books to browse in the basement, accessible from an adjacent street entrance.

The Soda Fountain at Woolworth Walk (25 Haywood St., 828/254-9210, www.woolworthwalk.com, Mon.–Thurs. 11 A.M.–6 P.M., Fri.–Sat. 11 A.M.–7 P.M., Sun. 11 A.M.–5 P.M., $1–6) is located in the restored 1938 F. W. Woolworth 5 and 10 building, which now houses Asheville's largest art gallery. The soda fountain isn't original, but it has been designed to look like the old Woolworth luncheonette. The lunch counter serves up the usual soda-fountain fare, including sandwiches, hot dogs, hand-dipped ice cream cones, malts, shakes, and floats.

The Sisters McMullen Cupcake Corner (1 Pack Sq., 828/252-9454, www.thesistersmcmullen.com, Mon.–Wed. 7:30 A.M.–6 P.M., Thurs.–Fri. 7:30 A.M.–9 P.M., Sat. 9 A.M.–9 P.M., $1–5) is located on Pack Square and serves up soups and sandwiches in addition to their signature cupcakes and whoopee pies.

The **French Broad Chocolate Lounge** (10 S. Lexington Ave., 828/252-4181, www.frenchbroadchocolate.com, Mon.–Thurs. 11 A.M.–11 P.M., Fri.–Sat. 11 A.M.–midnight, Sun. 1–10 P.M., $2–11) is exactly what it sounds like—a bar for chocolate lovers. In addition to serving wine, beer, coffee, and tea, there are artisan chocolates and desserts you can indulge in while reclining in plush leather lounge chairs. While the lounge may not be able to get its main ingredient locally, they do make use of locally sourced eggs, milk, and honey to create some pretty decadent desserts. The lounge also has Wi-Fi.

The **Double Decker Coffee Company** (41 Biltmore Ave., 828/505-2607, www.dbldecker. com, Mon. and Thurs. 11:30 A.M.–9 P.M., Fri.–Sat. 11:30 A.M.–11:30 P.M., Sun. 11:30 A.M.–7 P.M., $1–6) is, as you might have guessed, located in an old double-decker bus on the corner of Biltmore and Aston. The bus is, in fact, a retired 1963 Bristol Lodekka that was once part of the British public transit system before finding her way first to Atlanta and then Asheville in 1999. This is a truly fun place to grab a coffee or latte (and they have dozens of options) and a pastry. You'll find yourself seated on a narrow vinyl bus seat with a tin ceiling overhead and free Wi-Fi, though chances are you'll find the quarters too small to stay very long.

If you have your pooch in tow, check out Asheville's **Three Dog Bakery** (21 Battery Park, 828/252-1818, www.threedogasheville.com, Mon.–Sat. 10 A.M.–6 P.M., Sun. noon–5 P.M., $1–15). Part of an international chain started by a pair of dog-loving friends, this restaurant is exclusively for your four-footed friends, serving up natural fresh-baked and pre-packaged meals and treats for Fido. The bakery also has a section for cats and their owners.

On the northern edge of town, **Greenlife Grocery** (70 Merrimon Ave., 828/254-5440, www.greenlifegrocery.com, daily 7 A.M.– 10 P.M., $2–8) not only carries all your typical natural food offerings, but also serves breakfast, lunch, and dinner at their deli. Greenlife carries local organic produce as well as local meats, breads, and cheeses, and has a full line of natural body and skin-care products.

Grove Arcade

Chorizo (1 Page Ave., 828/350-1332, www.chorizo-asheville.com, Sun.–Thurs. 9 A.M.–4 P.M. and 4–9:30 P.M., Fri.–Sat. 9 A.M.–4 P.M. and 4–10 P.M., $10–16) is one of several downtown restaurants owned and operated by Chef Hector Diaz. Best known for its namesake Latin sausage, which you can add to any meal for $1, Chorizo offers mid-priced fare ranging from burritos and enchiladas to quesadillas and whole-roasted fish (and they mean "whole fish"). Meal presentation is equal to what you would find in a fine restaurant, only the servings are super-size. A good pick and a great value for two is the Latin nachos, a heaping plate of chips loaded with marinated chicken strips, cheese, *pico de gallo,* tomatoes, black beans, and rice. Dining is available inside the restaurant under a tin-roofed ceiling with dangling blue-glass chandeliers or on the street. Chorizo's also has full bar service. Next door, **Modesto** (1 Page Ave., 828/225-4133, www.modesto-asheville.com, Mon.–Thurs. 11:30 A.M.–9:30 P.M., Fri.–Sun. 11:30 A.M.–10:30 P.M., $5–25), also owned by Hector Diaz, serves brick-oven pizzas as well as other Italian dishes and has an extensive tapas menu and full bar.

Thai Basil (1 Page Ave., 828/258-0036, www.thaibasilnc.com, Mon.–Fri. 11:30 A.M.–2:30 P.M. and 5–9:30 P.M., Sat. noon–3 P.M. and 5–9:30 P.M., $6–18) has an extensive selection of traditional Thai dishes. All entrées are available with a choice of chicken, pork, beef, salmon, catfish, prawn, vegetables, or tofu. If you like spicy foods, try the chef's special Chili Mussel: New Zealand green mussels stir-fried with chili paste, onions, jalapenos, zucchini, and basil. For a milder entrée, the Bangkok chicken in house sauce is a slightly tangy option. Try the fried banana with ice cream for dessert.

Carmel's Restaurant & Bar (1 Page Ave., 828/252-8730, www.carmelsofasheville.com, Mon.–Thurs. 11:30 A.M.–2:30 P.M. and 5:30–9 P.M., Fri.–Sat. 11:30 A.M.–2:30 P.M. and 5:30–10 P.M., Sun. 11:30 A.M.–3:30 P.M. and 5:30–9 P.M., $9–29) specializes in fresh organic ingredients and naturally raised meats. Consider trying one of the restaurant's specialty grilled pizzas, which range in flavors from spicy buffalo chicken to candied tomato and brie. For entrées, Carmel's signature meatloaf is the best. Made with locally raised beef and sausage and topped off with onion straws, it's served under a wild mushroom sauce with mashed potatoes and baby green beans on the side. The bar is open

till 11 P.M. on weeknights and midnight on weekends.

If you want an aperitif or light supper, check out **Sante Wine Bar** (1 Page Ave., 828/254-8188, www.santewinebar.com, Mon.–Thurs. 4–10 P.M., Fri.–Sat. 4 P.M.–midnight, Sun. 4 P.M.–close, wine pours $4.50). They offer a variety of salads and cheese boards. The salmon cucumber salad offers a zesty and refreshing starter, or you can try the Mediterranean board, which consists of a variety of full-flavor tangy cheeses from Spain and Italy alongside apricots and almonds. There is also an extensive dip menu; you can try three of them on one plate for $13. The bar has a full wine, champagne, and bar menu.

Biltmore Estate

There are five restaurants on the Biltmore estate, and while none are worth making a special visit to enjoy if you're on the estate for the day you'll likely have to eat at least one meal there, as there are no designated picnic areas. **The Stable Café** (Shops at the Stables, 828/225-6370, www.biltmore.com/visit/dining/stable, Mon.–Fri. 11 A.M.–3 P.M., Sat.–Sun. 11 A.M.–4 P.M., $10–18) is the most convenient place to eat if you'd like indoor seating close to the mansion. Keep in mind, however, that any dining venue close to the mansion is likely going to be overcrowded and involve a lot of waiting. The Stable Café serves up barbecue, ribs, trout, and quiche.

You can avoid the crowds a little more effectively by dining at one of the restaurants at the Biltmore Estate Winery. **The Arbor Grill** (Biltmore Winery, 828/225-6237, www.biltmore.com/visit/dining/arbor, daily noon–7 P.M., $7–20) is an outdoor restaurant with live music on weekends. The Arbor is open weather permitting from March to October due to its outdoor location. Fare includes mostly sandwiches and salads. If you're looking for steak or wood-fired pizza, then check out the **Bistro** (Biltmore Winery, 828/225-6231, www.biltmore.com/visit/dining/bistro, daily

11:30 A.M.–8:30 P.M., $13–17), which is right next door to the winery.

Biltmore Village

The Corner Kitchen (3 Boston Way, 828/274-2439, www.thecornerkitchen.com, Mon.–Sat. 7:30–11 A.M., 11:30 A.M.–3 P.M., and 5–9 P.M., Sun. 9 A.M.–3 P.M. and 5–9 P.M., $6–26) is a wonderfully cozy place to dine for breakfast, lunch, or dinner. Located in one of the village's 1890s cottages, the Corner Kitchen has Arts and Crafts decor with Tiffany light fixtures, cozy fireplaces with oak mantelpieces, and an enclosed porch with bar seating. The restaurant has a definite southern flair, serving a sweet mustard–glazed meat loaf with cheddar grits on the side and blackberry ketchup–glazed pork chop with fried green tomatoes for dinner. The Sunday brunch is definitely something to write home about: You can get a breakfast salad with bacon and blue cheese, eggs, and pecans, or homemade biscuits with ham, cheese, and hollandaise sauce. Be sure to order a mimosa to top off those Sunday victuals.

Chelsea's and the Village Tea Room (6 Boston Way, 828/274-4400, www.chelseastea. com, tea room lunch Mon.–Sat. 11 A.M.–3 P.M., tea 3:30–4:45 P.M., Sun. 10:30 A.M.–3 P.M., gift shop Mon.–Sat. 10 A.M.–5 P.M., Sun. 10:30 A.M.–3 P.M., $4–13) is a fun place to stop for lunch or snack. They serve soups, sandwiches, quiche, and a comforting and delicious cheese and tomato sandwich for lunch and also host a traditional English tea mid-afternoon. The tea room is located inside **Chelsea's Gift Shop,** which carries a selection of tea-related gifts and home decor and baby items, as well as chocolate truffles.

La Paz Restaurante & Cantina (10 Biltmore Plaza, 828/277-8779, www.lapaz. com, Mon.–Thurs. 11 A.M.–10 P.M., Fri.–Sat. 11 A.M.–11 P.M., Sun. noon–10 P.M., $6–17) serves up both Mexican and southwestern dishes. You could easily make a meal of their beef nacho appetizer, which comes with crispy nachos buried in ground beef, beans, tomato,

and Monterey Jack and cheddar cheese, along with guacamole, sour cream, and jalapeño peppers. They offer a two- or three-item combo platter, allowing you to select from among tacos, enchiladas, burritos, chimichangas, tostados, and tamales.

Fig (18 Brook St., Ste. 101, 828/277-0889, www.figbistro.com, Mon.–Sat. 11:30 A.M.–3 P.M. and 5:30–9 P.M., Sun. 10 A.M.–2 P.M., $10–26) serves up continental cuisine with a distinct French influence made from locally grown, organic, and seasonal ingredients. The presentation is enough to make anyone fall in love with the food, and the plates often look too pretty to eat. Nevertheless, you must try some of this bistro's unique dishes, which include a macaroni gratin served with applewood bacon as well as a scrumptious salmon in red wine blackberry sauce. For dessert enjoy traditional milk and cookies.

The Red Stag Grill (11 Boston Way, 828/398-5600, www.bohemianhotelasheville. com, daily 6:30 A.M.–10 P.M., $15–38) is located in the Grand Bohemian Hotel and is most charming because of its atmosphere, where hand-hewn beams cross overhead, soft lighting shines on solid oak floors, and sumptuous furnishings make one feel at home. The restaurant serves both traditional and unusual fare, ranging from hand-cut steaks to elk tenderloin.

Not actually in Biltmore Village but close by is **Southside Café** (1800 Hendersonville Rd., 828/274-4413, www.southsidecafea-sheville.com, Mon.–Sat. 11 A.M.–2:30 P.M. and 5–9:30 P.M., Sun. 9:30 A.M.–2 P.M., $5–14), which is locally famous for its pimento cheese with flatbread. They also offer other traditional Southern fare in some truly unique sandwich combinations, including their honey barbecue–basted salmon sandwich served on sourdough with smoked bacon, baby greens, and cippolini-onion mayonnaise. One of my favorites is the tangy Angus burger topped with melted blue cheese and caramelized onions. Southside also has a number of pasta, salad, and soup concoctions as well as a full bar.

INFORMATION AND SERVICES

Information

The **Asheville Convention & Visitors Bureau** (36 Montford Ave., 828/258-6129, www.exploreasheville.com, Mon.–Fri. 8:30 A.M.–5:30 P.M., Sat.–Sun. 9 A.M.–5 P.M.) is the best place to get oriented to the city. If you're traveling in autumn, you can check out area fall-color reports at www.fallinthemountains.com. The visitors center is right off the I-240 at Exit 4C and close to the downtown historic area. The visitors center has free parking and free Internet access.

Located adjacent to the Blue Ridge Parkway headquarters outside Asheville, the **Blue Ridge Parkway Visitor Center** (Milepost 384, 828/298-5330, daily 9 A.M.–5 P.M.) is the major orientation center to the Blue Ridge Parkway. In addition to exhibits on the Parkway's history and area flora and fauna, the destination center also shows a brief introductory film and has an information desk with maps and brochures on attractions and amenities throughout the Asheville area.

National Forest Offices (160 Zillicoa St., 828/257-4200, www.cs.unca.edu, Mon.–Fri. 8 A.M.–4:30 P.M.) has a small gift shop with books and trail maps available for purchase as well as souvenirs. Forest Service personnel are available to answer questions and provide information.

Emergency Services

Mission Hospitals (509 Biltmore Ave., 828/213-1111, www.missionhospitals.org) operates western North Carolina's only designated 24-hour Level II Trauma Center. For non-emergencies in the Asheville area, contact the **Asheville Police Department** (100 Court Plaza, 828/252-1110, www.ashevillenc.gov, Mon.–Fri. 8:30 A.M.–5 P.M.).

Media

NEWSPAPERS

The Asheville Citizen-Times (www.citizen-times.com) is a daily newspaper with information on all Asheville-area happenings—news coverage, movie listings, what's for sale, marriage announcements, and more.

The Mountain Xpress (www.mountainx.com) also reports on local news and events affecting Asheville and the surrounding region. The paper reports on the area's vibrant arts and culture scene as well.

RADIO AND TELEVISION

The Mountain Air Network, WCQS 88.1 FM, offers locally hosted music programs featuring classical and other music and talk programs. HIS Radio, WLFA 91.3 FM, and WSKY 1230 AM are Christian radio stations serving the Asheville area. WRES 100.7 FM plays a variety of music for all different tastes. WPVM 103.5 FM, also known as The Progressive Voice of the Mountains, is a talk–news radio station and is part of the Mountain Area Information Network.

WYFF 4, affiliated with NBC, is the local television station reporting on local, regional, and national news, traffic, weather, entertainment, and sports.

Libraries

Buncombe County Public Libraries (www.buncombecounty.org) offer a wide variety of books, tapes, videos, and other materials as well as providing reference and reader's advisory services and programs for both children and adults. The libraries also offer a Summer Reading Program, an online card catalog at www.buncombecounty.org, and Story and Toddler Time. Library branches convenient to tourist areas include **Pack Memorial Library** (67 Haywood St., 828/250-4700, Mon.–Wed. 9:30 A.M.–8 P.M., Thurs.–Fri. 9:30 A.M.–6 P.M., Sat. 9:30 A.M.–5 P.M.), **East Asheville Library** (902 Tunnel Rd., 828/250-4738, Tues. and Thurs. 9 A.M.–8 P.M., Wed. and Fri. 9 A.M.–6 P.M., Sat. 9 A.M.–5 P.M.), and **North Asheville Library** (1030 Merrimon Ave., 828/250-4752, Mon., Wed., and Fri. 10 A.M.–6 P.M., Tues. and Thurs. 10 A.M.–8 P.M., Sat. 10 A.M.–5 P.M.).

Gay and Lesbian Resources

Asheville, a city that prides itself on being a haven for divergent and eclectic views, has become a popular vacation getaway for gay and lesbian couples. An active arts scene, a variety of downtown shops, hiking and outdoor activities, friendly locals, and much more make this unique town the perfect getaway.

Downtown Asheville features four gay/lesbian bars, including a dance club: **Scandals** (11 Grove St., 828/252-2838, www.clubscandals.net), the premier gay nightclub for the Asheville area; **Club Hairspray** (38 N. French Broad Ave., 828/258-2027, www.clubhairspray.com); **O.Henry's** (237 Haywood St., 828/254-1891); and **Smokey's Tavern** (18 Broadway St., 828/253-2155).

Asheville provides many luxurious opportunities for gay/lesbian lodging. Several accommodations are gay and lesbian owned and operated or gay and lesbian friendly. There are also accommodations for gay and lesbian commitment ceremonies. For a full listing of gay-friendly hotels, visit www.romanticasheville.com/gayandlesbian.

Post Offices and Internet Access

There are a number of post offices in Asheville. The easiest and most centrally located post office for tourists to access is likely the downtown location just south of Patton Avenue (33 Coxe Ave., 828/271-6428, Mon.–Fri. 7:30 A.M.–5 P.M., Sat. 9 A.M.–1 P.M.). Another is located north off I-240 (725 Merrimon Ave., 828/271-6438, Mon.–Fri. 8 A.M.–5 P.M., Sat. 9 A.M.–1 P.M.).

While most lodging options in Asheville are going to have Wi-Fi access, if you're camping or just passing through and want to check email try **The Asheville Visitors Center** (36 Montford Ave., 828/258-6101, Mon.–Fri. 8:30 A.M.–5:30 P.M., Sat. 9 A.M.–5 P.M., Sun. 9:30 A.M.–5 P.M.), which provides free Wi-Fi connections. You can also get online at **The Asheville Regional Airport** (61 Terminal Dr., 828/684-2226, opens 4:30 A.M.) for free.

If you're in the downtown historic district you can log on for free at **Malaprop's Bookstore/Café** (55 Haywood St., 828/254-6734, Mon.–Sat. 9 A.M.–9 P.M., Sun. 9 A.M.–7 P.M.) or at **True Confections** in the Grove Arcade (1 Page Ave. Ste. 147, 828/350-9480, Mon.–Thurs. 7:30 A.M.–9 P.M., Fri. 7:30 A.M.–11 P.M., Sat. 9 A.M.–11 P.M., Sun. 9 A.M.–8 P.M.).

You can also gain access to the Internet on public computers at the libraries.

GETTING THERE
Air

The **Asheville Regional Airport** (61 Terminal Dr., 828/684-2226, www.flyavl.com) is located about 15 miles south of downtown Asheville at Exit 40 off I-26. The airport is served by AirTran (www.airtran.com), Continental (www.continental.com), Delta (www.delta.com), and US Airways (www.usairways.com).

The airport offers short-term and long-term parking. The cost for short-term parking is $1.50 for 20–40 minutes, $2 for 40–60 minutes, $2.75 for 60–80 minutes, and $0.50 for each additional 20 minutes. The daily maximum for short-term parking is 24 hours at $12. The cost for long-term parking is $1 for the first hour, $1 for each additional hour, and $7 daily maximum. The short- and long-term parking lots are located directly across from the terminal building and are open 24 hours a day, seven days a week. Both lots are wheelchair-accessible. An overflow lot is located next to regular parking. The Department of Public Safety will provide lost car assistance, tow truck call-out, key retrieval, and battery jump start free of charge on a staff-available basis. You may be required to sign a liability waiver for some services.

Car

If you're coming into Asheville from the west you'll take I-40 into town and then get on the bypass around the city, I-240, to access most of the attractions. Signs from the interstate will clearly point you to downtown, visitor information services, and attractions. From the east, you'll also come in on I-40, taking I-240 to access visitor attractions.

Approaching from the south, take I-26 north all the way to Asheville, and then follow the signs for I-240. From the north, visitors will enjoy a very scenic drive down I-26, which intersects I-240.

GETTING AROUND
Car Rentals
There are five national car rental services with counters in the Asheville Regional Airport: Avis (828/684-7144), Budget (828/684-2273), Enterprise (828/684-3607), Hertz (828/684-6455), and National Alamo (828/684-8572).

Car Rental locations away from the airport are Hertz (891 Patton Ave., 828/225-1776), Thrifty Car Rental (835 Brevard Rd., 828/665-9995), and Avis (1 S. Tunnel Rd., 828/299-3644).

Parking
Asheville is something of a nightmare to drive in, despite its small-city status. Streets tend to be haphazardly marked (or marked too late), and the downtown has a number of one-way streets. Couple this with the local drivers who are lax about obeying basic traffic laws, and you have a bit of a free-for-all on the streets not unlike what you might find in Europe. Street parking in the downtown area is a mess of its own. There is metered parking available throughout the historic area, but good luck finding a vacant spot. Hedge your bets, save yourself some time and headache, and opt for one of the city parking garages instead.

On-street parking is allowed for a period of two hours or less for a cost of $1 per hour to be paid by meter at each parking space. On-street parking is free after 6 P.M. as well as on Sundays and holidays. A city parking lot with meters is located on Biltmore Avenue. There are also three parking garages. **The Civic Center Garage** (29 Rankin Ave.), Asheville's largest city garage, provides 550 spaces and is open 24 hours daily with an attendant on duty 10 A.M.–7 P.M. It is

located off Haywood Street, adjacent to the Asheville Civic Center. Entrances can be found off Vanderbilt Place and Rankin Avenue. The main exit is located on Rankin Avenue. The Civic Center Garage allows visitors to park free for the first hour with a charge of $0.50 per hour or fraction of an hour afterwards, with a daily limit of $4. Right next door is **Rankin Avenue Garage** (12 Rankin Ave.), also open 24 hours a day with an attendant on duty 10 A.M.–7 P.M., and located between Haywood Street and Rankin Avenue just north of College Street. Two entrances can be found off Walnut Street and Rankin Avenue with a pedestrian entrance on Haywood Street. This garage has a daily limit of $6. **Wall Street Garage** (45 Wall St.) can be found across the street from the Grove Arcade on Otis Street between Wall Street and Battery Park Avenue. The entrance is located on Otis Street. Free parking is given for the first hour with a charge of $0.75 for each additional hour or fraction of an hour, with a daily limit of $8. It is open 24 hours a day with an attendant on site 10 A.M.–7 P.M.

Public Transportation and Trolley Tours
The **Asheville Transit System** (828/253-5691, www.ashevillenc.gov) has 24 bus routes that service the city of Asheville and other local areas Monday–Saturday 6 A.M.–11:30 P.M. The routes originate from the Downtown Transit Center (49 Coxe Ave.), which provides amenities such as clean restrooms, indoor and outdoor seating, and an on-duty information assistant. Asheville Transit also provides paratransit transportation to all qualifying individuals who are unable to use the bus due to a handicap. To sign up or arrange transportation through the paratransit program, call 828/258-0186.

You can also take a tour of Asheville with **Asheville Historic Trolley Tours** (37 Montford Ave., 828/681-8585, www.ashevilletrolleytours.com, adults $19, children 6–17 $12, family of four $45). The trolleys offer narrated 90-minute tours on the history and lore of the city. You can, however, hop on and off the trolley at any point, as the trolley serves all of Asheville's major attractions and stops at each attraction once an hour daily from 9 A.M. to 4:30 P.M. Ghost Trolley Tours run from March through November on Saturday at 7:30 P.M. Adult tickets can be purchased for $20. Admission for children 6–17 is $12. Ghost tours leave from Tod's Tastys at 102 Montford Avenue. Advance reservations are required. Call 888/667-3600.

Gray Line Trolley Tours of Asheville (36 Montford Ave., 866/592-8687, www.graylineasheville.com, adults $20, children 5–11 $10) offers similar services departing from the Asheville Visitor Center every hour on the half hour and various other area attractions with 90-minute history tours and the same hop-on/hop-off privileges as Asheville Historic Trolley Tours. The service runs daily from 10:30 A.M. to 3:30 P.M.

Taxis

You won't see a lot of taxis running around town in Asheville, so your best bet is to call if you need one. There are a number of providers in the city, including **A Red Cab Company** (194 Haywood Rd., 828/232-1112), **Yellow Cab Company** (393 Haywood Rd., 828/253-3311), and **New Blue Bird Taxi Co.** (194 Haywood Rd., 828/258-8331).

ASHEVILLE AREA

Lake Lure Area

Lake Lure is formed by the waters of the Rocky Broad River and, despite its isolation and the winding mountain roads that lead to it, it has become a popular retreat for vacationers and retirees. The lake is located about 45 minutes southeast of Asheville and is known for its unique crucifix shape.

Lake Lure was the vision of Dr. Lucius B. Morse, who visited Hickory Nut Gorge in the early 1900s and determined the area was well

© FRENCH C. GRIMES

Lake Lure

suited for a resort community with a lake. Morse purchased the land around Chimney Rock, a total of 400 acres, for $5,000 in 1902, and formally established Chimney Rock Mountains, Inc. as the landholder. The company eventually acquired 8,000 acres, including the valley that would ultimately form Lake Lure.

Morse's vision became reality in 1925, when the Carolina Mountain Power Company was created with the intent of damming the Rocky Broad River for the purpose of both electrical power generation and creating a recreational lake. The dam was completed in 1926, and the full impoundment of the lake was completed in 1927. Growth in the area was slowed considerably by the onset of the Great Depression, but over time Lake Lure became a major destination for vacationers seeking escape from the heat of southern lowlands.

Today the dam on Lake Lure still powers a working hydroelectric plant. The lake itself covers 720 acres and has some 27 miles of shoreline. Lake depths range from 35 to 120 feet. Surrounded by granite mountains, Lake Lure sits at an elevation of just under 1,000 feet.

The village of Chimney Rock is small and touristy. The numerous shops in town tend to carry mostly the same wares—T-shirts, moccasins, and shot glasses. And you'll find more of the same in the gift shop at Chimney Rock Park. Don't be deterred, however, as the views of Lake Lure from Chimney Rock are not to be missed.

SIGHTS
◖ Chimney Rock Park

Chimney Rock Park (Hwy. 64/74A, 800/277-9611, www.chimneyrockpark.com, Apr.–Nov. daily 8:30 A.M.–7 P.M., Dec.–Mar. daily 9:30 A.M.–6 P.M., adults $14, children 6–15 $6, under 6 free) became a state park after it was purchased in 2007 by the State of North Carolina from the Morse family, which had owned the property since 1902, at a total cost of $24 million. Chimney Rock has long been a favored tourist attraction in western North

Carolina with its twisting trails to stunning views across Lake Lure. Its steep-walled landscape was the film set for many of the scenes in *The Last of the Mohicans.*

The park is, of course, best known for Chimney Rock, the 315-foot solid granite spire that rises over Hickory Nut Gorge at an elevation of 2,280 feet, providing long-range views over Lake Lure and 75 miles into the distance on clear days. A 26-story elevator inside the mountain allows visitors of any physical ability access to the scenery.

Chimney Rock Park is a good place to try rock climbing, with rappelling for beginners as well as opportunities for more advanced climbers. The park offers two-hour climbing clinics for $35 as well as half-day and full-day instruction, all provided by certified climbing instructors from Fox Mountain Guides.

If you're an avid bird-watcher, take a walk along the mostly level Hickory Nut Falls Trail, which leads to the base of Hickory Nut Falls, a 404-foot waterfall cascading over a granite face. In spring, you can enjoy an abundance of wildflowers along this path, and, in July, the trail is blush pink and white with lush rhododendron blossoms. Watch for black-throated blue warblers, rose-breasted grosbeaks, solitary vireo, and Swainson's warblers.

Other points to hit include climbing to the top of Chimney Rock to take in the view, experiencing the unique natural rock formation of the Opera Box, and climbing up to Exclamation Point for a view that places you 1,400 feet above the park entrance.

SPORTS AND RECREATION
◖ Boating

Lake Lure Tours (2930 Memorial Hwy., 828/625-1373, www.lakelure.com, Apr.–Oct. daily 10 A.M.–6 P.M., Mar. and Nov. Sat.–Sun. only, call for hours, hourly cruise adults $14, seniors $12, children 4–12 $6, lunch cruise $20, sunset cruise and dinner $55) offers scenic, sunset, and dinner cruises on the lake as well as boat rentals. Even if you don't want to rent your own boat, take advantage of the company's many boat tours to get out on the lake

© FRENCH C. GRIMES

pontoon boat rides on Lake Lure

and experience the views. Scenic pontoon boat tours run hourly from 10 A.M. until 4 P.M. The lunch cruise is for groups of 10 or more only and requires prior reservations. Sunset and dinner cruises run Friday–Sunday only and require prior reservations.

The lake itself is stunningly beautiful—generally a bright cerulean with a milky surface, with the mountains rising just beyond it to the west. Many of the mountains have exposed and eroded granite faces as they huddle in to form the steep walls of Hickory Nut Gorge. If you elect to take a sunset cruise in summer, you'll have the opportunity to see the sun set right down the center of the gorge.

But part of the allure of touring the lake by boat is seeing the residences on its shores, which range from little cottages to 12,000-square-foot mansions. Over 70 percent of the homes on the lake are vacation homes. As you putter around the shorelines, your tour guide will likely share with you tales of the families living along the lake, from those who fish from their windows to those who have built sprawling houses alongside the tiny early-20th-century cottages of their grandparents. You'll see the very first home built on Lake Lure between

1925 and 1927, a tiny cottage that stands in stark contrast to the lakefront mansions that dominate the shores today. That first house is only 500 square feet.

Among the sites you'll see on a Lake Lure Tour are the shorefronts where *Dirty Dancing* was filmed in 1987. You'll also learn about the submerged town of Buffalo, the remains of which can still be found in the deepest part of the lake more than 100 feet below the surface. Divers claim a church with bell intact still stands in a soggy grave at the bottom.

Lake Lure Marina, which is owned and operated by the same folks who run Lake Lure Tours, also offers motorized and non-motorized boat rentals. Options include pontoon boats, kayaks, canoes, paddle boats, and hydro-bikes with prices ranging from $10 to $80 per hour depending on the rental selected. The marina also has a lakeside beach with water slides that is open daily Memorial Day weekend through Labor Day weekend. Daily beach passes are $8 for adults, $7 for seniors, and $6 for children.

If you come to Lake Lure with your own boat, there are three public boat docks on the lake, but you must get a Lake Lure permit before docking. Boat permit fees vary widely, depending on your type of boat, the season you are visiting, and how long you plan to boat on the lake. You can purchase permits at the Lake Lure Marina or **Town of Lake Lure Municipal Center** (828/625-9983, www.townoflakelure. com/boat_permit_fees). There are no personal watercraft allowed on the lake.

Fishing

If you plan to fish on Lake Lure or on the Rocky Broad River, make sure you have a North Carolina fishing license. Among the specimens you might catch in the area are largemouth bass, smallmouth bass, trout, catfish, and pan fish.

You can take advantage of guided fishing trips on the lake, too. There are several providers in the area, including **Lewis No Clark Expeditions** (828/223-0269, www.lewisno-clark.com), which offers private guided fishing trips on the lake as well as professional instruction in casting, knot tying, and rod and reel selection and use. All equipment is provided. **Rob's Guide Service** (828/625-5121, www.robsguideservice.org) also offers fishing guide service on Lake Lure for all skill levels. **Pro Bass Fishing** (828/693-7529) provides 4-to-6-hour trips on the lake with all equipment furnished.

Golf

Lake Lure has a number of publicly accessible golf courses, a couple of them enjoying lake views. They're all open year-round, though they are busiest in summer and fall. Among them is the **Town of Lake Lure Golf Course** (658 Memorial Hwy., 828/625-4472, www. townoflakelure.com, daily 8 A.M.–5:30 P.M., 9-hole $17–22, 18-hole $19–32), a Donald Ross–designed nine-hole course located right on Highway 64/74A just over a mile west of Chimney Rock. **Apple Valley Golf Course** (309 Winesape Rd., 800/260-1040, www. rumblingbald.com, daily 8 A.M.–8 P.M., early $58–63, twilight $38–40, late $28), an 18-hole Dan Maples–designed course, is one of two courses on the Rumbling Bald Resort on Lake Lure. The second is **Bald Mountain Golf**

Course (112 Mountains Blvd., 800/260-1040, www.rumblingbald.com, daily 8 A.M.–8 P.M., early $58–63, twilight $38–40, late $28).

ACCOMMODATIONS
Inns and Bed-and-Breakfasts

There are a number of funky and nostalgic motor inns in Chimney Rock that might remind you of childhood road trips, but if you're looking for a bit more luxury and comfort, seek out one of the area's inns or consider renting a house. If you want to be right on the lake, check into **The Lodge on Lake Lure** (361 Charlotte Dr., 828/625-2789, www.lodgeon-lakelure.com, $160–314), one of the only waterfront accommodations on the lake. Long before the 1930s lodge was purchased by an international banker who turned it into an inn, the lodge had served as a retreat for the North Carolina Highway Patrol and later for the U.S. Army Air Corps. Decorated with furniture and eclectic antiques from South Africa, the home country of one of its owners, Horst Brunner, the lodge's guest rooms and common areas feature private balconies and light-capturing floor-to-ceiling windows overlooking the waters of Lake Lure. The great room houses a magnificent 20-foot stone fireplace with a millstone mortared into its center and massive hand-hewn ceiling beams.

The **1927 Lake Lure Inn & Spa** (2771 Memorial Hwy., 888/434-4970, www.lake-lure.com, standard accommodations and jacuzzi rooms $109–225, beachside signature and suites $99–149, suites $149–245, *Dirty Dancing* cabins $199–275) is situated right across the road from Lake Lure within walking distance of the Lake Lure Marina. The inn is operated by the owners of Lake Lure Tours. The inn has 69 guest rooms and suites as well as three cabins for rent. Guests have access to the pool as well as complimentary Wi-Fi. Even if you don't stay at the inn, you might want to pay a quick visit to this place to see the collection of art and antiques in the hotel lobby, halls, and public areas. Outside visitors are welcome to take a self-guided tour daily from 9 A.M. to 5 P.M. Among the objects you'll see are an 1870s Baccarat crystal chandelier over the main staircase, a self-winding clock, a collection of 19th-century upright music boxes from around the world in the inn lobby, and china cabinets filled to brimming with historic paraphernalia. Guests and non-guests of the inn can enjoy the on-site **Allure Spa** (Tues.–Thurs. 9 A.M.–5 P.M., Fri.–Sat. 9 A.M.–6 P.M., Sun. by appt.).

The Esmeralda (910 Main St., 888/897-2999, www.theesmeralda.com, $130–250) is conveniently located in Chimney Rock and has 14 elegant guest rooms comfortably furnished with Ethan Allen furniture and Bose Wave music systems. All the rooms have Wi-Fi, and many offer views of Hickory Nut Gorge. The most striking feature of The Esmeralda is its gorgeous lobby with stone fireplace and staircase made of mountain laurel branches. Guests enjoy complimentary wine and cheese in the evenings as well as an on-site restaurant, Parise's New American Bistro.

Vacation Rentals

The Arbor at Lake Lure (2494 Memorial Hwy., 828/625-1171, www.arborlakelure.com) offers guest cottages and cabins for rent, many with views of Chimney Rock Mountain. The lake house rental, as its name implies, offers lakefront lodging. Most of the accommodations here have private decks with hot tubs, gas log fireplaces, and king-size beds. The fully equipped kitchens come stocked with breakfast fixings. The decor is classic country with quilt-covered beds, rocking chairs, and wood-paneled walls.

Ivivi Lodge (161 Waterside Dr., 828/625-0601, www.ivivilodge.com, $5,000 a week) is the most unique vacation rental option on Lake Lure if you're willing to splurge and have a large family group to justify the cost—the lodge will accommodate up to 14 people. Mixing South African and European interiors with exterior designs Frank Lloyd Wright would appreciate, the lodge offers an environment where modern architecture mingles readily with the natural environment. Sharp lines and floor-to-ceiling windows define the inn's architecture, and the burnt orange tones of the exterior blend delicately into the surrounding trees. Inside the great room, sunlight pours through walls of glass that offer stunning views of Lake Lure and the mountains beyond. The furniture is contemporary, yet soothing earth tones invite guests to linger awhile and soak up the sunshine. There is no skimping on the minutiae at Ivivi. The same South African themes carry over into the lodge's rooms, all of which offer scenic views of Lake Lure. Again, the details delight the senses—bathroom sinks constructed to look like bowls, towel warmers, deep whirlpool baths (bubble bath provided), and constant gentle music pouring from in-room stereos.

Rumbling Bald Resort (112 Mountains Blvd., 800/419-3854, www.rumblingbald.com) has over 100 vacation rentals available ranging from private single-family homes to condominiums. Some properties are lakefront while others have mountain views or face one of the resort's two golf courses. Guests have access to all of the resort amenities, including swimming pools, tennis, and fitness center. Two golf courses and spa treatments are available for additional fees. There are also three restaurants at the resort.

Distinctive Mountain Lodging (2975 Memorial Hwy., 877/371-5100, www.distinctivemtnlodging.com) offers more than a dozen private residences for rent in the Lake Lure and Chimney Rock area, including lakefront homes with private docks and homes with incredible views of Hickory Nut Gorge.

A bit father afield than the other lodgings listed here, **(The Cottages at Spring House Farm** (219 Haynes Rd., 877/738-9798, www.springhousefarm.com, $245–325) is a place you want to check out if you're seeking the ultimate in solitude. North Carolina's very first eco-retreat, Spring House Farm is a 92-acre farm with miles of hiking trails through forest and meadow and along pond and stream. There are only six cottages on the property, each of them utterly secluded from the rest. Constructed of local timber, the cottages feature stone fireplaces or wood-burning stoves, front-porch hot tubs, and rustic, comfortable decor that invite languor and serenity. If you're not in a rush, spend a day here listening to raindrops crackle on maple leaves, curled up with a book and a cup of cocoa. Longtime proprietors Arthur and Zee Campbell have made every effort to ensure the comfort and privacy of their guests. For breakfast, they provide a kitchen stocked with fresh eggs, locally made jams and jellies, and homemade bread. Upon request, the Campbells will even give guests a tour of their 1826 home, the carefully restored Albertus Ledbetter House, which earned its place on the National Register of Historic Places in 2001. The Cottages at Spring House Farm is a couples-only retreat.

Camping

As a second-home destination, Lake Lure doesn't offer much in the way of camping options, but there are a handful of campgrounds in the area. Among them is **Hickory Nut Falls Family Campground** (639 Main St., 828/625-4014, www.hickorynutfallsfamilycampground.com, Apr.–Oct.), which offers tent and RV sites with full hookups. Some sites are riverfront. The campground is only a quarter mile from Chimney Rock Park. Pets are not allowed. Hickory Nut Falls also sells propane gas.

In Lake Lure, **Hitching Post Campground** (620 Girl Scout Camp Rd., 828/625-1138, www.hitchingpostcampground.com, tent camping $20, RV camping $30, bunkhouses $40, apartments $65) offers full hookups, dump station, bathhouse, fishing pond, and playground.

FOOD
Chimney Rock

Riverwatch Deli and Grill (379 Main St., 828/625-1030, Thurs.–Tues. 11 A.M.–6 P.M., winter hours may vary, $4–7) has dining overlooking the Rocky Broad River and serves sandwiches made with high-quality Boar's Head deli meats. This is a good, reliable spot to grab lunch. **Old Rock Café** (431 Main St., 828/625-2329, daily 11 A.M.–4 P.M., $6–8) is a quick and easy option directly adjacent to

the entrance to Chimney Rock Park. You place your order at the register here, and the service is lackluster at best, but they have served consistently good hamburgers every time I've eaten here, and they offer riverside seating on their deck outside. The chicken wraps, stuffed with fried chicken, lettuce, cheese, tomatoes, and ranch dressing are also pretty good, as are the especially crispy fries. Don't come here for any atmosphere besides the Rocky Broad, however, as lunch and dinner are served in plastic baskets lined with paper. You can also access the Rocky Broad Riverwalk, a scenic walkway along the river, from the rear of the restaurant.

Parise's New American Bistro (910 Main St., 828/707-2229, www.theesmeralda.com/parise_bistro, Feb.–Nov. daily 7:30 A.M.–2 P.M. and 5:30–9 P.M., Dec.–Jan. Mon.–Tues. 9 A.M.–3 P.M., Wed.–Sat. 9 A.M.–3 P.M. and 5–8 P.M., Sun. 9 A.M.–4 P.M., $15–29) is the new restaurant of The Esmeralda, a luxury inn on the west side of Chimney Rock.

Lake Lure

Beachside Grill (2771 Memorial Hwy., 828/625-0937, www.lakelure.com, Mon.–Thurs. 7 A.M.–5 P.M., Fri.–Sun. 7 A.M.–7 P.M., $5–7) offers salads, sandwiches, and burgers in a casual setting across the road from Lake Lure. They also have blue-plate specials Monday through Thursday and an all-you-can-eat buffet on Sundays. Next door is **The Veranda Restaurant** (2771 Memorial Hwy., 828/625-2525, www.lakelure.com, Tues.–Sat. 5–9 P.M., Sun. 10:30 A.M.–2:30 P.M., $16–34), which is also part of the Lake Lure Inn property and offers dining indoors or on the veranda overlooking the lake. Entrées include trout, snapper, salmon, rack of lamb, and filet mignon, and the restaurant offers a full wine list. Early-bird specials from 5 to 6:30 P.M. provide three courses for $14.99, a substantial discount from the regular menu. Reservations are recommended.

Larkin's on the Lake (1020 Memorial Hwy., 828/625-4075, www.larkinsonthelake.com, daily 11:30 A.M.–9 P.M., $19–37) is the only restaurant actually situated on Lake Lure, and boaters can dock here for dinner. Larkin's top eats are its barbecue baby-back ribs and its porterhouse pork chop glazed in apple cinnamon sauce. One of my favorites is the teriyaki brochette with its melt-in-your-mouth tender chunks of filet mignon skewered with pineapple, onion, and peppers. The restaurant has an extensive wine list. Service here is usually quite excellent. You'll want to make reservations if you want a lake-view table.

INFORMATION AND SERVICES
Information
The **Lake Lure Visitor Center** (2926 Memorial Hwy., 877/625-2725, www.hickory-nut.org) is located right next door to the Lake Lure Marina and is operated by the Hickory Nut Gorge Chamber of Commerce. The visitors center has public restrooms, as does the adjacent marina.

Post Office
The post office in Chimney Rock (366 Main St., 828/625-4847, Mon.–Fri. 8:30 A.M.–4:15 P.M.) is easy to find, being located in the center of town just east of the Chimney Rock Park entrance.

GETTING THERE
If you're coming into the Chimney Rock and Lake Lure area from Asheville, then the best route to take is ALT 74 west; there are signs for the exit on both I-240 and I-40 in Asheville. If you're coming from points south, take I-26 north to Hendersonville, then take Highway 64 to Bat Cave and turn right. Chimney Rock and Lake Lure are both on Highway 64. Approaching the area from the north or east, take I-40 east toward Asheville but exit well before at Exit 103, and follow Highway 64 to Lake Lure.

MOUNT PISGAH AND BEYOND

South of Asheville, the Blue Ridge Parkway passes through the Pisgah and Nantahala National Forests, a wild hinterland of remote mountain peaks and curling back roads. This is the landscape that inspired Charles Frazier's best-selling novel *Cold Mountain,* which was made into a motion picture, and a fearless hiker can head into the backcountry to hike the namesake mountain. Or one can hike the steep trek to the top of Mount Pisgah for 360-degree views of the Blue Ridge and, on a clear day, glimpses into the Smokies.

What we know today as the Pisgah National Forest was actually once owned by George Vanderbilt. He bought 80,000 acres of the area in 1895, which meant his landholdings stretched from the Shining Rock Wilderness Area 20 miles north to the Biltmore Estate

in Asheville. Vanderbilt sold timber rights on 69,000 acres for $12 an acre in 1912. He named the area Pisgah Forest, a name which the U.S. Forest Service kept when they acquired the property in 1914. Vanderbilt's widow, Edith, sold the property for $5 an acre.

Vanderbilt was something of a pioneer in the field of forestry management. Even though he allowed for logging on his land, he directed logging contractors to limit damage to small growth trees and to cut no trees under 16 inches in diameter.

It was really right here that forest management was born in America. Gifford Pinchot organized the Society of American Foresters in 1900, after being the first forester at Vanderbilt's Biltmore Estate. Pinchot's goal was to show how forest management could both

HIGHLIGHTS

【 Carl Sandburg Home National Historic Site: The home of the American author and poet is located on a 250-acre farm in Flat Rock (page 155).

【 Flat Rock Playhouse: The state theater of North Carolina offers Broadway-quality plays in Flat Rock (page 156).

【 Brevard Music Center: Known for its summer music festival, the Brevard Music Center has been training young performing artists since 1936 (page 158).

【 Shining Rock Wilderness: Once part of George Vanderbilt's Pisgah Forest, Shining Rock Wilderness is the largest wilderness area in North Carolina (page 163).

【 Highest Point on the Blue Ridge Parkway: The Richland Balsam Overlook offers the highest elevation on the Parkway at 6,047 feet (page 166).

LOOK FOR **【** TO FIND RECOMMENDED SIGHTS, ACTIVITIES, DINING, AND LODGING.

MOUNT PISGAH

improve the landscape and make use of it for income. He became Chief of the U.S. Division of Forestry in 1898, and seven years later the U.S. Forest Service was started as its own entity under the U.S. Department of Agriculture.

PLANNING YOUR TIME

If you're an avid outdoors person, then allow yourself at least three or four days to explore the Mount Pisgah area of the Blue Ridge Parkway. This will give you the opportunity to not only drive what I consider to be the most scenic section of the Parkway and take in the views, but also plenty of time for some longer hikes, fishing, and rafting or rock climbing if

you're into more adventuresome sports. The region also has several beautiful small towns with darling bed-and-breakfasts, several fine restaurants, and first-rate art and craft galleries carrying the work of regional artisans.

Because of the Parkway's high elevation in this area, it can be chilly in this region even in mid-summer. Thus, the best time to visit the region for comfortable weather is in the summer. Peak fall color season in October is best avoided if you don't like crowds. If you like the idea of having the Parkway largely to yourself, then mid- to late spring is a good time to visit when the weather is still cool, and there are often some warm days in September as well.

MOUNT PISGAH

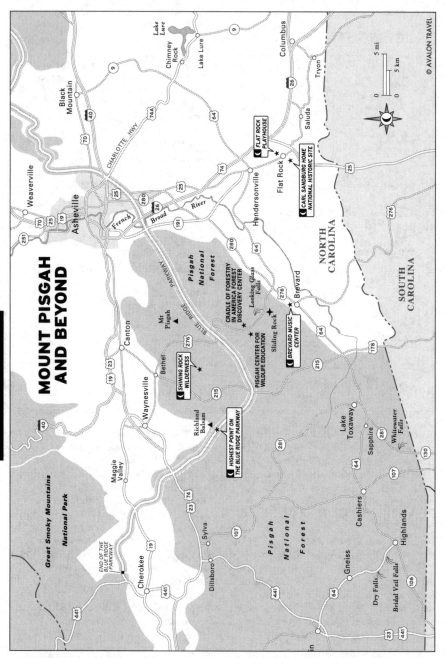

MOUNT PISGAH AND BEYOND

Hendersonville

Just south of Asheville off I-26, Hendersonville is perhaps best known for its historic downtown, which is listed on the National Register of Historic Places. Most of the historic structures here date to the late 19th and early 20th centuries. Interestingly enough, Hendersonville is also home to the angel referenced in Asheville native son Thomas Wolfe's novel *Look Homeward, Angel*. She stands today at the Oakdale Cemetery.

Other writers have left their mark here as well, including Carl Sandburg, who spent the last two decades of his life at his home just south of Hendersonville near Flat Rock. One will also find the critically acclaimed Flat Rock Playhouse here. The state theater of North Carolina, the playhouse is considered one of the best in the nation, offering an eight-month season running through October.

Hendersonville's Main Street is an attractive place to spend an afternoon. It's a bit of a challenge to drive through downtown, as the flower planters jutting out into the street make it something of a maze, and there are also a lot of stoplights, but the area is thriving with shops and restaurants as well as a variety of painted fiberglass apple slices, reflective of the area's orchard industry. If you arrive in town via Route 64 from Chimney Rock, you will likely notice the acres and acres of apple and peach orchards as well as in-season fruit stands where you can pick up produce and locally made ciders in summer and fall.

SIGHTS
Mineral and Lapidary Museum of Henderson County

A must-see stop is the Mineral and Lapidary Museum of Henderson County (400 N. Main St., 828/698-1977, www.mineralmuseum.org, Mon.–Fri. 1–5 P.M., Sat. 10 A.M.–5 P.M., free), which has displays of common North Carolina minerals and gems as well as a nest of dinosaur eggs from China, which you're welcome to

touch. The museum is located in the basement of an old bank building on Main Street and doesn't look like much on first entering. The dinosaur eggs that most people come to see are likely from the Hadrosaurs family, which lived 50 to 100 million years ago. The eggs feel like cracked rocks. There are other fossils here as well, including fish fossils from Wyoming, and gems from around the world. Look for the Ocean Jasper from Madagascar, which is distinguished by its colorful circular bands. There is a small gift shop in the already small museum where you can buy gems and minerals in the rough as well as polished. You can also purchase and cut open your own geode, a sphere-shaped rock with a hollow cavity lined with crystals.

Henderson County Heritage Museum

The Henderson County Heritage Museum (1 Historic Courthouse Sq., 828/694-1619, www.hendersoncountymuseum.org, Wed.–Sat. 10 A.M.–5 P.M., Sun. 1–5 P.M., donation) is located inside Hendersonville's historic courthouse in the 100 block of Main Street. It has exhibits on the history of Henderson County from the stories of the Cherokee who once lived here, through pioneer settlement, to the modern era. Even if you don't feel like touring the museum, be sure to at least walk by the beautiful 1904 courthouse with gold-colored dome. Courthouse tours are available on Wednesdays at 2 P.M.

Hendersonville Depot

The Hendersonville Depot (Maple St., 828/243-0226, www.avmrc.com, Sat. 10 A.M.–2 P.M., free) is the town's original 1902 depot, though today it houses the Apple Valley Model Railroad Club. Toy-train enthusiasts and kids alike will enjoy the display of the club's HO-scale railroad, which occupies 420 square feet and has 600 feet of track.

MOUNT PISGAH

Hendersonville's historic courthouse, home to the Henderson County Heritage Museum

© FRENCH C. GRIMES

Wolfe's Angel

The angel statue referenced in Thomas Wolfe's most famous novel, *Look Homeward, Angel,* can be viewed at Hendersonville's Oakdale Cemetery (Hwy. 64 W., 828/697-3084) located on Highway 64 west between Blythe and Church Streets. The marble angel is protected today by a wrought-iron fence, and a historical marker is located on Highway 64 west just under a mile from downtown.

Western North Carolina Air Museum

Antique-aircraft enthusiasts will enjoy a visit to the Western North Carolina Air Museum (Hendersonville Airport, 828/698-2482, www.wncairmuseum.com, Apr.–Oct. Wed. noon–5 P.M., Sat. 10 A.M.–5 P.M., Sun. noon–5 P.M., Nov.–Mar. Wed. noon–5 P.M., Sat.–Sun. noon–5 P.M., free), which has restored and replica antique vintage airplanes, including a 1900s Nieuport 11 reproduction and a 1945 Stearman N4S.

Apple Orchard Tours

Henderson County is loaded with fruit orchards, and many of them have tours available or on-farm fruit stands and markets. Some even have pick-your-own produce opportunities. If you'd like more information about visiting some of the area orchards, contact the Blue Ridge Farm Direct Market Association (828/697-4891, www.ncapples.com), a local cooperative of Henderson County apple growers formed in 1936.

ENTERTAINMENT AND EVENTS
Entertainment

The first Friday of every month, downtown Hendersonville's art galleries, antiques shops, and gift stores stay open late for the **First Friday/Gallery Stroll** (401 N. Main St., 828/697-2022, www.downtownhendersonville.org, 5–9 P.M.). In addition to the galleries being open late, some have artists demonstrating their crafts.

MOUNT PISGAH

In the summer, the Hendersonville visitors center hosts **Music on Main Street** (201 S. Main St., 800/828-4244, www.historichendersonville.org, June–Aug. Fri. 7–9 P.M., free) every Friday night. The musical lineup varies from week to week, ranging from oldies to classic rock. Parking lot and seating opens at 5:30, and you'll want to bring a lawn chair or a blanket. Pets and alcoholic beverages are not permitted. Call the visitors center to learn what bands are performing on any given Friday.

Summer fun is endless in this little town. On Monday nights you'll find the **Monday Night Street Dances** (201 S. Main St., 800/828-4244, www.historichendersonville.org, July–Aug. Mon. 7–9 P.M., free), which feature traditional Appalachian music and dancing, usually clogging. Again, bring your lawn chair and blanket (unless you plan to dance, too). No pets or alcohol are allowed, and parking and seating opens at 5:30.

The **Blue Ridge Performing Arts Center** (538 N. Main St., 828/693-0087, www.brpac.org, box office Tues.–Sat. noon–6 P.M.) is a small 100-seat theater and home to the local Absolute Theater Company. Throughout the year, the theater hosts performing artists, whether local, national, or international, in music, comedy, dance, and drama. Visit the websites for upcoming performances, showtimes, and tickets.

Events

The **North Carolina Apple Festival** (Main St., 828/697-4557, www.ncapples.com, free) takes place on Labor Day weekend each September and celebrates the importance of the region's orchards to the local economy with nine blocks of craft vendors, booths of North Carolina apple growers, live music, and food in downtown Hendersonville. Apple orchard tours are available as part of the festival, too. The King Apple Parade occurs on Labor Day. For more information on event times, visit the website.

SHOPPING

With smaller versions of some of downtown Asheville's favorite destinations like the Mast

General Store and Kilwin's (with its delectable fudge and ice cream!) and plenty more, Hendersonville has a thriving downtown 16-block historic district with most shops along Main Street and one block down on side streets. The town has many blocks of art galleries, antiques shops, gift shops, bookstores, and toy stores.

Art and Antiques

On the upper end of downtown is **The Arts Council of Henderson County** (538 N. Main St., 828/693-8504, www.acofhc.org, Tues.–Fri. 1–5 P.M., Sat. 1–4 P.M., and by appointment), which has a gallery carrying the work of masters of southern folk art as well as frequent exhibits of pieces from the artists of the River Arts District in Asheville.

All Nations Trading (514 N. Main St., 828/698-4888, www.spiritfeather.com, Mon.–Sat. 10 A.M.–5 P.M.) carries the handmade jewelry and art of the Native American Southwest, including turquoise and silver, pottery, kachina

Main Street in Hendersonville
© FRENCH C. GRIMES

MOUNT PISGAH

dolls, and fetish carvings. Represented tribes include the Lakota Sioux, Navajo, Zuni, and Pueblo.

The Revolving Arts Gallery (511 N. Main St., 828/692-9996, www.therevolvingartsgallery.com, Mon.–Thurs. and Sat. 11 A.M.–6 P.M., Fri. 11 A.M.–8 P.M.) carries rotating exhibits of regional artists and has several artist studios on-site. The gallery also has regular workshops, lectures, and musical entertainment throughout the year.

Wickwire (330 N. Main St., 828/692-6222, www.wickwireartgallery.com, Mon.–Sat. 10 A.M.–6 P.M., Sun. 1–4 P.M.) is a fun stop. The gallery carries both fine and folk art and has two stories of gallery and retail space featuring oil painting, handmade furniture, photography, and handcrafted jewelry.

Red Step Artworks (142 3rd Ave. W., 828/697-1447, www.redstepartworks.com, Tues.–Sat. 10 A.M.–5 P.M.) is worth taking a quick stroll off Main Street. The gallery feature handmade crafts from over 30 regional North Carolina artists, including handcrafted jewelry and wood-fired and salt-glazed stoneware. The gallery owners also do custom orders of jewelry and dinnerware.

Village Green Antique Mall (424 N. Main St., 828/692-9057, Mon.–Sat. 10 A.M.–5 P.M., Sun. 1–5 P.M.) is the largest antiques dealer downtown with 12,000 square feet of items for sale, including a used-book store upstairs. **Jane Asher's Antiques & Fine Traditions** (344 N. Main St., 828/698-0018, Mon.–Sat. 10 A.M.–5 P.M., Sun. 1–5 P.M.) carries a wide array of European furniture as well as estate jewelry, sterling silver, china, and crystal. **Nana's Antiques** (122 W. Allen St., 828/697-8979, Tues.–Sat. 10 A.M.–6 P.M., Sun. 1–5 P.M.) is located in a 1920s bungalow one block off Main Street on the corner of Allen and Church Streets and features the wares of several antiques dealers. Items available for sale include wicker furniture, vintage baby items, glassware, books, historic tools, linens, jewelry, and even architectural pieces.

Gifts

Speranza's Weather House (100 6th Ave. E., 877/210-2344, www.theweatherhouse.com, www.weatherequipment.com, Mon.–Fri. 9:30 A.M.–5 P.M., Sat. 10 A.M.–3 P.M.) is a pretty unique gift shop, carrying everything you need to track the forecast, decorative and functional, including thermometers, barometers, rain gauges, rain chains, weather vanes, atomic clocks, and wireless weather stations. **Mast General Store** (527 N. Main St., 828/696-1883, www.maststore.com, Mon.–Fri. 10 A.M.–5 P.M., Sat. 10 A.M.–4 P.M., Sun. 1–6 P.M.) is one of several locations of this popular western North Carolina general store to be found in the Blue Ridge region. Located in a restored 1905 emporium, the store carries outdoors clothing and gear, nostalgic mercantile items, and barrel candy.

Dancing Bear Toys (418 N. Main St., 828/693-4500, www.dancingbeartoys.com, Mon.–Sat. 10 A.M.–6 P.M., Sun. noon–5 P.M.) is an upscale toy store carrying Playmobil, Melissa and Doug, and Thomas the Tank toys as well as nostalgia-inspiring toys from whoopee cushions to erector sets. **Mountain Lore Books & More** (408 N. Main St., 828/693-5096, Mon.–Thurs. 10 A.M.–5 P.M., Fri.–Sat. 10 A.M.–6 P.M., Sun. noon–5 P.M.) is an independent bookseller carrying a wide array of new titles as well as audio books, magazines, greeting cards, stationery, and gifts. Dogs are welcome!

Rabbit & Company (124 4th Ave. E., 828/692-6100, www.rabbitandcompany.com, Mon.–Sat. 9 A.M.–6 P.M.) is a half block off Main Street and carries wine, craft beers, gift baskets, kitchen gadgets, cookbooks, and gourmet cooking items. **American Doll** (206 N. Main St., 828/692-6422, www.americandollshoppe.com, Mon.–Sat. 10 A.M.–5 P.M.) carries a wide array of goods for avid doll collectors young and old, including custom dolls, American Girl dolls, and Bitty Baby dolls and accessories.

ACCOMMODATIONS

Hendersonville supports an array of large chain hotels, including Best Western, Days

Inn, Comfort Inn, Quality Inn, and Ramada Limited, but if you really want to experience the historic and small-town feel of this place, consider choosing one of the town's many inns and bed-and-breakfasts.

Downtown Historic District

Claddagh Inn (755 N. Main St., 828/693-6737 or 866/770-2999, www.claddaghinn.com, $90–175) is the closest bed-and-breakfast to Hendersonville's downtown shops and restaurants, being one block off Main Street. Listed on the National Register of Historic Places, the inn has 16 guest rooms, all with private baths and some with fireplaces and claw-foot tubs. Guests enjoy a full breakfast as well as an evening social hour. Wi-Fi is available throughout the inn.

The **Waverly Inn** (783 N. Main St., 800/537-8195, www.waverlyinn.com, $189–325) has 15 individually decorated guest rooms, one of them pet friendly. Many of the rooms have claw-foot soaking tubs, and all have private bathrooms. Full breakfast is served each morning, and guests can enjoy an evening social hour at 5 P.M. Complimentary Wi-Fi is also available.

Elizabeth Leigh Inn (908 5th Ave., 828/698-9707, www.elizabethleighinn.com, $225) is a beautiful old Victorian home built in 1893. The inn has four light-filled bedrooms, all with private baths and fireplaces. Inn guests enjoy a guest pantry, full breakfast each morning, free Wi-Fi, and massage services with appointment.

Melange Inn and Gardens (1230 5th Ave. W., 800/303-5253, www.melangebb.com, rooms $139–169, Rose Suite $169–219) has four rooms and one suite, all with private baths and Wi-Fi access. Some rooms have fireplaces, whirlpool tubs, and private porches. All guests enjoy a full breakfast and access to the gardens found behind the inn.

Outside the Downtown Area

Echo Mountain Inn (2849 Laurel Park Hwy., 828/693-9626, www.echoinn.com,

$85–195) is about three miles from downtown Hendersonville, occupying a hilltop above the town with lovely mountain views to the east. Built in 1896, the stone inn is beginning to show some wear, particularly in the common areas, but if you're seeking some quiet away from town this is a good choice, particularly if you have kids. Most rooms are spacious with televisions and mini-fridges, and there is a swimming pool available for guests. The inn also offers complimentary Wi-Fi as well as use of the computer room for guests without laptops. Morning breakfast is a simple continental with cereal, muffins, toast, fruit, yogurt, coffee, tea, and juice.

Pinebrook Manor (2701 Kanuga Rd., 877/916-2667, www.pinebrookmanor.com, $149–269) is located three miles from downtown Hendersonville and has four sumptuously decorated suites, all with private baths and some with fireplaces. Located on a five-acre estate with private gardens, this is an ideal location for romantic getaways if you're seeking an out-of-town location. They serve a full gourmet breakfast.

FOOD
Casual Fine Dining

Hendersonville is one of those rare towns where it's almost difficult to track down a bad meal. The variety and flavor richness of the local culinary scene is pleasantly surprising, and you can start testing out the foodie waters at **Hannah Flanagan's** (300 N. Main St., 828/696-1665, www.theoriginalhannahflanagans.com, daily 11 A.M.–2 A.M.), an Irish pub that's a good place to stop if you're looking for a relatively quick sit-down meal. The menu includes Irish specialties like shepherd's pie as well as corned beef and cabbage. The pub also has an extensive beer selection including the expected Guinness Stout as well as oatmeal porter and hard apple cider.

Square One Bistro (111 S. Main St., 828/698-5598, www.square1bistro.com, Sun.–Mon. and Wed.–Thurs. 11 A.M.–9 P.M., Fri.–Sat. 11 A.M.–10 P.M., $6–20) is a local favorite in large part because the food here is so darn fresh…and good. The restaurant specializes in using local organic ingredients, natural meats, and sustainably fished seafood. Start off with the baked brie in a puff pastry with dribbles of blackberry jam and honey, and then indulge in one of the restaurant's high-flavor entrées. My favorite is the bistro steak—a peppercorn-crusted cut of meat served with buttermilk blue cheese—though the turkey escalope with Yukon gold mashed potatoes is a good one, too. The bistro offers "small plates" for the health- and calorie-conscious, and there's a full wine list and live music. The feel here is a warm one, with exposed masonry walls and displays of local artwork on the walls.

Never Blue (119 S. Main St., 828/693-4646, www.theneverblue.com, Tues.–Thurs. 11 A.M.–9 P.M., Fri.–Sat. 11 A.M.–10 P.M., $5–28) is a fun place to grab a bite. It has a garage door that rolls up, opening the dining room to the street. This is a good place to dine if you'd like to try several different dishes for the price of one since the tapas menu allows for small servings of several options like Spanish-style flatbreads with Serrano ham and Manchego cheese and Cuban sandwiches. Never Blue has a full bar with lots of fun specialty drinks including martinis, shooters, and sangrias. One of my favorite martinis is Envy, which features blueberry vodka and turns bright green when you stir it up. On Thursdays, all martinis are $7.

Perhaps the pizza at **West First Wood-Fired Pizza** (101B W. 1st Ave., 828/693-1080, Tues.–Sat. 11 A.M.–2 P.M. and 5–10 P.M., $7–13) is so good because it's made by genuine bakers. Whatever the reason, you've got to try it. All the pizzas here have a handmade organic wheat crust as their base, and all are topped with freshly grated romano cheese. That's just the beginning. Some of their tempting and unusual offerings include a goat cheese pizza, a shrimp pizza, and yes, believe it or not, a potato pizza flavored with rosemary, gorgonzola cheese, walnuts, and caramelized red onions. For dessert, sweep your palate clean with the tangy lemon zest cheesecake.

Quick Bites
Savannah's on Main (117 S. Main St., 828/696-9052, www.savannahsonmain.com, Wed.–Sat. 10 A.M.–5 P.M., $6–15) has light lunch and afternoon tea fare, including salads and fruit and cheese plates, as well as a wide offering of teas. The associated gift shop carries women's clothing and accessories as well as home decor and gift items.

INFORMATION AND SERVICES
Information
Henderson County Travel and Tourism (201 S. Main St., 800/828-4244, www.historichendersonville.org, Mon.–Fri. 9 A.M.–5 P.M., Sat.–Sun. 10 A.M.–5 P.M.) is located on the southern edge of the downtown historic area. You can also obtain more information specifically about Hendersonville's downtown area through **Downtown Hendersonville, Inc.** (401 N. Main St., 828/697-2022, www.downtownhendersonville.org), which is a nonprofit association of downtown merchants and local citizens and also the administrator of the town's Main Street Program.

Emergency Services
Pardee Hospital (800 N. Justice St., 828/696-1000, www.pardeehospital.org) offers 24-hour emergency services, as does **Park Ridge Hospital** (100 Hospital Dr., 828/684-8501, www.parkridgehospital.org).

Internet Access
Free Wi-Fi is available along Hendersonville's Main Street from 6th Avenue to Allen Avenue, so if you need to check your email you can set your laptop up anywhere.

GETTING THERE
Hendersonville is about 24 miles from Asheville and is most easily accessed from I-26 by taking Exit 49B and following U.S. 64 west 1.5 miles to the historic downtown. If you're coming in from the Chimney Rock and Lake Lure area, get on U.S. 64 west at Bat Cave and follow

it all the way to Hendersonville, pass under I-26, and then turn left onto Main Street, and you'll find yourself right in the middle of the historic district.

GETTING AROUND

Hendersonville likes its shoppers and tourists, so parking options in the downtown area are ample. There is free parking along Main Street, though take note of time limitations. There is also metered parking available for $0.25/hour with a three-hour maximum in four downtown lots one block east of Main Street along King Street. A fifth metered and leased parking lot is available one block west of Main Street on Church Street. You can also park for free at the Hendersonville visitors center at 201 South Main Street.

Flat Rock

Once a place of summer escape for the well-heeled of the South Carolina Low Country, Flat Rock was home to vast estates belonging to affluent plantation owners, Charlestonians, and even a few Europeans during the 19th century. Flat Rock is often called "the little Charleston of the mountains." The entire village of Flat Rock is currently listed on the National Register of Historic Places. It is best known for the Flat Rock Playhouse and as the country home of poet and author Carl Sandburg.

◖ CARL SANDBURG HOME NATIONAL HISTORIC SITE

Located right across the street from the Flat Rock Playhouse, the Carl Sandburg Home National Historic Site (81 Carl Sandburg La., 828/693-4178, www.nps.gov/carl, daily 9 A.M.–5 P.M., closed Christmas day, $5 for house tours) is worth a visit even if you're not a fan of one of America's favorite poets. The Sandburgs' 240-acre farm occupies an alternately open and wooded hillside overlooking a circular pond. Here Carl and Lilian Sandburg lived with their three daughters and two grandchildren after moving from Michigan in 1945. Sandburg wanted a quiet and secluded place to write, and his wife wanted the space to raise her award-winning goats. During the Sandburgs' residence, the homeplace was actually known as Connemara Farms, and Lilian raised over 200 dairy goats here and was recognized as a champion breeder of Toggenburg goats. Sandburg spent the last 22 years of his life in Flat Rock.

The walk to the Sandburg home is just under half a mile up a hill, and the admission fee is for the house tour—you can actually stroll the trails on the farm for free. Sandburg's home, which was originally built in 1838, has a collection of the author's books, notes, and papers numbering more than 10,000. Tours of the home are offered daily. This is not your typical historic house tour, either. The Sandburg home looks much as the Sandburgs left it, with books and papers scattered about and unpretentious furnishings.

A short walk from the house is the barn complex where you can see Sandburg's 1962 Willys Jeep, a gift he received for writing the movie script for *The Greatest Story Ever Told*. You're welcome to pet the resident goats as well.

The site has a small visitors center and gift shop in the basement of the house as well as public restrooms near the pond. You can, of course, purchase books of Sandburg's poetry, his famous biography of Abraham Lincoln, and a variety of books on the poet himself.

Each summer the Flat Rock Playhouse Vagabond Players present weekly performances at the amphitheater based on the life and works of Carl Sandburg. On Memorial Day each year, the home hosts the Sandburg Folk Music Festival.

© DEBORAH HUSO

Carl Sandburg Home National Historic Site in Flat Rock

MOUNT PISGAH

ENTERTAINMENT AND EVENTS

◖ Flat Rock Playhouse

Founded in 1952, the Flat Rock Playhouse (2661 Greenville Hwy., 828/693-0731, www.flatrockplayhouse.org) is, without doubt, the most popular attraction in the area. Make ticket reservations early, as shows sell out fast. Expect to attend with a full house. The small theater serves nearly 100,000 patrons each year. The show season typically runs April through December, and ticket prices vary. The casts of the playhouse's numerous dramas come from all over the country to produce musicals as well as comedy and drama, including well-known favorites like *Seven Brides for Seven Brothers* and *The Man of La Mancha* as well as newer offerings like *The Woman in Black.*

On first arriving for a show you may be alarmed by the parking arrangements, which jam cars in one behind the other with no apparent way out. But the parking here has been staged as well as the shows, and you'll find yourself amazed at how quickly you can get out of the parking lot. There is no wait at all.

ACCOMMODATIONS

In Town

Flat Rock Inn (2810 Greenville Hwy., 800/266-3996, www.flatrockbb.com, call for rates) is located in an 1888 Victorian home within walking distance of shops and restaurants in Flat Rock and has four guest rooms available, all with private baths, and two with private porches. Breakfast is served each morning with Kona coffee (one of the innkeepers is a native of Hawaii).

Outside Town

The Lake House Lodge & Spa (447 Lily Pad La., 828/693-5070, www.highlandlake.com, $149–229) is a beautiful 60-acre lakefront resort nestled in quiet woods with lodge rooms, cottages, and vacation homes available for rent. The lodge has an on-site spa offering massage, facials, wraps, and waxing.

The **Highland Lake Inn** (86 Lily Pad La., 800/635-7166, www.hlinn.com, rooms $99–239, suites $179–299, cottages $129–449) is located a few minutes outside Flat Rock on 26 private acres next to a 40-acre scenic lake. There are a variety of accommodations available here, including lodge rooms, suites, cabins, and vacation rental homes. A southern country breakfast buffet is available each morning to all guests except those in rental homes. The inn offers many complimentary amenities, including a swimming pool, tennis courts, bicycles, and boats. Season's Restaurant is on-site and has live piano music on Friday and Saturday evening as well as during Sunday brunch.

FOOD
Casual Fine Dining
Season's Restaurant (86 Lily Pad La., 828/696-9094, www.hlinn.com/seasons, Mon.–Sat. 7:30–10 A.M., 11:30 A.M.–2 P.M., and 5–9 P.M., Sun. 7:30–9:30 A.M., 10:30 A.M.–2 P.M., and 5–8 P.M., $19–28) is part of the Highland Lake Inn and is best known for its prime rib, though the restaurant also has an extensive seafood menu, including calamari, halibut, and salmon. The Sunday brunch and dinner buffets are especially popular among the locals and cost $24 per person. Buffet selections include cheese-studded soft scrambled eggs and organic cheese grits. Be sure to try the New York–style cheesecake drizzled in maple syrup for dessert. During the winter Season's shuts down the Sunday dinner buffet, and winter hours vary.

Quick Bites
Flat Rock Village Bakery (2710 Greenville Hwy., 828/693-1313, Mon.–Sat. 7 A.M.–5 P.M., $5–11) is run by the same talented folks who operate West First Wood-Fired Pizza in neighboring Hendersonville. The signature feature of this bakery-café is its wood-fired organic breads, which you'll find in every sandwich (or pizza) you order. The havarti and prosciutto panini served on either sourdough or focaccia will make you melt. The kids' menu is first-rate, too—grilled cheese or peanut butter and jelly on organic nine-grain bread.

The Back Room (2702C Greenville Hwy., 828/697-6828, www.flatrockwineshoppe. com, Tues.–Sat. 11 A.M.–midnight, $6–24) is located next door to the Flat Rock Wine Shoppe and serves up a variety of soups and sandwiches as well as lasagna and shrimp kabobs after 5 P.M. Diners here can build their own pasta bowls, selecting pasta, sauces, meats, cheeses, and veggies, and after 9 P.M. the restaurant has an array of munchies available, including warm pimento cheese dip with chips and zesty pulled-pork nachos. The Back Room has live music nightly, including open mic on Wednesdays. Check the website for upcoming performers.

INFORMATION AND SERVICES
Henderson County Travel and Tourism (201 S. Main St., 800/828-4244, www.historichendersonville.org, Mon.–Fri. 9 A.M.–5 P.M., Sat.–Sun. 10 A.M.–5 P.M.) provides visitor information services for both Hendersonville and Flat Rock. You can also obtain additional information on the village of Flat Rock online through the Flat Rock Merchants Association (www.flatrockonline.com).

MOUNT PISGAH

Brevard

Known for the Brevard Music Center, which trains young musicians and also hosts a first-rate summer music festival, Brevard is also coming into its own as a visual arts destination. The nearby Shining Rock Wilderness and Pisgah National Forest are an outdoor recreation lover's paradise with hikes to dozens of waterfalls, challenging backcountry hikes, rock climbing, kayaking, and horseback riding. Transylvania County, where Brevard is located, is known as the Land of Waterfalls, in fact, with over 250 falls in the area.

Brevard is also known for its unusual white squirrel population. And no, these are not albino squirrels, but an unusual color variant of the eastern gray squirrel. About 25 percent of Brevard's squirrel population is white, and if you'd like to get a glimpse of the critters, the best place to do so is on the campus of Brevard College.

ENTERTAINMENT AND EVENTS
◖ Brevard Music Center
The Brevard Music Center (349 Andante La., 888/384-8682, www.brevardmusic.org) is a nationally and internationally known center for study, drawing as many as 2,000 applicants a year who compete for 400 study slots.

At Brevard, students from all over the country and the world live, learn, and socialize with their faculty and with the music center's guest artists, who often stay in residence for several days. Concerts here give you the opportunity to experience the talent of the nation's (and often the world's) best music students often accompanied by top-flight guest artists in genres from opera to country. Among the artists you may encounter at Brevard are Yo Yo Ma, André Watts, Joshua Bell, and Frederica Von Stade. The music center is best known for the Brevard Music Festival concerts, which run June through early August and range in price from free to $50.

SHOPPING
Art Galleries
While Brevard may be best known as a music venue, the town also has an extensive collection of art galleries that continues to grow—as of late 2009 there are just under a dozen art galleries in this town of only 6,500 people. Brevard hosts a Gallery Walk every fourth Friday of the month, April through December, where all the art galleries are open from 5 to 9 P.M. for special evening viewings. For more information on local galleries, visit www.artsofbrevard.org. As you wander around downtown, be sure to note the 16 metal animal sculptures created by North Carolina metal artists and sculptors. My favorite is the *White Squirrels* sculpture at City Hall, which features Brevard's unusual resident mascot.

The **Bluewood Gallery** (36 W. Jordan St., 828/883-4142, www.bluewoodgallery.com, Tues.–Sat. 9:30 A.M.–5:30 P.M.) features fine-art photography. Among the local artists they feature are Sean Raphael Parrish, who creates unusual hand-colored black-and-white photographs of people and buildings, and Jeff Miller, a digital photographer who makes beautiful scenes of the surrounding mountains.

The **Red Wolf Gallery** (8 E. Main St., 828/862-8620, www.redwolfgallerync.com, Mon.–Sat. 10 A.M.–5 P.M., Sun. 1–5 P.M.) has an unusual collection of modern art and sculpture, including works in metal and clay from all over the world.

If you don't have a lot of time, at least be sure to visit **Number 7 Fine Arts and Crafts Cooperative** (12 E. Main St., 828/883-2294, www.number7arts.com, Mon.–Sat. 10 A.M.–5 P.M.), which features 25 local artisans and carries everything from painted glassware to mixed-media presentations. One of the Cooperative's artists, Carol Weeks, continues to use her SLR camera, a Pentax 35mm, to capture the vivid colors of leaves, rocks, and water in her nature photography. Like so many of the artists in these mountain towns, she takes her inspiration from the stunning natural canvas of the surrounding Appalachian landscape.

The **Transylvania Community Arts Council** (349 S. Caldwell St., 828/884-2787, www.artsofbrevard.org, Mon.–Fri. 10 A.M.–4 P.M.) is located four blocks off Main Street. It has both permanent and changing exhibits featuring the work of local artists in all mediums and is the home of the local arts council.

Gifts

The Proper Pot (36 W. Main St., 828/877-5000, www.theproperpot.com, Mon.–Sat. 9:30 A.M.–5:30 P.M.) is a large kitchen and specialty food and gift store in the center of Main Street. They carry wines, both regional and international, plus a variety of artisan cheeses, chocolates, sauces, and kitchen implements.

Across the street is **Continental Divide** (35 W. Main St., 828/884-5484, Mon.–Sat. 10 A.M.–6 P.M., Sun. noon–5 P.M.), a unique store carrying a small and pricey selection of nautical gift items as well as beautifully made cherry furniture and a collection of decorative globes.

SummerBrooke Gardens Tea and Garden Gift Shoppe (15 W. Main St., #1, 828/884-2625, www.summerbrookegardens.com, Mon.–Sat. 10 A.M.–5 P.M.) carries fine china tea-service items, loose-leaf teas, silk flowers, honey, and a variety of gift items. The shop usually has at least one sample tea available for tasting.

If you have kids in tow, check out the upscale toy store at the corner of Main and Broad. **O. P. Taylor** (2 S. Broad St., 828/883-2309, www.optaylors.com, Mon.–Sat. 10 A.M.–6 P.M., Sun. 1–5 P.M.) has a full array of Playmobil items and a shop devoted to toy train collecting. You can also pick up a plush white squirrel as a souvenir of Brevard.

ACCOMMODATIONS
Hotels

There are a couple of chain hotels in Brevard, including the **Hampton Inn** (275 Forest Gate Dr., 828/883-4800, www.hamptoninnbrevard.com, $95–149) and the **Holiday Inn Express** (2228 Asheville Hwy., 828/862-8900, $89–145).

Inns and Bed-and-Breakfasts

The **Red House Inn** (266 W. Probart St., 828/884-9349, www.brevardbedandbreakfast.com, $99–179) is within walking distance of downtown restaurants and shopping. The home, built in 1851, has an interesting history, having served as a general store, courthouse, railroad station, and school over the course of its career. A relatively new lodging addition to Brevard, the Red House Inn has five guest rooms, all decorated simply but colorfully, and all with private baths. The bathrooms feature ceramic tile showers. Guests enjoy a full English breakfast with locally produced bacon and sausage and eggs and coffee roasted right in Brevard. Complimentary Wi-Fi is available to all guests.

The **Inn at Brevard** (315 E. Main St., 828/884-2105, www.theinnatbrevard.com, $150–225) has 14 guest rooms and is a good option for families with children who want a bed-and-breakfast experience, as the inn has several rooms with two beds. They also offer a full breakfast.

Camping

Our 100 Acre Woods Campground (9855 East Fork Rd., 828/398-0968, www.our100acrewoods.com, open year-round, $26.75) is a primitive tent-only campground with five sites. Each site has three to five acres, offering you the ultimate in camping seclusion. Free Wi-Fi is available, as are showers. The campground has some pretty unique amenities, including the opportunity for a gourmet chef to come to your camp site and cook your dinner for you.

Ash Grove Resort Cabins & Camping (749 East Fork Rd., 828/885-7216, www.ashgrove.com, open year-round, tent and RV sites $24–40, cabins $110–160) has 19 RV and tent sites with water and electric hookups available. Campground amenities include a hot tub, bonfire pit, horseshoes, badminton, and a small on-site waterfall. There's a dump station on the property.

Davidson River Campground (1 Davidson River Cir., 828/862-5960, www.recreation. gov, open year-round, single sites $20, double sites $40, $5 extra for electrical hookup) is located just outside Brevard on Route 276 in the Shining Rock Wilderness Area. This Pisgah National Forest campground has 160 sites, some with river access, and hot showers. There are no hookups, but the campground does have a dump station. It is the most convenient campground to the hiking and fishing opportunities in the Shining Rock Wilderness.

Cascade Lake Campground (1679 Campground Rd., 828/877-6625, www.cascadelakerecreationarea.com, Apr.–Oct., $15–45) has 160 campsites located and is located right next door to the Dupont State Forest between Brevard and Hendersonville. The campground has its own private beach, and there are two boat ramps available as well as canoes and paddle boats for rent. RV sites with electric, water, and sewer hookups are available, and the campground has a country store and laundry.

FOOD
Casual Fine Dining
Hobnob (192 W. Main St., 828/966-4662, www.hobnobrestaurant.com, Mon.–Sat. 11:30 A.M.–2:30 P.M. and 5–9 P.M., Sun. 11 A.M.–2 P.M., $7–27) is probably my top pick for Brevard, just because of the fun diversity of the menu—where else can you get seafood lasagna with shrimp and scallops? My personal favorite is the chicken saltimbocca topped with sliced prosciutto, cheese, and sage and baked in a marsala wine sauce to give it a little kick.

I like **The Quarry** (14 S. Gaston St., 828/877-2244, www.thequarryrestaurant. com, June–Aug. Mon.–Tues. 5–9 P.M., Wed.–Thurs. 11 A.M.–2 P.M. and 5–9 P.M., Fri. 11 A.M.–2 P.M. and 5–10 P.M., Sat. 5–10 P.M., Sun. 11 A.M.–2 P.M. and 5–9 P.M., Sept.–May Mon.–Thurs. 5–9 P.M., Fri.–Sat. 5–10 P.M., $5–22) for its warm atmosphere with stacked rock walls in the dining room and intimately gathered tables. They offer piano music daily at 6 P.M. from June through August and at 6 P.M. Thursday–Saturday from September through May. The piano music definitely makes you feel like falling in love again over dinner if you've brought that special someone along. The Quarry has a strong seafood touch to their menu with entrées like stuffed grouper, trout picatta, and three seed–encrusted ahi tuna, though they do offer prime rib, steak, and chicken entrées as well. Reservations are recommended but not required.

Jordan Street Café (30 W. Jordan St., 828/883-2558, Sun.–Thurs. 5–9 P.M., Fri.–Sat. 5–10 P.M., $8–30) is a great little bistro with outdoor patio dining and live music on select evenings. The best picks here are the bacon-wrapped tenderloin for dinner, and the buffalo chicken wrap and the Jordan burger for lunch. They also feature a pizza of the day and quesadilla of the day and homemade desserts.

Quick Bites
Rocky's Soda Shop (50 S. Broad St., 828/877-5375, June–Aug. daily 10 A.M.–9 P.M., Sept.–May daily 10 A.M.–5:30 P.M., $4–8) is one of my favorite stops in Brevard. With its 1950s-style lunch counter and soda fountain, the place offers an easy step back into time. In addition to all the ice cream–related concoctions you can imagine, from malts to banana splits, Rocky's also has burgers, sandwiches, soups, and salads.

Bracken Mountain Bakery (42 S. Broad St., 828/883-4034, Nov.–Apr. Tues.–Fri. 7:30 A.M.–5 P.M., Sat. 8 A.M.–5 P.M., May–Oct. Mon.–Fri. 7:30 A.M.–5 P.M., Sat. 8 A.M.–5 P.M., $1–4) is a good place to pick up breakfast, an afternoon snack, or some crusty bread for a picnic lunch. In addition to their homemade loaves of everything from sourdough to honey cracked wheat, they carry a wide array of cookies, scones, muffins, and pies.

Dolly's Dairy Bar (124 Pisgah Hwy., 828/862-6610, www.dollysdairybar.com, daily 11 A.M.–9 P.M., $2–6) is the perfect place to stop after an afternoon spent scaling the slippery surface of Sliding Rock. Serving up soft-serve and hand-dipped ice cream, the dairy bar is located at the intersection of Routes 276 and 280 just south of the Shining Rock Wilderness Area.

INFORMATION AND SERVICES
Information
Transylvania County Visitors Center (175 E. Main St., 800/648-4523, www.visitwaterfalls.com, Mon.–Fri. 9 A.M.–5 P.M., Sat. 10 A.M.–4 P.M.) offers brochures and maps on the area. If you would like to get information on the national forest, stop by the **Pisgah Ranger Station** (1001 Pisgah Hwy., 828/877-3265, www.ncnatural.com/NCUSFS/Pisgah/pisgdst.html, Mon.–Fri. 8 A.M.–5 P.M.). It has exhibits on the area's waterfalls, flora, fauna, and history as well as a small gift shop, information desk, and restrooms. Across the parking lot from the ranger station visitors center is the Andy Cove Nature Trail, a 0.7-mile self-guided nature walk through the woods.

Emergency Services
Transylvania Regional Hospital (260 Hospital Dr., 828/884-9111, www.trhospital.org) is a 24-hour facility.

Mount Pisgah Area

The Mount Pisgah Area of the Parkway is a land of towering mountains, many of which are bisected by Parkway tunnels. There are nine alone between Asheville and Mount Pisgah, which you'll recognize as you approach from the north by the radio tower on the summit as well as by its chopped-off appearance.

Much of this region east of the Blue Ridge belonged to George Vanderbilt's estate, and was known as Pisgah Forest. Louis Carr, who purchased timber rights to almost 70,000 acres of Pisgah Forest from Vanderbilt in 1912, built railroads in the mountains to bring out the timber, and many of today's roads in the national forest exist on those former railroad beds.

In 1914, the U.S. Forest Service bought over 78,000 acres of the Vanderbilt estate to create Pisgah National Forest, the first-ever national forest created from purchased land. Other logging operations besides Carr's operated in these mountains well into the 1920s, though the landscape today has largely recovered and bears very little trace of the industrial logging that occurred here nearly a century ago. Today the Pisgah National Forest consists of 512,670 acres.

MOUNT PISGAH
Hiking
THE PISGAH SUMMIT TRAIL
- Distance: 3.2 miles round-trip
- Duration: 3 hours
- Elevation gain: 712 feet
- Difficulty: Strenuous
- Trailhead: Mount Pisgah Summit Trail parking area, Milepost 407.7

If you're in good physical shape, the Summit Trail to the top of Mount Pisgah (5,721 ft.) is well worth a hike. The beginning portion of the trail is mostly level and rife with wildflowers, including lilies, trillium, and goldenrod. After about half a mile, you'll come to a lovely cascading spring. This will also be the end of pleasant relatively level walking.

From here the trail begins to ascend, and the trail grows steeper, requiring some scrambling over rocks and tree roots. You'll pass by a couple of benches through this area, and you may want to take advantage of the opportunity to rest.

The last third of the trail is quite strenuous

with hundreds of rock steps leading up to the 360-degree view at the top. If you're not in good shape, this last section can be a killer. The view is worth the climb, however. You'll arrive on a wooden viewing platform with the radio tower overhead; on a clear day the mountains form an endless blue sea as far as the horizon, and the blunt summit of Cold Mountain is also visible.

Accommodations and Food

Though you'd never suspect it from the relatively rustic facade, the **(Pisgah Inn Restaurant** (Milepost 408.6, 828/235-8228, www.pisgahinn.com, daily 7:30–10:30 A.M., 11:30 A.M.–4 P.M., and 5–9 P.M., $6–29) offers meals that easily qualify as first class, at least on most days. The dining room overlooks the mountains to the east, though it's not unusual for this high-elevation location to be shrouded in thick white fog, which creates its own otherworldly atmosphere. At supper here you'll be served by waiters in crisp white shirts and black bow ties whose focus on service is more than welcome, particularly after a long day of hiking (and yes, casual hiking attire and boots are perfectly acceptable here, even at dinner time). Service at breakfast and lunch tends to be a bit more hit or miss, and some of the waitstaff can be downright inattentive if the restaurant is busy, which it often is. The restaurant's signature dish is Pisgah Pasta in a white wine sauce. Other especially good entrée offerings include tournedos of beef tenderloin and ricotta cavatelle. One of my lunchtime favorites is the Black and Blue Salad, which has incredibly tender beef tips laid over a bed of greens with blue cheese crumbles, fried onion straws, and tomatoes. Breakfast is equally decadent. My picks are the candied pecan cakes and the omelet Florentine. They also serve decadent desserts like French silk pie drizzled in chocolate sauce and served with strawberries, ice cream, and sliced almonds—plenty of replenishing fare for the avid outdoors types who frequent the place.

The **Pisgah Inn** (Milepost 408.6, 828/235-8228, www.pisgahinn.com, $120–235) is the only lodging offering along this stretch of the Parkway unless you're willing to take a long side trip to Brevard, Waynesville, or Asheville for overnight accommodations. Disappointingly ordinary when compared to the restaurant, the inn is showing its age, even in its supposedly updated rooms. Furnishings and amenities are what you'd expect of a mid-range hotel—nothing fancy here—but the major highlight is that every room comes with a balcony overlooking the undulating ridgelines of the Pisgah National Forest.

The **Mt. Pisgah Campground** (Milepost 408.8, 828/648-2644, $16) is a large campground with over 50 tent sites and 62 RV sites as well as a dump station. Adjacent to the campground, the **Mt. Pisgah Country Store** (Milepost 408.6, 828/235-8228, www.pisgahinn.com, Apr.–Oct. daily 8 A.M.–8 P.M.) not only carries basic camping and picnicking supplies but also has a launderette available. If you're interested in picnicking, the **Mt. Pisgah Picnic Area** (Milepost 407.8) is located just south of the Summit parking area on the right. Tables are accessible via a short walk into the woods from the parking lot.

LOOKING GLASS ROCK

Visible from various overlooks along the Parkway south of Mount Pisgah, Looking Glass Rock is readily recognizable by its smooth, bald white face. One of the best viewpoints is from the Cradle of Forestry Overlook at Milepost 411.

COLD MOUNTAIN

Since the publication of Charles Frazier's best-selling novel *Cold Mountain* and the subsequent movie, this isolated peak (elevation 6,030 ft.) in the Pisgah National Forest has gained some status as a tourist attraction, though few people actually hike to the summit, as it's a steep 10 miles one-way. Most travelers opt for a picture instead, and the best vantage is from the Cold Mountain Overlook, at Milepost 411.9 just south of the Pisgah Inn.

◖ SHINING ROCK WILDERNESS

Traversing the mountain roads between the art towns of Brevard and Waynesville and accessible off the Blue Ridge Parkway south of Mount Pisgah at Milepost 411.9, Highway 276 provides road access into the Shining Rock Wilderness, part of the much larger Pisgah National Forest and originally owned by George Vanderbilt.

Highway 276 is definitely worth a side trip off the Parkway. It is part of the Forest Heritage Scenic Byway, a 79-mile loop that crosses the Parkway twice and takes drivers on a scenic tour of a large section of the Pisgah National Forest. The route between Brevard and the Parkway follows a mountain stream whose banks are laden with rhododendron. Hemlocks, chestnut oaks, and mountain laurel line the roadway, which has occasional overlooks and picnic tables for pausing to enjoy the deep green woods.

Cradle of Forestry in America Forest Discovery Center

The first stop off the Blue Ridge Parkway on Highway 276 is the Cradle of Forestry in America Forest Discovery Center (1001 Pisgah Hwy., 828/877-3130, www.cradleof-forestry.org, Apr.–Nov. daily 9 A.M.–5 P.M., $5, children 15 and under free). While the center has a very brief and informative exhibit on the history of the Pisgah National Forest and the evolution of forest management in America, this is probably a site you can skip unless you have kids. Most of the exhibits are geared toward youngsters: Kids will enjoy the underground tunnel where they can learn about forest creatures that burrow under the earth, and they can also play an interactive forest management game. There is also a short movie on the birth of forestry in America, a gift shop, café, and restrooms. The whole facility seems to suffer from an excess of staff—after a point it can verge on the annoying, as they can be found around every corner offering assistance. The center

© DEBORAH HUSO

Sliding Rock in the Shining Rock Wilderness

MOUNT PISGAH

also hosts special events from April through October, including musical performances and art and photography exhibitions. Most events require an additional admission fee.

Sliding Rock

Sliding Rock is a beloved natural waterslide that plunges children and brave adults into 55-degree water in summertime. The smooth rock face, worn slick by centuries of water wear, provides a glass-like surface for sliding at full speed into a six-foot-deep pool below. Located four miles south of the Cradle of Forestry, Sliding Rock receives 1,000 to 2,000 visitors a day at the height of summer. The entry fee to the area is $1 per person.

Looking Glass Falls

Among the lovely natural features accessible just off Highway 276 are Looking Glass Falls, a 60-foot sheet of water cascading over a granite face with a deep, chilly swimming hole at its base. George Vanderbilt once owned this waterfall as part of his Pisgah Forest. Even when he logged much of the acreage, he directed that

© DEBORAH HUSO

Looking Glass Falls in the Shining Rock Wilderness

25 acres around Looking Glass Falls should remain untouched.

Pisgah Center for Wildlife Education

The Pisgah Center for Wildlife Education (1401 Fish Hatchery Rd., Pisgah Forest, 828/877-4423, www.ncwildlife.org, Mon.–Sat. 8 A.M.–4:45 P.M., free) offers a great opportunity to explore a mountain trout hatchery that supplies trout to 15 counties in the western part of the state. Visitors are welcome to feed the trout, which include brook, rainbow, and brown. The Pisgah Center also has a backyard wildlife garden and an auditorium that shows a film several times daily on the natural history of the North Carolina mountains and the work of the North Carolina Wildlife Resources Commission to preserve the landscape. There is also a gift shop on-site where visitors can purchase books, wildlife-related gifts and T-shirts, and toys.

The center offers an incredible array of programs and workshops for the public, including introductory fly-fishing workshops, programs on how to use GPS, guided nature hikes, guided fishing trips, and programs for kids. Program offerings, times, and prices vary, so call for details.

Horseback Riding

There are 100 miles of horse trails in the Pisgah National Forest, many of which provide you access to waterfalls. If you don't have your own mount along, contact **Pisgah Forest Stables** (476 Pisgah Dr., Brevard, 828/883-8258, www.pisgahstables.com, Mon.–Sat. 10 A.M.–4 P.M., 1-hour backwoods ride $35, 2-hour mountaintop ride $70, 3-hour mountaintop ride $95, waterfall ride $100) in Brevard. They offer one-, two-, and three-hour rides as well as a stunning three-hour waterfall trip to Twin Falls.

Rock Climbing

There are a lot of opportunities for rock climbing in the Shining Rock Wilderness Area of the Pisgah National Forest. The most popular climb is up the bald face of Looking Glass Rock, which has a difficulty rating of 5.5 to 5.11 for free climbs and ratings of A0 to A5 for aided climbs, depending on which of the 138 climbing routes you take. Climbs are not permitted on Looking Glass Rock between January 15 and August 15 due to nesting peregrine falcons in the area.

If you want to climb in the Shining Rock Wilderness Area during those times, consider climbing Cedar Rock, which has about the same rating for difficulty as Looking Glass with 36 routes available. For more information on rock climbing in the Shining Rock Wilderness Area, contact the Pisgah Ranger District at 828/877-3265—though you may have trouble finding an expert on the subject of climbing, as the Forest Service employs a fair number of volunteers.

If you want to hire a climbing guide or have never tried rock climbing and would like some instruction, **Fox Mountain Guides and Climbing School** (3228 Asheville Hwy., 888/284-8433, www.foxmountainguides.com, open year-round) in Pisgah Forest, a crossroads just north of Brevard at the entrance to the Pisgah National Forest, offers full- and half-day climbing and rappelling trips throughout the Brevard area, including trips up Looking Glass and Cedar Rocks.

The **Appalachian Mountain Institute** (21 Cherry Ridge Rd., 828/553-6323, www.appalachianmountaininstitute.com, daily 8 A.M.–5 P.M., closed Christmas and Thanksgiving), also in Pisgah Forest, offers guided rock climbing as well for beginners through advanced, as does **Pura Vida Adventures** (152 Hendersonville Hwy., Pisgah Forest, 772/579-0005, www.pvadventures. com, open year-round, daily morning trips 8 A.M., afternoon trips 2 P.M.).

Boating and Fishing

The Davidson and French Broad Rivers, both of which bisect Transylvania County, are popular with kayakers and canoers. The Upper Davidson and North and West Forks of the French Broad are ideal for adventurous kayakers, offering rapids up to Class IV, while the wide and slower-moving waters of the French Broad offer ideal conditions for a canoe trip. **Pura Vida Adventures** (152 Hendersonville Hwy., Pisgah Forest, 772/579-0005, www. pvadventures.com) offers guided white-water and float trips on kayaks. They also offer kayak rentals.

The Davidson River has also been ranked as one of the top 100 trout streams in the United States and is best known for its large brown trout. Area streams are loaded with rainbow, brown, and brook trout as well as smallmouth bass. One good resource for those who prefer to go it alone and skip the guide service is the **Western North Carolina Fly Fishing Trail** (800/962-1911, www.flyfishingtrail. com), covering 15 great fly-fishing spots in Jackson County, which is bordered by the Blue Ridge Parkway on the northeast and has acres and acres of public lands in both the Pisgah and Nantahala National Forests between the state line with South Carolina and the area around Sylva and Dillsboro. You can order a

complimentary detailed map of the trail or check the map out online.

However, if you're not familiar with the area and want to be privy to some lesser-known fishing locations, it's a good idea to take advantage of a local guide service, as some of the best fishing spots are not in easily accessible places. Several local outfitters offer fishing equipment and guide service, including **Davidson Outfitters** (95 Pisgah Hwy., Pisgah Forest, 888/861-0111, www.davidsonflyfishing.com, daily 8 A.M.–6 P.M.), which has a complete fly shop and freshwater fishing equipment, and offers float and wade guided fishing trips.

If you'd like the fun of tubing the Davidson River, check out the options at **Davidson River Rafting** (Pisgah Hwy., 828/243-0522, May–Sept. daily 10 A.M.–7 P.M.), which is located next to Dolly's Dairy Bar at the Pisgah National Forest entrance on Route 276.

GRAVEYARD FIELDS TO WATERROCK KNOB
Graveyard Fields
THE GRAVEYARD LOOP TRAIL

- Distance: 1.8 miles round-trip

- Duration: 45 minutes

- Elevation gain: 300 feet

- Difficulty: Moderate

- Trailhead: Graveyard Fields Overlook parking area, Milepost 418.8

The Graveyard Loop Trail offers an easy hike to Yellowstone Falls through a tunnel of rhododendron and then a side trail through low-growing briars and wildflowers, remnants of a 1925 fire, that make the landscape here reminiscent of the rugged West. Graveyard Fields gained its name, however, from the stumps of spruce and fir trees that were uprooted along these slopes by a windstorm 500 to 1,000 years ago, making it look like a barren landscape of black headstones. This is a very popular trail in the summer, so much so that you may find it difficult to find parking at the trailhead.

The first portion of the trail is paved and

descends quickly through a tunnel of rhododendron. Note how the forest floor on either side of the trail is carpeted in the waxy green leaves of galax. The paved trail ends at a boardwalk that passes through more rhododendron as well as mountain laurel. Then it opens onto a golden stream loaded with large boulders. In summer, you'll often see hikers taking a dip here.

From the boardwalk, the trail becomes more eroded from the heavy traffic it receives and passes over a log bridge that traverses a tiny amber-colored stream. In August, watch for ripe blueberries along the trail—many locals come here with pails in hand purely for the sake of picking berries to take home.

A long series of steps will lead you to the bottom of the Lower Falls, which is not unlike the Yellowstone Falls of Wyoming's famous national park in its coloration. Beneath the cascading water, the rock is golden-toned. On hot days, you may see youngsters climbing up the falls to slide down the lower half of the slick rock face, but don't try this yourself. This is not a monitored recreation area like nearby Sliding Rock, and the falls are a dangerous place to go climbing. There is, however, a nice swimming hole at the base of the falls.

You will leave the Lower Falls the same way you came in, but if you'd like to continue your hike, veer right where the trail forks to enter the area known as Graveyard Fields. The landscape quickly opens to low shrub growth, and much of the area will be pelted with ripe blueberries toward the end of summer. For a short space the trail parallels a split-rail fence, providing an overview of the young landscape rich in wildflowers and low-growing shrubs and bisected by a golden brown stream. This area has some unusual high-elevation bogs, and you'll see many hikers in summer venturing out into the shrub growth to pick wild blueberries, blackberries, and gooseberries.

This trail will loop around Graveyard Fields and back to the parking area, though you can also elect to hike an additional 0.8 mile one-way to the Upper Falls by taking a trail off to the right after you've traveled almost a mile from the Lower Falls. This will increase the length of your hike by at least an hour and a half, as the trek to the Upper Falls is steep.

Black Balsam Trailhead Spur

Just south of Graveyard Fields, take a little side trip to the Black Balsam Trailhead parking area along a spur road, Forest Road 816, at Milepost 420.2. This road provides some stunning views of the stubby slopes of Graveyard Fields as well as Mount Pisgah and Looking Glass Rock. The road is paved but not well-maintained, so expect to dodge some crater-like potholes. It's worth the short trip, however, just for the photo opportunities from the pull-offs along the way as you look west into the long dark-green wilderness of the Pisgah National Forest.

Devils Courthouse Overlook

At Milepost 422.4, the Devils Courthouse Overlook provides a view of the spiny backbone of the ridge known as Devils Courthouse. You can also take a 20-minute walk from here to the top of the spiny ridge for 360-degree views into the Pisgah and Nantahala National Forests.

◖ Highest Point on the Blue Ridge Parkway

The landscape south of Graveyard Fields is among the highest and most lonesome along the Parkway, as it winds through national forest land, providing uninterrupted views of wilderness peaks in all directions. At Milepost 431 is the highest point on the Blue Ridge Parkway at Richland Balsam. Here the Parkway climbs to 6,047 feet. An overlook at the highest point offers long blue vistas to the south and west. This area of the Parkway, because of its high elevation, is dominated by a spruce-fir forest so dense it makes the mountainsides appear almost black with the deep shades of the conifers. Be sure to note, if you're here in late spring or summer, the amazing profusion of wildflowers at this overlook.

Waterrock Knob

The **Waterrock Knob Visitor Center** (Milepost 451.2, 828/775-0975, May–Sept.

© FRENCH C. GRIMES

highest point on the Blue Ridge Parkway

daily 10 A.M.–5 P.M.) is located at an elevation of 5,810 feet. The visitors center is small and features a small gift shop as well as a guide to the mountain peaks within view. The parking area here is a popular place from which to watch the sunset over the Smokies. There are restrooms with pit toilets but no running water.

THE WATERROCK KNOB TRAIL

- Distance: 1.2 mile round-trip

- Duration: 1 hour

- Elevation gain: 600 feet

- Difficulty: Strenuous

- Trailhead: Waterrock Knob Visitor Center parking area, Milepost 451.2

The Waterrock Knob Trail offers what is arguably one of the most worthwhile hikes along the Parkway. Though the trail is only a half mile in length one-way, the hike is strenuous, a continuous uphill climb.

Most visitors to Waterrock Knob take the paved trail to the visitor platform—a steep trek of about a quarter mile—take in the view, and then return to the parking area. If you're in

pretty good shape, however, keep going beyond where the paved trail becomes a dirt and rock path up the mountain. The views from the summit of Waterrock Knob (6,292 ft.) are well worth the steep hike. With each step, new views open and compel the hiker upward through huckleberry brambles and scenic rock outcroppings. If you make the hike in late summer, you'll also likely be rewarded with the opportunity to pick ripe blackberries and blueberries.

As you climb, you'll experience a little bit of a rock scramble in places and a few opportunities to enjoy views of the Smokies to the north and west and Maggie Valley to the east. You'll know you've reached the summit when you come to a clearing with a bench to your left. Walk past the bench to another rock outcropping and enjoy views of the mountainous skyline to the southeast. If you follow the trail a few steps further, you can overlook the Waterrock Knob parking area as well as look west for views of the summits of Clingmans Dome (6,643 ft.), Mount LeConte (6,593 ft.), and Mount Guyot (6,621 ft.), the highest peaks in the Great Smoky Mountains National Park.

MOUNT PISGAH

Waynesville

Waynesville, just west of Asheville, looks like a town one might expect to see in a Norman Rockwell painting—a picturesque Main Street where all the storefronts are occupied, tidy brick sidewalks, and curving iron lampposts. Home to one of the famous Mast General Stores, Waynesville has also earned a reputation in recent years as being an arts destination. In all, the town is home to more than a dozen art galleries. Local rumor has it that that's more per capita than New York City has.

SIGHTS
Museum of North Carolina Handicrafts

A bit off the main drag in Waynesville but worth a visit is the **Museum of North Carolina Handicrafts** (49 Shelton St., 828/452-1551, May–Oct. Tues.–Sat. 10 A.M.–4 P.M., adults $5, students $3). Located on the edge of town, the museum is housed in the former residence of Will Shelton, superintendent of the Navajo Indian School in Shiprock, New Mexico. The museum displays Native American artifacts collected by Shelton and other historic handicrafts like a pine and walnut table made in 1845 and owned by the Caldwell family, who once lived in the nearby Cataloochee Valley (now part of the Great Smoky Mountains National Park). The museum also has an extensive collection of North Carolina's famous Seagrove pottery. Seagrove is a small community in central North Carolina. The first potters in that area began making functional stoneware prior to the American Revolution. The tradition continues to this day with many descendants of the original potters still at the wheel. The Seagrove area has been recognized by the state legislature as "the official birthplace of North Carolina traditional pottery."

SHOPPING
Art Galleries

The **Blue Owl Studio** (11 N. Main St., 828/456-9596, www.blueowlinc.com, Mon.–Sat. 10 A.M.–5:30 P.M., Sun. noon–5 P.M.) is one of the many galleries on Waynesville's Main Street. Artist Penny Wagner operates the studio with her husband, Gary. She paints pictures, mostly of black bears, onto pieces of wood reclaimed from old barns torn down by local craftsmen. Gary then helps her in transferring the original art to canvas and wood using the giclée process of printing. The couple does all the work themselves.

Textures (142 N. Main St., 828/452-0058, www.texturesonmain.com, Mon.–Sat. 10 A.M.–5 P.M., Sun. noon–5 P.M.) specializes in modern art and pottery but also carries sleek and unusual woodcraft by local artisan and gallery co-owner John Gernandt, who works in cherry, poplar, maple, walnut, and white oak to create unusual side tables, desks, and coffee tables. Also on display here is textile art, much of it produced by the artisans of a local textile group known as Glint as well as by John's weaver wife, Suzanne.

Twigs & Leaves Gallery (98 N. Main St., 828/456-1940, www.twigsandleaves.com, Mon.–Sat. 10 A.M.–5:30 P.M., Sun. 1–4 P.M.) is a good place to check out if you want to see the works of dozens of artists all in one place. With two floors of gallery space, Twigs & Leaves features fine art, jewelry, crafts, and furniture, all of it handmade by primarily regional artisans. Gallery owner Kaaren Stoner creates remarkable patterns of twigs and leaves in her clay creations, which range from pots and vases to birdhouses and salt and paper shakers.

Just down the street is **Gallery 86** (86 N. Main St., 828/452-0593, www.haywoodarts. org, Mon.–Sat. 10 A.M.–5 P.M.), the gallery of the Haywood County Arts Council. The gallery offers changing exhibits by local artists and artisans.

My favorite gallery in Waynesville is **Ridge Runner Naturals** (33 N. Main St., 800/525-3009, www.theridgerunner.com, Mon.–Tues. and Thurs.–Sat. noon–6 P.M., Sun. 1–5 P.M.), which features the beautiful oil and watercolor

© FRENCH C. GRIMES

Main Street, Waynesville

ENTERTAINMENT AND EVENTS
Music
Waynesville hosts **Mountain Street Dances** on select Friday evenings late June through early August in front of the historic courthouse on Main Street from 6:30 to 9 P.M. There's live mountain music and cloggers perform; clogging teams offer instruction to the audience. If you don't plan on dancing, bring a lawn chair or blanket.

Folkmoot USA (112 Virginia Ave., 828/452-2997, www.folkmootusa.org, check website for prices) occurs the last two weeks in July and is a celebration of international culture through the lens of folk music and dance. Performers come from all over the world to share their musical skills, and since the festival's beginning in 1984, it has featured folk musicians from over 100 nations.

Art
Art After Dark is held the first Friday of every month May to October in downtown Waynesville. Local shops and galleries stay open until 9 P.M., with some offering refreshments and musical entertainment.

ACCOMMODATIONS
Lodges and Inns
Waynesville has a number of chain hotels, including Best Western and Days Inn, but if you're interested in atmosphere, look for a local touch. **The Waynesville Inn Golf Resort and Spa** (176 Country Club Dr., 800/627-6250, www.thewaynesvilleinn.com, standard rooms $89–109, Deluxe Gold View rooms $105–125, junior suites $130–150, Donald Ross Suite $149) is one such option, with 115 rooms in a beautiful setting with mountain views in all directions. The resort has 27 holes of golf on three Donald Ross–designed courses. Guest also have access to an on-site spa, two resort restaurants, and a swimming pool.

About 13 miles from Waynesville in a scenic high-elevation setting is **The Swag** (2300 Swag Rd., 800/789-7672, www.theswag.com, Swag House rooms $490–750, Chestnut Lodge

landscapes of Jo Ridge Kelley, who paints romantic landscapes of the Smoky and Blue Ridge Mountains and has recently begun to paint vibrant abstract waterscapes. The shop also sells the photography of Ed Kelley, which includes panoramic landscapes of the Great Smoky Mountains and Blue Ridge Parkway.

Gift Shops
Blue Ridge Books (152 S. Main St., 828/456-6000, www.brbooks-news.com, Mon.–Thurs. 8 A.M.–8 P.M., Fri.–Sat. 8 A.M.–9 P.M., Sun. 8 A.M.–6 P.M.) is an independent bookseller and newsstand two blocks down from the Mast General Store. The shop carries *New York Times* bestsellers, which they discount 25 percent, as well as a good selection of general fiction and nonfiction and regional books. They have over 1,000 magazine titles and major daily newspapers for sale as well as an area with kids' books and small tables and chairs. The bookstore has coffee and sweet treats for sale as well as free Wi-Fi access both indoors and outside on the covered deck.

MOUNT PISGAH

rooms $650–695, cabins and suites $695–785), a country inn that has become synonymous with stunning mile-high views, round-the-clock gourmet dining and delicacies, and family-style camaraderie—all while sharing a mile-long border with the Great Smoky Mountains National Park and private access to miles of secluded hiking trails. Few lodgings can boast such utter isolation and superb access to nature while still providing all the most treasured amenities of city life, but The Swag is one. From the base of its curling driveway in the rolling green foothills of Maggie Valley to the woods and rhododendron-encrusted pinnacle where the log lodge is perched is a difference in elevation of 1,100 feet. Visitors who arrive here in spring or fall will not only experience an ear-popping change in elevation but a two-week change in season from the driveway's base to its endpoint at The Swag. The inn has 16 rooms, including a two-story cabin. And while the setting is worlds away from everything, the resort itself is always bustling with activity and does not offer the isolation from humanity suggested by its high elevation and proximity to wilderness. It really is something like a high-elevation house party. Only a few steps from the front door is the 6.5-mile Cataloochee Divide Trail along the eastern border of the national park as well as access to dozens of other hiking venues, including a short trip to the top of Gooseberry Knob, where gourmet picnic lunches are served on Wednesdays.

Bed-and-Breakfasts

The **❰ Inn at Iris Meadows** (304 Love La., 828/456-3877, www.irismeadows.com, $225–300) is an early-20th-century home with sprawling porches overlooking the town. The inn, which has seven rooms, all with private baths and fireplaces and Wi-Fi, as well as one wheelchair-accessible room on the main floor, is probably the finest accommodation in Waynesville proper. If you like waking up to morning light, check into the Butterfly Room, a warm and sunny room on the 2nd floor with an adjoining whirlpool bath and access to the inn's second-story veranda with porch swing.

Many of co-owner Becky's own photographs and paintings of flowers and butterflies can be found throughout the inn, mirroring the sloping, lush gardens outside, where irises by the hundreds bloom in late spring.

❰ Oak Hill on Love Lane Bed and Breakfast (224 Love La., 828/456-7037, www.oakhillonlovelane.com, $150–235) is right next door to the Inn at Iris Meadows and is equally as comfortable and beautifully decorated. The inn has five spacious rooms and a shady front porch with wicker furniture where guests can relax. The bed-and-breakfast is decorated with consigned paintings by local artists, all of which are available for purchase. The old coal fireplaces in the bedrooms have been converted to gas logs. The innkeepers provide a full snack pantry with iced tea, coffee, cookies, and chips. The Victorian inn, built in 1898, is also listed on the National Register of Historic Places. Oak Hill's bathrooms are its best feature, as all have thick, plush towels and locally made Hazelwood Soap Company soaps and toiletries, all freshly scented in lavender, as well as evening turndown service with chocolates on the pillows and bedside beverage. The inn offers complimentary Wi-Fi and a three-course breakfast. Your morning repast might consist of fresh seasonal berries on glacé served with a puff pastry quiche stuffed with bacon, cheese, spinach, and onion. If you're too full for the final course, which will likely be an oversized muffin, the innkeepers will bag it for you to take on the road or trail with you.

The Yellow House (89 Oakview Dr., 828/452-0991, www.theyellowhouse.com, rooms $149–175, suites $185–265) has 10 rooms and suites in a historic late-19th-century house on a hilltop above Waynesville with beautiful long-distance mountain views. Most rooms are spacious and sumptuously decorated. Some have fireplaces, jetted bathtubs, and private balconies. Guests enjoy a full breakfast each morning and can have it served in their rooms, in the dining room, or on the veranda. Evening hors d'oeuvres are available as well as complimentary coffee, tea,

Oak Hill on Love Lane Bed and Breakfast in Waynesville

soft drinks, and snacks. The inn has one pet-friendly suite.

FOOD
Casual Fine Dining
The Sweet Onion (39 Miller St., 828/456-5559, www.sweetonionrestaurant.com, Mon.–Sat. 11:30 A.M.–9 P.M., $7–25) is popular with locals and has a wide range of offerings. Food here is predictably good, though stay away from the country-fried steak, which can't even be cut with a steak knife. Safe standbys include the shrimp and grits and the catfish, which is dusted in cornmeal and is best served with fried okra.

Chef's Table (30 Church St., 828/452-6210, www.chefstable-nc.com, Tues.–Sat. 5–9 P.M., Sun. 11 A.M.–2 P.M., $14–30) offers an upscale dining opportunity in Waynesville with a menu heavy on seafood, including Carolina Low Country shrimp and grits, an interesting calamari Caesar salad, and a grilled jumbo shrimp salad with crab meat and blueberries thrown in.

If you're seeking a warm and rustic atmosphere with a relaxed pace, try **The Old Stone Inn** (109 Dolan Rd., 828/456-3333, www.old-stoneinn.com, Mon.–Sat. 5:30–8 P.M., $7–27). Since they're only open a few hours for dinner, making advance reservations is recommended. The place is cozy with a blazing fire often filling the dining room with a golden glow and the exposed-beam ceilings adding to the overall historic atmosphere. Start your meal with the pecan baked brie served with crackers. For dinner, the porterhouse pork chop or lump crab cakes are both reliable choices. If you can still stuff dessert in, try the white chocolate bread pudding served with bananas Foster sauce. The Old Stone Inn is located above downtown Waynesville. Take Depot Street from Main Street, and then turn left on Love Lane. Then take another left onto Dolan Road. The inn will be on your left.

Quick Bites
Whitman's Bakery (18 N. Main St., 828/456-8271, Wed.–Sat. 7 A.M.–5 P.M., $1–8) is a local

favorite for lunch. Established in 1945, the bakery carries a sumptuous array of sandwiches. Expect to wait in line if you arrive during the noon hour.

The Chocolate Bear (170 N. Main St., 828/452-6844, www.thechocolatebears.com, Mon.–Sat. 10 A.M.–8 P.M., Sun. noon–6 P.M.) is one of my favorite stops on Main Street. This decadent shop is serviced by 18 chocolatiers, two of them local, and it carries a sumptuous array of gigantic truffles, chocolate-covered treats of all descriptions, and gelato. Be sure to try the sweet and salty dark chocolate–covered potato chips as well as the chocolate-covered blueberries and animal crackers.

Vin Wine & Tapas Bar (20 Church St., 828/452-6000, Thurs.–Fri. 4–9 P.M., Sat. noon–9 P.M., Sun. 1–5 P.M.) is located inside the Classic Wineseller and is a good place to stop for before-dinner drinks and appetizers, including tapas, cheese boards, and dessert items.

The Patio (26 Church St., 828/454-0070, www.patio-nc.com, Nov.–Mar. Mon.–Sat. 10 A.M.–4 P.M., Apr.–Oct. Mon.–Sat. 10 A.M.–4 P.M., Sun. 10 A.M.–3 P.M., $5–9) is my favorite place in Waynesville to grab a quick lunch. The food is fast but healthy. Best here are the quiche and soup of the day as well as the grilled chicken wrap, rolled up with bacon, romaine lettuce, tomatoes, onion, and parmesan cheese soaked with Caesar dressing. There is some inside seating, but it's most pleasant to eat on the outside patio, which is decorated with blooming baskets of flowers and metal art on the adjacent brick walls.

INFORMATION AND SERVICES
Information
The **Haywood County Tourism Development Authority** (1233 N. Main St., Ste. 1-40, 800/334-9036, www.smokeymountains.net, Mon.–Fri. 8:30 A.M.–5 P.M.) offers brochures and maps on Waynesville and the surrounding area.

Emergency Services
Haywood Regional Medical Center (262 Leroy George Dr., 828/456-7311, www.haymed.org, 24 hours) is accessible from the Lake Junaluska exit off Highway 23/74. Stay in the middle lane, take a left, and at the next light you will take a right onto Hospital Drive; follow the signs. The **Haywood County Sheriff's Office** (1620 Brown Ave., 828/452-6666) can also provide emergency assistance.

GETTING THERE
The easiest way to reach Waynesville from the Blue Ridge Parkway is to exit at Highway 23/74 north. You will go about seven miles and then take Exit 102A onto Highway 276, which will take you right into downtown Waynesville.

Sylva and Dillsboro

Sylva and Dillsboro are separate towns, but given the fact that they run right into each other, you might not even notice the separation. The two village neighbors are tucked into a valley formed by the Tuckasegee River and look a bit like Main Street America circa 1950. Victorian houses and brick storefronts line the streets, and there is a certain amount of serenity here.

In the 1850s, the first wagon road to cross the Smokies came through Dillsboro and some three decades later came the railroad. At that time, Dillsboro was the main town with Sylva being nothing more than a railroad siding. That situation has since reversed, with Sylva now being the more populous of the two.

Dillsboro, however, is home to a thriving little craft community that you can easily miss if you're just breezing through town. Be sure to head down the back streets and check out the local artisans, some of whom have been plying their craft here in the village for nearly three decades.

SIGHTS
Heinzelmännchen Brewery

The Heinzelmännchen Brewery (545 Mill St., 828/631-4466, www.yourgnometown-brewery.com, Tues.–Fri. 11 A.M.–6:30 P.M., Sat. 11 A.M.–5 P.M.) is a must-stop if you're in Sylva. A microbrewery run by a German-born brewmeister, Heinzelmännchen makes light and fresh German beers. The brewery does not have their beers on tap (though several local eateries do), but you can purchase beer to take home in a growler or a keg. The store sells beers, ales, and stout, as well as root beer and birch beer. The first Friday of every month, the brewery offers samples of its brews as well as samples of cuisine from local restaurants during an event they call Food and Beer Pairing. The brewery features food from local restaurants that carry their brew.

Jackson County Green Energy Park

The Jackson County Green Energy Park (100 Green Energy Park Rd., 828/631-0271, www.jcgep.org, Mon.–Fri. 9 A.M.–5 P.M.) is a relatively new addition to Dillsboro. It's a methane-powered business incubator and features a glass blowing, blacksmithing, and pottery studio. The energy park also has a sculpture garden. Visitors can take tours of the energy park on Wednesdays and Thursdays between 2 and 4 P.M. to learn how the park is powered by methane gas. Call before you visit to make sure artisans will be on-site demonstrating their work.

SHOPPING
Art Galleries
SYLVA

Though not nearly as prosperous as the neighboring town of Waynesville, Sylva has its own burgeoning arts community on Main Street. **It's By Nature** (678 W. Main St., 828/631-3020, Tues.–Sat. 10:30 A.M.–5:30 P.M.) hosts the work of dozens of regional artists, including

the eye-catching red glazed pottery of Eileen Lovinger Black, and the fluid and mesmerizing photographs of LeAnne Fowler, a dancer who creates black and white images of moving fabric and water.

Gallery One (640 W. Main St., 828/293-3407, Mon.–Fri. 11 A.M.–4 P.M.) is the gallery of the Jackson County Arts Council and features rotating exhibits of local artists as well as artist demonstrations and workshops.

North Carolina native Matthew Turlington has his own gallery in Sylva. **The Penumbra Gallery** (528 W. Main St., 828/631-5278, www.penumbragallery.com, Tues.–Sat. 11 A.M.–4 P.M.) displays his black-and-white photographs of the surrounding mountains and some stark and nostalgic nighttime images of downtown Sylva. Turlington says some of his pictures take years of waiting to create, like his picture "Main Street Sylva," which shows the town under a full moon with no cars, a setting he had to use the utmost patience to find. Turlington does all of his own developing, printing, matting, and framing, giving himself control over and income from the entire production process.

DILLSBORO

Dillsboro has a substantial arts community that has suffered in recent years with the removal of the Great Smoky Mountains Railroad from Dillsboro to neighboring Bryson City. Thus far, most of the local artisans have remained, but they don't get nearly the traffic they once did. It's a pity because you could easily spend two or three hours exploring the local studios and galleries, which number about a dozen, often finding the artists themselves hard at work on looms and pottery wheels.

A good place to start your tour is the **Oaks Gallery** (29 Craft Circle, Riverwood Shops, 828/586-6542, www.oaksgallery.com, Mon.–Sat. 10 A.M.–5 P.M.), owned and operated by Susan and Bob Leveille. Susan, a longtime weaver and niece of Lucy Morgan, founder of the Penland School of Crafts outside Spruce Pine, North Carolina, has resided in Dillsboro for more than 30 years. You might find Susan working at her loom, and you can always purchase some of her finely woven textiles, but she also sells the work of more than 100 other area artisans. Those wares include pewter hammered into everything from spoons to decorative items by the descendants of Ralph Silas Morgan (brother to Lucy Morgan), who started the family's pewter work in the 1930s.

Riverwood Pottery (60 Craft Circle, Riverwood Shops, 828/586-3601, www.riverwoodpottery.com, Mon.–Sat. 10 A.M.–5 P.M.) is another good place to stop. The showroom is small, and it is easy to miss the real treat here—watching sixth-generation North Carolinian Brant Barnes deftly drive his potter's wheel in the studio behind the shop, where he shapes everything from bowls and vases to hanging planters. With more than 35 years of pottery making under his belt, Brant is mesmerizing to watch, as curving urns take shape in silky wet clay under his craft-roughed hands. One of his signature styles is earthen-colored glazes featuring mountain blueberry brambles.

© FRENCH C. GRIMES

potter Brant Barnes at work at Riverwood Pottery in Dillsboro

Also at the Riverwood Shops is **Maggie J's Jewelry** (59 Craft Circle, Riverwood Shops, 828/371-3711, www.maggiejs.com, Mon.–Sat. 10 A.M.–5 P.M.), where you can purchase metalsmith Maggie Joynt's unusual jewelry from carved petal necklaces to gorgeous dangling earrings loaded with miniature hoops.

You can see another local potter at work at **Tree House Pottery** (148 Front St., 828/631-5100, www.treehousepotterync.com, Mon.–Sat. 10 A.M.–5 P.M., Sun. 11 A.M.–4 P.M.). Owner-artists Joe Frank McKee and Travis Berning specialize in horsehair and raku pottery but also feature the work of seven other potters in their shop. McKee and Berning also head up the **Western North Carolina Pottery Festival** (148 Front St., 828/631-5100, www.wncpotteryfestival.com, $2), which takes place the first Saturday in November and features area potters throwing, firing, and selling their wares.

Dogwood Crafters (90 Webster St., 828/586-2248, www.dogwoodcrafters.com, Mar.–Dec. daily 10 A.M.–6 P.M.) is the shop of the Dogwood Crafters Cooperative, which was begun in 1976 by a dozen local mountain artisans. Today the cooperative has about 100 members and an eclectic mix of local crafts for sale, including shuck dolls, tatted lace, quilts, birdhouses, stained glass, and baskets.

ACCOMMODATIONS
Inns and Bed-and-Breakfasts
SYLVA

Sylva's finest accommodations are actually not in town at all but in the mountains surrounding the village. Among them is the **Galvladi Mountain Inn** (400 North Fork Rd., 877/631-0125, www.galvladi.com, $200–375), which is situated on 250 acres and is built of handcrafted round logs and features more than one soaring stone fireplace. There are five rooms here, all of them warmly furnished with rocking chairs, sofas, or overstuffed armchairs situated to take in the views from the large windows. Some have whirlpool tubs, fireplaces, and private patios, and all have private baths. The inn has its own private hiking trails, a fitness center, and ample porches for relaxing. Breakfast, lunch, and dinner are included in the price of the room, and picnic lunches are available.

The **Balsam Mountain Inn** (68 Seven Springs Dr., 828/456-9498, www.balsam-mountaininn.com, $145–229) is a century-old three-story inn with 50 individually decorated guest rooms. The inn holds much of its early-20th-century charm with simple, comfortable furnishings as well as wide hallways whose walls are filled with local artwork. Guests are welcome to use the 2,000-volume library, and the inn's 100-foot-long two-story porch provides ample opportunity for whiling away the evening in a rocking chair while taking in the mountain views. The property is situated at over 3,500 feet. There is an on-site restaurant serving breakfast and dinner daily as well as lunch on Saturdays and Sundays. Pets are permitted with an additional fee.

© FRENCH C. GRIMES

Dillsboro Inn

DILLSBORO

The **Squire Watkins Inn** (657 Haywood Rd., 800/586-2429, www.squirewatkinsinn.com, $115–135) offers the best accommodations in Dillsboro. It is located just off the Highway 23 and 441 intersection behind the Huddle House. The simple two-story frame house on the western edge of town had a quieter location before 441 was widened to four lanes, but the Squire Watkins is still the place to go if you're seeking relative peace and quiet. The house features double porches on the front where you can relax with a glass of wine in the evenings. If you're lucky, you might get to enjoy the singing of tree frogs and summer rain to drown out the adjacent highway noise. The inn has four rooms of varying sizes, all of them simply and cheerfully decorated by the innkeepers, who have owned and operated the Squire Watkins since 1983. The Dogwood Room on the front of the house, adjacent to the second-story porch, is my favorite room. It is outfitted with sunny yellow and light green curtains, bedspreads, and furniture and features a painted

wood floor, a small sitting area facing a window alcove, and a tiny but sufficient bathroom with shower. Often guests will gather in the downstairs parlor and play the piano or guitar in the evenings. The innkeepers are gems, too. As longtime residents of Dillsboro, they know the area intimately and will happily act as your personal concierge.

The **Dillsboro Inn** (146 N. River Rd., 828/586-3898, www.dillsboroinn.com, $125–275) is another lodging option just outside town on the banks of the Tuckasegee River. Located on a hydroelectric dam that generates a nice waterfall just outside the inn's front door, the Dillsboro Inn has a decidedly laid-back atmosphere that includes nightly campfire marshmallow roasts with the innkeepers. If you're traveling with children, pets, or in a large party, the Dillsboro Inn might be a good option, as they have several large suites with as many as three beds, small kitchenettes, sitting areas, and private patios overlooking the river, and three rooms that are pet-friendly. The rooms are a bit rough around the edges with rustic wood-paneled walls, wide plank floors, and furnishings that have seen some wear in some cases. Avoid ground-floor suites, as they tend to be noisy with guests walking overhead. Bathrooms, however, are spacious, and most rooms have Wi-Fi access, though you might have to move around to find the signal. The Dillsboro Inn is really for people who like to socialize. If you're looking for peace and quiet, the Squire Watkins is a better choice.

Camping

Fort Tatham Campground (175 Tatham Creek Rd., 828/586-6662, www.carefreervresorts.com, Apr.–Oct., $19–24) is a scenic campground with 92 total sites and 75 permanent campsites. Full hookups are available, as are laundry and shower facilities. The campground has a dump station, pool, and playground. The campground is six miles south of Dillsboro on U.S. 441.

Savannah Creek RV Resort (50 Timber Leaf Dr., 828/631-5111, www.scrvr.com, open year-round, daily $30, weekly $180, monthly $450 plus electric) is an RV-only campground with lovely mountain views, a fishing pond on-site, weight rooms, and even an outdoor kitchen. Full hookups, laundry, and showers are available. There is also a pool and camp store. Savannah Creek has 25 campsites and is located in Sylva, five miles from Dillsboro.

FOOD
Sylva
Lulu's Café (612 W. Main St., 828/586-8989, www.lulusonmain.com, Mon.–Sat. 11:30 A.M.–8 P.M., $7–17) offers the most varied menu in town with everything from a fresh poached-salmon salad to an Asian noodle salad. The restaurant also specializes in vegetarian fare, but you can get meat dishes here, too. Among them is the tropical pork tenderloin with a glaze of orange and Jamaican jerk spices. Another tasty option is the restaurant's black beans cooked with onions, garlic, cumin, oregano, and lime and served over brown rice.

You can also get the black beans on the side with most entrées.

Restaurant 553 (553 W. Main St., 828/631-3810, www.restaurant553.com, Mon.–Sat. 5–9 P.M., $5–30) is a good place go if you want white tablecloth atmosphere and romantic outdoor seating after dark. The menu is traditional with filet mignon, lobster tail, Cornish game hen, and rib-eye steak. Many dishes are served in a tangy blue cheese cream sauce.

Dillsboro
Opened in 2009, **Kosta's Family Restaurant** (828/631-0777, www.kostasdillsboro.com, Mon.–Sat. 11 A.M.–9 P.M., Sun. 11 A.M.–3 P.M., $6–15) is popular among the locals, most likely for its reasonable rates and large portions. While the starter salad you can add to any entrée for $1 seems like a deal, skip it—the salad is pretty much all iceberg lettuce. Order the soup of the day instead. Food here is traditional Greek, Italian, and American with an excess of lettuce and white bread, unfortunately, though the staff will serve wheat upon request. Stick to the Greek and Italian dishes for happiest results. The Greek lasagna, spaghetti with meatballs, and gyro platter are all good choices.

West Carolina Internet Café (475 Haywood Rd., 828/586-5700, www.westcarolinacafe.com, daily 8 A.M.–7 P.M.) serves light fare, including deli salads, bagels, croissants, and sweet treats, along with a variety of gourmet coffees and teas and fruit smoothies. In addition the café has free Wi-Fi, computers for use, and printing, copying, and fax services. Computer usage is $1 per 5 minutes, $5 for 30 minutes.

The **Jarrett House** (100 Haywood St., 828/586-0265, www.jarretthouse.com, daily 11:30 A.M.–2:30 P.M. and 4:30–7:30 P.M., $12–16) isn't for everyone, as food is served family-style here. The food isn't bad, though—typically home-style country fare, including country ham, red-eye gravy, fried chicken, and catfish all with plenty of buttered potatoes, green beans, candied apples, and biscuits. There's no such thing here as not getting enough to eat.

The **Dillsboro Smokehouse** (403 Haywood St., 828/586-9556, daily 11 A.M.–9 P.M., $5–18) is a local favorite beloved for its barbecue baby-back ribs as well as a full selection of other barbecue entrées. Be sure to order your ribs with the piping-hot sweet-potato fries. If you're not into barbecue, then try the rolled taco, which you can order with sliced roast beef or chicken stuffed into a soft flour shell with Monterey Jack and cheddar cheese, onions, and green chiles topped with sour cream and salsa. The smokehouse serves locally crafted Heinzelmännchen root and birch beer.

INFORMATION AND SERVICES
Information
The Jackson County Chamber of Commerce (773 W. Main St., 800/962-1911, www.mountainlovers.com, Mon.–Fri. 9 A.M.–5 P.M., Sat. 10 A.M.–2 P.M.) is located in a beautiful Victorian house on the western end of Main Street just below the Jackson County Courthouse.

Emergency Services
Harris Regional Hospital (68 Hospital Rd., 828/586-7000, www.westcare.org) is most easily accessible off Highway 23/74 at Exit 85 in Sylva and has 24-hour emergency services.

MOUNT PISGAH

CHEROKEE INDIAN RESERVATION AND MAGGIE VALLEY

The North Carolina entry point to the Great Smoky Mountains National Park, the Cherokee Indian Reservation, is home to the Eastern Band of the Cherokee Nation, the descendants of those who avoided the Trail of Tears to the Oklahoma Territory in 1838, or those who returned years later. Tourism has brought prosperity to the town of Cherokee as well as the nearby off-reservation town of Maggie Valley. The Museum of the Cherokee Indian is a must-see starting point to understanding the long history and culture of the tribe, and many galleries and shops in town offer the opportunity to purchase locally made Cherokee crafts. Of course, tourism has also brought some of the glitz more reminiscent of the western side of the Smokies, including the palatial Harrah's Casino. The benefit, however, is that the casino regularly hosts big-name artists like Miranda Lambert and George Jones.

Just south of Cherokee is a venue for those seeking quiet, the small town of Bryson City, where one can stay overnight at one of many small bed-and-breakfasts or hop aboard the Great Smoky Mountains Railroad for scenic trips through the mountains. To the north of Cherokee and accessible via winding Highway 19 is the strip town of Maggie Valley. Stretching for miles on either side of the highway through what would otherwise be a scenic mountain valley, Maggie Valley is mostly a whirlwind of motels, miniature golf courses, theaters, and tourist traps. It is perhaps the attempt of the North Carolina side of the Smokies to answer the hoopla of Tennessee's Pigeon Forge, though on a much smaller scale.

HIGHLIGHTS

(Museum of the Cherokee Indian: This beautifully done museum offers the history and artifacts of the Cherokee from ancient times to the present (page 185).

(Qualla Arts and Crafts Mutual: The oldest Native American craft cooperative in the country showcases and sells locally made Cherokee crafts (page 187).

(Harrah's Casino: The Cherokee-owned casino offers big-name shows and 24-hour gaming that financially supports the community initiatives of the Eastern Band of the Cherokee (page 188).

(_Unto These Hills:_ This summer outdoor drama tells the story of the Cherokee removal from North Carolina (page 188).

(Mingo Falls: Cascading over 120 feet, this lovely waterfall is just outside the town of Cherokee and accessible via a quick hike (page 189).

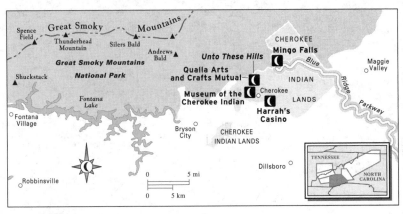

LOOK FOR (TO FIND RECOMMENDED SIGHTS, ACTIVITIES, DINING, AND LODGING.

PLANNING YOUR TIME

Allow yourself at least one full day in Cherokee so you have time to fully explore the highlights that will give you a grounding in the region's Native American history. Those include the Museum of the Cherokee Indian, the Oconaluftee Indian Village, Qualla Arts and Crafts Mutual, and the outdoor drama _Unto These Hills_. A second day will give you time to either hit some of the amusements of nearby Maggie Valley, like Ghost Town in the Sky, or to explore the village of Bryson City and ride the Great Smoky Mountains Railroad.

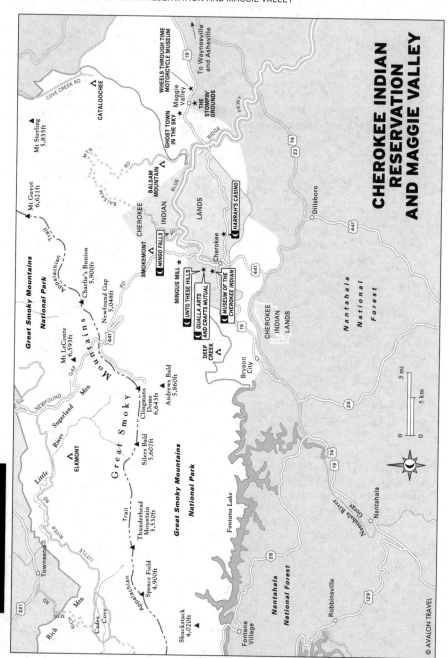

CHEROKEE INDIAN
RESERVATION
AND MAGGIE VALLEY

To Waynesville and Asheville

WHEELS THROUGH TIME MOTORCYCLE MUSEUM
THE STOMPIN' GROUNDS
GHOST TOWN IN THE SKY
Maggie Valley

CATALOOCHEE
COVE CREEK RD

Mt Sterling 5,835ft

Mt Guyot 6,621ft

Great Smoky Mountains National Park

BALSAM MOUNTAIN

BALSAM MTN RD

BLUE RIDGE PKWY

Appalachian Trail

Charlie's Bunion 5,900ft

SMOKEMONT

MINGO FALLS

CHEROKEE INDIAN LANDS

HARRAH'S CASINO

Newfound Gap 5,048ft

Mt LeConte 6,593ft

NEWFOUND GAP RD

441

MINGUS MILL
UNTO THESE HILLS
QUALLA ARTS AND CRAFTS MUTUAL
MUSEUM OF THE CHEROKEE INDIAN

Cherokee

441

Dillsboro

441

23

74

Clingmans Dome 6,643ft

Andrews Bald 5,860ft

DEEP CREEK

19

CHEROKEE INDIAN LANDS

Mountains

Great Smoky

Sugarland Mtn

Silers Bald 5,607ft

ELKMONT

Little River

NEWFOUND GAP

River

Bryson City

Nantahala National Forest

28

Thunderhead Mountain 5,530ft

Great Smoky Mountains National Park

Fontana Lake

74

19

Nantahala

Appalachian Trail

Spence Field 4,900ft

Shuckstack 4,020ft

28

Nantahala River

Nantahala Gorge

RICH MTN RD

LITTLE RIVER RD

Townsend

321

Cades Cove

Rich Mtn

Fontana Village

Robbinsville

129

5 mi
5 km
0
0

© AVALON TRAVEL

CHEROKEE INDIAN RESERVATION AND MAGGIE VALLEY

Maggie Valley

More strip than town, Maggie Valley is one of the eastern gateways into the Smokies, the last town before entering the Cherokee Indian Reservation and Great Smoky Mountains National Park. Many of the attractions are hokey at best, but there are some genuinely good clogging shows here as well as an annual motorcycle festival (and Harley rentals!).

Maggie Valley is located on the western edge of Haywood County, which claims to have the highest average elevation of any county in the East with 13 peaks rising over 6,000 feet.

SIGHTS
Ghost Town in the Sky
Ghost Town in the Sky (16 Fie Top Rd., 828/926-1140, www.ghosttowninthesky.com, May Fri.–Mon. 10 A.M.–6 P.M., June–mid-Sept. daily 10 A.M.–6 P.M., mid-Sept.–Oct. Fri.–Sun. 10 A.M.–6 P.M., adults $29.95, children $24.95) has been a part of the attraction scene in Maggie Valley for half a century, quite a claim for an amusement park. But that's not even the biggest news about this place: Even more remarkable is that the cowboy who plays the Apache Kid has served in the role since the 1960s.

Even if you enjoy the thrilling rides of amusement parks, Ghost Town in the Sky may come across as a bit cheesy with its Wild West theme in the middle of the Smoky Mountains, but keep your judgment in check and just enjoy the rides, which include the Cliff Hanger roller coaster. As its name suggests, this ride clings to the side of Buck Mountain, offering incredible views if you're brave enough to enjoy them.

Any visit to Ghost Town in the Sky begins with a 15-minute chairlift ride up the mountain since the 90-acre amusement park is situated at 4,000 feet. The park has rides for all ages and thrill-seeker levels as well as shootouts, cancan girls, tribal dancing, bluegrass bands, and a saloon.

Wheels Through Time Motorcycle Museum
Wheels Through Time Motorcycle Museum (2914 Soco Rd., 828/926-6266, www.wheelsthroughtime.com, daily 9 A.M.–5 P.M., adults $12, seniors $10, children $6, group rate for six or more $10 each) is a draw for the motorcyclists that flock to the Smokies for great rides through the mountains. Unbelievably, it draws some half a million visitors a year, who come to see their favorite machines on two wheels displayed in historical review. The museum also hosts regular openings and exhibitions throughout the year with even more bikes to check out. Visit the website for days and times.

ENTERTAINMENT AND EVENTS
Entertainment
Maggie Valley is known for its musical entertainment, and there are more than half a dozen venues in town where you can enjoy live music. The best among them is **Carolina Nights** (3732 Soco Rd., 828/926-8822, www.maggievalleyusa.com, showtime 6:15–9 P.M., $29.95 dinner, show, and all taxes), a dinner theater that presents one major musical show a year and, despite the theater's location in the Appalachian Mountains, the genres you'll enjoy here will not necessarily be country. Dinners are served cafeteria-style.

The **Stompin' Grounds** (3116 Soco Rd., 828/926-1288) holds a Clogging Competition the first weekend in May, and the American Clogging Hall of Fame World Championships is held on the fourth Saturday in October. The Stompin' Grounds is home to the American Clogging Hall of Fame, which honors America's clogging history and the cloggers of today. The public is always welcome to attend the competitions here—and should. If you think clogging is a hokey mountain dance done by old ladies in puffy skirts, then you need to check

COURTESY OF GHOST TOWN IN THE SKY

the Apache Kid at Ghost Town in the Sky

this place out. You've never seen clogging like this before.

Events

Thunder in the Smokies (3374 Soco Rd., 828/246-2101, www.handlebarcorral.com, $15) is a motorcycle rally held each year in both April and September with organized rides through the countryside, live music, including gospel on Sunday, vendors, and bike games. Thousands of bikers attend every year and take rides together on the Parkway, into Asheville, and into Cherokee. **Gryphon Bikes** (871 Soco Rd., 828/926-4400, www.gryphonbikes.com, daily rental $109–215, 3-day rental $294–429, 5-day rental $465–675) offers Harley rentals by the day if you don't have your own bike.

SPORTS AND RECREATION
Skiing and Snowmobiling

The **Cataloochee Ski Area** (1080 Ski Lodge Rd., 800/768-0285, www.cataloochee.com, Nov.–Mar. hours vary, lift tickets $33–53, equipment rental $20–23) has 16 slopes and trails open to skiers and snowboarders as well

as Tube World (www.tubemaggievalley.com, $25) with a mechanical tow to the top. Ski lessons and rentals are available. Even the chairlift rides here are fun, as they offer a chance to sit back and enjoy the long-distance Smoky Mountain views. There are 50 skiable acres; the top elevation is 5,400 feet, with a vertical drop of 740 feet. For ski reports, call 800/768-3588.

ACCOMMODATIONS
Hotels

Maggie Valley is loaded with hotels and motels of all descriptions, many of them 1950s-style motor inns. If you're looking for accommodations with more amenities and more plush surroundings, you might prefer to stay at an inn or bed-and-breakfast in the neighboring town of Waynesville or stay in a vacation rental. Your best bet for hotels, at least in Maggie Valley, is more likely a chain option. That being said, there are a few locally owned hotels that provide more updated overnight lodgings. Among them is the **Jonathan Creek Inn** (4324 Soco Rd., 800/577-7812, www.jonathancreekinn.com, standard rooms $50–110, creek rooms $65–125, rooms with hot tub and fireplace $75–150, villas $150–395), which has a mixture of lodging options available, including creekside rooms, rooms with whirlpool baths, rooms with hot tubs, and even villas. All are comfortably if simply furnished and offer a peaceful setting in the midst of town. Guests have use of the hotel's indoor heated pool, a creekside hot tub, game room, stocked trout stream, Internet station in the lobby, and free Wi-Fi.

Smoky Falls Lodge (2550 Soco Rd., 877/926-7440, www.smokyfallslodge.com, standard rooms $89, larger rooms with fireplaces $109–199, 3-bedroom apartment $229) is another private option on the main drag in Maggie Valley. With creekside rooms, many with fireplaces, and cozy, rustic furnishings, this hotel option is more peaceful than it appears from the street. All guests enjoy complimentary Wi-Fi, and the lodge is motorcycle friendly, offering covered parking for bikers. The Grizzly Grill offers dining on-site.

Best Western Mountainbrook Inn (3811 Soco Rd., 800/213-1914, www.bestwestern.com/mountainbrookinn, $80–159) offers 50 rooms, all with microwave, fridge, and coffee maker as well as free Wi-Fi. Guests enjoy complimentary continental breakfast each morning as well as access to an outdoor pool and indoor spa. The **Comfort Inn** (3282 Soco Rd., 866/926-9106, www.comfortinnmaggie.com, $49–269) has 68 rooms with microwaves, fridges, and high-speed Internet access. Some hot-tub rooms are available, too. Guests can enjoy the hotel's indoor pool or take a break in one of the rocking chairs in the hotel gazebo.

The **Ramada Limited** (4048 Soco Rd., 800/305-6703, www.ramada.com, $115–213) has creekside rooms with private balconies if you're interested in a little more than the standard hotel atmosphere. The hotel has whirlpool and family suites available as well as microwaves and refrigerators in each room. Guests enjoy use of the indoor heated pool and hot tub and complimentary continental breakfast each morning.

Cabins

Boyd Mountain Log Cabins & Christmas Tree Farm (445 Boyd Farm Rd., 828/926-1575, www.boydmountain.com, $165–385) offers overnight accommodations in restored antique log cabins on a 130-acre Christmas tree farm. The cabins are on the rustic side but are fully equipped with kitchens and everything you need to set up housekeeping for a couple of days. One-, two-, and three-bedroom cabins are available, and all feature covered porches with rocking chairs for taking in the views. There is also on-site fishing available on three stocked ponds and a stream.

Equestrian lovers might consider staying at **Cataloochee Ranch** (119 Ranch Dr., 800/868-1401, www.cataloocheeranch.com, main ranch house $152–215, Silverbell Lodge $205–247, cabins $247–268, romance cabins $320, 2- and 3-bedroom cabins $446), which has a variety of rustic log cabins available for rent as well as lodge rooms. Accommodations are simple and sparse but comfortable with many cabins offering fireplaces and decks with lovely views. Half- and full-day horseback riding is available for ranch guests and non-guests with rates starting at $45 for guests. Breakfast and dinner are included in the room and cabin rates.

Camping

Creekwood Farm RV Park (4696 Jonathan Creek Rd., 800/862-8110, www.creekwoodfarmrv.com, $30–48) has 125 sites, some on the river, and all with full hookups. Sites also have access to cable TV hookups.

Stone Bridge RV Resort (1786 Soco Rd., 828/926-1904, www.stonebridgervresort.com, $25–42) has 300 campsites for tents and RVs. In addition to full hookups this luxurious campground has Wi-Fi, cable TV, three bathhouses, laundry facilities, 46 campsites on a stocked trout creek, basketball courts, horseshoe pits, an arcade, dump station, and firewood and ice available on-site.

Rippling Waters Creekside RV Park (3962 Soco Rd., 828/926-7787) is open year-round, and has laundry and bathrooms available as well as full hookups.

FOOD

Joey's Pancake House (4309 Soco Rd., 828/926-0212, www.joeyspancake.com, Fri.–Wed. 7 A.M.–noon, $4–8) is probably a standout because it's one of the few options for breakfast in Maggie Valley, and it has consistently fast and friendly service. Here you'll find omelets of all descriptions, breakfast crepes, biscuits and gravy, country ham—all the usual yummy suspects.

J. Arthur's Restaurant (2843 Soco Rd., 828/926-1817, www.jarthurs.com, May–Oct. daily 4:30–9 P.M., Nov.–Apr. Wed.–Thurs. 4:30–9 P.M., $4–28) is one of the most popular in Maggie Valley and has a huge dining room and a menu that's almost as big. While they're well appreciated for their prime ribs and steak, their gorgonzola cheese salads are the best. If you want to eat on the lighter side, J. Arthur's also has a huge salad bar served with as many warm rolls with butter as you can stand to eat.

Grizzly Grill (2550 Soco Rd., 877/926-7440, www.thegrizzlygrill.com, $5–16) is best known for its barbecue, which you can have sweet, medium, or hot on more than a few of the menu offerings, from pork and chicken plates to pulled-pork sandwiches. The restaurant also serves steaks, burgers, and pizza.

INFORMATION AND SERVICES
Information

The **Haywood County Tourism Development Authority** (1233 N. Main St., Ste. 1-40, Waynesville, 800/334-9036, www.smokeymountains.net, Mon.–Fri. 9 A.M.–5 P.M.) is in Waynesville just down the road. Take Highway 19 north, and turn right on Highway 74/23, and follow the visitors center signs to downtown.

Emergency Services

Haywood Regional Medical Center (262 Leroy George Dr., 828/456-7311, www.haymed.org, 24 hours) in neighboring Clyde offers 24-hour emergency service.

Post Office

The **Maggie Valley Post Office** (4280 Soco Rd., 828/926-0679, Mon.–Fri. 8:30 A.M.–4:30 P.M.) is located right next door to the Jonathan Creek Inn on Highway 19.

GETTING THERE

To reach Maggie Valley from the south, take I-85 north to I-985 north, which becomes Highway 365/23 north. Then follow Highway 23/441 north to Dillsboro. At Dillsboro, take Highway 23/74 east to Waynesville/Maggie Valley. Take Exit 102B for Maggie Valley. If you're coming in From Asheville, take I-40 west. Take Exit 20 for Maggie Valley. From points west, take I-40 towards Asheville, but get off the interstate at Exit 20 before reaching Asheville.

Cherokee

While Cherokee has become more famous in recent years due to the addition of a Harrah's Casino to the town, the things you really don't want to miss here include the numerous museums, villages, and galleries providing insight into the heritage and history of the Cherokee Nation. The people who live here are the descendants of those who didn't take the Trail of Tears to Oklahoma.

The southern Appalachians have been home to the Cherokee and their early ancestors for thousands of years. At its height, prior to European contact in the mid-1600s, the Cherokee Nation consisted of 36,000 people occupying 140,000 square miles of territory in eight present-day southern states.

By the mid-18th century, many Cherokee had become farmers and sent their children to white schools, and some had even converted to Christianity. Most felt they were safe from encroachment by white settlers because of King George III's Proclamation of 1763, which stated that there would be no white settlement in the Appalachian Mountains and points west. By the 1780s, however, the U.S. Civilization Policy was in full effect with the intent of assimilating all Native Americans, including the Cherokee.

Prospects for the Cherokee went from bad to worse in 1835, when Major Ridge, without full approval of the Cherokee Nation or Chief John Ross, signed the Treaty of New Echota. The treaty allowed for the sale of the Cherokee homeland to the federal government for $5 million. In addition, all Cherokee were required to abandon their homes and move west to Indian Territory. Some 16,000 Cherokee, including Chief John Ross, made the journey. Some Cherokee, however, applied to become U.S. citizens, separated from the Cherokee Nation, and occupied their own privately owned reservation, what is today known as the Qualla Boundary. The current residents of North Carolina's Cherokee Indian Reservation are the descendants of those few who managed to stay behind.

Cherokee didn't gain its place as a tourist destination until the 1950s, when the Museum of the Cherokee Indian was founded. It was at this time that tourists began to see "roadside chiefs" in Cherokee, local men dressed in popularized Indian garb including elaborate headdresses. You can still find some of these "roadside chiefs" in town, as they continue their efforts to appeal to a visitor demographic that craves the popular over the realistic.

The Qualla Boundary is a prosperous, if touristy, place loaded with gift shops, restaurants, and hotels. The reservation covers 100 square miles, and some 14,000 members of the Eastern Band of the Cherokee currently reside here.

Most visitors travel into Cherokee via Highway 19 from Maggie Valley, coming across Soco Gap, an area that is loaded with roadside fruit stands and junk shops, selling everything from boiled peanuts to overstock dishware.

SIGHTS
◖ Museum of the Cherokee Indian

The Museum of the Cherokee Indian (589 Tsali Blvd., 828/497-3481, www.cherokeemuseum. org, June–Aug. Mon.–Sat. 9 A.M.–7 P.M., Sun. 9 A.M.–5 P.M., Sept.–May daily 9 A.M.–5 P.M., adults $9, children 6–13 $6, 5 and under free) is the place you should start your exploration of the Cherokee Indian Reservation. This well-organized museum provides a good overview of the Native American history of the mountains of western North Carolina beginning with exhibits on the Paleo Indians who lived in the area during the last Ice Age. The museum traces many Cherokee traditions and crafts, including the tribe's well-known and beautiful basket weaving, to origins as early as 7500 B.C. There are many examples of woven and coiled baskets on display as well as dozens of examples of historic Cherokee pottery and effigy bowls, which are made in the shapes of humans or animals.

Among the museum's most interesting exhibits is one on Sequoyah, the only recorded historical figure to have created a complete writing system without having first been literate in another language. Sequoyah took the Cherokee's native tongue and developed a written language from it. Take a few moments to listen to the Cherokee alphabet, and see if you can follow the complex characters, each one of which stands for a syllable. Sequoyah, who was the son of a white father and a Cherokee mother, completed his writing system in 1821.

The Cherokee, in fact, developed their own newspaper in the written language that Sequoyah developed, and you can view an 1870 Cherokee printing press here as well.

The Museum of the Cherokee Indian also briefly reviews the story of William Holland Thomas, a 12-year-old white orphan who moved to the Oconaluftee River region of western North Carolina and was adopted by a Cherokee Chief called Yonaguska or Drowning Bear. Yonaguska and his people applied for U.S. citizenship under the Treaty of 1817 once they saw removal would otherwise

GROWING MATERIALS FOR ART

While the average visitor to Cherokee doesn't think about it, most of the Cherokee crafts one sees for sale in the town are made using natural local resources, from clay to oak trees. But some of the natural resources on which the Cherokee depend to make their beautiful and functional wares are fading from the landscape.

Among them is the butternut tree, which the Cherokee have used for generations as a source of both dye for baskets and textiles and wood for carving. The butternut has been subject to a blight similar to that of the American chestnut, so the local Qualla Arts and Crafts Mutual has partnered with the University of Tennessee to re-establish butternut trees on the reservation. They have developed a blight-resistant butternut and have begun planting its seedlings in the town of Kituwah with seedlings also available for locals to plant in their yards.

Local craftspeople are also encouraging their neighbors to plant river cane, which is used in the crafting of many of the beautiful Cherokee baskets you'll find at the Qualla Arts and Crafts Mutual and other shops in town. River-cane habitat has shrunk over recent decades to 2 percent of its original size, so today Cherokee artists and residents are planting the cane for a dual purpose – to supply local art and to promote soil conservation and stream restoration.

Carolina in 1866. The federal government acknowledged the Eastern Band two years later, establishing today's reservation out of lands purchased by Thomas. You can read the fictionalized version of the story in Charles Frazier's *Thirteen Moons*, which is available for purchase in the museum gift shop along with a host of other books on Cherokee history, culture, and language, including Cherokee-English dictionaries and a Cherokee-language version of *Thirteen Moons*.

The museum gift shop also sells locally made Cherokee handicrafts as well as T-shirts and souvenirs. On the lawn of the museum is an example of the Cherokee Bear Project, which features the artistry of more than a dozen local artists who have painted bears to represent the landscape, history, and heritage of the Smoky Mountains. In front of the Museum of the Cherokee Indian is "Sequoyah Syllabeary," a bear painted to resemble Sequoyah, the creator of the Cherokee alphabet.

Oconaluftee Indian Village

The Oconaluftee Indian Village (Drama Rd., 866/554-4557, May–Oct. daily 9 A.M.–5 P.M., adults $15, children 6–12 $6, 5 and under free) is located on a hillside just above the Museum of the Cherokee Indian and interprets an 18th-century Cherokee community. The outdoor living-history museum has a variety of costumed interpreters demonstrating everything from basket weaving and beadwork to finger weaving and pottery making.

The village also features a model of a partially underground sweathouse and replicas of 1700s log homes like those in which the Cherokee would have lived. The most interesting demonstration here is probably the canoe-making process, where interpreters burn out the shell of a canoe from a log with the slow but effective use of fire. Burning out the hull of a canoe in this way typically takes six months, but it saved on the backbreaking labor that would have been required of manually digging out the wood. Throughout the day interpreters hold scheduled talks on Cherokee life and customs as well as hold demonstrations of

be inevitable. Young Thomas ultimately became an attorney and advocated for Yonaguska and his tribe, even going so far as to gain them some of the funds the Cherokee received under the Treaty of New Echota. It was Yonaguska's people as well as some Cherokee who hid in the mountains and escaped removal that ultimately formed the Eastern Band of the Cherokee. They were formally recognized as their own distinct nation by the state of North

© FRENCH C. GRIMES

craft demonstration at Oconaluftee Indian Village in Cherokee

traditional dance and battle reenactments. The village also offers hands-on classes in pottery and basketry at the outdoor village classroom for $35 per person.

The one problem here is that the interpreters do not volunteer information on the history of their crafts or the process of their work, making the experience a rather flat one for visitors who aren't comfortable enough to ask questions on their own. You can elect to take a guided tour of the village (adults $20, children 6–12 $12, 5 and under free), which are offered daily on the hour between 10 A.M. and 4 P.M. But be sure to ask about these tours at the ticket booth, as no one is likely to volunteer information on them.

The village has a small gift shop at the exit where you can purchase crafts made by village interpreters.

SHOPPING

Cherokee is in many ways a nostalgic place. Apart from the casino and the ever-growing sprawl of new chain hotels and restaurants, the town adjacent to the Oconaluftee entrance to the Great Smoky Mountains National Park has changed very little. There are gift shops by the dozens here. Most of them, however, carry the same standard fare—T-shirts, shot glasses, Minnetonka moccasins, and jewelry (most of it from the American Southwest, not from local craftspeople). You can purchase some locally made pottery and basketry in many of these shops, but places focusing on locally made native crafts are few and far between. Be prepared, however, when you do find locally made crafts. Years ago you could purchase Cherokee baskets and pottery for very low prices, but today crafters know their worth, and even small items can be on the pricey side.

◖ Qualla Arts and Crafts Mutual
The Qualla Arts and Crafts Mutual (645 Tsali Blvd., 828/497-3103, www.cherokee-nc.com, June–Aug. daily 8 A.M.–7 P.M., Sept.–Oct. daily 8 A.M.–6 P.M., Nov.–May daily 8 A.M.–4:30 P.M.) is located across the street from the Museum of the Cherokee Indian and is a must-see even if you don't plan to buy any local crafts. The shop has a large gallery showcasing both historic and current Cherokee crafts. Many of the works on display have been created by local, living artists whose biographies are recounted alongside their artistry in clay, basketry, and wood. Take the time to admire, in particular, the intricacy of the patterns and perfect handiwork of the river-cane mats and baskets on display as well as the double river-cane baskets made extra sturdy for carrying heavy loads and sometimes even water.

The Qualla Arts and Crafts Mutual also has three rooms devoted to displays of crafts for sale, all of them locally made by native Cherokee. The shop represents the work of over 350 tribal members. Here you can purchase river cane, white oak, and honeysuckle baskets of all sizes, a wide array of the beautiful and simple Cherokee pottery from wedding vases to effigy bowls, smooth wood carvings, cedar bead necklaces, handmade dolls, beautiful beadwork belts and sashes, and finely woven textiles.

CHEROKEE AND MAGGIE VALLEY

Other Shops

The **Native American Craft Shop** (1847 Tsali Blvd., 828/497-6790, www.greatsmokiesart. com, daily 9:30 A.M.–6 P.M.) is on Highway 441 on the left as you approach the national park entrance. The Native American Craft Shop carries many locally made Cherokee baskets of pine needle, river cane, and white oak, as well as Cherokee-made pottery. In addition, the store carries Native American crafts from all over the United States, including deerskin shirts, hand-carved animals, turquoise jewelry, and books on Native American history and culture. The one problem with this beautiful shop is the poor customer service, and the same goes for their associated shop, the **Great Smokies Fine Arts Gallery** (6 Acquoni Rd., 828/497-5444, www. greatsmokiesart.com, daily 10 A.M.–6 P.M.), which carries limited-edition fine-art prints, upscale rustic and unusual home furnishings, Native American artwork and crafts, and also provides custom framing. The gallery is located in the Great Smokies Center across the road from the Best Western.

Bearmeat's Indian Den (4210 Wolfetown Rd., 828/497-4052, www.bearmeats-indianden.com, daily 9 A.M.–6 P.M.) is an Indianowned and -operated store featuring a wide array of locally made Cherokee crafts as well as Cherokee healing herbs and herb-based skin-care and health products. The store also has a farmers market carrying hoop cheese, country ham, honey, jams, jellies, peanuts, and pickles. Bearmeat's is located on Highway 19 north in Cherokee.

Though one mile south of downtown Cherokee, **The Old Mill 1886** (3082 U.S. 441 N., 828/497-6536, www.cherokeemill.com, Mon.–Sat. 10 A.M.–5 P.M., open Sat. only in winter) is worth a visit and is one of the newest retail establishments in Cherokee. This oldtime country store carries antiques, Civil War and Indian artifacts, locally made Cherokee crafts from over 60 artisans, corn meal, cheeses, and preserves. You can still see the mill's authentic grinding equipment, though the mill is no longer operational.

ENTERTAINMENT AND EVENTS

(Harrah's Casino

Added to the Cherokee landscape in 2007, Harrah's Cherokee Casino & Hotel (325 Paint Town Rd., 828/497-7777, www.harrahscherokee.com, 24 hours) has drawn a fair amount of traffic away from other worthy attractions in the town. Nevertheless, the casino has helped the Eastern Band of the Cherokee prosper, as it helps fund tribal initiatives like the building of new schools and community buildings and services. The Eastern Band owns the casino; Harrah's only manages it.

The casino features over 80,000 square feet of round-the-clock gaming space with some 3,300 games. Those include a wide array of slot machines, video poker, live digital blackjack, and baccarito. Even if you're not into gaming, Harrah's is the best spot in town for entertainment. The 1,500-seat pavilion draws big names in music and comedy with headliners like Willie Nelson, Martina McBride, Kenny Rogers, Big & Rich, and Tom Jones. Check the website for upcoming shows, and call 866/370-3705 to order tickets.

The casino also has its own hotel, five restaurants, and retail shops with many package deals available that combine gaming with an overnight stay.

(Unto These Hills

The popular outdoor drama *Unto These Hills* (Drama Rd., 866/554-4557, June–Aug. Mon.–Sat. 7 P.M., adults $18–22, children 6–12 $8–10, 5 and under free) has been a Cherokee tourist attraction since 1950 when the Mountainside Theater first opened. The evening drama recounts the history of the Cherokee from first contact with Europeans through the romanticized story of Tsali, the legendary Cherokee hero who hid from the authorities during the removal to the Indian Territory and died fighting to remain in his homeland.

The actors in this beloved outdoor drama are not actors at all but descendants of the Cherokee who held onto their North Carolina homeland. While you're waiting for the show to begin, take note of the Cherokee Eternal Flame, which burns continuously just off-stage. The flame was lit from coals brought from a similar eternal flame maintained on the Cherokee Reservation in Oklahoma to which the original caretaker of the "sacred fire" was banished along with most of the rest of the Cherokee people on the Trail of Tears in 1838 and 1839.

You can order tickets by phone, on the website, or pick them up at the main box office at the intersection of Drama Road and Tsali Boulevard. The ticket office is open Monday–Saturday 9 A.M.–4 P.M. You can also purchase tickets at the Mountainside Theater from 4 P.M. until showtime.

Festivals

The town of Cherokee holds more than a dozen festivals throughout the year, most of them occurring at the Cherokee Indian Fair Grounds adjacent to the Museum of the Cherokee Indian. One that is a true local event is the **Ramp It Up Festival,** which is held each year in March to coincide with the opening of trout season. Those who attend will feast on both mountain trout and local ramps, enjoy local music and craft vendors, and watch horseshoe tournaments.

In May and October, the town hosts **"Cruise the Smokies" Spring Cherokee Rod Run,** a gathering of vintage vehicles from Model Ts to Stingrays. In July, the **Festival of Native Peoples and Cherokee Art Market** fills the fair grounds with Native American vendors from all over the southeast as well as with dancing, storytelling, and singing performances. For more information on Cherokee events, visit www.cherokee-nc.com.

SPORTS AND RECREATION
Hiking
◖ MINGO FALLS

- Distance: 0.2 miles one-way
- Duration: 20 minutes

Mingo Falls

© DEBORAH HUSO

- Elevation gain: Minimal
- Difficulty: Easy
- Trailhead: Just before entering the park from Cherokee on Highway 441, take a right onto Big Cove Road. Go 5.2 miles to Mingo Falls Campground, and turn right. You'll see the sign for the trailhead upon entering the campground.

If you want to see one of the Great Smoky Mountains' beautiful waterfalls without the effort of a strenuous hike, the trail to Mingo Falls is perfect. It's also one of the few easy trails in the Smokies that isn't mobbed with visitors and is a great stroll for young children as well. The hardest part of the trail is the 170 steps you have to climb at the outset, but after that the trail slopes gently upward alongside a tumbling stream.

The trail is prettiest in June and July when the mountain laurel and then the rhododendron are in bloom. The trail is rocky but short,

CHEROKEE AND MAGGIE VALLEY

and after curling around a large rock ledge on the left, the falls will rise immediately in front of you. Step up onto the bridge in front of the falls, which roll along alternately wispy and rushing vertical paths for a breathtaking drop of 120 feet into Cove Creek.

Fishing

The Cherokee Indian Reservation provides some often-overlooked opportunities for trout fishing. The reservation has over 30 miles of trout streams as well as three trout ponds, and waters throughout the Qualla Boundary are restocked with brook, rainbow, and brown trout twice weekly. The trout are raised at the **Cherokee Tribal Hatchery** (Big Cove Rd., 828/497-5520, Mon.–Fri. 8 A.M.–4 P.M.), which welcomes visitors.

The open season for Enterprise Waters (tribally stocked trout streams) is from the last Saturday in March until the last day in February. Those public fishing areas include Raven Fork from its confluence with Straight Fork downstream to the Oconaluftee River and then down the Oconaluftee to the reservation boundary at Birdtown. Bunches Creek and the fish ponds in Big Cove as well as Soco Creek on U.S. 19 are also open to public fishing. All other waters are not open to public fishing and can only be fished by members of the Eastern Band of Cherokee Indians.

A good place for family fishing is the **Oconaluftee Islands Park,** which is right in the center of town adjacent to Highway 441. A popular destination for picnicking, swimming, and fishing, the park is always loaded with activity. Situated on a small island in the middle of the Oconaluftee River, it's a good place to bring the kids, though perhaps not the best spot for peace and quiet. The park has public restroom facilities.

If you want to fish on the Cherokee Indian Reservation, you must purchase a tribal fishing permit. A one-day permit costs $7. For more information on where to purchase permits and for a map of fishing areas, contact the **Fish & Game Management Enterprise of** **the Eastern Band of the Cherokee Nation** (800/438-1601).

Golf

You might be surprised to learn that the Cherokee Indian Reservation has its own 18-hole golf course beneath the peaks of the Smokies, but it does. Opened in 2009, **Sequoyah National** (79 Cahons Rd., 828/497-3000, www.sequoyahnational.com, daily 8:30 A.M.–7:30 P.M., $65–110) is a Robert Trent Jones II–designed course located three miles from Cherokee in nearby Whittier. The course has rental clubs available, a pro shop, a driving range, and golf lessons.

ACCOMMODATIONS

Cherokee is one of those places where you're generally better off going with the chain hotels rather than the mom-and-pop operations, most of which are beginning to show their age. You'll find more modern furnishings and amenities in some of the newer chain hotels. If you're looking for a bed-and-breakfast experience, then check out the options in nearby Dillsboro or Bryson City.

Hotels

Harrah's Cherokee Casino & Hotel (777 Casino Dr., 828/497-7777, www.harrahscherokee.com) is probably the nicest place to stay in town, particularly if you like being close to the action. The hotel has 576 rooms, including 29 luxury suites. Hotel guests can enjoy an on-site fitness center, indoor pool and hot tub, and free parking in the casino's garage. The 15-story hotel is actually quite beautiful, with walls of glass to take in the views of the Smoky Mountains. The lobby with its soaring ceilings and stone fireplace displays a vast collection of contemporary Cherokee art. There are also five restaurants on-site.

Best Western Great Smokies Inn (1636 Acquoni Rd., 828/497-2020, www.greatsmokiesinn.com, $55–119) is located in the midst of downtown Cherokee adjacent to Sacunooke Village on Highway 441 north; it has convenient access to shopping and dining and is close to the Oconaluftee entrance to the Great Smoky Mountains National Park. The hotel has 152 rooms available as well as a restaurant, Myrtle's Table, on-site. Guests can enjoy use of the outdoor pool in season, and continental breakfast is provided free November through March. The hotel also offers a free shuttle to Harrah's Casino.

Fairfield Inn and Suites (568 Painttown Rd., 828/497-0400, www.marriott.com/fairfieldinn, $99–189) has 100 rooms and suites, continental breakfast, and high-speed Internet. **Comfort Suites** (1223 Tsali Blvd., 828/497-3500, www.comfortsuites.com, $60–159), with 91 rooms, offers continental breakfast, and an outdoor pool and hot tub.

Hampton Inn (185 Tsalagi Rd., 828/497-3115, www.cherokeehampton.com, $59–139) is located on Highway 19 south and has 67 rooms, all with high-speed Internet access. All guests enjoy a hot breakfast bar and free shuttle to Harrah's Casino. In the same neighborhood on Highway 19 south is the **Holiday Inn** (37 Tsalagi Rd., 828/497-3113, www.hicherokeenc.com), which has 154 rooms available, all with free high-speed Internet access. The hotel also has indoor and outdoor pools, a fitness center, and the Chestnut Tree Restaurant on-site.

Camping

Great Smoky Mountains RV and Camping Resort (17 Old Soco Rd., 828/497-2470, $30) has 251 sites available, including hookups. **Indian Creek Campground** (1367 Bunches Creek Rd., 828/497-4361, www.indiancreekcampground.com, tent sites $27–31, cabins $50–135) offers fishing access on the stocked tribal waters of Bunches Creek right from your campsite—if you are lucky enough to have a creekside site. The campground has 68 campsites, most with sewer hookup, though creekside sites do not have sewer hookups. They also have a playground, camp store, laundry, and dump station. Reservations recommended, especially for creekside sites. Cabins are also available.

Yogi in the Smokies (317 Galamore Bridge Rd., 828/497-9151, www.jellystone-cherokee. com, campsites $27–62, rental cabins $55–169) is a Jellystone Park camping resort with riverside campsites and 31 rustic rental cabins, some of them pet friendly. There are 152 sites, as well as a heated pool, fishing, camp store, and laundry.

Cherokee KOA (92 KOA Campground Rd., 828/497-9711, www.koa.com/where/nc/33173, $33–54) has more than 200 sites, as well as indoor and outdoor pools, hot tubs, and saunas. They offer mini-golf, an outdoor movie screen, fishing, and many more activities.

River Valley Campground (2978 Big Cove Rd., 828/497-3540, www.cherokeesmokies.com/rvcampground, $25–35) has 73 full hookup sites, and 42 tent sites with water and electric; 45 of the sites are seasonal. Guests can tube, swim, and fish in the Raven Fork River, which flows through the campground. River Valley also has a camp store, recreation room, laundry, and cable TV.

FOOD

Myrtle's Table (Hwy. 441 N. and Acquoni Rd., 828/497-2020, www.greatsmokiesinn.com/dining.html, Apr.–Nov., $9–20) is located at the Best Western Smokies Inn on Highway 441 and specializes in country-style cooking.

Brushy Mountain Smokehouse and Creamery (664 Casino Trail, 828/497-7675, www.brushymtnsmokehouse.com, daily 11 A.M.–9 P.M., $3–19) is the kind of place where, if you have room left after the lunch or dinner buffet piled high with smoked meats, endless sides, and a large salad bar, you've got a bigger appetite than most. But this place offers dessert, nevertheless—80 flavors of premium ice cream, to be exact. The ice cream is good, and it should be—it's made right at the restaurant. If you go for dinner, be sure to try the hickory-smoked St. Louis–style ribs. They are only available after 4 P.M.

Granny's Kitchen (1098 Painttown Rd, 828/497-5010, www.grannyskitchencherokee.com, Apr.–Nov. Tues.–Thurs. 11 A.M.–8 P.M., Fri.–Sun. 7 A.M.–8 P.M., $7–11) is a family-owned and -operated restaurant serving up classic southern home cooking served in a buffet style. The buffet menu changes daily, but don't worry—the fried chicken is on there everyday.

Sycamores on the Creek (777 Casino Dr., 828/497-8706, www.harrahscherokee.com, Sun. and Wed.–Thurs. 5–9 P.M., Fri.–Sat. 5–10 P.M., $8–42) is the newest restaurant at Harrah's Casino. They offer an excellent selection of steaks, chops, and seafood. Start with the jumbo shrimp cocktail, and then enjoy several southern tastes brought together in the pecan, pear, and blue cheese salad. Any of the steaks are a good bet for the main course, but the herb-encrusted lamb chops are excellent. If it is Friday or Saturday, place your bets on the prime rib.

Pizza Inn (920 Tsalagi Rd., 828/497-9143, www.pizzainn.com, June–Sept. Sun.–Thurs. 11 A.M.–10 P.M., Fri.–Sat. 11 A.M.–11 P.M., Oct.–May Sun.–Thurs. 11 A.M.–9 P.M., Fri.–Sat. 11 A.M.–10 P.M., $3–20) is a regional chain located in the Riverwalk at Riverbend shopping area. There isn't much in the way of atmosphere here—in fact you may see a dirty floor and experience lackluster service—but the pizza is consistently good, greasy and loaded with cheese just like pizza should be, and they offer a $7 pizza buffet at lunchtime as well as riverside seating both indoors and on the deck.

INFORMATION AND SERVICES
Information

The **Cherokee Welcome Center** (498 Tsali Blvd., 800/438-1601, www.cherokee-nc.com, daily 8:15 A.M.–5 P.M.) is located kitty-corner across the street from the Museum of the Cherokee Indian on Highway 19/441 and has brochures for area attractions, restaurants, and accommodations. Public restrooms are available here, and there is also a stop here for the Cherokee Transit.

Emergency Services

The **Cherokee Indian Hospital** (1 Hospital Rd., 828/497-9163) and the **Cherokee Police** (828/497-4131) provide emergency services.

GETTING THERE AND AROUND
Car

If you're traveling into Cherokee from the east, take I-40 west from Asheville to Exit 27 for the Great Smoky Mountains Expressway (U.S. 74). Continue on U.S. 74 to Exit 74, and take Highway 441 to Cherokee. If you're coming in from the Tennessee side, take I-40 east from Knoxville into North Carolina. Leave the interstate at Exit 27 (Great Smoky Mountains Expressway). Continue on U.S. 74 to Exit 74, and take Highway 441 to Cherokee.

Public Transportation

The Cherokee-Gatlinburg-Pigeon Forge Shuttle Service (866/388-6071, www.cherokeetransit.com, May–Sept. daily 8 A.M.–12:30 A.M., Oct. daily partial schedule, $7–14) offers four round-trips daily between Cherokee and the towns of Gatlinburg and Pigeon Forge on the Tennessee side of the Smokies. The route traverses the Newfound Gap Road through the Great Smoky Mountains National Park with a 10-minute stop at Newfound Gap for photos. Pickups and drop-offs occur at three locations: Cherokee Transit Ticket Booth in Cherokee, Gatlinburg Welcome Center in Gatlinburg, and Patriot Park in Pigeon Forge. Local transit service is available at all three pickup and drop-off locations.

Cherokee Transit also offers local service around town, running every half hour from 7 A.M. until 12:30 A.M. daily May through October. There are sheltered transit stops all over town. Fare is $1 each time you board or $2 for a full-day pass.

Bryson City

This quiet Main Street town at the lesser-known Deep Creek entrance to the Great Smoky Mountains National Park is the ideal place for travelers who want to take in the Smokies at a slower pace. There are a handful of lovely bed-and-breakfasts here, a soda fountain on Main Street, an old-time drive-thru on the edge of town (where waitresses still wear roller skates), and access to some of the less-traveled reaches of the national park. Bryson City also holds some claim to fame as the burial place of celebrated southern Appalachian writer and naturalist Horace Kephart, best known as author of *Our Southern Highlanders,* published in 1913, which detailed his experiences living among the people of the Smokies region. The book was somewhat unique for its time in that it did not portray the mountain people in a derogatory way. Later in life he was a tireless campaigner for the establishment of the Great Smoky Mountains National Park.

SIGHTS
Great Smoky Mountains Railroad
The Great Smoky Mountains Railroad (225 Everett St., 800/872-4681, www.gsmr.com, Jan.–Mar. adults $34, children 2–12 $19, Apr.–Sept. and Nov.–Dec. adults $49, children 2–12 $29, Oct. adults $53, children 2–12 $31) offers a variety of traveling options if you're interested in seeing Smoky Mountain scenery by rail. The train departs from Bryson City for gourmet dinner trains and mystery trains through the Smokies as well as for half- or full-day excursions into the Nantahala Gorge. Combination tickets that allow for a train ride and a white-water-rafting trip are also available. A variety of seating options are available, including 1920s coach seating, open-air cars, and club cars with cocktail tables.

Rafting excursion prices include round-trip train fare, lunch, an eight-mile guided white-water-rafting trip, and hot showers. If you're up for the rafting trip, this is a fun way to do it, and you'll likely enjoy the ride if you're a train enthusiast. If you're taking the ride exclusively to enjoy the scenery, however, skip it. Better scenery awaits on road trips in the Great Smoky Mountains National Park and surrounding national forests without having to sit passively on a train for more than four hours.

The railroad also has special holiday trips throughout the year, including Polar Express and Great Pumpkin Patch Express rides. Check the website or call for schedule information and details on special train rides and packages.

While you're waiting to board, consider paying a visit to **Smoky Mountain Trains** (100 Greenlee St., 828/488-5200, www.smokymountaintrains.com, adults $9, children $5), a museum adjacent to the Bryson City Depot with displays of over 7,000 Lionel engines, cars, and model railroad accessories.

SHOPPING
Most of the shopping in Bryson City can be found along Everett Street in the area of the Great Smoky Mountains Railroad station. While there are plenty of shops, there's nothing particularly noteworthy about any of them, as most tend to carry very similar selections of souvenirs and gifts. Among the options are the **Bryson General Store** (115 Everett St., 828/488-8010, Mon.–Thurs. 10 A.M.–6 P.M., Fri.–Sat. 10 A.M.–7 P.M., Sun. noon–5 P.M.), which carries upscale gifts including home decor, Vera Bradley items, clothing, shoes, and handbags. **Watershed Trading Company** (281 Everett St., 828/488-6006, www.watershedtrading.com, Mon.–Sat. 10 A.M.–6 P.M., Sun. noon–5 P.M.) specializes in rustic decor and woodsy home accents. **Madison's on Main** (110 Main St., 828/488-3900) carries upscale home accents, jewelry, specialty chocolates, and gourmet gifts.

The Cottage Craftsman (44 Frye St., 828/488-6207, www.thecottagecraftsman.com) is a Bryson City gem. Located in a cute yellow Arts and Crafts cottage near the train depot, it features only the work of local and regional artists, ranging from fine art and baskets to gourmet food.

ENTERTAINMENT AND EVENTS
Singing in the Smokies

Singing in the Smokies (1130 Hyatt Creek Rd., 828/497-2060, www.theinspirations.com, $15–20, children 12 and under free) is the largest gospel singing festival in the United States, and it takes place three times a year at Inspiration Park just off Highway 19 east of Bryson City. The event is hosted by The Inspirations, a Swain County–based southern gospel group that formed in 1964. While the faces have changed over the years this four-part harmony group's sound has not, and the group has been honored as America's Favorite Gospel Group six times; it's not unusual to hear them on national radio airwaves.

Singing in the Smokies festivals are held annually over Independence Day weekend, Labor Day weekend, and on the third weekend in October. You'll not only hear The Inspirations but several other well-known gospel groups, which may include The Sneed Family, Chuck Wagon Gang, and Land of the Sky Boys with Little Ernie Phillips.

SPORTS AND RECREATION
Rafting and Tubing

The **Nantahala Outdoors Center** (13077 Hwy. 19 W., 888/662-2199, www.noc.com) is probably the best-known river outfitter in the region and offers the greatest variety in both river offerings and difficulty levels in the western North Carolina region. The Nantahala Outdoors Center (NOC) is not just headquarters for white-water rafting operations, however. It is something of a village unto itself with three restaurants, a pub, lodging facilities, and even shopping. NOC has several outposts from which it launches river trips, but if you come to the main campus 20 miles outside Bryson City on Highway

74 west, you'll find yourself on the Nantahala River in the midst of the Nantahala River Gorge. This is good white water for family excursions, as it's exciting without being terrifying (Class II to Class III, $37–99). NOC also offers trips on the Chattooga with its Class IV and V rapids ($89–300), plus the Ocoee ($46–91), French Broad ($46–79), Cheoah ($135–149), Nolichucky ($22–109), and Pigeon River ($19–40). NOC also rents kayaks to independent river explorers, provides shuttle service, and offers other trips and courses such as fly fishing ($50–400), kayak fly fishing ($200–400), wilderness medicine ($149–1,950), and adventure photography ($500–550). River rafting is typically available from early spring through fall, though the season varies depending on the river and rainfall.

Rolling Thunder River Company (10160 Hwy. 19 W., 828/488-2030, www.rollingthunderriverco.com, raft with guide $34–37, guide-assisted $28–31, rental non-guided $18–21, single funyak $26–28, double funyak $24–26, high-performance funyak $30–32) also offers guided whitewater rafting trips on the Nantahala.

Tuckasegee River Outfitters (4909 Hwy. 74, 828/586-5050, www.tuckfloat.com, self-guided trips $10–25, guided trips $20–35) rents rafts, kayaks, or tubes for fun family-friendly floats down the gentle Tuckasegee River. Trips take 2–4 hours. Keep an eye out for wildlife: Spotting blue heron, kingfishers, or even bald eagles is not uncommon. There are rapids, but just enough to be fun, not serious white water. A nice touch is the free shuttle that takes you up the river at the start of your adventure, so when you get off the river you're at the outfitters and your car—no bus ride back in wet clothes. Dry off and check out the snack bar and gift shop.

J. J.'s Tubes (1651 Toot Hollow Rd., 828/488-3018, www.bjsdeepcreekrentals.com) is located just outside the Deep Creek entrance to the Great Smoky Mountains National Park, making it the most convenient tube rental option in Bryson City. It's not just lazy floating; there are also some fast sections along this mountain stream, as well as good spots to stop and swim. Rent a tube and ride Deep Creek as many times as you like.

Zip Line

If you're interested in trying out the new sport of zip-lining while in the North Carolina mountains, check out **Nantahala Gorge Canopy Tours** (10345 Hwy. 19 S./74 W., 877/398-6222, www.nantahalagorgecanopytours.com, $69). Located 12 miles west of Bryson City at the Falling Waters Adventure Resort, this zip-line outfitter offers nine zip-line sections on 20 scenic acres. You will probably be going too fast to notice, but the landscape through which you'll be zipping is loaded with mountain laurel, rhododendron, and flame azalea. All equipment is provided, including helmet and full-body harness. You'll also be accompanied by a canopy ranger. Participants must be at least 10 years of age and 70–250 pounds.

ACCOMMODATIONS
Inns and Bed-and-Breakfasts

The **《 Folkestone Inn** (101 Folkestone Rd., 888/812-3385, www.folkestone.com, $109–153) is located just minutes from the Deep Creek entrance to the Great Smoky Mountains National Park and is arguably the best lodging available in Bryson City. Nestled in a rolling pasture just beneath the peaks of the Smokies, this farmhouse has offered visitors a quiet escape for more than two decades. There are 12 rooms at the inn, all with different themes and decor. My personal favorite is the Wrens and Warblers room, an upstairs bedroom with private balcony decorated with bird prints, antique decoys, and fluffy flowered bedclothes and pillows. It's a perfect spot for avid bird-watchers, as it overlooks the feeders on the inn's north lawn. Antique claw-foot tubs abound here as well, and the Folkestone has an expansive front porch with porch swing and rocking chairs

providing a front-row seat to the evening chorus of bull frogs and scenes of summer fireflies. Breakfast is included with lodgings, and dinner is available on Friday and Saturday night with advance notice. The inn allows well-behaved and supervised children over 10. There is no smoking allowed indoors.

The **Hemlock Inn** (911 Galbraith Creek Rd., 828/488-2885, www.hemlockinn.com, rooms $144–196, suites $239–299, cabins $144–300) is a rustic country inn on 50 lovely acres on a mountaintop above Bryson City. The inn has 22 simple and comfortable rooms as well as three cabins available for rent. There are no TVs, but there are lots of rocking chairs for taking in the views.

Camping

There isn't much for campgrounds around Bryson City. Your best bet is going to be the National Park Service camping just inside the Deep Creek entrance to the park: **Deep Creek Campground** (800/365-2267, Apr.–Oct., $17) is located just north of Bryson City at the end of Deep Creek Road. Located just inside park boundaries, this campground has 92 sites, some along the scenic creek. Bathhouses are available, but no showers. This campground, despite its seemingly isolated location, is popular with locals, some of whom arrive early to have a better pick of campsites.

Deep Creek Tube Center & Campground (1090 W. Deep Creek Rd., 828/488-6055, www.deepcreekcamping.com, campsites $21–33, cabins $63–169) is located right on Deep Creek a mile from the national park entrance and offers tube rentals ($4 for all day) as well as full hookups and rustic cabins.

FOOD
Restaurants

For typical southern comfort food there are several options in Bryson City, including **The Station Restaurant** (225D Everett St., 828/488-1532, daily 8 A.M.–10 P.M., $4–20), which serves rotisserie-cooked meats and homemade desserts and has full bar. The

Bar-B-Que Wagon (610 Main St., 828/488-9521, Tues.–Sat. 11 A.M.–8 P.M.) offers hickory-smoked pit barbecue made on-site.

Standard Italian fare is available at **Anthony's Italian Restaurant** (103 Depot St., 828/488-8898, Sun.–Thurs. 11 A.M.–9 P.M., Fri.–Sat. 11 A.M.–10 P.M., $2–15). They have hand-tossed pizza, homemade Italian specialties, and subs.

The Filling Station Deli and Sub Shop (145 Everett St., 828/488-1919, www.thefillingstationdeli.com, Mon.–Sat. 10 A.M.–4 P.M., $3–7) lets you fill up with High Test—at least that's what they call the famous Cuban sandwich loaded with Cuban pork, ham, Genoa salami, and Swiss cheese. For lighter but equally pleasing options, ask about the quiche of the day or try the seasonal fruit plate with honey yogurt and homemade banana bread. As evidenced by the menu names, gas station memorabilia abounds. Save room for dessert, because right next door is **Soda Pops** (141 Everett St., 828/488-5379, www.sodapops.us, spring/fall Mon.–Sat. noon–8 P.M., summer daily noon–9 P.M.), which is Bryson City's 1940s- and '50s-themed soda fountain. Stop in to see the extensive collection of Coca-Cola memorabilia and enjoy a treat whipped up with Mayfield premium ice cream.

(Naber's Drive-In (1245 Main St., 828/488-2877) is one of my favorite stops in Bryson City. Apart from the sheer fun of being served by waitresses on roller skates (some of whom look as if they've likely been working here since the place opened), Naber's sundaes can't be beat. They're huge—order one with two spoons if you have company along. The drive-in also fronts the Tuckasegee River and is conveniently located on Highway 19 to Cherokee on the eastern outskirts of town.

Groceries

The **Bryson City IGA** (345 Main St., 828/488-2584, 8 A.M.–9 P.M.) has a good selection of groceries for campers and picnickers and is the only good-sized grocery store in town.

INFORMATION AND SERVICES
Information

The **Swain County Chamber of Commerce** (210 Main St., 828/488-3681, www.greatsmokies.com, Mon.–Fri. 9 A.M.–5 P.M.) has two locations in Bryson City, the main one on Main Street across from the Courthouse, and the satellite office in a caboose on Everett Street kitty-corner from the Great Smoky Mountains Railroad station.

Emergency Services

The **Swain County Hospital** (45 Plateau St., 828/488-2155) offers 24-hour emergency services and is located north of downtown off Richmond Street.

Post Office

The Bryson City post office (130 Slope St., 828/488-3481, Mon.–Fri. 9:30 A.M.–5 P.M., Sat. 10 A.M.–noon) is just north of Highway 19 in downtown.

GETTING THERE

If you're traveling into Bryson City from the east, take I-40 west from Asheville to Exit 27 for the Great Smoky Mountains Expressway (U.S. 74). Continue on U.S. 74 to Bryson City. If you're coming in from the Tennessee side, take I-40 east from Knoxville into North Carolina. Leave the interstate at Exit 27 (Great Smoky Mountains Expressway). Continue on U.S. 74 to Bryson City.

GREAT SMOKY MOUNTAINS NATIONAL PARK

Covering more than half a million acres, the Great Smoky Mountains National Park is the "great park" of the East, drawing some 10 million visitors annually. It is, in fact, the most-visited national park in the country. And while many perceive the Smokies as a "drive-through" destination since the park features only one major highway, this vast wilderness area is actually home to hundreds of miles of quiet back roads (paved and unpaved), some 800 miles of hiking trails, and 16 mountain peaks over 6,000 feet. The park is also home to more than 1,800 black bears, 80 Canadian elk, and some 100,000 living organisms, making it one of the most diverse collections of flora and fauna in the southern Appalachians. Its biological diversity is the major reason the park was named an International Biosphere Reserve and World Heritage Site.

The Smokies, which receive just over $1.50 in federal funding per visitor each year, depend heavily on donations and volunteers to keep the park running smoothly. The park's lack of personnel and inability to monitor visitor usage is sometimes painfully evident. This problem is most obvious at the park's numerous historic structures, which have been extensively vandalized over the years.

From residences and churches to old schools and mills, the park's historic buildings number over 90. Between 1925 and 1944, the states of North Carolina and Tennessee purchased over 6,600 tracts of land to create the Great Smoky Mountains National Park. While some of that land belonged to logging companies, many

© FRENCH C. GRIMES

HIGHLIGHTS

◖ Newfound Gap Road: This 30-mile scenic highway bisects the Great Smoky Mountains National Park and is the most popular route through the park, with long-distance views and streamside driving (page 202).

◖ Roaring Fork Motor Nature Trail: Offering a one-way loop tour of the old Roaring Fork community, this route takes drivers past Appalachian homesteads and bubbling streams (page 204).

◖ Cades Cove: One of the park's most popular areas, Cades Cove has the largest collection of intact historic Appalachian structures in the national park (page 204).

◖ Clingmans Dome: The highest point in the national park at 6,643 feet, Clingmans Dome has an observation tower offering 360-degree views (page 209).

◖ Alum Cave Bluffs Trail: One of the park's most popular hikes, the Alum Cave Bluffs Trail offers access to an unusual rock formation that makes it one of the most arid places in the east; the trail also provides some of the park's loveliest long-distance views (page 211).

◖ Fontana Dam: The highest dam in the eastern United States, Fontana is 480 feet tall (page 228).

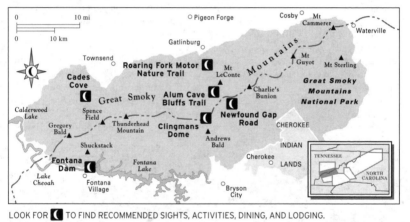

LOOK FOR ◖ TO FIND RECOMMENDED SIGHTS, ACTIVITIES, DINING, AND LODGING.

tracts were the farms, homes, and businesses of hundreds of mountain families. Almost since the park's establishment, the National Park Service has made extensive efforts to preserve some of the historic buildings to interpret the lives of the people who once lived here.

PLANNING YOUR TIME

While most visitors to the Great Smoky Mountains National Park give the park no more than a day's visit, focusing their exploration on an auto tour of the Newfound Gap Road, the only way to do the Smokies justice is

to spend at least three or four days here, more if you can spare the time. The park is a hiker's paradise with some 800 miles of trails, and most of the park's most scenic areas are accessible only if you get out and walk.

You can get a good overview of the park by spending one day in the Cataloochee Valley, home to the park's reintroduced elk as well as several historic Appalachian structures and quiet hiking trails, then another seeing the sights along the Newfound Gap Road, and then spending a third day either exploring the historic structures and trails of Roaring Fork or the more

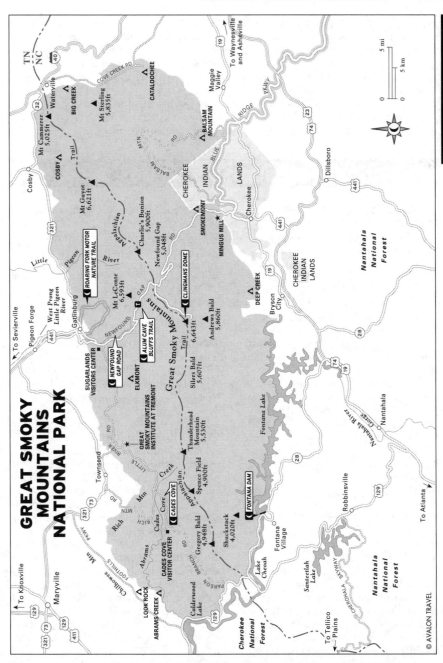

GREAT SMOKY MOUNTAINS NATIONAL PARK

© AVALON TRAVEL

popular Cades Cove. If you have more time and enjoy outdoor adventures, make plans for some day hikes. The park visitors centers have tons of resources on the Smokies' hiking trails.

The Great Smoky Mountains National Park is busiest in mid-summer and October, so if you want to avoid mobs of people (and I do mean mobs) but still wish to enjoy mild weather, consider visiting in spring or September. You can enjoy more open vistas as well as a lot fewer fellow travelers in the park if you visit in winter—as long as you don't mind the cold. If you do end up visiting the park in the high season and want to get away from the crowds, steer clear of the Newfound Gap Road and Cades Cove and opt for some of the park's many little-explored back roads or hiking trails instead.

Exploring the Park

Established in 1934, the Great Smoky Mountains National Park (865/436-1200, www.nps.gov/grsm, free) was the first of three National Park Service units to be established in the southern Appalachians during the Great Depression. The establishment of the Blue Ridge Parkway followed in 1935, and then in 1936, Shenandoah National Park, the Smokies' sister park in Virginia, was officially designated.

What is unique about these three parks is that, unlike the great parks of the West, all three were carved out of privately held land that was purchased by the states. In the case of the Smokies, most of the land that today makes up the national park was owned by logging companies, and much of the landscape here was heavily logged during the first third of the 20th century. In fact, by 1940, 65 percent of what is now the Great Smoky Mountains National Park had been logged.

The Smokies are something of an eastern rainforest in that they receive more than 80 inches of rainfall annually. This helps account for the park's diverse flora and fauna and its designation as an International Biosphere Reserve.

VISITORS CENTERS

The Great Smoky Mountains National Park has three visitors centers, one in North Carolina and two in Tennessee. The most easily accessible are the Oconaluftee Visitor Center on the Newfound Gap Road just inside the park at the Cherokee, North Carolina, entrance and the Sugarlands Visitor Center just inside the park on the Newfound Gap Road at the Gatlinburg, Tennessee, entrance. To make the most of your visit, especially if this is your first time in the park, pick up a Smokies Starter Kit for $5 at any of the visitors centers. The kit will provide you a road and trail map for the park as well as information on top day hikes and auto tour booklets for some of the park's most popular scenic drives.

Oconaluftee Visitor Center

The Oconaluftee Visitor Center (1194 Newfound Gap Rd., 865/436-1200, Nov.–Apr. daily 8:30 A.M.–4:30 P.M., May daily 8:30 A.M.–5 P.M., June–Aug. daily 8 A.M.–6 P.M., Sept.–Oct. daily 8:30 A.M.–6 P.M.) is the best place to begin your tour of the Great Smoky Mountains National Park if you're starting from the North Carolina side. The visitors center, which is two miles north of Cherokee on U.S. 441, has a small exhibit area detailing some of the early history of the park, an information desk, and a small bookstore. The current visitors center will soon be replaced by a new structure scheduled to open in 2011.

Sugarlands Visitor Center and Park Headquarters

The busiest information center in the park, the Sugarlands Visitor Center (1420 Little River Rd., 865/436-1200, Dec.–Feb. daily 8 A.M.–4 P.M., Mar. and Nov. daily 8 A.M.–5 P.M., Apr.–May and Sept.–Oct. daily 8 A.M.–6 P.M., June–Aug. daily 8 A.M.–7 P.M.)

is located off the Newfound Gap Road just inside the Tennessee entrance two miles south of Gatlinburg. The visitors center has a natural-history museum that provides an overview of the park's flora, fauna, and geology. There is also an introductory surround-sound film running here throughout the day as well as a large bookstore carrying volumes on just about anything you'd want to know about the Smokies.

Cades Cove Visitor Center

Located about halfway around the popular Cades Cove Loop Road on the western end of the park, the Cades Cove Visitor Center (Cades Cove Loop Rd., 865/436-1200, Dec.–Jan. daily 9 A.M.–4:30 P.M., Feb. and Nov. daily 9 A.M.–5 P.M., Mar. and Sept.–Oct. daily 9 A.M.–6 P.M., Apr.–Aug. daily 9 A.M.–7 P.M.) is 12 miles southwest of Townsend. The visitors center has all the brochures and maps you'll need to explore the park as well as a large bookstore.

PROGRAMS
Park Ranger Programs

Park ranger programs are held regularly at various locations throughout the park and include guided walking tours of historic areas like the Mountain Farm Museum along the Oconaluftee River or hands-on demonstrations at park visitors centers about the wild creatures that call the Smokies' home. Ranger programs also include guided nature and native plant walks and early-morning hayrides around Cades Cove.

The Cades Cove Visitor Center, in particular, offers some fun programs in peak season, including blacksmithing demonstrations, musical entertainment, and basket-making demonstrations. Night hikes are available as well, some of them to the top of Clingmans Dome. Campground amphitheaters regularly host ranger talks and musical entertainment.

For a complete and updated list of ranger programs available in the park, including dates and times, pick up a copy of the Smokies Guide at any park visitors center.

Programs are seasonal, starting in the spring and continuing through summer and fall.

Junior Ranger Program

If you have kids in tow, be sure to stop by one of the national park visitors centers and inquire about the Junior Ranger Program. Most of the visitors centers have Junior Ranger booklets for sale ($2.50 each) with various offerings dependent on your child's grade level. The books offer various activities for children to help them learn about leaf identification, park history, and how to look for particular flora and fauna while traveling around the park. Kids who complete their Junior Ranger booklets are formally inducted as Junior Rangers by a park staff member and get a Junior Ranger badge free of charge.

The park also offers ranger programs geared specifically to kids, many of them hands-on learning experiences. Among the offerings are a blacksmithing workshop at the Mountain Farm Museum adjacent to the Oconaluftee Visitor Center where kids will get a chance to make their own dinner bell, as well as wading programs where kids can get their feet wet in park streams while looking for salamanders and water insects.

The *Smokies Guide,* available for free at all park visitors centers, has a schedule of all Junior Ranger programs available.

Smoky Mountain Field School

The Smoky Mountain Field School (865/974-0150, www.outreach.utk.edu/Smoky, Mar.–Oct., $9–155) offers a more in-depth way to explore the richness of the Smokies and obtain a greater understanding and appreciation of the mountains' flora and fauna, landscape, and beauty. Partnering with the University of Tennessee, the Great Smoky Mountains National Park offers one- and two-day programs from spring through fall in a variety of subjects, including the edible and traditional plants of the Smokies, insects of the Smokies, stream life, wildflower identification, orienteering, search and rescue, and backpacking. The programs take place at various locations

GREAT SMOKY MOUNTAINS

throughout the park and require advance reservations; check website for availability and to register. Programs are primarily for adult learners, but several family programs are offered that are appropriate for children 6–12.

ENTRANCE STATIONS

The Great Smoky Mountains National Park is unusual among the nation's parks in that it charges no entrance fee. Friends of the Smokies have donation boxes at Cades Cove, Newfound Gap, Cataloochee, Clingmans Dome, Deep Creek, and Roaring Fork Motor Nature Trail as well as at the three in-park visitors centers. The money they collect supports various park programs and services. Past projects include over a million dollars in support of ongoing efforts to combat the hemlock woolly adelgid, donation of hybrid vehicles to the park, purchase of a search-and-rescue vehicle for the park, and various other conservation and preservation efforts.

The park has 17 points at which you can enter the park by automobile, though the vast majority of those entrances are via gravel roads. If you're up for an adventure, aren't on a schedule, want to enjoy driving the park without experiencing traffic and crowds, and want to see some of the backcountry without hiking, consider some of these less-traveled, if slower, routes.

DRIVING TOURS

For better or worse, the vast majority of visitors to the Great Smoky Mountains National Park barely get out of their cars except to take pictures at overlooks. You can increase your enjoyment of the park's many driving tours by taking some time to explore the history behind what you're seeing and to experience some hikes along the way, too. Even if you're not physically able to do much hiking, consider enjoying one of the park's many **Quiet Walkways,** designated pathways through the woods at various stops along the park's roads that range from a few hundred feet to several miles. Most of them are level, easy walks that let you get close to nature without a lot of physical effort. Watch for the Quiet Walkways signs as you drive around the park.

◖ Newfound Gap Road

The Newfound Gap Road is the most popular route for visitors to take through the park. It extends 30 miles from Cherokee to Gatlinburg and takes about half a day to drive if you take the time to visit some of the sites along the way.

Your first stop along the Newfound Gap Road, also known as Highway 441, will be the Oconaluftee Visitor Center, where you can pick up park maps and guidebooks. Adjacent to the visitors center is the Mountain Farm Museum, where you can explore several original historic structures representing farm life in the Smokies at the turn of the 20th century. You can also access the level and scenic 1.6-mile Oconaluftee River Trail from here, which goes all the way into the town of Cherokee and makes for a leisurely and easy stroll.

Mingus Mill is the next stop along the Newfound Gap Road. It was one of the first historic structures to be restored in the park, and it became an attraction here in 1937, after CCC workers completed its restoration. It is one of 80 such historic structures in the park.

As you travel the first several miles of the Newfound Gap Road, notice that the Oconaluftee River parallels the road to your right. Occasional pull-offs will give you the opportunity to take pictures of this scenic river that was sacred to the Cherokee Indians, many of whom still live on the Cherokee Indian Reservation adjacent to the national park's Oconaluftee entrance. Consider getting out of your car and spending some time enjoying the sounds of rushing water. Notice the variety of flora along the river, including yellow birch trees, the pointed green leaves of the doghobble vine, hemlocks, and lady ferns.

After you've traveled about seven miles, you'll come to the first of several Quiet Walkways along the Newfound Gap Road. Most of these walkways offer short strolls through the woods and the opportunity to get away from the traffic that can often be found on the Newfound Gap Road in summer and fall.

Soon you'll begin to climb, entering a higher elevation landscape with occasional scenic views. If you're wondering about all the gray, dead trees on the mountainsides, these are eastern hemlocks, which are under attack by the invasive hemlock woolly adelgid. The park has some 137,000 acres of hemlocks, most of which will soon be gone forever.

About halfway through your journey on the Newfound Gap Road you'll come to the Oconaluftee Valley Overlook (parking area on the left). Views from this overlook as well as others in the park are not always very clear. The Great Smoky Mountains National Park has, in fact, the worst air quality of any national park in the country, and not all of the haze you'll see is the natural cloud drift for which the park is named. Some of it is the result of air pollution from power plants and automobiles.

At about 16 miles into your journey, a spur road off to the left leads to Clingmans Dome (6,643 ft.), with an observation tower at the summit.

Once you return to the Newfound Gap Road the way you came in on the Clingmans spur road, your next stop will be the overlook at Newfound Gap on your right. At 5,048 feet it is the highest point on the Newfound Gap Road and is probably the most-visited spot in the park.

As you descend on the Newfound Gap Road, you'll find yourself following the course of the West Prong of the Little Pigeon River. There are numerous pull-offs that provide access to the river for photography, fishing, or even wading.

Just before you leave the park, you'll have one last scenic overlook at mile 27: The Campbell Overlook, with views of Mount LeConte (6,593 ft.).

As you end your journey along the Newfound Gap Road, passing through a forest of red maples, white oaks, tulip trees, and dogwoods, remember that this landscape was once cleared for farming, home to the prosperous Sugarlands Valley community. Today the forest has reclaimed the land, demonstrating

HOW TO FIND THE BEST FALL COLOR

Visitors flock to the Great Smoky Mountains National Park for its spectacular autumn color displays, easily making fall the park's busiest season. During peak fall weekends it is not unusual to find traffic jams along the park's main roads. The result, unfortunately, can be a rather unpleasant fall color-viewing experience.

Because most visitors to the park view autumn's colorful stage show from their cars, just getting out and taking a walk can put distance between you and the swarm of visitors. Keep in mind that fall color can be found anytime between mid-September and early November in the Smokies because of the park's varying altitudes. Color begins in the higher elevations in September and gradually descends down the mountainsides. Thus, one doesn't have to visit the park in mid-October to see spectacular shows of autumn leaves.

To find a little peace and color in October, try a walk along the Oconaluftee River Trail with trail access at the Oconaluftee Visitor Center on the Newfound Gap Road just west of Cherokee. A stroll along the Chasteen Creek Falls Trail, accessible from the Smokemont Campground, also offers delightful glimpses of autumn leaves, as do any of the trails veering off from the Deep Creek Campground, which is located on Deep Creek Road 2.5 miles north of Bryson City.

Some of the most spectacular specimens for fall viewing are found in middle to lower elevations, like the sugar maple, which can range in color from rich scarlet to orange and yellow. Tulip poplars also dominate the Smokies, often blanketing whole mountainsides with dazzling yellow leaves. If you stroll along streams or in other damp areas you may see sweet gums, late bloomers in the fall season, that display star-shaped leaves in luscious purple, red, and yellow, often on the same tree.

how quickly nature takes over when man's influence is removed.

◖ Roaring Fork Motor Nature Trail

The Roaring Fork Motor Nature Trail is one of my favorite drives in the park. To reach it turn onto Historic Nature Trail–Airport Road at traffic light #8 in Gatlinburg, and follow the signs. Just before you enter the national park to start on your loop drive, you'll notice Mynatt Park to your right, a lovely place to picnic right alongside Twin Creeks. This is a safe and fun place for children to fish, and it also has a nice streamside picnic area with restrooms.

Before you actually reach the start of the one-way five-mile loop tour, you'll travel a little ways on Cherokee Orchard Road, which, in the 1920s and '30s, was a commercial orchard covering nearly 800 acres. Once you reach the start of the loop tour, you'll have the opportunity to purchase an auto tour booklet from a roadside exhibit for $1.

The Motor Nature Trail passes through a dense hardwood forest (keep your eyes open for black bear, particularly if you're traveling early in the morning or just before dusk), with the first stop being at Ogle Place, a two-room cabin surrounded by rocky ground and rhododendron thickets. Although you'd never guess from looking at the rustic cabin, this was one of only a handful of homes at the turn of the 20th century that had running water, which the owners pumped into the house from the spring using wooden troughs!

Much of the Motor Nature Trail follows the old roadbed of the Roaring Fork community, which was built by hand in the 1850s and served as the road to the community of White Oak Flats (present-day Gatlinburg). Some 25 families lived along Roaring Fork. As you climb up and through the cove hardwood forest, roll down your windows and take in the sounds of the woods. There are two overlooks along the trail that offer nice views, though they're getting increasingly overgrown each year.

If you enjoy hiking, there are two waterfall hikes accessible from the Roaring Fork Motor Nature Trail. The first climbs almost three miles to Rainbow Falls and is fairly strenuous. The second is a more moderate hike to Grotto Falls, a waterfall you can actually walk behind.

The real treat along this route, besides the opportunity it provides to simply get away from the crowds and enjoy a leisurely drive, is the access to the old homeplaces. As you descend on the trail and the road begins to parallel the beautiful cascading stream of Roaring Fork, you can visit three more residences, including the homes of Jim Bales, Ephraim Bales, and Alfred Reagan.

Be sure to park and get out and explore these three homesites. You'll be amazed, in particular, at how the Ephraim Bales Cabin seems to be plotted right in the midst of a boulder field. It was something all the residents here contended with, and it made farming a challenge.

As you gradually descend toward town again, be sure to note the Thousand Drips Falls to your left. Though not a spectacular cascade, it's an unusual one with multiple thin streams of water coursing over the face of the rock. Also, make a point of stopping at Ely's Mill at the end of the trail. Built in the 1920s, the mill was not used to grind corn or wheat but rather the waterwheel powered the equipment in a woodworking shop that was once located here. Today, the mill is a shop selling locally made crafts and Appalachian antiques.

Stay on the Roaring Fork Motor Nature Trail as it exits the national park and follow it back to Highway 321 in Gatlinburg. Note that the Roaring Fork Motor Nature Trail is closed during the winter.

◖ Cades Cove

Cades Cove is the most popular loop auto tour in the Great Smoky Mountains National Park. The route is accessible by taking Little River Road west from the Sugarlands Visitor Center for 25 miles or by entering the park at Townsend on Highway 73 and then taking a right on Little River Road and going 16 miles to the Cades Cove entrance. The loop tour is

11 miles, but you should allow at least two hours for the trip, more if you plan to spend some time exploring the historic structures along the way or taking some hikes that veer off the loop. This auto tour is most popular in the hour or so before sunset, so if you want to avoid the crowds visit early in the morning or even midday (though you're most likely to see wildlife in early morning or evening).

If you take the tour during peak visitation hours, be prepared for slow going and be respectful of others on the loop tour by pulling off onto the shoulder if you want to stop and take pictures or observe wildlife. It's often the drivers who just stop in the middle of the road that make the Cades Cove loop a sometimes-nightmare to drive. If you do get sick of the backup there are two opportunities along the drive where you can take a road off to the left and shorten your loop tour.

Cades Cove is undoubtedly the best place in the park to see wildlife. You can be almost guaranteed sightings of white-tailed deer and wild turkey, no matter the time of day. And black bears are a common sight here as well.

Look for them in the branches of old apple trees, where they and their cubs often laze away the afternoon.

As you drive along, enjoy the scenery. This is one of the most beautiful areas of the park accessible by car, with hazy blue mountains rising up above the valley floor where fields are often a rich gold when viewed in evening light. The Park Service has maintained the rural nature of the cove, keeping mowed and fenced fields so that the community here looks much as it would have at the turn of the 20th century.

Among the numerous tour stops along the way is the Methodist Church, the most photographed structure in the park. Stop your car, climb the steps into the church, and imagine yourself in another time. Many visitors have left little hand-written prayers on scraps of paper at the altar, and weddings are still held here on occasion. Behind the church is a quiet cemetery. As you walk the grounds, notice how many children's graves there are, indicative of an era when infant mortality was high.

About halfway around the loops is the Cades

© FRENCH C. GRIMES

Cades Cove, one of the most beautiful areas of the park accessible by car

© FRENCH C. GRIMES

cantilever barn in Cades Cove

Cove Visitor Center, which has a large gift shop with books on the history of the Smokies, the region's flora and fauna, and outdoor recreation. Also here are the only public restrooms available on the loop tour.

Alongside the visitors center is the Cable Mill Area. This is the busiest section of the loop tour—if people get out of their cars only once in Cades Cove, it will be here. Nevertheless, take some time to explore the historic structures here, including the Cable Mill, where you can buy cornmeal and whole-wheat flour ground on-site. In high season, there will be an interpreter at the mill demonstrating how it works.

The other key feature of the Cable Mill Area is the Gregg-Cable House, built in 1879 by Leason Gregg, who purchased land for his home from John P. Cable.

Around the Gregg-Cable House you will see the usual features of a mountain farm, all of which are original but moved to this site from other places. They include a smokehouse, corn crib, sorghum mill, and a drive-through barn that allowed farmers to pull their wagons inside and pitch hay directly into the loft in short order. You'll also see a cantilever barn; this construction method originated in Europe centuries ago and its deep overhangs allowed farmers to provide shelter to both animals and farm equipment.

As you continue your loop tour around Cades Cove you'll see three more homes, including the Dan Lawson Place, Tipton Place, and Carter Shields Cabin. As you drive this section of the loop tour, keep your eyes on the open fields to the north on the left-hand side of the road. There are many old apple trees here, and it's not uncommon to see a bear and maybe even her cubs taking an afternoon nap in the trees.

After you pass Sparks Lane on your left, you'll continue the loop back to where you started near the entrance to Cades Cove Campground. Consider stopping by the camp store for an ice cream cone before heading on your way.

Cades Cove is closed to vehicle traffic until 10 A.M. on Wednesday and Saturday mornings, when it is available for exclusive use of bicyclists.

Newfound Gap Road

This is the most heavily traveled route through the Smokies, being the main byway between Cherokee and Gatlinburg, and in summer months it's not unusual to experience traffic jams here. Nevertheless, for anyone new to the Smokies the Newfound Gap Road remains the best option for getting a good overview of the park and also provides access to some of its most famous features, including Clingmans Dome, the highest point in the national park.

The route the current Newfound Gap Road follows has provided passage over these mountains in some form or another for centuries, though residents of these mountains didn't realize that Newfound Gap at 5,046 feet was the lowest pass through the mountains until 1872. The name of the gap comes from the discovery by Swiss geographer Arnold Henry Guyot, for whom the park's second-highest peak is named, that the "newfound" gap provided

easier passage than the previously used Indian Gap more than a mile west.

A drive along the Newfound Gap Road will take you on a tour that covers some 3,000 feet in elevation, allowing you to experience the varied forest types of the Smokies as well as the differing temperatures wrought by vertical climate.

SIGHTS
Oconaluftee Visitor Center and Mountain Farm Museum

The Oconaluftee Visitor Center and Mountain Farm Museum (865/436-1200, Nov.–Apr. daily 8:30 A.M.–4:30 P.M., May daily 8:30 A.M.–5 P.M., June–Aug. daily 8 A.M.–6 P.M., Sept.–Oct. daily 8:30 A.M.–6 P.M.) will likely be your first stop as you explore the sights along the Newfound Gap Road if you're entering the park from the North Carolina side. At the visitors center you can pick up park maps and guides as well as view exhibits on the people who lived and worked in what is now the Great Smoky Mountains National Park before its establishment in 1934. The park service recently broke ground on a new Oconaluftee Visitor Center, which will open sometime in 2011. The public restrooms in the current visitors center are in the basement, accessible only by going outside and around to the back of the building.

Be sure to spend at least a few minutes exploring the Mountain Farm Museum adjacent to the visitors center via a short walk alongside the Oconaluftee River. You can pick up a walking-tour map for $1 at the visitors center or from a covered box at the start of your walk. The first structure you'll notice on your tour of this outdoor museum is the farmhouse, which was originally constructed by John Davis about 1900. Also on-site here are a meathouse, blacksmith shop, corn crib and gear shed, apple house, and a barn. The barn is the only structure here original to this site alongside the Oconaluftee River; all the other

© FRENCH C. GRIMES

view from Newfound Gap

structures were moved here to create the outdoor museum.

During peak tourist seasons, living-history interpreters will likely be present at the farmhouse demonstrating early-20th-century cooking techniques and talking to visitors about life on an Appalachian farmstead before the establishment here of the national park. You'll also likely see hogs in a pen near the barn. Most farm families kept hogs both because they were easy to raise, often foraging in the forest, and because they typically produced several litters each year. Farmers generally captured hogs in the fall, fattening them up in pens before butchering.

As you leave the farm notice the split-rail fence to your left. Split-rail fences were common in the mountains because they were sturdy and could be built without digging holes for posts, an important feature in soil that was rocky. Few farmers fenced livestock; rather fences were used to keep livestock out of gardens and fields.

Mingus Mill

About a half mile west of the Oconaluftee Visitor Center is Mingus Mill (daily 9 A.M.–5 P.M., Mar. 15–Nov.). The mill is operational and open to visitors from spring through fall and is accessible via a short walk from the mill parking area. Built in 1886, Mingus Mill operated for nearly 50 years, grinding corn into meal and wheat into flour for local farmers.

If you step inside the mill, you can watch corn and wheat being ground by large millstones. You can even purchase cornmeal or whole-wheat flour ground at Mingus Mill to take home with you as an edible souvenir!

Mingus Mill is not powered by a waterwheel; rather it has always operated under the power of a turbine. The mill race sends water flowing into the turbine, where it pours down inside the turbine tower, generating the power to turn the gears and millstones. Shortly after Mingus Mill was restored in the late 1930s, local miller John Jones operated the mill on a lease from the National Park Service until the early '40s when the mill closed down for a second time.

view from the Webb Overlook on the Newfound Gap Road

© FRENCH C. GRIMES

The park service reopened the working mill as an attraction in the late 1960s.

Webb Overlook

About 13 miles from the Oconaluftee Visitor Center (17 miles if you're traveling from the Sugarlands Visitor Center), you'll come to the Webb Overlook on your left. The elevation here is about 4,500 feet. From here you'll have your first good view of Clingmans Dome, the park's highest peak, to the northwest.

Deep Creek Valley Overlook

In another mile is the Deep Creek Valley Overlook, which is one of the park's most popular, as it offers long-distance views of pristine wilderness as far as the eye can see. This view looks to the southwest into the roadless wilderness of the Deep Creek Valley.

Oconaluftee River Valley Overlook

At the halfway point on the Newfound Gap Road is the Oconaluftee Valley Overlook. The parking area is to the left, but the vast view is across the road looking to the southeast. Here you'll see the deep cut of the valley formed by the Oconaluftee River and the forces of both erosion and plate collision. Before you leave this overlook, consider spreading a blanket and having a picnic under the lovely birch trees whose silver papery trunks line the edge of the parking lot.

◖ Clingmans Dome

As you approach the highest area of the Newfound Gap Road, a spur road off to the left will take you on a seven-mile side trip to Clingmans Dome, the highest peak in the park and also the highest mountain in Tennessee at 6,643 feet. A short but steep half-mile trail will take you from Clingmans parking area to an observation tower at the summit. On a clear day you can enjoy 360-degree views, even seeing as far as Mount Mitchell. However, don't be surprised if you're fogged in, as the peaks of the Smokies seem to spend most of their time in the clouds. But wait a little while if you can: The weather here is ever changing, and a fog can drift away in a matter of minutes.

Newfound Gap

The Newfound Gap overlook is the most visited spot in the park, and if motorists get out of their cars at one place, this will be it. The elevation here is 5,048 feet, the highest point on the Newfound Gap Road.

The first thing you'll notice as you enter the overlook parking lot is the Rockefeller Memorial to your left. This simple stone terrace commemorates the $5 million donation the Rockefeller Foundation made to help the states of Tennessee and North Carolina purchase the land to create the Great Smoky Mountains National Park.

President Franklin D. Roosevelt dedicated the national park at Newfound Gap in 1940. The memorial actually straddles the state line between Tennessee and North Carolina, and the Appalachian Trail passes through here as well.

Take some time to enjoy the view from Newfound Gap. You'll likely see the Smokies'

signature haze settling in the folds of the mountains. Notice the stone walls that line the overlook, most of them built by Civilian Conservation Corps workers in the 1930s. More than 4,300 CCC boys worked in the park during the Great Depression.

You might notice it's a bit cooler here than at the park entrances—in fact, you can expect temperatures at Newfound Gap to be at least 10 to 15 degrees cooler than in Cherokee or Gatlinburg.

Morton Overlook

Situated at an elevation of 4,837 feet, the Morton Overlook affords an incredible view of the V-shaped valley of the West Fork of the Little Pigeon River. You can probably also see the Newfound Gap Road twisting away below you on its way to Gatlinburg. Also look for the twin peaks of Chimney Tops to your left. You can hike to the top of Chimney Tops on a steep trail requiring hand-over-hand climbing from the trailhead, which is eight miles from the Sugarlands Visitor Center and accessible from the Newfound Gap Road.

River Pull-Offs

Between the Sugarlands Visitor Center and the trailhead for Alum Cave Bluffs along the Newfound Gap Road are many pull-offs that allow you to pause and take in the sounds and sights of the West Prong of the Little Pigeon River. Even in summer the water is a chilly 55 degrees, allowing it to act as an air-conditioner for the surrounding landscape. If you're visiting the park in early to mid-summer you'll probably be treated to gorgeous displays of Rosebay rhododendron along the river, but even if you're traveling outside of bloom season, enjoy the dark-green foliage of the riverside thickets.

Campbell Overlook

About three miles from the Sugarlands park entrance in Tennessee is the Campbell Overlook, which offers views of Mount LeConte. With an elevation of 6,593 feet, LeConte is the third-highest peak in the Smokies and also the *tallest*

West Prong of the Little Pigeon River along the Newfound Gap Road

mountain east of the Mississippi in that it rises over a mile from its actual base to its summit.

Sugarlands Visitor Center

The Sugarlands Visitor Center (865/436-1200, Dec.–Feb. daily 8 A.M.–4 P.M., Mar. and Nov. daily 8 A.M.–5 P.M., Apr.–May and Sept.–Oct. daily 8 A.M.–6 P.M., June–Aug. daily 8 A.M.–7 P.M.) is the most heavily visited in the park and has a large exhibit area on the park's geology, flora, and fauna. While you're here, consider taking a stroll along the 1.9-mile Gatlinburg Trail, which departs the visitors center near the restrooms. This is one of only two trails in the park where pets are allowed, and it makes for a nice nature stroll, being mostly level, as it wends its way through the woods and along the West Prong of the Little Pigeon River.

HIKING
Clingmans Dome

- Distance: 1 mile round-trip
- Duration: 30–45 minutes
- Elevation gain: 330 feet
- Difficulty: Moderate
- Trailhead: At the Clingmans Dome parking area located seven miles off the Newfound Gap Road via a spur road just east of Newfound Gap (the spur road is closed Dec.–Mar. each year)

The hike to Clingmans Dome is probably the most popular short hike along the Newfound Gap Road. Clingmans is not only the highest peak in the park but also the highest mountain in Tennessee at 6,643 feet. A short but steep half-mile paved trail will take you from Clingmans parking area to an observation tower at the summit. Even though the trail to the summit is paved and wide, it's still strenuous because of the extreme elevation gain in a short distance, so don't think this will be an easy stroll.

As you hike, notice the surrounding landscape of thick undergrowth and stunted and windswept trees. You may be surprised, if you're visiting Clingmans Dome in summer, at the richness of life on the summit. Wildflowers by the thousands line the path, and in late summer you can pick sweet wild raspberries along the trail.

GREAT SMOKY MOUNTAINS

© DEBORAH HUSO

While it's possible to experience incredible long-distance views from Clingmans Dome, don't be surprised if you're fogged in. Because of its high elevation the mountaintop is often blanketed in haze, and you may only be able to see a few feet in front of you.

The observation tower at the summit rises 45 feet above the surrounding landscape, allowing you to rise above the tree line for 360-degree views on a clear day.

At the top of the tower, the National Park Service has signage to help orient you with diagrams of the surrounding mountains. If you're lucky and arrive here on a clear day, you may be able to see the highest peak east of the Mississippi, Mount Mitchell (6,684 ft.), which is just north of Asheville, North Carolina.

You may be alarmed by the tree die-off on the summit of Clingmans Dome. The forest here is mostly spruce-fir, and invasive species and air pollution have both taken their toll on the trees. The invasive balsam woolly adelgid has killed more than 70 percent of the Smokies' Fraser firs, and you can see their silvery skeletons stretching away in all directions. Pollution plays a role, too. The Smokies receive the highest deposits of sulfur and nitrogen in the form of acid rain of any other national park in the United States. Rain on the high summits like Clingmans Dome has five to ten times the acid content of natural precipitation. Much of that acid moisture arrives here in the form of cloud cover, though Clingmans also receives an astounding 82 inches of rainfall each year.

◖ Alum Cave Bluffs Trail

- Distance: 11 miles round-trip

- Duration: 7–8 hours

- Elevation gain: 2,560 feet

- Difficulty: Strenuous

- Trailhead: Alum Cave Bluffs Trailhead parking area on the Newfound Gap Road 8.6 miles from the Sugarlands Visitor Center

The Alum Cave Bluffs Trail is one of the most popular in the park, with good reason.

The five-mile hike to the summit of Mount LeConte (6,593 ft.) offers an ever-changing landscape of mountain streams, unusual rock formations, and long-distance views. If you plan to hike this trail come early, as the two parking areas fill up quickly.

The first stretch of the trail makes a moderate climb through mature northern hardwood and hemlock forest, and you'll be amazed by the size of some of the trees here. The path parallels Alum Cave Creek and is lined with an abundance of rhododendron thickets, which are profuse with white and pink blossoms in mid-June and July.

The first mile and a half of the trail offers many lovely views of small cascades tumbling over rocks. As you hike along, look for salamanders—the park has 27 species. Salamanders love the Smokies' temperate rainforest climate. The easiest to spot will be the black-bellied salamander, which often grows longer than six inches.

At about 1.5 miles, you'll come to a feature known as Arch Rock, which is less an arch than a narrow tunnel formed by centuries of freeze and thaw conditions on this mountainside. Several stone steps lead right through Arch Rock, and after this landmark you'll notice the trail begins to climb more steeply and steadily. As the elevation changes, so does the forest around you, which begins to display more spruce and fir trees.

After another half-mile of climbing you'll reach an area known as Inspiration Point, which affords views of steep, jagged, and boxy slopes often enveloped by streaks of fog. The landscape has changed to one of heath balds and is more open with scrubby undergrowth, including mountain laurel and blueberries. You'll also see abundant evidence of landslides on the surrounding slopes.

The halfway point of this trail is at Alum Cave Bluffs. These arching rock formations create a rain shelter that is less a cave than an overhang that allows them to have such an arid climate in their shadow that precipitation never reaches the dry and dusty soil beneath them. Among the unusual minerals that

GREAT SMOKY MOUNTAINS

© DEBORAH HUSO

stream along the Alum Cave Bluffs Trail, one of the park's most popular trails

can be found at Alum Cave Bluffs is oxalate, a rare mineral that occurs only in the world's most arid climates, making this spot quite an anomaly. Even if it's pouring rain, you'll never feel moisture here. So even though the Smokies are one of the wettest places on the East Coast (Mount LeConte receives over 80 inches of precipitation a year), Alum Cave Bluffs is one of the driest.

The vast majority of hikers turn around at Alum Cave Bluffs and head back to their vehicles, but if you have the time and energy, keep going. Your journey will be rewarded. The trek becomes more consistently steep and challenging as you proceed past Alum Cave along narrow rock ledges, often using the assistance of steel cables to pull your way along. But as you hike, you'll enjoy ample long-distance views (if it's not raining!), revealing slopes devastated by hemlock die-off as well as your first opportunity to see the summit of LeConte.

As you hike, pause to notice the rhododendron, doghobble, and lush green ferns along the path to help take your mind off the steady steep climb, which will persist for most of the remaining two miles to the summit. The last steep section of trail will require you to climb

along narrow rock ledges, then you'll emerge into a spruce forest so dense it will seem like dusk even in the middle of the day. Take note of all the colorful mushrooms, richly growing lichen and moss, and small gnarled trees. This is also a good place to look for salamanders and snails.

Soon you'll intersect with the Rainbow Falls Trail, which leads you to the summit of LeConte in short order. Hopefully you've made reservations for an overnight stay at LeConte Lodge, the park's hike-in lodging facility. There is no electricity or running water available at the lodge, but there is hot food and propane-heated cabins, which after your hike will seem like a luxury.

If the weather is clear, you can easily see 60 miles from the summit. The best place for watching sunsets is Cliff Top, which is accessible via a spur trail from the lodge; if you're here for sunrise, hang out at Myrtle Point. Return via the same route.

HORSEBACK RIDING

The **Smokemont Riding Stable** (828/497-2373, www.smokemontridingstable.com, Apr.–Nov. daily 9 A.M.–5 P.M., $8–48) offers guided trail rides of one to 2.5 hours. The 2.5-hour ride departs at 9 A.M., noon, and 3 P.M. and takes you along Chasteen Creek to the Chasteen Creek waterfall. Wagon rides along the Oconaluftee River to the old Beck farmstead and back are also available. Riders do not have to be experienced, as basic instruction is provided in advance of all trail rides. Reservations for both the horse and wagon rides are preferred. The Smokemont Riding Stable, which is adjacent to the Smokemont Campground, also sells firewood and ice for campers.

On the Tennessee side of the Newfound Gap Road, the **Sugarlands Riding Stables** (865/436-3535, www.sugarlandsridingstables. com, mid-Mar.–May and Sept.–Nov. daily 9 A.M.–4 P.M., June–Aug. daily 9 A.M.–6 P.M., $25–50) also offers guided horseback rides of one, 1.5, or two hours. Loop trails will take you up through mountain terrain and then back down. You'll pass mountain creeks and see small cascades while you keep an eye out for the abundant wildlife.

CAMPING

The **Smokemont Campground** (800/365-2267, $17–20) is located off the Newfound Gap Road 3.2 miles from the Oconaluftee Visitor Center. It's open year-round, and reservations are required mid-May–October. The campground is shady and close to the Oconaluftee River and, like many of the park's campgrounds, exceedingly buggy in the summer months. The campground has restrooms with shower facilities as well as a dump station for RVs. There are 142 sites available. Firewood and ice are available for purchase at the Smokemont Riding Stable.

PICNICKING
Collins Creek Picnic Area

Located 4.9 miles from the Oconaluftee Visitor Center along the Newfound Gap Road, the Collins Creek Picnic Area is nice in that it offers a large picnic shelter for family gatherings but unpleasant in that its low-elevation forested location makes it a prime spot for mosquitoes and gnats in summer. Unless the weather is cool, you might want to plan your picnic lunch for a higher elevation. There are restrooms here, however.

Chimneys Picnic Area

On the Tennessee side of the Smokies, the Chimneys Picnic Area offers a pleasant place to lunch alfresco. Located on the Newfound Gap Road 4.6 miles east of the Sugarlands Visitor Center, the Chimneys Picnic Area has dozens of picnic tables, many of them overlooking the West Prong of the Little Pigeon River in a cove hardwood forest loaded with rhododendron and impressive large boulders. There are charcoal grills available as well as restrooms. Chimneys is easily the most pleasant and picturesque picnicking spot in the park.

Roaring Fork and Greenbrier Cove

Accessible just outside Gatlinburg, these two entrances into the Great Smoky Mountains National Park offer quiet auto tours along rambling streams as well as access to several waterfall hikes, preserved Appalachian cabins, and some escape from the crowds.

The Roaring Fork Motor Nature Trail is paved and one-way and provides a quiet retreat by foot or automobile as well as lots of opportunities for wildlife sightings. If you travel the route in early morning or in the evening, your chances of spotting one of the park's ubiquitous black bears rummaging through forest mast are pretty high, as this section of the park is known for its black bear sightings. The Motor Nature Trail meanders through a deep forest of sun-obstructing hemlocks, delicate tulip trees, chestnut oaks, maples, and glossy-leafed magnolias. The understory is thick with giant rhododendrons that cradle white rippling and sometimes roaring streams. You can spend as little as an hour puttering along this route or

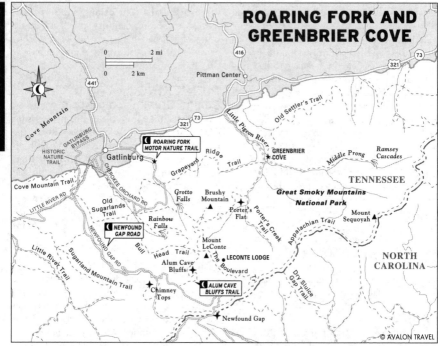

as much as a day if you care to explore one or more of the many hiking trails here.

The second half of the one-way Motor Nature Trail actually lies in the original road-bed of the 19th-century Roaring Fork community. Many original Appalachian homes are visible along this route and accessible via a short walk from the road.

ROARING FORK

The Roaring Fork area of the national park is accessible only from Gatlinburg by turning onto Airport Road at traffic light #3. This feeds directly into Cherokee Orchard Road, which hooks up with the Roaring Fork Motor Nature Trail after a couple of miles. Due to its abundant rainfall and temperate climate, the Roaring Fork area is mostly cove hardwood forest dominated by maple, white oak, magnolia, chestnut oak, and tulip tree. You will also notice a substantial hemlock forest here.

Most people come into Roaring Fork to explore the remnants of the small community that once thrived here. Originally settled in the mid-19th century, Roaring Fork supported a few tub mills, a store, a church, and a school. And all of it was located on a dead-end road, now part of the Roaring Fork loop.

Sights
OGLE PLACE

The Noah "Bud" Ogle Place is the first you will see along this trek, while still on Cherokee Orchard Road. An interpretive trail here with self-guiding brochures in a box next to the trail will guide you around this homestead that Bud and Cindy Ogle came to occupy in 1879. Reportedly a local land assessor said the property was not fit for farming, and if you take note of all the rocks around you, you'll easily see why. But the Ogles carved out a living here, even having running water brought

© FRENCH C. GRIMES

Alfred Reagan Place on Roaring Fork

into the house from a spring via a flume. In addition to subsistence farming, the Ogles also operated a tub mill.

EPHRAIM BALES CABIN

Once you've looped around the upper part of the Roaring Fork Motor Nature Trail, you'll come to the Ephraim Bales Cabin, a small dogtrot cabin built around the turn of the 20th century where Ephraim and Minerva Bales lived with their nine children. Notice again the rocks everywhere: The Bales owned 70 acres here and managed to farm 30 of them. You may find the cabin small and dark as you enter, but that's because windows and doors were viewed only as an opportunity for heat to escape in winter. The larger room here would have served as the main living area, while the smaller was the kitchen. Extra beds would have been placed in the dogtrot.

ALFRED REAGAN PLACE

The colorful Alfred Reagan house was once the home of a relatively prosperous farmer and entrepreneur who owned a mill, blacksmith shop, and store in Roaring Fork. While the exact date of the home's construction is unknown, the original log cabin of the home, which Reagan eventually covered with sawn boards, was likely built in the late 1880s or early 1890s. The house is readily recognizable by its blue and yellow doors, courtesy of early Sears and Roebuck paint. Reagan charged one gallon of corn per bushel to grind corn, a typical fee of the era, and was likely more successful than his neighbors because he worked so hard to diversify his income with many operations. Reagan's Mill is across the road from the house and is all that is left of the Reagan family's outbuildings.

Hiking
RAINBOW FALLS

- Distance: 5.5 miles round-trip

- Duration: 4 hours

- Elevation gain: 1,600 feet

GREAT SMOKY MOUNTAINS

- Difficulty: Strenuous
- Trailhead: Rainbow Falls parking area on the Cherokee Orchard Road outside Gatlinburg. From town, turn onto Airport Road at traffic light #8 and follow signs to Cherokee Orchard.

While the Rainbow Falls Trail climbs all the way to the summit of Mount LeConte, most hikers here take the trail only to the falls and then return, which is no wonder—the hike is steep pretty much without relent and involves a lot of picking your way over rocks and tree roots. That being said, if you're in good shape this can make for a worthwhile hike after a good rain when the falls are spilling over at full throttle.

The first part of the trail passes through what was once an 800-acre orchard loaded with 47 varieties of apple trees and maintained by its owner, M. M. Whittle, for more than two decades under a lease agreement after the park was established.

The higher you hike, the greater becomes the distribution of boulders throughout the woods, making it look something like a cemetery for giants. Take note of LeConte Creek to your right as you ascend. There are many lovely cascades encased in showers of rhododendron thicket. You will also see a lot of large deadfall in these woods, most of them fallen eastern hemlocks brought down by the hemlock woolly adelgid.

You'll know you're getting close to the falls once you start crossing log foot bridges over the creek. The third bridge is just below Rainbow Falls, and if you hike a little further the falls will come into view. Rainbow Falls is not a spectacular gushing cloud of water but rather a thin vertical spire dropping straight down from the top of a cliff. It is actually prettiest in winter, especially if you are fortunate enough to come after a long stretch of cold days that freeze the water into an otherworldly hourglass.

Unless you wish to continue another 3.5 miles to the summit of LeConte, you can turn around at this point and return via the same route.

GROTTO FALLS

- Distance: 3 miles round-trip
- Duration: 2 hours
- Elevation gain: 500 feet
- Difficulty: Moderate
- Trailhead: Grotto Falls parking area on the Roaring Fork Motor Nature Trail

A less-strenuous waterfall hike from the Motor Nature Trail is the Grotto Fails Trail. From the parking area, the trail climbs relatively gently for about 500 feet through a deeply shaded forest of virgin hemlock. Conifer needles cushion the wide path, as it winds through the increasing diversity of maples, ghostly beeches, and silverbells.

You might run into some llamas on this trail, as this is the route used to supply the hike-in LeConte Lodge on the summit of Mount LeConte, and a roped train of llamas makes this trek as many as three times a week loaded down with supplies.

A mile and a half in, 25-foot-high Grotto Falls is a treat for kids of all ages because you can walk right under the falls and mute the world as you stand behind the water's deafening cascade. Don't worry, you won't get too wet, nothing more than a mist will settle over your clothes and hair.

MOUNT LECONTE

The only lodging facility within the national park, **LeConte Lodge** (865/429-5704, www.leconte-lodge.com, Mar.–Nov., adults $116, children $85, includes accommodations, dinner, and breakfast) is almost an attraction in itself. That's because the lodge is accessible only by hike, not by vehicle. It is located at the summit of Mount LeConte (6,593 ft.), the base of which is skirted by the Roaring Fork Motor Nature Trail, and consists of a gathering of rustic cabins with no electricity or running water but ample 60-mile views on a clear day.

Several of the hiking trails that veer off the Roaring Fork Motor Nature Trail provide access to LeConte Lodge, including the Bull

INVASIVE SPECIES ON THE RAMPAGE

It has become an all too common sight in the forests of the Blue Ridge and Smoky Mountains: the tall gray ghosts of hemlocks decimated by the hemlock woolly adelgid (HWA). Like non-native pests before it, including the famous chestnut blight at the turn of the 20th century, HWA threatens to overhaul significant portions of the Appalachian ecosystem. As you drive around Roaring Fork and Greenbrier Cove, in particular, you'll notice its influence on the forest landscape.

A tiny aphid-like insect, generally recognizable only by the woolly white sac in which it coats itself on the underside of hemlock needles, HWA was first discovered on the East Coast in the 1950s. It eventually showed up in Shenandoah National Park in Virginia in 1988, where it has since destroyed 95 percent of the park's hemlocks.

Until recently, foresters have depended on an insecticidal soap known as M-PedeR and soil injections consisting of a pesticide called MeritR to help fight HWA, but neither represents a long-term, practical, or financially feasible option for saving the hemlocks.

A biological solution, however, has been in the works for several years. Several southern universities, including Clemson, Virginia Tech, the University of North Carolina, and the University of Tennessee have been working diligently to raise and distribute predator beetles, another non-native species that feeds exclusively on HWA. The result has been hope for the Great Smoky Mountains National Park, which has 137,000 acres of hemlock forest. The park began working to treat its hemlocks with the help of predator beetles, insecticide injections, and spraying as soon as they saw evidence of the adelgid's presence.

The park's first release of predator beetles occurred in May 2002, but it will be years, most biologists say, for the predator beetles to reproduce on a scale large enough to suppress HWA on their own. Thus far, the Park Service has released 400,000 predator beetles in the park.

While hemlocks may not be an economically valuable tree species, their value to the forest ecosystem is substantial. A common sight along streams, hemlocks regulate ground and water temperatures year-round with their thick canopies. Native brook trout, for example, are quite dependent on hemlocks for shade and cool water. Some species of warblers are known to nest only in hemlocks.

In places where hemlock die-off has been substantial, invasive plants like garlic mustard are coming in to take its place, creating yet another round of problems. The National Park Service has treated over 100,000 hemlocks, through soil or direct injections, along roadsides and in old-growth conservation areas. An additional 400 acres of trees have been treated with insecticidal soap.

For more information about the hemlock woolly adelgid, visit www.saveourhemlocks.org.

Head Trail, Rainbow Falls Trail, and Trillium Gap Trail. Trillium Gap Trail is on the route that the lodge llamas hike three times a week to bring in supplies. The shortest route to the summit is the Alum Cave Bluffs Trail accessible from the Newfound Gap Road, but this is also the route with the most elevation gain in the shortest distance. The Boulevard Trail, which comes in off the Appalachian Trail from Newfound Gap, is generally regarded as the easiest trek to the lodge, but also the longest at eight miles.

LeConte Lodge has a long history. It was built in 1934, before the national park was officially established, and has served as an overnight base for hikers ever since, resting as it does on the fourth-highest mountain east of the Mississippi.

There are no hot showers here, but every cabin comes with a bucket for sponge bathing that you can fill up with hot water from the single hot-water spigot at the lodge kitchen. There are flush toilets available in a separate building. Supper is the same every night. It's hearty hiker's fare—beef tips in brown gravy, mashed potatoes, green beans, spiced apples, cookies, and hot cocoa or coffee—who cares about calories after hiking at least five miles uphill to get here? In the morning, breakfast is equally as ample with pancakes, eggs, Canadian bacon, grits, and biscuits.

If you're accustomed to sleeping in a tent or a trail shelter, LeConte Lodge will be the ultimate in luxury. However, if you prefer hotel rooms with 400-count sheets and cushy mattresses, this place might feel a little bit like hell, with bunk beds in cramped drafty cabins with wire over the windows to help deter the bears. But chances are that after you've made the hike up here you'll just be glad for a dry place to sleep.

If you'd like to stay here, plan well in advance. The lodge easily books up a year in advance, especially for weekends and during fall color season.

GREENBRIER COVE

Greenbrier Cove was one of many communities in what is now the national park. Members of the local Whaley family first moved into the cove in the early 1800s. They were later joined by the Ownby clan, and, at the height of its population, about two dozen families lived here, almost all of them Whaleys or Ownbys. Most families here engaged in subsistence agriculture, occupying small farms of 50 to 100 acres. If you're a Dolly Parton fan, you might find it interesting to know that the songstress's ancestors Benjamin C. Parton and his wife, Margaret, moved to the cove in the 1850s. Their descendants moved out of the cove when the national park came. Dolly is Benjamin Parton's great-great-granddaughter.

Greenbrier Cove is a bit north of the Roaring Fork area, accessible six miles north of Gatlinburg on Route 321 on the right. Greenbrier Cove Road is a dead-end road that follows the boulder-laden course of the Little Pigeon River for six miles. Lined with old-growth virgin red oak, hemlock, and maples, as well as thick leafy rhododendron stands, the road leads to a host of peaceful hiking trails, including the tough eight-mile round-trip trek to Ramsay Cascades and back.

Horseback Riding

Smoky Mountain Riding Stables (1720 E. Parkway, 865/436-5634, www.smokymountainridingstables.com, mid-Mar.–May and Sept.–Nov. daily 9 A.M.–4 P.M., June–Aug. daily 9 A.M.–6 P.M., $25–50) offers one- and two-hour trail rides into the national park around Greenbrier Cove. Either guided ride takes you up wooded trails along and sometimes through mountain streams. Chances are good you will see deer, turkey, or maybe a black bear. From Gatlinburg traffic light #3 go four miles east on Highway 321 north.

Hiking
PORTER CREEK TRAIL

- Distance: 1 mile one-way to Porter's Flat
- Duration: 1 hour
- Elevation gain: 300 feet
- Difficulty: Easy
- Trailhead: From U.S. 321 take the Greenbrier Cove Road 4.1 miles, park on the traffic loop, and look for gate and signs.

A nice little leg-stretcher, the Porter Creek Trail passes through a wildflower wonderland in spring and past old Appalachian homesites, cemeteries, and an Appalachian cantilever barn, testament to the people who once made these mountains their home.

At about 0.7 mile, you'll see a set of block steps leading up to the old Ownby Cemetery, which dates to the 1900s. Descendants of Greenbrier Cove residents still maintain the cemetery and sometimes replace headstones.

At approximately one mile you will come to Porter's Flat, site of the first settlements of Greenbrier Cove by the Whaley family. The old road that the trail has followed ends here.

If you opt to continue another 0.8 mile, the Porter Creek Trail leads to a waterfall, the soft and bridal veil–like Fern Falls. Return to the parking area via the same route.

Little River Road

Little River Road courses for about 13 miles along the banks of Little River between the park's Sugarlands Visitor Center near Gatlinburg and the park's Townsend entrance at Highway 73. This is often the route park visitors take to Cades Cove, which is located southwest of Townsend. This is a windy stretch of road and the going is slow, almost hypnotic, as you weave back and forth along the curling and scenic stream. But it's definitely worth a drive if you have the time, being the most scenic way to access Cades Cove as well as having a number of worthy sights to check out along the way, including the National Historic District at Elkmont and a number of pleasant hikes.

SIGHTS
Elkmont

The area where the Elkmont Campground is today located along Little River Road was originally begun as a logging town in 1908 by the Little River Lumber Company. The town quickly became a tourist destination, being especially popular with fishermen. In 1912 the Wonderland Park Hotel was built here, and cottages proliferated. The National Park Service granted cottage owners lifetime leases to their properties once the park was established and then continued to renew the leases in intervals of 20 years until 1992. Originally, the park service planned to tear down the hotel and cottages, but the area now known as the Elkmont Historic District is now listed on the National Register of Historic Places. The park service hopes to restore some of the older buildings, though the Wonderland Park Hotel has since collapsed.

The big attraction at Elkmont these days, however, is the synchronous fireflies that live there. As their name suggests, these fireflies synchronize their flashing patterns, though no one knows why they do it. The fireflies have become so popular here that during their expected peak flashing period each year the National Park Service closes the entrance to the Elkmont Campground to private vehicles (save for registered campers) between 5 P.M.

© FRENCH C. GRIMES

Little River

and midnight. The only vehicles allowed in are the trolleys from Gatlinburg that have been lined up specifically to take visitors in to see the natural light show! Trolleys leave from the Sugarlands Visitor Center. To find out when the next synchronous firefly show will likely be, call 865/436-1200.

Great Smoky Mountains Institute at Tremont

The Great Smoky Mountains Institute at Tremont (9275 Tremont Rd., 865/448-6709, www.gsmit.org) is a residential environmental learning center located along the Little River Road in the Great Smoky Mountains National Park. If you want to have a deeply enriching experience in the Smokies, then this is the way to do it. Tremont is a private nonprofit organization that works hand in hand with the National Park Service to provide workshops, youth and family camps, and programs that use the national park as an outdoor classroom. The institute offers environmental learning opportunities to children from elementary age to adult and also provides training for teachers as well as classroom curricula.

Courses here include multiple-night guided backpacking adventures, guided hikes with naturalists, Elderhostel hikes, geology workshops, photography workshops, bird-watching courses, and even courses in environmental interpretation. Tremont also offers a Southern Appalachian Naturalist Certification program. Camps and workshops run from 1 to 10 days, depending on the subject covered. Multiple-day offerings include meals and lodging at the institute. Tuition ranges from $25 to $950, depending on what courses you select. Advance reservations are required.

The Institute is easily accessible by taking the Townsend entrance into the park on Highway 73 and then turning right onto Little River Road. The Institute will then be on the left.

HIKING
Laurel Falls

- Distance: 2.5 miles round-trip
- Duration: 1.5 hours
- Elevation gain: 400 feet
- Difficulty: Moderate
- Trailhead: Parking area located 3.9 miles west of the Sugarlands Visitor Center on Little River Road

Laurel Falls is easily the most popular waterfall hike in the park, both because it is relatively short and easy, which most of the park's waterfall hikes are not, and because the trail is paved and can accommodate baby strollers. The first part of the trail is the steepest, making a gradual uphill climb through a forest of maples, pines, and mountain laurel, which will likely be in full bloom mid-June to early July.

The trail affords some lovely views into the Little River Valley and has a few resting benches along the trail, so you can sit and enjoy the scene if you like. The trail continues to climb around rock faces. You'll notice the trees are smaller here, as this area of the park was logged in the 1920s.

At 1.3 miles you'll reach the falls, which drop about 75 feet and form a lovely wide cascade. This is a popular spot, and you'll likely find it impossible to get a picture of the falls without people in it, as children and parents alike love to wade here and hop around from one rock to the other in the pool below the falls. You can return via the same route.

CAMPING

Elkmont Campground (800/365-2267, Mar.–Nov., $17–23) has 220 campsites, 55 of them located alongside the Little River. Reservations are required from mid-May through October. There is no dump station available.

Cades Cove

After the Newfound Gap Road, Cades Cove is the most popular section of the park, receiving about two million visitors annually. It is home to the park's largest collection of preserved Appalachian structures, including churches, homes, and barns. Cades Cove is stunningly beautiful and also one of the best places in the park to see black bears, but no matter what time of day you travel this road by car you'll often find bumper-to-bumper traffic. Enjoying the cove by bike is a much better option, and you can do so on Wednesday and Saturday mornings until 10 A.M., when the loop is closed to vehicular traffic.

Native Americans never lived in Cades Cove, though they frequently hunted here, camping

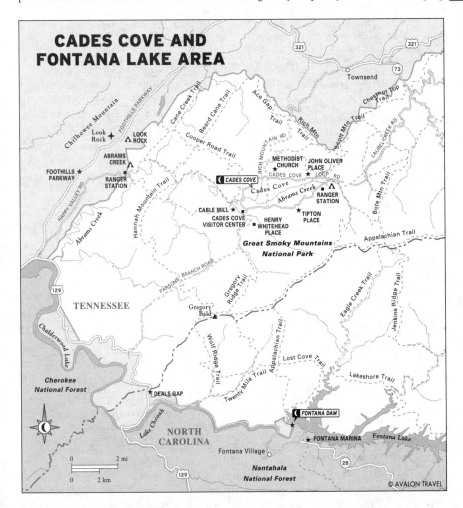

CADES COVE AND FONTANA LAKE AREA

© AVALON TRAVEL

BLACK BEARS:
THE SMOKIES' BIGGEST ATTRACTION

The Great Smoky Mountains National Park is home to about 1,500 black bears, and, not surprisingly, they represent the biggest attraction to park visitors. One of the most common places for seeing black bears in the Smokies is the Cades Cove Loop. Here, in early morning or just before dusk (and occasionally in the middle of the afternoon), black bears can be found lounging in apple trees or turning over rocks looking for insects at road's edge.

But even as the bears represent a delight to visitors, they can also represent a problem, especially when park visitors have little to no experience with wildlife.

Because a lot of bears in the Smokies have become accustomed to seeing people, many have lost their natural fear of humans. And bears that become accustomed to humans, especially humans who provide them with a food source, end up being problem bears. These are the bears that raid campers' food stores, break into vehicles, and approach visitors.

In 2000, two black bears killed a female tourist in the Great Smoky Mountains National Park near the Elkmont Campground. As far as park officials were able to tell, the unfortunate visitor did nothing to provoke the attack; she just panicked and ran. By the time the rangers got to her, it was too late. Neither of the bears had a history of problems, but because they attacked a human both were euthanized. Various Appalachian Trail shelter closures take place pretty much every year due to bear activity.

Black bears rarely attack humans and, unlike grizzlies, almost never attack in defense of food or young. But when black bears do attack, the attack is almost always predatory in nature. This was the case for the woman killed in the Smokies.

Since the early 1990s, black bear populations in the Smokies have been increasing steadily. That's mainly because oak forests in the region have been especially productive over the last couple of decades. Since acorns are a primary food source for black bears, their numbers have increased as well.

Park staff does their best to educate visitors in the hopes of eliminating the opportunity for bear-human conflict. As you tour the park, you may notice placards on picnic tables and in campgrounds, and advisories on the park radio station, advising you not to approach bears and to be wary of how you store food. Right now, backcountry hikers can camp only in designated areas and must store their food suspended between trees, away from the area where they sleep.

Remember to enjoy the park's bears (and other wildlife, too) at a distance. Instead of approaching, use your binoculars or the zoom lens on your camera to enjoy up-close wildlife watching, and employ the following tips:

- Never feed bears. This habituates them to humans and human food sources.

- Always store food in appropriate receptacles when camping, and, if in doubt, ask park rangers for advice.

- Place garbage in bear-proof receptacles if available. Otherwise, don't take garbage outside until you are ready to dispose of it.

- Thoroughly clean outdoor grills in picnic areas and campgrounds after use.

- Remember to report nuisance bear activity to park officials.

In the unlikely event that you should be approached by a black bear, make a lot of noise and wave your arms. Throw sticks or stones at the bear if necessary. This will deter a bear from approaching closer in most instances. But don't run if the bear charges – this will make the bear see you as prey. Besides, bears can run up to 30 miles per hour, so you don't have a chance of outrunning one. Slowly back away, don't turn your back, and make a lot of noise. Often, bears make bluff charges. If a black bear actually makes contact, fight back with anything available to you. The bear may consider you too much trouble and leave you alone.

© FRENCH C. GRIMES

Cable Mill at Cades Cove

in the valley for weeks and even months at a time. White settlers first began filtering into Cades Cove in the 1820s and by 1850 nearly 700 people lived in the cove, most of them farming the wide and lush bottomland settled between the mountains. Among the family names you'll see on the headstones of old cemeteries in the cove are Cable, Oliver, Tipton, Shields, and Sparks.

The new residents found plentiful game here, including white-tailed deer and bear, and took full advantage of the abundance of the earth, so much so that by the time the national park was established there were only some 30 white-tailed deer left in Cades Cove. As you'll notice, however, the deer population has fully recovered.

Everyone who lived in the valley farmed, even if farming was not their sole occupation. Some operated mills, the first of which were small tub mills only suitable for grinding corn. Gristmills were the cove's first industry, followed by blacksmithing, and later, in the 1830s, even an iron forge that employed local Cherokee.

The families here grew orchards and made peach and apple brandy from their harvest. Everyone had vegetable gardens, and most farmers grew large fields of corn and wheat, sometimes rye and barley as well. In addition to eating wild game, most families also raised and butchered their own hogs.

Chestnuts were a not insignificant industry for cove families as well. Before the chestnut blight decimated the Smokies' American chestnut population between 1925 and 1940, families gathered chestnuts by the thousands, carrying bushels of them to Maryville and Knoxville to sell.

When the states of North Carolina and Tennessee began purchasing land for the national park, one of the first large tracts purchased was right here in Cades Cove in 1927. Most families took the money for their land and left the cove willingly. But not all. John Oliver, who was the great-grandson of one of the cove's first settlers, fought the state of Tennessee for six years to hold on to his land, but he eventually lost the battle. Some residents were given lifetime rights to

SURPRISING BEAR FACTS

Unlike their western cousin the grizzly bear, black bears, in general, are not very large. Adult males are typically four to six feet long and weigh in anywhere from 100 to 400 pounds. Females are typically smaller. The Eastern black bear found in the Smokies is usually uniformly black with a square head and round, erect ears.

Though black bears are considered predators, their diets are more than 75 percent vegetative matter, such as nuts, acorns, grasses, berries, and fruits. They also eat insects and carrion and occasionally prey on other animals. They are opportunistic eaters, too, and will feed on human food scraps, garbage, pet food, and birdseed. You will most likely see bears close to wooded areas where they can easily find food and cover.

Black bears may go into hibernation as early as late October. They emerge between mid-March and mid-April. Their most common den sites are not, as legend would have us believe, caves, but hollow trees. Cubs are born in mid- to late January while mothers are denning. Common litter sizes are 1-3 cubs, and cubs stay with their mothers until they are 16-18 months old. It is not uncommon in the Smokies to see mother bears with two or three cubs in tow. Make sure to never get between a bear and her cubs.

Bears can live up to 30 years in unhunted populations, but most live 10-15 years. In unprotected areas, bears' most common causes of mortality are hunting and vehicle collisions. Adult bears have no natural predators and are not very susceptible to parasites or disease.

their homes, and community life went on here to some degree well into the 1940s. The last school closed in 1940, the post office in 1947.

An 11-mile one-way loop tour will take you on a journey around the cove to explore the many remnants of its human history.

SIGHTS
John Oliver Place

The first stop on the loop tour of Cades Cove, the John Oliver Place was the first cabin built in the cove in the 1820s, and interestingly enough, the Oliver family continued to own this property up until the national park was established over 100 years later. Notice the notched corners on the cabin that allow gravity to hold the house together. Residents would have used mud in the chinks to keep out the weather and would have had to replace the chinking periodically as it wore away.

Methodist Church

Built in 1902 at a cost of $115, this church has two front doors, which usually is a sign that the seating was segregated, with men on one side and women on the other, but that was never the case here. Likely the church's builder, J. D. McCampbell, had borrowed the plans from another church of similar design.

Cable Mill Historic Area

Your first stop at the Cable Mill Historic Area will likely be the **Cades Cove Visitor Center** (865/436-1200, Dec.–Jan. daily 9 A.M.–4:30 P.M., Feb. and Nov. daily 9 A.M.–5 P.M., Mar. and Sept.–Oct. daily 9 A.M.–6 P.M., Apr.–Aug. daily 9 A.M.–7 P.M.), which has a large bookstore as well as public restrooms. From here you can begin your tour of the historic area. While all of the structures you see are original, most have been moved here from other locations.

The only structure original to this site is **Cable Mill** (mid-Mar.–Nov., demonstrations mid-June–mid-Aug. daily 9 A.M.–5 P.M.), built around 1870 by John P. Cable; one of Cable's sons operated the mill into the early 20th century. Cable built a gristmill and a sawmill here, both powered by the same wheel. He was also a farmer and maintained a large bell on a pole

© FRENCH C. GRIMES

Methodist Church in Cades Cove

here, which customers could ring to draw Cable in from his fields when they needed mill services.

Also here is the prosperous-looking Gregg-Cable House, which was built in 1879 on Forge Creek Road. Historians believe it was the cove's first frame house built with sawed lumber; the lumber was sawed at Cable Mill. The Leason Gregg family lived in this house for a short time, but in 1887 John's children Rebecca and Dan bought the house. Rebecca operated a boardinghouse here and raised her brother's children after he was diagnosed with mental illness. She owned some 600 acres of land in the valley and lived a long life in this home. She died in 1940 at age 96; the house was then moved to its new location here near the Cable Mill.

There are several typical farm outbuildings in the Cable Mill area as well, including both a cantilever barn and a drive-through barn, a corn crib, sorghum mill, smokehouse, and blacksmith shop.

Tipton Place

On the southern edge of Cades Cove are several more houses, including the Tipton Place, which was built by Col. Hampton Tipton in the 1870s for his daughters, who were known locally as Miss Lucy and Miss Lizzie. The two sisters were both schoolteachers in the cove. The James McCaulley family also lived here a time, and McCaulley had his own blacksmith shop, which still stands near the house. Across the road is the farm's cantilever barn and corn crib.

BIKING

Cades Cove is the best place to bike in the Great Smoky Mountains National Park because, unlike many other roads in the park, the Cades Cove loop is not steep and winding nor, at certain times, occupied with heavy motor vehicle traffic. You can bike the 11-mile loop tour through Cades Cove without the inconvenience of motor traffic on both Wednesday and Saturday mornings until 10 A.M., May through September. During those times the cove is closed to automobiles. Bike rentals are available at the **Cades Cove Store** (865/448-9034, www.explorecadescove.com, Sun.–Tues. and Thurs.–Fri. daily 9 A.M.–5 P.M., Wed. and Sat. daily 7 A.M.–5 P.M.) for $4–6 per hour. The last rentals are available at 2:30 P.M.

HORSEBACK RIDING

Cades Cove Riding Stables (865/448-9009, www.cadescovestables.com, mid-Mar.–early Jan. 9 A.M.–4:30 P.M., 1-hour guided horseback ride $25, 30-minute guided carriage ride $8, guided hayride $6–8) offers trail rides along a nature trail within the cove for half-hour and one-hour rides. They also offer half-hour horsedrawn carriage rides through Cades Cove daily. Another option is to take a hayride—you'll be pulled by a truck, not a horse, but this is a great way to see Cades Cove since the hayride travels the entire loop road. At various times the park service will have a ranger ride along to provide interpretive

© FRENCH C. GRIMES

Henry Whitehead Place in Cades Cove

history along the entire route. Call for times of carriage and hayrides.

SCENIC DRIVES AND MOTORCYCLE TOURS
Parson Branch Road

If you have a full day to spend touring the southwest corner of the Great Smoky Mountains National Park, consider taking a side trip on the Parson Branch Road. Accessible by taking a right turn just past the Cades Cove Visitor Center parking area, this 10-mile scenic drive will take you on a one-way gravel back road through one of the most isolated areas of the park; you'll come out at Highway 129 just north of Deals Gap on the western boundary of the park. Drive carefully and slowly on this route, and allow yourself at least an hour. The road is full of potholes, and you will ford more than 15 small streams. Don't be worried, however, if you're driving a sedan. The road is not very steep and the fords are shallow.

Shortly after turning onto the Parson Branch Road (which allows two-way traffic for the first

two miles), you'll see the **Henry Whitehead Place** on your left. The story of this house is an interesting one. It was built by Henry Whitehead, a widower with three daughters. He built the home when he remarried to Matilda Shields Gregory, who had been abandoned by her husband and left alone with a small child. Her neighbors came together in the emergency to build her a tiny log cabin, which still stands, connected by a roof overhang to the residence her second husband built her.

Much of the journey follows a small stream, which you will cross and re-cross many times on your drive. Roll down the windows of your vehicle, and take in the sounds of tumbling water and birdsong. As you drive gradually uphill notice the enormous hemlock die-off in the surrounding forest. These trees have all been the victim of the invasive hemlock woolly adelgid. One of the best times of year to take this scenic road tour is from mid-June to mid-July, when the walls of rhododendron along the roadway will be in full bloom.

You'll know you're about halfway to Highway

129 when you crest the top of a mountain and see the trailheads for the Hannah Mountain and Gregory Bald Trails. From here you'll descend. Take note of the many scenic cascades along Parson Branch. You might even want to pause and fish in one of the deep, shady pools here. Once you reach Highway 129, you'll need to take a right if you want to head back toward Townsend or Gatlinburg.

Deals Gap

Highway 129 from Deals Gap to Chilhowee Lake is not technically inside the Great Smoky Mountains National Park, but it hugs the park's southwestern boundary and is a popular route for motorcyclists. That's because this stretch of mountain highway features 318 curves in only 11 miles. You can reach this area, known as the Tail of the Dragon, from Tennessee by taking the Foothills Parkway south from Highway 321 west of Townsend or from North Carolina by taking Highway 129 north from Robbinsville. The area is directly accessible from the national park by taking the Parson Branch Road directly out of Cades Cove, but keep in mind that Parson Branch Road is not paved.

Whether you are in a motorcycle or a car, exercise caution on Highway 129 west of Deals Gap. It's not just the sheer number of curves that boggle the mind here, but the incredible tightness of many of them. There will be many sections of road where it's not safe to go faster than 15 mph. More than a few motorcyclists have been killed and seriously injured on this road. If you're in a car, you'll feel outnumbered by the two-wheeled variety of transportation on this route. The drive is a pretty one, though, with lots of pull-offs where you can let faster traffic pass or from which you can enjoy the views of Chilhowee Lake. There are also pull-offs right on the lake for fishing access, and some have picnic tables.

If you want to prove that you rode the Tail of the Dragon, plenty of photographers set up shop on the overlooks here to take pictures of you on your ride; later you can download photos of yourself from their website for a fee. You can get more information about this famous ride at www.tailofthedragon.com.

Be sure to pick up your Tail of the Dragon T-shirt at the **Deals Gap Motorcycle Resort** (17548 Tapoco Rd., 800/889-5550, www.dealsgap.com, Mar.–Nov. Sun.–Thurs. 8 A.M.–7 P.M., Fri.–Sat. 8 A.M.–8 P.M., hotel rooms $60–80, tent sites $12–16), which has a retail shop carrying Tail of the Dragon merchandise as well as gas and convenience items. There is also a motorcycle hotel and camping resort here, and Dragon's Den Grill and Pub.

CAMPING

Cades Cove Campground (800/365-2267, $17–20) is located adjacent to the popular Cades Cove auto tour at the west end of Little River Road. The campground has 159 sites. On-site is a camp store with bicycle rentals available. They also sell camping supplies, firewood, ice, and park guidebooks. A snack bar has hot dogs and sandwiches for sale as well as soft-serve ice cream cones. There is also a picnic area adjacent to the campground. The campground is open year-round, but reservations are required mid-May through October. There is also a dump station available.

Fontana Lake Area

The community of Fontana wouldn't exist were it not for the dam from which it takes its name. The village was established in 1941 as a town for the workers who built the dam, and, at its height, it supported a population of 6,000 people. Construction on the dam began in 1942, and took only 36 months.

Fontana Dam was built to supply electricity to the ALCOA plant in nearby Marysville for the manufacture of aluminum. In the 1940s there was an urgent need for electricity to supply the industry powering World War II. The electricity produced by Fontana Dam ultimately went to supply power to atomic bomb research operations at Oak Ridge.

The Tennessee Valley Authority (TVA) bought over 1,000 individual tracts of land for Fontana Dam and Lake, resulting in the relocation of some 600 families. Those families' homes, farms, schools, and churches are now all covered by the lake, which flooded five communities. Fontana, like many TVA dams, was thus a mixed blessing. While it resulted in dislocation, it also brought electricity (and jobs) to rural residents in the wake of World War II. The dam also provides much-needed flood control to the region. This area of North Carolina and Tennessee receives more than 50 inches of rainfall a year, and the Little Tennessee River, on which Fontana is located, drains 2,650 square miles, most of it mountainous. Before the dam, devastating floods were an unfortunate part of life in the Little Tennessee River Valley. By anticipating weather conditions, TVA can draw down the dam to accommodate heavy rains. In a typical year, water levels at Fontana vary by as much as 50 feet.

Even today visitors are impressed by the size and scale of Fontana Dam, the highest concrete dam east of the Rocky Mountains. It took more than 2.8 million cubic yards of concrete to build it. It began producing power in January 1945 and continues to produce hydroelectric power today while also providing a popular recreation area at Fontana Lake.

◖ FONTANA DAM

Fontana Dam is the highest dam in the eastern United States at 480 feet and is something of an engineering wonder, particularly given the fact that it was built in the 1940s. It holds back the waters of Fontana Lake, a Tennessee Valley Authority (TVA) reservoir that hugs the Great Smoky Mountains National Park's southern border from Fontana Village almost to Bryson City. The **Fontana Dam Visitor Center** (Fontana Dam Rd., 828/498-2234, www.tva.gov/sites/fontana.htm, May–Nov. daily 9 A.M.–7 P.M., free) has exhibits on the history of the dam, a small gift shop, and a viewing platform overlooking the dam. The visitors center also has showers for hikers and sells backcountry camping permits, which might come as

Fontana Marina

© FRENCH C. GRIMES

a surprise until you realize that the Appalachian Trail crosses right over the dam.

You can also drive over the dam if you would like. The road dead-ends in the national park, but there is a picnic table and grill to the right of the road just on the other side of the damn, providing a lovely place to stop and enjoy the view of Fontana Lake.

FONTANA MARINA

If you have your own boat you can launch it on Fontana Lake at the Fontana Marina (50 Fontana Rd., 828/498-2129, www.fontanavillage.com, Sun.–Thurs. 8 A.M.–4 P.M., Fri.–Sat. 8 A.M.–6 P.M.), which is located on Highway 28 two miles south of Fontana Village. The marina also rents pontoon boats, personal watercraft, kayaks, canoes, and johnboats. Guided boat tours to historic areas across the lake are available. The tours go to the Eagle Creek and Hazel Creek areas, offering the opportunity to see the old copper mines, roads, and other remnants of lost communities that existed before the dam was built. Fontana Lake is 29 miles long with 238 miles of shoreline. Fontana Village resort has a phone service at the marina; Appalachian Trail thru-hikers can call for shuttle service to the resort for overnight lodgings if they want a respite from the trail. Shuttle service is $3.

FONTANA VILLAGE
Resort

Today Fontana Village (Hwy. 28 N., 800/849-2258, www.fontanavillage.com, rooms and suites $79–209, campground $25–35, cabins $89–309) is a rustic resort with 100 lodge rooms and 110 cabins available for rent, many of them the same structures that once served the workers on the Fontana Dam. The lodge also has houseboats available for rent on Fontana Lake and 20 campsites available for either tents or RVs. Guests have access to resort amenities, including an outdoor pool,

lazy river, and day spa, for an additional fee. The resort also has two on-site restaurants: **Wildwood Grill** (828/498-2211, www.fontanavillage.com, Apr.–Oct. Mon.–Thurs. 11:30 A.M.–9 P.M., Fri.–Sat. 11:30 A.M.–10 P.M., Sun. 11:30 A.M.–6 P.M., $5–12) and the **Mountain View Bistro** (828/498-2115, www.fontanavillage.com, daily 7:30 A.M.–2:30 P.M. and 5:30–8 P.M., $13–28). A general store sells groceries, gifts, firewood, and ice, but prices are steep—they definitely take advantage of the fact that there is nowhere else to shop within less than a 30-minute drive. Laundry facilities are also available.

Fontana Village also runs **Hazel Creek Outfitter** (828/498-2211, www.fontanavillage.com, Mar.–Nov. Sun.–Thurs. 8 A.M.–9 P.M., Fri.–Sat. 8 A.M.–10 P.M.). It is located at the general store complex and is a good place to rent mountain bikes or find out more about the guided hikes offered. White-water rafting is also available through a third party. Pickup for the trips is at the general store.

Fontana Riding Stables (828/498-2211, ext. 6911, Apr. and Sept.–Oct. Fri.–Sun., May–Aug. daily, hours vary) offers trips to explore the Nantahala National Forest as well as lakeside trails. Call ahead for ride departure times, availability, and cost.

Camping

Cable Cove Campground (Hwy. 28, 828/479-6431, www.main.nc.us/graham/hiking/rangerhq.html, Apr. 15–Oct. 31, $10) is a U.S. Forest Service campground with 26 campsites. This is a primitive campground with no water, electric, or shower facilities. From Fontana Village, take NC 28 south 4.7 miles. Then turn left onto Forest Road 520, and you'll see the campground in 1.4 miles.

Tsali Recreation Area Campground (Hwy. 28, 828/479-6431, www.main.nc.us/graham/hiking/rangerhq.html, Apr. 15–Oct. 31, $10) has showers, flush toilets, and 42 campsites.

Deep Creek

The Deep Creek entrance to the park, just south of Cherokee and a few miles north of Bryson City, is more popular with locals than tourists. Area kids enjoy tubing on Deep Creek in the summer, and families find it a great place to picnic and camp away from the park's mobs of visitors. There are also a number of hiking trails here, three of them providing access to waterfalls.

HIKING
Juney Whank Falls

- Distance: 0.6 mile round-trip
- Duration: 30 minutes
- Elevation gain: 120 feet
- Difficulty: Moderate
- Trailhead: Parking area at the end of Deep Creek Road across the creek from the Deep Creek Campground

Juney Whank Falls offers the shortest trek at Deep Creek. Visitors here follow a log bridge to a skinny waterfall surrounded by slick lichen-clad rocks. Along the short and somewhat steep path, enjoy the displays of fern and wildflowers. The falls itself drops about 90 feet total—40 above the log bridge where you'll stand to view it and 50 additional feet below.

Indian Creek Falls

- Distance: 2 miles round-trip
- Duration: 1 hour
- Elevation gain: 150 feet
- Difficulty: Moderate
- Trailhead: Parking area at the end of Deep Creek Road across the creek from the Deep Creek Campground

Just below Juney Whank Falls is a gentler, if longer, hike past wispy Tom Branch Falls to Indian Creek Falls. Following an old road-bed for about a mile, the hike offers a serene forested setting of dark hemlocks and towering rhododendron to a view of one of the park's loveliest falls. You might find the trail a bit muddy, as it's used by horses as well as hikers.

Cascading over rock layers for 60 feet into a deep pool at its base, Indian Creek Falls is so perfectly rendered that its stony terraces appear man-made.

ROAD TO NOWHERE

Just south of the Deep Creek entrance at the end of Lakeview Drive outside Bryson City is a lonely paved highway leading north into the park. Locals refer to the highway as the Road to Nowhere. Decades ago, park officials intended to build a parkway through the Smokies along Fontana Lake. The project was never completed, and the highway stops abruptly about six miles into the park at a man-made stone tunnel. Locals whose families were driven from their homes in this region of the park to make way for Fontana Lake call the road "a broken promise," as government officials had vowed to build a road along the lake's northern edge to provide access to family gravesites.

Cars have never passed through the stone tunnel at the end of Lakeview Drive, but today the visitor on foot can. Beyond the dank and cavernous tunnel is a 26-mile hiking trail that weaves along the northern edge of Fontana Lake. Even car-bound visitors, however, can experience breathtaking views of the Smokies plunging into Fontana Lake from various overlooks along the Road to Nowhere.

CAMPING
Deep Creek Campground (800/365-2267, Apr.–Oct., $17) is located just north of Bryson City at the end of Deep Creek Road. Located

just inside park boundaries, this campground has 92 sites, some along the scenic creek. Bathhouses are available, but no showers. This campground, despite its seemingly isolated location, is popular with locals, some of whom arrive early to have a better pick of campsites.

Cataloochee Valley and Balsam Mountain

For those who want to experience some of the human history of the Smokies without enduring the crowds of Cades Cove, Cataloochee Valley is the place to go. Located northwest of Maggie Valley and just off I-40, this entrance to the park has become more popular in recent years (due to the introduction of elk here about a decade ago), but it's still the most peaceful place to explore the homes, churches, and schools of the Smokies' European American settlers.

One of five historic districts in the national park, Cataloochee was at one time the most populated area in the region that is now the national park. The 1910 census recorded 1,250 people in the valley, which by that time had been inhabited for nearly 100 years by European Americans. White settlers first came into Cataloochee in the 1830s. Most of the valley's residents left by the early 1940s, however, in the wake of the establishment of the Great Smoky Mountains National Park.

Accessing the valley and the elk requires patience. Cove Creek Road is winding and narrow, alternately paved and graveled, and there are no national park signs to direct an unknowing visitor. After zigzagging up and around a mountainous stretch known as the Cataloochee Divide, you'll be transported suddenly into an open valley of endless serenity—miles of rolling grass cradled lightly in the arms of blue-green mountain peaks and watered by pristine and frigid streams. Like its sister Cades Cove, the Cataloochee Valley preserves the remnants of a once-thriving Appalachian community.

To reach the Cataloochee Valley, take Exit 20 off I-40 onto Highway 276. You'll then take an immediate right onto Cove Creek Road. From here, it's about 12 miles into the valley on a road that is alternately paved and graveled and quite twisty in some places. This road actually follows portions of the old Cataloochee Turnpike, which originally started as an Indian trail. Allow yourself about half an hour.

Just before you descend into Cataloochee Valley, take a few moments to stop at the overlook on your right just after the road turns from gravel to paved after the intersection with Big Creek Road. Climb the short paved trail to the Cataloochee Valley overlook and take in the sweeping vista of the valley below and the mountains stretching out before you

Cataloochee Valley

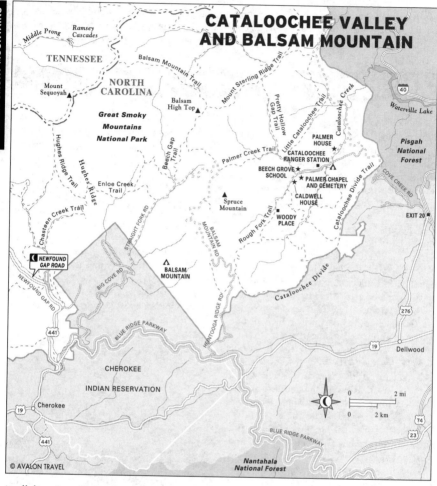

in all directions. Today you will see mostly forested mountainsides, but for the residents of Cataloochee the scene would have been quite different, with cleared land opening up the valley floor and cutting into the bottom of the mountainsides. If you listen carefully, you will hear the distant tumble of Cataloochee Creek below you.

The valley is open to vehicle traffic from 8 A.M. to sunset. Cataloochee is most heavily visited in the evenings before sunset, when tourists come in to see the elk grazing in the open fields. If you prefer to avoid the crowds, come into the valley around midday. You can still see the elk if you get out into the woods and do some hiking, as they normally take shelter in the forest during the daytime.

SIGHTS
Palmer Chapel and Cemetery

The first structure you'll notice as you enter the valley is Palmer Chapel, built in 1898, which now stands empty along Cataloochee Creek, its doors opening to the forest instead of

© FRENCH C. GRIMES

Palmer Chapel in the Cataloochee Valley

to the road. Up the hill behind the church lies a ragged cemetery, where graves marked and unmarked, sunken and new, bear the names of the valley's early settlers—Caldwell, Palmer, Noland, Bennett, and Barnes. The preachers here were circuit riders who typically visited one Sunday a month. Each year the descendants of Cataloochee's original residents gather here at Palmer Chapel for a reunion to share food, attend church services, and care for the cemeteries of their families.

Beech Grove School

The Beech Grove School is the only school building left in the Cataloochee Valley. Built in 1901, the school was open from November through January and sometimes into February and March. Today the school stands empty among overgrown weeds and woods, a left-over desk or two turned askew on dusty floors, blackboards curling away in the humidity.

Caldwell House

Beyond the school is the Caldwell House, a two-story white frame structure with paneled interior walls, attesting to the prosperity of its former master, Hiram Caldwell. Built in 1906, the home has three large bedrooms upstairs. Notice the remnants of insulating newspaper on the walls and ceilings as well as the wood paneled walls.

Palmer House

If you return the way you came and then take a left onto Big Creek Road you'll come to the Palmer House, which was once a log home with a dogtrot connecting its two ends. In the early 1900s, as its owners grew more prosperous, they covered the exterior with weatherboarding. Note as you wander around the interior of the home the remnants of fancy wallpaper on the walls as well as the sturdy rock fireplaces and glass-fronted kitchen cupboards. When Jarvis Palmer inherited this home from his father, he soon began adding onto the home to accommodate boarders. The Palmers owned three miles of trout stream, which they stocked, and charged for fishing. They made further money by renting rooms in the house and in the bunkhouse they built across the road.

THE ELK OF CATALOOCHEE

Elk had not lived in the Smokies since the mid-1800s, but in 2001, 52 elk were released in the Cataloochee Valley, a relatively isolated cove in the northeast corner of the Great Smoky Mountains National Park, as part of an experimental reintroduction of these animals to the area. Since then, the elk population has nearly doubled, and the elk can often be found not just in Cataloochee but also around the Oconaluftee Visitor Center and Smokemont Campground. Interestingly enough, one of the park's elk has been especially adventurous, making extended trips to the Tennessee side of the Smokies and even to Hot Springs, North Carolina.

Adult male elk generally weigh 600 to 700 pounds, while females are a bit smaller, typically weighing around 500 pounds. Males can look especially impressive when their antlers are in full bloom, with some having antlers five feet across. Elk eat mostly grass, bark, buds, and acorns. Healthy adults do not have any natural predators in the Smokies, though black bears, coyotes, and even bobcats will prey on calves or injured elk. Females generally give birth to one calf a year.

SCENIC DRIVES

Most of the 10 million people who visit the Great Smoky Mountains National Park every year do so via the Newfound Gap Road, so the best way to avoid the crowds is to steer clear of this main thoroughfare into the park. There are a lot of driving alternatives that provide access to beautiful mountain woodlands, high ridges, and boulder-laden streams with virtually no other vehicle traffic—if you have the time and are willing to take some gravel roads and drive slowly. Make use of the Great Smoky Mountains Trail Map, available at any of the park visitors centers for a small fee, as it shows all of the road accesses into the park and will help you get around if you choose to head off the beaten path.

Balsam Mountain Road

The Heintooga Ridge Road/Balsam Mountain Road is only accessible from the Blue Ridge Parkway near Soco Gap at Milepost 458, where a spur road takes off to the northwest. The Heintooga Ridge Road after several miles becomes the Balsam Mountain Road, a stretch of road that is something of a hiking trail for cars. This gravel byway penetrates the park interior just west of the Cataloochee Valley and north of the Cherokee Indian Reservation. It covers about 14 miles of forested mountain ridge.

While you're still on the paved spur road, be sure to stop briefly at the **Mile High Overlook** (elevation 5,250 ft.) on the left side of the road, which offers westward views into the endless sea of blue mountains that makes up the Great Smoky Mountains National Park.

About 3.5 miles after turning off the Blue Ridge Parkway you'll arrive at **Black Camp Gap.** There are a few picnic tables here, and this is also where you officially enter the Great Smoky Mountains National Park. At the **Heintooga Overlook and Picnic Area** you'll have the opportunity to continue your journey on the 14-mile one-way Balsam Mountain Road, a lonely graveled back road that will take you on a nearly private tour of the northeast corner of the national park.

Keep in mind that, since this road is one-way once you're on it, you have to follow it to its end, which will take about an hour and a half if you don't stop to hike along the way. Because the road is graveled and narrow, the pace is slow, but visitors here are few. Even in the summer and fall seasons you're unlikely to come across more than a handful of other travelers on this route. The road is well maintained, too, so you can feel comfortable driving the family sedan on it.

If you enjoy wildflowers, summer is an excellent time to tour the Balsam Mountain Road. The roadside for the first several miles

©FRENCH C. GRIMES

Straight Fork

crowding around you on all sides. After about 11 miles, you'll notice a small stream cascading down the slopes. Shortly, your route will begin to parallel **Straight Fork,** a scenic boulder-laden stream and one of the tributaries of the Oconaluftee River. At 13 miles the road becomes two-way again, and you'll have many opportunities to pull off and take photos of the cascading waters of Straight Fork, which you will follow out of the park and onto Straight Fork Road, which cuts through the Cherokee Indian Reservation and rejoins Highway 441 at Cherokee.

HIKING
Woody Place

- Distance: 2 miles round-trip

- Duration: 1 hour

- Elevation gain: None

- Difficulty: Easy

- Trailhead: At the dead end of the road just past the Caldwell House in Cataloochee Valley

This wide and level trail to the former home of Jonathan Woody offers a pleasant hike through the forest alongside a pretty stream. It is not uncommon to see elk foraging in the woods near the trail, but remember to keep your distance from these large animals, particularly during rutting season. The hike offers a cool escape on summer days, as it passes through hardwood forest, and the trail is bordered by green ferns and arching rhododendron.

You will cross the stream several times on this hike with the help of log bridges. As you cross, note how the old road on which you are walking fords the stream, providing crossing for horses and wagons.

After you've continued your forest walk for about a mile, the trail will open to a sunny clearing where the two-story white frame Woody house stands. Covered in lap siding and shingled with hand-cut shakes, the home looks much as it would have when the Woody family

is loaded with wildflowers, including wild bergamot, tall coneflowers, bright-yellow clumps of oxeye, black-eyed susans, and milkweed that is often peppered with butterflies. Roll down your car windows and enjoy the sounds of the woods, which are made up of spruce, hemlocks (many of them dying), dogwoods, tulip poplars, oaks, cherries, and birch. Watch the play of sunlight on the leaves, and watch for the roadside blackberry brambles that in August are loaded with ripe fruit. If you take this route in mid-June through early July, you'll likely see rhododendron in bloom.

For the first 4.5 miles, the road descends slowly but then begins to climb again. Watch for a small waterfall to your right after about 5.5 miles. At 7.5 miles you'll find access to the **Palmer Creek Trail,** which provides hiking access into the Cataloochee Valley. It's about a 4.5-mile hike to Cataloochee Road from here.

After you've traveled 8.5 miles you'll see the trailhead for the **Balsam Mountain Trail,** and from here the road descends again, more sharply this time. Soon, you'll see rhododendron

Woody Place in the Cataloochee Valley

© FRENCH C. GRIMES

lived here at the turn of the 20th century. Take some time to sit on the front porch and listen to the adjacent stream, and imagine how it must have felt to live here when Cataloochee was a busier and thriving community.

Many of the park's historic structures have been damaged by vandalism, and one thing that distinguishes the Woody house from others you will see in the park (especially those one can visit without a hike) is that there is no graffiti marring the walls. Remember to respect these emblems of life in the Smokies long ago, and leave no trace when you depart. As you wander around the Woody residence, note that this was a prosperous home. Carved mantelpieces remain intact in the home's main rooms, and there are three large bedrooms upstairs.

Adjacent to the residence is an old springhouse. As you walk around be alert for snakes, who seem to enjoy this clearing for sunning themselves in the afternoon. Return to your vehicle via the same trail.

CAMPING

The **Cataloochee Campground** (800/365-2267, Mar.–Oct., $17) is one of the park's more secluded camping options, though you may often find it full on summer weekends. The campground is open year-round and has 27 campsites, some of them on Cataloochee Creek, as well as restrooms (the only ones in the valley apart from portable toilets). There are no hookups here and no bathhouse.

The **Balsam Mountain Campground** (800/365-2267, May–Oct., $14) is a very small and surprisingly popular national park campground accessible off the Heintooga Ridge Road spur off the Blue Ridge Parkway at Milepost 458. With 46 campsites, it's a good place to camp if you're planning on exploring some of the trails accessible off the Balsam Mountain Road. There are restrooms but no showers. This somewhat crowded campground nestled on a narrow ridge also has its own half-mile nature trail.

Practicalities

INFORMATION

Park headquarters is located adjacent to the **Sugarlands Visitor Center** (1420 Little River Rd., 865/436-1200, Dec.–Feb. daily 8 A.M.–4 P.M., Mar. and Nov. daily 8 A.M.–5 P.M., Apr.–May and Sept.–Oct. daily 8 A.M.–6 P.M., June–Aug. daily 8 A.M.–7 P.M.) but is not open to the public. Sugarlands is the park's main visitors center.

EMERGENCY SERVICES

For emergency services in the Great Smoky Mountains National Park, you can always call 911. But you can also contact park headquarters, particularly if the issue is a fire or safety hazard, at 865/436-9171. Emergency services are also available through the Cherokee Police Department at 828/497-4131, or the Gatlinburg Police Department at 865/436-5181.

GETTING THERE

The easiest route if you're coming into the Great Smoky Mountains National Park from the north or west is to take I-40 from Knoxville,

Tennessee, to U.S. 66 at Exit 407. U.S. 66 will feed into U.S. 441 south to Gatlinburg. Stay on 441 all the way to the park entrance. While the simplest route, this is also the busiest, and it could take you a full hour or more to reach the park. An alternate option is to take Exit 435 off I-40 and follow U.S. 321 to Gatlinburg.

If you've flown into McGhee-Tyson Airport outside Knoxville, then your best bet is to avoid Knoxville altogether and head south on Highway 129 to Maryville. At Maryville, take U.S. 321 north to the park entrance at Townsend or to Pigeon Forge, where you will take a right onto U.S. 441 and follow it into the national park.

If you're coming in from the south, take U.S. 441 north to Cherokee, North Carolina. U.S. 441 takes you right to the park's Oconaluftee entrance.

From the east, follow I-40 west of Asheville, North Carolina, to U.S. 23/74 (the Great Smoky Mountains Expressway). Stay on the Expressway until you reach the exit for U.S. 441 north, and follow 441 into Cherokee.

There is no public transportation to the park.

TENNESSEE FOOTHILLS

The Tennessee side of the Smokies, home to country music legend Dolly Parton, has often gotten bad marks among more cultured travelers and those more interested in scenery and outdoor recreation than theme parks and dinner theaters. With its outlet malls, bungee jumping, and Ripley's museums, this area has a fair amount to entice a younger set and perhaps very little, on the surface, to draw the independent traveler. But not so fast: One wouldn't want to overlook unique places like the Great Smoky Arts and Crafts Community outside Gatlinburg, which features studio and gallery tours of over 100 local artists and crafters. Even the Dollywood theme park might surprise you—carefully designed to emphasize greenery and scenery, the park is home to the largest gathering of publicly visible, non-releasable

bald eagles in America, a real carriage works, a blacksmith shop, and dozens of venues for first-rate bluegrass and country music. The foothills also offer access to outfitters who can provide white-water rafting, horseback riding, and even back-road Hummer tours through the Smokies.

Prior to the creation of the Great Smoky Mountains National Park and World War II, the advent of which brought jobs and rural electricity to the area with the establishment of the Tennessee Valley Authority, the Tennessee Foothills were a largely impoverished area, and there is still an often startling difference between rich and poor in the region. On the whole, however, tourism and the industry drawn here by the region's countless reservoirs have given East Tennessee a level of

© DEBORAH HUSO

HIGHLIGHTS

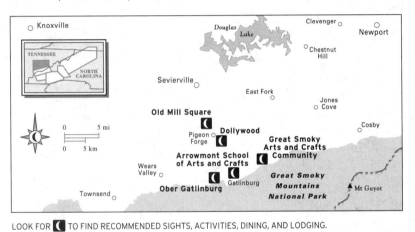 **Arrowmont School of Arts and Crafts:** Arrowmont is a nationally recognized school of traditional arts instruction established in 1945 (page 241).

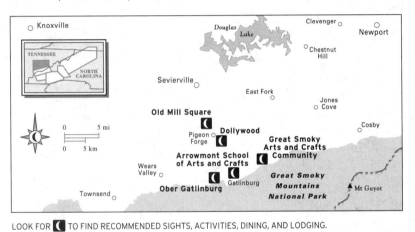 **Great Smoky Arts and Crafts Community:** The largest community of independent artisans in the nation, the Great Smoky Arts and Crafts community has more than 100 members (page 243).

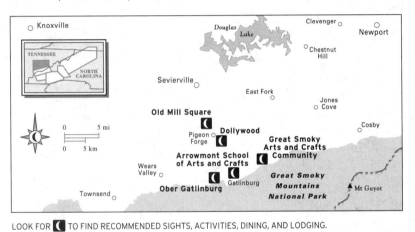 **Ober Gatlinburg:** The largest aerial tramway in the country takes visitors to Gatlinburg's mountaintop ski resort (page 246).

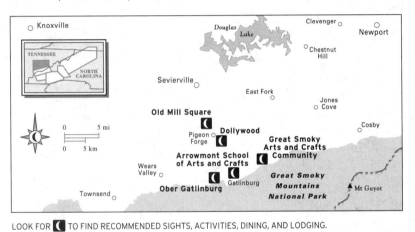 **Dollywood:** Grounded in the history, culture, and music of the southern Appalachians, Dollywood is the country legend's namesake theme park (page 255).

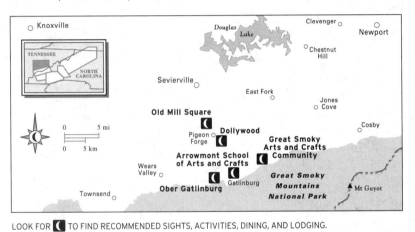 **Old Mill Square:** A still-operating gristmill in Pigeon Forge is now the centerpiece of a square of shops devoted to reviving Appalachian arts (page 259).

TENNESSEE FOOTHILLS

LOOK FOR TO FIND RECOMMENDED SIGHTS, ACTIVITIES, DINING, AND LODGING.

economic prosperity that has drawn a strong influx of retirees and vacation homeowners to the region in the last decade. The result is a sometimes bewildering mix of cultural identities that nevertheless makes the region worthy of a visit, whether your preference is amusement and water parks or local crafts and outdoor recreation.

PLANNING YOUR TIME

Depending on your level of interest in sometimes over-the-top attractions, you could spend anywhere from a weekend to more than a week in the Tennessee Foothills and still not do all there is to do. If you're interested in the Appalachian heritage crafts of the Smokies, then you should allow at least half a day if not a full day to explore the Great Smoky Arts and Crafts Community outside Gatlinburg. Allow another day to take in the many attractions of Gatlinburg itself from Ober Gatlinburg to Ripley's Aquarium of the Smokies.

If you are brave enough to withstand the masses in Pigeon Forge, then be sure to visit Old Mill Square, as well as spend a day at Dollywood, which is loaded with great musical shows and has many demonstrating heritage crafters. Allow two or three days if you want to explore the town's numerous and sometimes

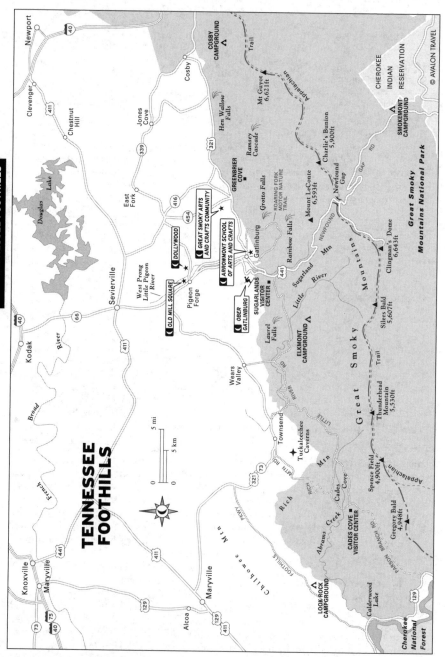

TENNESSEE FOOTHILLS

© AVALON TRAVEL

ridiculous amusements, ranging from Titanic Pigeon Forge to indoor sky diving.

Those seeking a little more peace and serenity on the Tennessee side will probably want to stick to the Townsend area.

There really is no ideal time to visit the Tennessee Foothills—at least the Gatlinburg and Pigeon Forge area—to avoid masses of tourists, as both towns enjoy pretty heavy visitation even in winter when special events keep the local tourism economies bustling through the colder weather. That being said, the busiest time, as with the rest of the Smokies, is undoubtedly mid-summer and fall.

Gatlinburg

Though not as built up as its neighbor Pigeon Forge, Gatlinburg is definitely a tourist town. During busy seasons, the main street through town is almost impassable by car. But past the T-shirt shops and neon-lighted Ripley's museums are some worthwhile places to check out, including the Great Smoky Arts and Crafts Community and the Arrowcraft Gallery. And if you get a little ways outside of town, you can find some peaceful inns as well.

Gatlinburg, though it has the distinction of being called a "city," is only two miles long by five miles wide, its growth likely curbed by the national park on its southern border and the steep mountainsides that border it everywhere else.

What is today known as Gatlinburg was once the community of White Oak Flats, and some local families can trace their roots to that era. How the town's name changed to Gatlinburg is something of a mystery and maybe more legend than truth, but the local story claims that a man named Radford Gatlin opened a general store here in the 1850s, and as part of his agreement to handle the post office operations the community postmark became Gatlinburg.

Gatlinburg is known for many things, not the least of which is its number of wedding chapels. There are 15 of them, and the city has become known as the "wedding capital of the South" over the years. Each year 600,000 people come to Gatlinburg to get married or to witness a wedding, making romance quite an industry here. Only Las Vegas is a more popular place to say "I do."

SIGHTS
◖ Arrowmont School of Arts and Crafts

The Arrowmont School of Arts and Crafts (556 Parkway, 865/436-5860, www.arrowmont.org, June–Oct. Mon.–Sat. 8:30 A.M.–4:30 P.M., workshops $275–1,400) was founded in 1945. Prior to 1945, the campus had been the Pi Beta Phi settlement school, founded in 1912, a philanthropy project of the Pi Beta Phi women's fraternity, which sought to bring basic education and health services to the children of the extremely impoverished area. Early on, the fraternity recognized the unique nature of the crafts that the mountain people produced. This led to the school providing a weaving teacher and later more vocational education. In 1926 the fraternity established the Arrowcraft shop to market the handicrafts of the local people. Today the school has a gallery showcasing exhibits of regional artists and provides weekend and one- and two-week workshops for adults in spring, summer, and fall. If you want to get close to the true and historic culture of the Smokies, signing up for a workshop here is the way to do it. You will come out surprisingly proficient in the craft you choose because instruction is intensive and focused. They offer classes in both contemporary and traditional art in areas such as fiber arts, pottery, metal and jewelry, and many others.

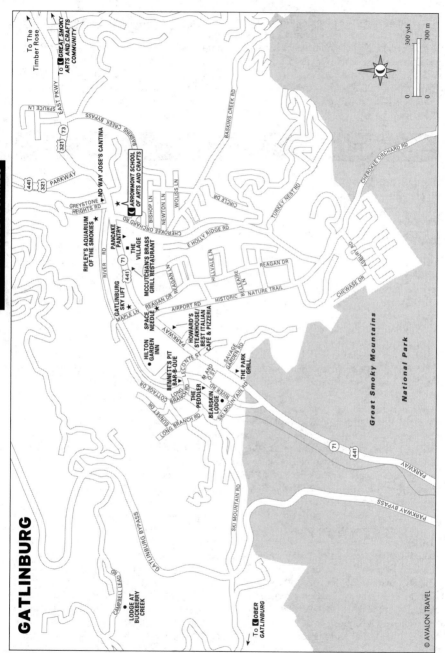

GATLINBURG

To The
Timber Rose

To GREAT SMOKY
ARTS AND CRAFTS
COMMUNITY

EAST PKWY

SPRUCE LN

BASKINS CREEK BYPASS

321 73

441 321 PARKWAY

GREYSTONE
HEIGHTS RD

NO WAY JOSE'S CANTINA

ARROWMONT SCHOOL
OF ARTS AND CRAFTS

BISHOP LN

NEWTON LN

WOLISS LN

CIRCLE DR

BASKINS CREEK RD

CHEROKEE ORCHARD RD

RIPLEY'S AQUARIUM
OF THE SMOKIES

PANCAKE
PANTRY

RIVER RD

71

441

VILLAGE

McCUTCHAN'S BRASS
GRILL RESTAURANT

TURKEY NEST RD

E HOLLY RIDGE RD

GATLINBURG
SKY LIFT

MAPLE LN

REAGAN DR

AIRPORT RD

SPACE
NEEDLE

HOWARD'S
STEAKHOUSE/
BEST ITALIAN
CAFÉ & PIZZERIA

REAGAN LN

HILLVALE LN

BELLAIRE LN

REAGAN DR

CHEWASE DR

OLD ASBURY DR

HISTORIC NATURE TRAIL

HILTON
GARDEN
INN

BENNETT'S PIT
BAR-B-QUE

LECONTE ST

PARKWAY

THE PARK
GRILL

SAVAGE
GARDEN RD

THE PEDDLER

LONG BRANCH RD

COTTAGE RD

BEARSKIN
LODGE

SUNSET DR

LONG BRANCH RD

M AND M RD

RIVER RD

SKI MOUNTAIN RD

SKI MOUNTAIN RD

GATLINBURG BYPASS

CAMPBELL LEAD RD

LODGE AT
BUCKBERRY
CREEK

To OBER
GATLINBURG

Great Smoky Mountains

National Park

71

441

PARKWAY

PARKWAY BYPASS

300 yds

300 m

© AVALON TRAVEL

Ripley's Aquarium of the Smokies

There are tons of Ripley's attractions in Gatlinburg as well as in neighboring Pigeon Forge. Unless you have kids in tow, however, you can probably skip them, as they are, for the most part, cheesy at best. One exception is Ripley's Aquarium of the Smokies (88 River Rd., 888/240-1358, http://gatlinburg. ripleyaquariums.com, May–Sept. daily 9 A.M.– 11 P.M., Oct.–Apr. Sun.–Thurs. 9 A.M.–9 P.M., Fri.–Sat. 9 A.M.–11 P.M., adults $19, children 6–11 $10, children 2–5 $4), which is the largest aquarium in Tennessee, holding some 1.4 million gallons of water. My favorite part is the 340-foot-long glidepath that takes you on a journey under the shark lagoon where sand tiger sharks, nurse sharks, and even stingrays glide overheard. The aquarium has dive shows every two hours. Displays here allow you to touch horseshoe crabs and stingrays as well as watch colorful tropical fish swim through a coral reef display.

There are two restaurants in the aquarium as well as a huge gift shop selling a pretty massive collection of marine-themed toys and gifts.

Gatlinburg Sky Lift

The Gatlinburg Sky Lift (865/436-4307, www.gatlinburgskylift.com, Apr.–May daily 9 A.M.–9 P.M., June–Aug. daily 9 A.M.– 11 P.M., Sept.–Oct. daily 9 A.M.–9 P.M., adults $12, children $9) is essentially a ski lift that takes you to the top of a mountain where you can catch a sparkling view of Gatlinburg after dark (which is the best time to go) and also all the darkness beyond, including the sloping shadows of the mountains of the national park. The lift climbs 1,800 feet, dropping you off for a visit to the mountaintop snack bar and gift shop. The lift is located on the Parkway in the center of downtown—you can't miss it.

Space Needle

The Space Needle (115 Historic Nature Trail, 865/436-4629, www.gatlinburgspaceneedle.com, Sun.–Thurs. 10 A.M.–11 P.M., Fri.–Sat. 9 A.M.–midnight, winter hours may vary, adults $7.25, seniors $5, children 5–12 $3, children 4 and under free) is another of Gatlinburg's over-the-top attractions that has its redeeming qualities. If you're looking for a way to kill time after dark, take the elevator to the top of this 407-foot tower at the center of downtown for some glistening views of downtown Gatlinburg at nightfall. If you reach the top of the Space Needle just after sundown, you'll be able to trace the faint outlines of Mount LeConte and Greenbrier Pinnacle to the northeast. Below the space needle is a 25,000-square-foot arcade with video games, laser tag, a virtual reality roller coaster simulator, a gift shop, and restrooms.

SHOPPING

While Gatlinburg is home to some 400 specialty shops, most of those along the Parkway that cuts through the center of town are decidedly touristy. To find locally made items and higher-quality merchandise that might make for a meaningful souvenir for years to come, you have to dig a little deeper.

◖ Great Smoky Arts and Crafts Community

An often overlooked treasure of Gatlinburg's otherwise "touristy" atmosphere is the Great Smoky Arts and Crafts Community (800/565-7330, www.gatlinburgcrafts.com). Established in 1937, it is the largest independent organization of artisans in the United States with more than 100 studios, shops, and galleries located along its eight-mile loop on Glades Road, Buckhorn Road, and Highway 321 about three miles east of downtown Gatlinburg.

What's special about this community is not just the crafts but the fact that visitors can actually interact with the artists, many of whom own and operate their own galleries. Be sure to look for the Great Smoky Arts and Crafts signs, however, which ensure the galleries display the genuine handiwork of local and regional artisans. You can pick up a map of the community at one of Gatlinburg's visitors centers. If you

TENNESSEE FOOTHILLS

WEDDING CAPITAL OF THE SOUTH

Even the most cursory drive through Gatlinburg will clue you in to the fact that this is a popular place to get married. Wedding chapels abound in the town and surrounding hills, and some 20,000 couples tie the knot here every year. Las Vegas is the only place in America with more weddings than Gatlinburg. That's why the town has come to be known as the "wedding capital of the South."

A few celebrities have even jumped the broom here, including Billy Ray Cyrus and Patty Loveless. But why?

Part of the reason is that Tennessee requires no blood tests or waiting period before getting married, making it a relatively easy place to get hitched. Plus, there are plenty of things to drive romance here, including the beautiful scenery and oodles of romantic accommodations. But then comes the question: Which came first, the cabin rentals with heart-shaped whirlpool tubs or the couples seeking nuptials?

We may never know.

But if you are thinking about tying the knot while you're here there are plenty of places to do it. There are more than a dozen chapels in town, ranging from white Victorian churches encrusted in gingerbread trim to log cabin chapels in the woods. You can call 865/453-5502 for information about obtaining a Tennessee marriage license. You can also browse the many chapel options in town with the help of the Gatlinburg Wedding Chapel Association (www.gatlinburgweddingassociation.com).

want to cover the studio tour in its entirety, allow a full day.

Among the shops here is **Licklog Hollow Baskets** (1360 E. Parkway, 865/436-3823, daily 10 A.M.–5 P.M.), where owners Billie and Lisa Canfield sell many of their own creations, including baskets and ironwork. Lisa used her basket-weaving art to help pay for college, but then ended up pursuing it as a career. Other artisans, like David Ogle, owner of **Ogle's Broom Shop** (680 Glades Rd., 865/430-4402, Mon.–Sat. 10 A.M.–5 P.M.), have been part of the cultural landscape of these mountains as long as they can remember. David and his wife, Tammi, are third generation broom makers, David's grandfather having run the shop in the 1940s. A fourth-generation Appalachian chair maker can be found at **The Chair Shop** (830 Glades Rd., 865/436-7413, Mon.–Fri. 9 A.M.–5 P.M., Sat. 10 A.M.–4 P.M.). At the **Paul Murray Gallery** (1003 Glades Rd., 865/436-8445, www.paulmurray.com, Dec.–Mar. Mon.–Sat. 11 A.M.–4 P.M., Apr.–June Mon.–Sat. 11 A.M.–5 P.M., July–Sept. Mon.–Sat. 11 A.M.–6 P.M., Oct.–Nov. daily 11 A.M.–6 P.M.), Canadian-born painter Murray displays his moving portraits of residents of the mountains of Kentucky and Tennessee. An especially popular stop on the loop tour of the community is **Alewine Pottery** (623 Glades Rd., 866/469-7687, www.alewinepottery.net, daily 9 A.M.–5 P.M.). Master potter Robert Alewine and his students make all the pottery available for purchase here, and you can usually watch them at work. You'll be amazed by the intricate leaf patterns and dazzling colors Alewine creates here in clay. A maple leaf on a vase looks as real here as one you might pick off the forest floor.

At **Otto Preske – Artist in Wood** (535 Buckhorn Rd., 865/436-5339), you can meet someone who has been part of the Great Smoky Arts and Crafts Community for more than a quarter of a century. Preske carves custom wooden mantelpieces with forest scenes of deer and elk, portraits of the persona of the west wind, and long-ago Indian warriors using traditional wood-carving tools. At the **Turtle Hollow Gallery** (248 Buckhorn Rd., 865/436-6188, Mar.–Dec. daily 10 A.M.–6 P.M., Jan.–Feb. Thurs.–Sat. 10 A.M.–6 P.M.), see the works of sculptor Ross Markeley, who has lived and worked in Gatlinburg for 17 years. He carves animals, humans, and unusual sculptures of human body parts in limestone, bronze, marble, and wood.

The Village

A quaint little retail haven in the center of downtown Gatlinburg is The Village (634 Parkway, 865/436-3995, www.thevillage-shops.com) with its fountain and Bavarian-style shops, most of which offer a more upscale atmosphere than the rest of the main drag through town. The Village, which curls away into its own little courtyard away from the main street through town, actually developed because the owners who purchased the property in 1965 were not quite sure what to do with it, having only 24 feet of frontage on the Parkway. The concept of The Village developed as a way to draw people from the main street back into a cozy gathering of shops that might otherwise have been no more than an alleyway.

The concept has worked. More than two dozen specialty shops and cafés now occupy The Village. One of my favorites is **Smoky Mountain Babies** (865/430-9550, Mar.–Nov. daily 10 A.M.–10 P.M., winter hours may vary), which carries high-end baby clothes and toys. If you're in the market for deck shoes, river sandals, or hiking boots to ensure your readiness for outdoor adventure, then check out **The Hayloft-Comfort Shoes** (800/245-2668, daily 10 A.M.–10 P.M.). **The Silver Tree** (865/430-3573, daily 10 A.M.–10 P.M.) is a whole store dedicated to silver jewelry, while **Simply Animals** (865/436-5849, daily 10 A.M.–10 P.M.) carries clothing, collars, toys, and treats for pets—you're welcome to bring in your pooch as well. Early risers can come by **The Donut Friar** (865/436-7306, daily 5 A.M.–10 P.M.) for fresh donuts, pastries, bread, lattes, and cappuccinos. You don't have to get there by 5 A.M., but don't wait too long—the donuts often sell out. If you happen to just be walking by, the smell is almost impossible to resist.

Winter hours for all the shops in The Village are speculative at best. Stores there are not required to have set hours from mid-December to March and will modify their schedule based

The Village in Gatlinburg

on customer traffic, weather, or whim. The weekends are your best bet in the winter.

Downtown Galleries

The Arrowcraft Gallery (576 Parkway, 865/436-4604, www.craftguild.org, May–Nov. Mon.–Sat. 10 A.M.–8 P.M., Sun. 10 A.M.–6 P.M., Dec.–Apr. Mon.–Sat. 10 A.M.–6 P.M., Sun. 10 A.M.–6 P.M.) is one of the most beautiful shops in town, located next to traffic light #6 across from River Road. One of four galleries of the Southern Highland Craft Guild that can be found in the southern mountains, Arrowcraft carries the handmade crafts of guild members, including beautifully turned wooden bowls, blown glass ornaments that sparkle like Christmas lights in the window, handmade jewelry, woven coverlets and table linens, and lovingly crafted toys.

Beneath the Smoke (467 Parkway, 865/436-3460, www.kenjenkins.com, Apr.–Dec. Mon.–Sat. 10 A.M.–8 P.M., Jan.–Mar. 10 A.M.–6 P.M., winter hours may vary) is the gallery of award-winning internationally known photographer and Gatlinburg native Ken Jenkins. The two-story gallery features hundreds of Jenkins' wildlife and landscape photographs from North America and around the world. Allow yourself some time to explore the gallery and peruse Jenkins' moving portraits of black bears, cougars, and eagles as well as his vibrant pictures of some of America's most treasured landscapes from the peaks of the Smokies to the sand and wind-carved rockscapes of the southwestern United States.

Downtown Gifts

Jonathan's (733 Parkway, 877/218-0442, Apr.–Dec. daily 9 A.M.–11 P.M., Jan.–Mar. daily 9 A.M.–8 P.M.) is tucked in among a horde of typical tourist traps on Gatlinburg's main drag right in the midst of the busiest section of the Parkway. The store has a nice selection of casual resort clothing as well as hiking boots, Minnetonka moccasins, and Life is Good clothing and gear, as well as gifts for children.

Maples' Tree (639 Parkway, 800/598-0908, www.maplestree.com, daily 9 A.M.–11 P.M., winter hours may vary) is just down the street and carries factory-made quilts, quilted purses, comfy nightwear for kids and adults, Jim Shore figurines and ornaments, and some home decor and garden items.

ENTERTAINMENT AND EVENTS
Annual Wildflower Pilgrimage

Gatlinburg's Annual Wildflower Pilgrimage (865/436-7318 ext. 222, seminars and classes $10–50) occurs each year across four days in April. During the festival the Great Smoky Mountains National Park offers more than 170 different programs to celebrate the arrival of spring blossoms, including guided hikes, motorcades, lectures, and outdoor programs.

Gatlinburg Fine Arts Festival

Gatlinburg Fine Arts Festival (888/240-1358, www.gfaf.net, free) occurs the third weekend in May and features a juried art show with

participating artists from all over the country, as well as live music and food vendors. The fair is held at Ripley's Aquarium and along River Road.

Gatlinburg Craftsmen's Fair

The Gatlinburg Craftsmen's Fair (303 Reagan Dr., 865/436-7479, www.craftsmenfair.com, adults $6, 12 and under free) occurs twice annually during a week in July and then two weeks in October at the Gatlinburg Convention Center. The fair has been going strong for more than three decades and features some 200 craft demonstrators in pottery, woodworking, jewelry making, painting, leather work, and basket weaving from all over the southern Appalachians. Not only do they offer their handmade wares for sale, but most of the artisans demonstrate their craft throughout the day. As part of the festivities, regional musicians fill the convention center with the sounds of dulcimer, banjo, and fiddle. Call or check the website for the current year's dates.

Gatlinburg Winter Magic

Gatlinburg Winter Magic (800/568-4748, www.gatlinburgwintermagic.com) runs from mid-November through February each year. The event kicks off in early November with a chili cook-off and the illumination of the city with over three million twinkling lights, all of them LED bulbs. The last weekend in November, the streets of town are filled with storytellers and carolers for Tunes & Tales, while the Gatlinburg Convention Center is decorated with dozens of Christmas trees. The Fantasy of Lights Christmas Parade occurs the first Saturday of December. What makes the parade particularly unique is that it occurs at night, turning the Parkway through the town center into a moving and rolling spectacle of lights.

SPORTS AND RECREATION
◖ Ober Gatlinburg

Ober Gatlinburg (1001 Parkway, 800/251-9202, www.obergatlinburg.com, daily

10 A.M.–7 P.M., single-session lift tickets $15–47, two-session lift tickets $52–89) is a mountaintop resort overlooking Gatlinburg that offers skiing on eight slopes; there are also 10 lanes for snow tubing with a 50-foot vertical drop. Skiing is typically available mid-December to early March. Ober Gatlinburg also has a year-round indoor ice skating rink in the center of the resort's mall. The resort is open year-round except for a maintenance shutdown of about one week, usually in the spring. Hours of operation are extended in the summer and during ski season, sometimes as late as midnight to accommodate night skiing. The biggest attraction here outside of ski season is the 120-passenger aerial tramway—the largest in the United States—that takes visitors from downtown Gatlinburg to the top of Mount Harrison at 2,700 feet. Ober Gatlinburg also has an 1,800-foot alpine slide that simulates a bobsled ride, offering a ride down the ski trails and through the woods.

Among the warm-weather attractions here are water slides, scenic chair lifts, musical entertainment, and a wildlife exhibit. The Ober Gatlinburg Restaurant and Lounge offers dining with long-distance views, and there are also several snack bars and cafés at the mall.

Just a warning, though—the resort is on the cheesy side, so unless you're coming here to ski, you might want to skip it. Even if you're not interested in visiting the amusement park, however, you might still want to purchase a tramway ticket, as the 10-minute ride up the mountain from downtown offers stunning views of Mount LeConte. The cost to ride the tramway only is $10 for adults and $8.50 for children. If you don't take the tramway, you can access the resort by taking Ski Mountain Road at traffic light #10.

White-Water Rafting

The Pigeon River, which flows along I-40 in the Cherokee National Forest just north of the Great Smoky Mountains National Park, is a great place to test your white-water mettle. Rapids here are mostly Class I to III with a handful of Class IV thrown in to whet your whistle for bigger water in the future, so it's a good rafting location for families and beginners on the water. Most local outfitters cover a five-mile stretch of river around Waterville by I-40 Exit 451. The scenery along this route is lovely with several calm water spots. Rhododendron, dogwoods, redbuds, pears, maples, and oaks create a canopy over the gorge, where an occasional Canadian goose or river otter sidles by.

There are about a dozen local outfitters that offer white-water rafting on the Pigeon River. Among them is **Rafting in the Smokies** (247 E. Parkway, 865/436-5008, www.raftinginthesmokies.com, June–Aug. Tues.–Thurs. and Sat. from 11 A.M., $35–39)—their guides are great. Rafting may also be offered on Sunday, Monday, and Friday and later than Labor Day, dependent on conditions. Call ahead for availability and reservations (required). Once your trip is scheduled, check in at their outpost in Hartford at Exit 447 off I-40.

Nantahala Outdoors Center's Great Outpost (888/905-7238, www.noc.com) is adjacent to the national park entrance on the southern edge of Gatlinburg. NOC is seeking LEED (Leadership in Energy and Environmental Design) certification from the U.S. Green Building Council for the renovated structure it is occupying. The already regionally well-known outfitter provides white-water rafting, kayaking, and float trips on seven area rivers, including the Pigeon River. NOC's Great Outpost also offers guided fly-fishing trips, guided hikes, mountain biking, and outdoor education classes and nature tours.

Other outfitters include **Smoky Mountain Outdoors** (453 Brookside Village Way, 800/771-7238, www.smokymountainrafting.com), which offers white-water and float trips and funyak rentals.

Zip Line

Zip Gatlinburg (905 River Rd., 877/494-7386, www.zipgatlinburg.com, daily 10 A.M.–8 P.M., $50–75) offers a canopy tour featuring nine cables, seven swinging platforms, and two sky bridges. Call or check website booking calendar for available tour times. Reservations can be made online.

Hummer Tours

Off Road Voyages (175 Parkway, 866/998-6924, www.offroadvoyages.com, daily 10 A.M.–4 P.M., $42–75) offers military Hummer (as in Humvee) tours of the Smokies, taking passengers on wild rides up steep mountainsides, through slushy ravines, up 30-degree side slopes, and across creeks to explore the Smoky Mountains on a wild and bumpy ride. This isn't for everyone, especially if you don't like your teeth knocking together, but if you're not into hiking this might be one avenue of experiencing the woods outside the confines of an air-conditioned automobile. Off Road also offers white-water packages in conjunction with Hummer tours.

If you want to rent your own Hummer or a Jeep for exploring on your own, check out **Southland Car and Jeep Rentals** (1011 E. Parkway, 865/436-9811, www.southlandcarjeeprental.com, Apr.–Oct. daily 8 A.M.–8 P.M., Nov.–Mar. Mon.–Sat. 9 A.M.–6 P.M.).

ACCOMMODATIONS

It would be pretty hard not to find a place to stay in Gatlinburg. The town has 12,000 rooms available, and on any given night some 45,000 tourists are spending the night here. And that's in a town where the resident population numbers only 3,500. Unfortunately, the sheer number of choices makes it difficult to sort the good lodgings from the bad. That being said, if you like being close to the action there are dozens of hotels right in town, some with rooms overlooking the busy Parkway, and others a block or so off the main street that provide easy access to attractions and shopping without the associated noise. And keep in mind that, no matter the season, downtown Gatlinburg will be going strong till midnight. Because Gatlinburg enjoys frontage on several rivers and streams pouring down out of the Smokies, even some of the most basic hotels

offer accommodations with stream-front balconies. If you plan to stay in town for several days or a week you might consider a vacation rental, of which there are thousands, to give you more bang for your buck. Many cabins and houses in the area rent by the week, offering you a better deal than the usual nightly charge. If serenity and luxury is what you're seeking, your best bet is probably one of about half a dozen bed-and-breakfasts occupying the curling back roads just outside of town.

Hotels

There are hotels of all descriptions in Gatlinburg, and pretty much all the major chains are represented here somewhere, including Best Western, Super 8, Hampton Inn, Sleep Inn, Days Inn, Clarion, and Comfort Inn as well as dozens of privately owned hotels. If you want to be guaranteed clean, comfortable rooms with reliable service, then your best bet is to reserve at one of the high-end chains, but there are plenty of local operations that are nice. Among them is the **Bearskin Lodge** (840 River Rd., 865/430-4330, www.thebearskinlodge.com, rooms $70–140, suites $110–170), a good hotel for families. It's within walking distance of Gatlinburg's attractions, shopping, and dining but not on the main drag through town, giving it a pretty quiet location. Bearskin Lodge is located on the West Fork of the Little Pigeon River, and many of the rooms have private balconies overlooking the water. Request a room on the west end corner of the hotel for the most privacy (so you're not looking across the river into someone else's hotel room) and for the largest suites with fireplaces and king beds. Kids and tired parents will love this place because it has both an outdoor heated pool and a lazy river that's wonderful to float around in an inner tube after a long day of hiking. There are also two gas fire pits in the pool area where you can roast marshmallows. There are a couple of drawbacks to this place, however: The staff can be downright careless and not particularly interested in the happiness of their guests (a fact of life in way too many accommodations in the area), and while the rooms are clean and orderly they are starting to show some wear. The Bearskin offers complimentary high-speed Internet access as well as continental breakfast.

Opened in 2009, **Hilton Garden Inn** (625 River Rd., 865/436-0048, www.gatlinburg.hgi. com, rooms $109–159, suites $149–169) is the first hotel in the state of Tennessee with LEED (Leadership in Energy and Environmental Design) certification. The green features that will be most readily apparent to guests are the hotel's use of compact fluorescent lightbulbs; motion detectors that turn room lights on and off; low-flow toilets, faucets, and showers; and recycling baskets in guest rooms. The five-story hotel has 112 rooms, each featuring the luxurious Garden Sleep System bed, complimentary Wi-Fi, and complimentary remote printing from guest rooms. The hotel has an outdoor swimming pool, a fitness center, and Stay Fit Kits where guests can check out supplies for yoga and pilates. On-site is a restaurant offering breakfast and dinner as well as all-day room service and a lounge bar.

Fairfield Inn and Suites (168 Parkway, 865/430-3659, www.marriott.com/gtlno, $59–169) is another good family hotel. Though located on the western edge of downtown and not really within easy walking distance of most shopping and restaurants, the hotel does have a trolley stop. Renovated in 2009, the hotel is crisp and new and features a beautiful pool with fountain and waterslide as well as an indoor pool and hot tub. The kids will love that it's right next door to mini-golf. Free continental breakfast is available each morning, and guests enjoy complimentary high-speed Internet access.

Westgate Smoky Mountain Resort and Spa (915 Westgate Resort Rd., 877/819-4028, www.wgsmokymountains.com, 1-bedroom suites $79–159, 2-bedroom suites $149–209, 3-bedroom suites $179–259) is a welcome bit of seclusion that is still convenient to both Gatlinburg and Pigeon Forge. The 70-acre resort has everything you need, from the Wild Bear Falls Waterpark to a hot stone massage at the Serenity Spa. Other amenities include a 24-hour fitness center, two heated pools, and an on-site restaurant and lounge.

Inns and Bed-and-Breakfasts

The **(Timber Rose English Lodge** (1106 Tanrac Trail, 877/235-4993, www.timber-rose.com, $99–159) is located within the Great Smoky Arts and Crafts Community. It was built to resemble an English estate lodge, and the Timber Rose's rambling, ornate architecture and garden cherubs initially seem at odds with the rustic mountain environment around it, but once you step out onto one of the private verandas that grace each of the lodge's five suites the Timber Rose seems perfectly placed. The northeastern view is one of rolling blue ridge after rolling blue ridge. The rooms here are almost as stunning as the view. Decorated in Victorian-era antiques with wood-burning fireplaces and flower-papered walls, they offer an Old World feel complimented by modern amenities—outdoor hot tubs, fully equipped kitchens, and spacious bathrooms. This is a couples-only lodge, and no breakfast is served. However, the suites' fully equipped kitchens provide cookware and utensils for making your own meals. No smoking is permitted indoors.

Also located in the midst of the Great Smoky Arts and Crafts Community, the **Buckhorn Inn** (2140 Tudor Mountain Rd., 866/941-0460, www.buckhorninn.com, rooms $175, cottages $170, guesthouses $195–320) has been welcoming guests since 1938. Nestled in woods and rhododendron stands, the inn overlooks the national park with long views of Mount LeConte, toasty fires, and lazy hammocks under the trees. The Buckhorn also offers dinner on-site. Lodge rooms are elegant, but the cottages' decor (and housekeeping) tends to be a bit on the shabby side, so opt for a lodge room if you can. Two-bedroom guesthouses are also available.

(The Lodge at Buckberry Creek (961 Campbell Lead Rd., 866/305-6343, www. buckberrylodge.com, lodge suites $180–265, gallery suites $225–325, grand suites $300–460) is situated above the town of Gatlinburg and is accessible via Ski Mountain Road.

Featuring what it terms as "camp-style suites," the lodge is anything but rustic, save for its decor. Here the crown moldings are made of cherry and birch with the bark still intact, and rooms are decorated in Adirondack-style furniture. Many of the suites feature views of Mount LeConte from their private verandas. The Lodge at Buckberry Creek is located on 26 private acres adjacent to the Great Smoky Mountains National Park on land that has belonged to the local McLean family for three generations. With its own trout fishing stream, hiking trails, and dining, Buckberry Creek offers enough amenities that guests just seeking a peaceful getaway could spend their entire visit on-site. The service is impeccable, and the staff really knows how to make you feel as if you are the most important person on earth.

Christopher Place Resort (1500 Pinnacles Way, 800/595-9441, www.christopherplace. com, rooms $165, suites $275–330, guesthouse $275) is a good place to lay your head if you're looking for a luxury bed-and-breakfast far from the more trammeled areas of the Smokies. Located about 15 miles from the Cosby entrance to the national park off Highway 32 south of Newport, Christopher Place seems like it's in the middle of nowhere, especially as you make the circuitous climb up English Mountain to the resort property. Once you arrive, you'll understand. The mansion house affords sweeping views of the Smokies to the east and has two long and broad verandas for taking in the scene. Christopher Place occupies 280 acres and has nine guest rooms and suites as well as a guesthouse. The inn features a grand spiraling staircase in the entranceway lighted by a crystal chandelier, and the curling stairway will lead you three stories up to the guest game room with pool table, guest fridge, and freshly baked cookies on the bar. The home is decorated with family antiques and memorabilia. The current owners had grandparents serving under the Kennedy and Johnson administration, and many historic photos of the era line the walls of the game room. Christopher Place offers dinner on-site with a changing menu. Dinner is served nightly at 7 P.M. and costs $40 per person. The public is welcome with advance reservations. The resort also has an English-library pub where you can order drinks as well as fish-and-chips or beer-boiled

Christopher Place Resort

© FRENCH C. GRIMES

shrimp cocktail. A three-course breakfast is served each morning overlooking the grand eastern view. The inn provides concierge services, including arranging white-water rafting, horseback riding, and guided fly-fishing in the Smokies.

Cabins

There are thousands of cabins and vacation rentals in and immediately around Gatlinburg, and since this is the "wedding capital of the South" many of the rentals cater to couples. Accommodations range from luxurious and tasteful to downright cheesy (think heart-shaped whirlpool tubs). The process of finding the right cabin can be overwhelming with so many offerings.

Be sure to get a clear understanding from the vacation rental operator as to how private your accommodations will be. Many of the city's rental agencies have dozens of cabins grouped together in relatively small spaces, which can quickly spoil your vision of a romantic evening in the hot tub with your spouse if you're staring across the deck at another couple doing the same thing right next door. Others can be right in the thick of residential communities, with their attendant children and dogs running around the neighborhood and local baseball parks shining their lights in your windows till midnight.

Mountain Rentals of Gatlinburg (209 Cartertown Rd., 866/482-1044, www.mountainchalets.com, 1-bedroom $75–145, 2-bedroom $85–200, 3-bedroom $95–165, 4-bedroom $125–275, 5 or more bedrooms $150–575) offers a variety of vacation rental properties. Some of the best options feature private porches with hot tubs, lofts with pool tables, gas fireplaces, full kitchens, and two master suites with whirlpool tubs and king-size beds, all in the same cabin.

Jackson Mountain Homes (1662 E. Parkway, 865/436-8876, www.jacksonmountain.com, 1-bedroom $110–205, 2-bedroom $120–240, 3-bedroom $130–315, 4-bedroom $215–675, 5-bedroom $275–640, 6-bedroom $500–675, 8-bedroom $575–1,100)

has vacation rentals all over Gatlinburg with a rental office on the outskirts of town on Highway 321 north. Many of the cabins feature multiple master-bedroom suites, pool tables, air hockey, hot tubs, gas log fireplaces, and multi-level decks. Rentals are consistently clean, outfitted with high-quality furniture, and armed with security systems to protect valuables. The staff at Jackson Mountain Homes is service-oriented, allowing for quick and easy check-in, including after-hours check-in.

Mountain Laurel Chalets (440 Ski Mountain Rd., 800/626-3431, www.mtnlaurelchalets.com, 1-bedroom $95–195, 2-bedroom $100–229, 3-bedroom $140–300, 4-bedroom $210–315, 5-bedroom $195–350, 6-bedroom $200–450, 7 to 12 bedrooms $400–1,000) seems to have the corner on the market when it comes to high-elevation vacation rentals overlooking Gatlinburg and the Great Smoky Mountains National Park from the twisting back roads accessible off Ski Mountain Road at traffic light #10, such as the three-story chalet I enjoyed, situated with a postcard-perfect view of Mount LeConte from its rear deck with hot tub. As with most vacation rentals in Gatlinburg, Mountain Laurel's homes are privately owned and individually decorated, though common amenities include multiple master suites, full kitchens, gas log fireplaces, hot tubs, and easy check-in procedures. All units are protected by alarmed security systems.

Camping

Twin Creek RV Resort (1202 E. Parkway, 800/252-8077, www.twincreekrvresort.com, Mar.–Nov., $60) is something of a luxury camping resort with 85 paved sites, heated pool and kiddie pool, hot tub, laundry, full hookups, laundry, Wi-Fi, cable TV, bathhouse, playground, decks at every campsite, and access to trolley service. The resort is north of Gatlinburg on Highway 321.

Camping in the Smokies Gatlinburg RV Park (1640 E. Parkway, 865/430-3594, $30–42) is also located on Highway 321 north of Gatlinburg right next door to Gatlinburg City

Hall. Situated along a stream with the national park behind it and shady sites, the resort offers full hookups, cable TV, laundry, bathhouse, and pool. There is trolley service to the campground.

Cosby Campground (127 Cosby Park Rd., 865/436-1200, www.nps.gov/grsm, $14) is located inside the Great Smoky Mountains National Park just inside the Cosby entrance to the park off Highway 321. This is one of the lesser-used national park campgrounds and is a great place to camp if you prefer to get away from the crowds you'll often find in other park campgrounds during periods of peak visitation. Located alongside Cosby Creek, the campground provides access to several hiking trails, including the Gabe Mountain Trail, which leads to Hen Wallow Falls.

FOOD
Casual Fine Dining

Great food can be a little tricky to find in Gatlinburg if you don't know where to look. Too many of the restaurants here, recognizing the fact that most of their customers are tourists and not locals, don't bother to go the extra mile to win back your service as second time. There are a few exceptions, however, and strangely enough, they tend to be owned by the same people, so obviously there are a few restaurateurs in town who know what they're doing.

◖ **The Peddler** (820 River Rd., 865/436-5794, www.peddlergatlinburg.com, Sun.–Fri. 5 P.M.–close, Sat. 4:30 P.M.–close, $19–38) is a local and tourist favorite and always packed to the gills. The restaurant has lovely riverside seating available in both the dining room and the bar, but unless you get there early your chances of getting one of those coveted tables are slim to none. The Peddler is best known for its steaks, though the charbroiled shrimp is darn good as well. All entrées come with unlimited access to a well-stocked salad bar, and there is a full bar available. The Peddler does not accept reservations but does allow guests to call ahead, so you can get your name on the waiting list before you head to the restaurant.

Bennett's Pit Bar-B-Que (714 River Rd., 865/436-2400, www.bennetts-bbq. com, Sun.–Thurs. 8 A.M.–10 P.M., Fri.–Sat. 8 A.M.–11 P.M., $5–22) is known, of course, for its hickory-smoked barbecue beef, pork, and chicken and gargantuan platters of food. This is southern-style cooking at its dripping best. The restaurant also has a soup and salad bar and breakfast buffet.

The Park Grill (1110 Parkway, 865/436-2300, www.parkgrillgatlinburg.com, Sun.–Fri. 5 P.M.–close, Sat. 4:30 P.M.–close, $13–33) is owned and operated by the same folks that run The Peddler, and some of the menu options are similar. The Park Grill, however, offers some great combo meals like prime rib and chicken or filet mignon and shrimp that come with the salad bar, a side, and fresh hot bread. The restaurant's sweet moonshine chicken is another good one to try. For dessert, grab a friend and order the dessert sampler, which comes with Jack Daniel's crème brûlée, berry cobbler, and chocolate cheesecake trufflette.

◖ **Howard's Steakhouse** (976 Parkway, 865/436-3600, www.howards-gatlinburg.com, Sun.–Thurs. 11 A.M.–10 P.M., Fri.–Sat. 11 A.M.–11 P.M., $13–50) has, hands down, absolutely the best steak burgers in town—and perhaps anywhere in the Smokies. They come with heart-attack-on-a-plate toppings like bacon, mounds of cheese, and even ham, but the taste is worth the risk. Howard's also serves up a surprisingly lean and tasty rib eye. The restaurant has a pub-style atmosphere with booths against the windows and a full bar. If the weather is nice, elect to eat on the outdoor patio overlooking the river. If it's evening, you might see some resident raccoons come out to the river to beg for scraps from the diners above. And while there are few places in the Smokies where you can describe the service as excellent, Howard's is an exception. The waitstaff here is attentive almost to a fault. No dirty plate will sit on your table for longer than two seconds.

Best Italian Café & Pizzeria (968 Parkway, 865/430-4090, www.bestitalian. com, Sun.–Thurs. 11 A.M.–10 P.M., Fri.–Sat. 11 A.M.–11 P.M., $11–23) is located right behind Howard's Steakhouse and is best known for its garlic rolls, which are topped with olive oil, garlic, parmesan, and romano cheese. For your main course, definitely try the filet tips linguini with some of the most tender beef tenderloin tips served up with pasta, onions, and green and red peppers.

For reasons that are unclear to me, the food in Gatlinburg tends to get progressively worse the closer you get to the center of the downtown tourist area. One exception to that is **McCutchan's Brass Grill Restaurant** (710 Parkway, 865/436-4345, www.mccutchans-brassgrill.com, daily 11 A.M.–10 P.M., $9–22), a family-friendly place owned by the same folks who operate Howard's Steakhouse, meaning many of the menu offerings are similar, including the to-die-for cordon bleu burger topped with bacon, blue cheese crumbles, and provolone cheese. I like the fact that the kids' menu doesn't sport the usual junk food fare but offers ham-and-swiss and turkey sandwiches as well as steak burgers.

No Way Jose's Cantina (555 Parkway, 865/430-5673, www.nowayjosescantina.com, daily 11:30 A.M.–10 P.M., $5–13) is a fun place to eat across the road from Ripley's Aquarium and offers pleasant seating on the river. The restaurant offers all the usual fare you'd expect from a Mexican restaurant, all of it reliably good. But the thing you have to order before your meal arrives is a basket of chips with the restaurant's homemade salsa. It's so bitingly fresh it tastes like the ingredients came right out of the garden.

Breakfast

◖ **Pancake Pantry** (628 Parkway, 865/436-4724, June–Oct. daily 7 A.M.–4 P.M., Nov.–May daily 7 A.M.–3 P.M., $6–10) is a perennial favorite of mine. I've been here a time or two, or three, and I always have to get my favorite dish—the wildberry crepe, which consists of five types of berries in compote stuffed inside three crepes with creamy ricotta cheese and powdered sugar on top. Diners start lining up at the door at 7 A.M., so get here early! But if you're late, don't worry—they serve breakfast until closing time.

Mountain Lodge Restaurant (913 E. Parkway, 865/436-2547, daily 7 A.M.–3 P.M.,

$3–8) is a local's favorite, without very much tourist traffic. It's located on Highway 321 north a fair distance from the downtown tourist area of Gatlinburg. It's easy to see why the locals like it: It's cheap and reliably good. Four people can eat here for under $20. The fare is typical country breakfast—pancakes, omelets, biscuits and gravy, and toast and grits.

Grocery Service

If you're renting a cabin in the Gatlinburg or Pigeon Forge area and don't want to contend with the hassle of grocery shopping to stock the fridge when you get there, **Smoky Mountain Grocery** (877/484-8853, www.smokymountaingrocery.com, $15 per delivery) will do your shopping for you and deliver groceries to your door on arrival or even pre-arrival if you request it. You can order online.

INFORMATION AND SERVICES
Information

Understanding the visitors centers in Gatlinburg is bit of a challenge. The **Gatlinburg Chamber of Commerce** (800-568/4748, www.gatlinburg.com) is located at East Parkway and operates the **Gatlinburg Welcome Center** (Hwy. 441 S., Memorial Day–Oct. daily 8 A.M.–7 P.M., Nov. daily 8 A.M.–5:30 P.M.). The City of Gatlinburg operates the visitors centers in town. The **Parkway Visitor Center** (520 Parkway, daily 10 A.M.–6 P.M.) is located at traffic light #3 in downtown Gatlinburg at the intersection of U.S. 441 and U.S. 321. The **Aquarium Welcome Center** (88 River Rd., daily 9 A.M.–9 P.M.) is located at traffic light #5 on Ripley's Aquarium of the Smokies Plaza.

Emergency Services

Fort Sanders Sevier Medical Center (709 Middle Creek Rd., 865/429-6100, www.fssevier.com) offers 24-hour emergency service. You can also contact the **Gatlinburg Police** (1230 E. Parkway, 865/436-5181) for assistance.

Media

Gatlinburg has its own cable channel,

WGAT-69, which you can tune into from your hotel room. Channel 69 offers 24/7 information on area attractions, events, shopping, and restaurants.

GETTING THERE

The heaviest traveled route into Gatlinburg is from I-40, and this is the route you will likely take if you're coming in from the north or west. Most visitors exit the interstate at U.S. 66 at Exit 407; 66 will feed into U.S. 441 south to Gatlinburg. However, while this is the simplest route, it is also the busiest. An alternate option is to take Exit 435 off I-40 at Knoxville, and follow U.S. 321 to Gatlinburg.

If you've flown into McGhee-Tyson Airport outside Knoxville, then your best bet is to avoid Knoxville altogether and head south on Highway 129 to Maryville. At Maryville, take 321 north to the park entrance at Townsend or to Pigeon Forge, where you will take a right onto U.S. 441 and follow it right into Gatlinburg.

If you're coming in from Asheville and points east, take I-40 west to Exit 443, and follow the Foothills Parkway to Highway 321 south, which leads right into Gatlinburg.

From the Atlanta area and points south, you can reach Gatlinburg by taking I-85 north to I-985 north, and then following I-985 to U.S. 23, which feeds right into Highway 23/441 in North Carolina. Stay on 441 to Cherokee, and drive through the Great Smoky Mountains National Park on the Newfound Gap Road to reach Gatlinburg.

GETTING AROUND
Parking

Parking in Gatlinburg is something close to a nightmare, in large part due to the traffic and the sheer number of people overwhelming what is still very much a small town. The most hassle-free and inexpensive option is to park at one of the two free park-and-ride lots and then take the trolley. The lots are located at the **Gatlinburg Welcome Center on the Spur** (Hwy. 441 S.) and the **City Hall**

Complex (1230 E. Parkway). Also free is the thrill of capturing an elusive space along River Road, which runs parallel to the Parkway along the West Prong of the Pigeon River between Ripley's Aquarium and Ski Mountain Road. The City of Gatlinburg operates two parking garages, **Ripley's Aquarium Garage** (88 River Rd.) and **Fred McMahan Parking Garage** (520 Parkway). Both garages are $1.75 for the first hour, $1 each hour after that, with a maximum daily charge of $6. There are also three municipal lots. The Anna Porter Public Library Lot (237 Bishop La.) and the lot at 303 Reagan Drive both charge a flat rate of $5 all day. Finally, the lot at 366 Parkway charges $0.75 per hour. If you pay to park, stick with these options. There are plenty of private parking lots, but they can get expensive. Guests at in-town hotels should just leave their cars in the hotel lot and walk or ride the trolley.

Gatlinburg Trolley System
The Gatlinburg Trolley (865/436-3897,

Gatlinburg Trolley

© FRENCH C. GRIMES

www.gatlinburgtrolley.org, daily 8 A.M.–midnight, winter Sun.–Thurs. 10 A.M.–6 P.M., Fri.–Sat. 10 A.M.–10 P.M., $0.50–1) provides access to all of the attractions of Gatlinburg and neighboring Pigeon Forge without the headache of finding parking. The trolleys make frequent stops at clearly marked shelters and stops in Gatlinburg as well as Pigeon Forge. There are 100 trolley stops in Gatlinburg alone. Key stops include the Gatlinburg Welcome Center, where you can park free and ride, as well as the Aquarium Trolley Stop. Special trolley routes also offer tours of the Great Smoky Mountains National Park, trips to Dollywood, and loops around the Great Smoky Arts and Crafts Community. Exact change is required. An interesting side note is that Gatlinburg's 20-trolley fleet is powered by a mixture of B20 biodiesel.

Pigeon Forge and Sevierville

Sevierville is the birthplace of country music legend Dolly Parton. It was here that Parton grew up with her 11 brothers and sisters, some of whom she adopted as her own as she grew into fame. A statue of Dolly, sculpted by well-known local artist Jim Gray, stands in front of the Sevierville Courthouse. The courthouse lawn is one of the few areas of town that still looks as it must have when Parton was growing up here. The rest of Sevierville and its next-door neighbor Pigeon Forge have become booming tourist destinations with over 11 million visitors each year. You may feel, when you arrive here, that all 11 million of those people have decided to come at the same time you have, but it's an illusion. The neon lights and gargantuan attractions that line the roadsides can easily make any visitor feel overwhelmed.

Pigeon Forge has perhaps rightfully earned its reputation as one of the East Coast's biggest tourist traps. If you have kids who need constant entertainment, from go-cart rides to bungee jumping, you'll have no problem finding what they crave. But if you're seeking access to some real culture, you'll have to look a little harder. Surprisingly, one of the best places to find it is Dollywood, an extremely well-designed amusement park with some first-rate country and bluegrass shows and genuine Appalachian crafters displaying their skills and wares.

The town of Pigeon Forge traces the origin of at least part of its name to 1820, when pioneer Isaac Love set up an iron forge here. His son went on to build a tub mill a decade later. That mill is now a National Historic Site, which you can visit at Old Mill Square on the Little Pigeon River. The mill continues to produce flour and cornmeal for use at local restaurants and for sale to the public.

Believe it or not, early settlers here found huge numbers of passenger pigeons along the banks of the Little Pigeon River, feeding on the nuts of the beech trees that bowed over the stream. Thus, Pigeon Forge found its name. But Pigeon Forge and Sevierville both remained quiet rural communities until the Great Smoky Mountains National Park was established here in 1934. Slowly, tourism had its effect on the area, and Pigeon Forge was formally incorporated in 1961.

With the opening of the amusement park that would eventually become Dollywood and the arrival of the World's Fair in neighboring Knoxville in 1982, awareness of eastern Tennessee as a tourist destination increased dramatically. But even though the town looks big with all its visitor services and attractions, its year-round resident population remains relatively small. Just over 6,000 people call Pigeon Forge home.

SIGHTS
Dollywood
Visitors just might catch a glimpse of Dolly Parton at Dollywood (1020 Dollywood Lane,

Pigeon Forge, 865/428-9488, www.dollywood. com, Apr.–Dec., $42–54), where she performs for the amusement park's opening for the season each April. Parton started the theme park in Pigeon Forge more than 20 years ago, and it has since become the town's premier attraction. But this isn't your average theme park. Dollywood has the look of an old-time Appalachian village and small southern town all at the same time with tree-lined streets, ponds, and streams. Rides are tucked into the

woods, hardly noticeable, and snack stands sell delightful treats.

And while Dollywood may be best known for Showstreet, where theaters offer up everything from bluegrass and country to square dancing, the park also employs several master craftsmen, honoring the Appalachian arts that Dolly knew as a child. In addition to candle making, blacksmithing, and wood crafting, the park also has its own wagon-making facility known as Valley Carriage Works.

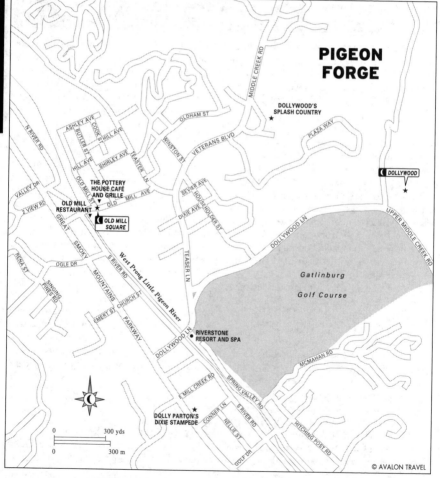

© FRENCH C. GRIMES

Valley Carriage Works at Dollywood in Pigeon Forge

The carriage shop takes actual orders for wagons and carriages and, in fact, built a replica Cherokee wagon to commemorate the 165th anniversary of the Trail of Tears. The wagon is currently on display at the Museum of the Cherokee Indian in Cherokee, North Carolina, and sports an 1838 one-cent piece inserted in the wood in honor of the year in which the Trail of Tears began. Normally, all Valley Carriage Works wagons and carriages carry a penny of the year they were built.

Dollywood, in partnership with the American Eagle Foundation, is also home to the largest gathering of non-releasable bald eagles in America accessible to the public. At Eagle Mountain, park visitors can watch the national bird in its native habitat. The eagles on display have been injured and could not survive in the wild, but they find a comfortable home in the trees here at Dollywood, and daily Wings of America shows put visitors in close contact with the birds.

Shows are held in various theaters and outdoor stages all over Dollywood, though most are concentrated along Showstreet. The music celebrates Dolly's bluegrass and country roots, and some of her relatives perform here. *Sha-Kon-O-Hey!* honors the people and culture of the Smokies with eight original songs Parton wrote for the Great Smoky Mountains National Park's 75th anniversary, which occurred in 2009. The Smoky Mountain String Band combines fiddles, bass, and banjo with down-home comedy. *Dolly's Family Reunion* features Parton's uncles and cousins singing some of Parton's own songs. If you'd like some indication of just how good the music is here, Dollywood has earned more Big E Entertainment Awards in recent years than any other amusement park in the world.

There are restaurants and food stands scattered throughout the park, so you'll never go hungry, though the meals can be a little bit pricey, especially considering what you paid to get into the park in the first place. One of my favorite snacks is the fresh berries and cream concoction available from a stand in the

Craftsman's Valley across from the Wings of America theater.

Rides here run the gamut, allowing plenty of fun for kids of all ages with old-time wooden roller coasters, water rides, and a country fair area with less intimidating options for the little ones. SkyZip offers five zip-line crossings through the park. The ride takes about an hour and a half and costs an extra $40. Two other additions to the park's collection of rides are a new steel coaster known as Mystery Mine and a fun one for younger kids and playful adults, River Battle.

Just in case you haven't spent enough money by the time you're getting ready to leave the park, there are loads of gift shops here. If you're looking for a souvenir, stick to the shops in Craftsman's Valley, where you can actually buy locally crafted goods, most of them made right here in the park—from beautiful leather belts to handblown glass.

The nice thing about Dollywood is really the people who work here, however. These are not "I'm just here for the summer" college kids who don't care about your happiness. Most of the staff is made up of retirees who are here to have fun and enjoy making visitors happy. You won't find a friendlier bunch anywhere.

Parking at Dollywood is $8 per vehicle. You can save yourself some cash, however, by parking your car at Old Mill Square and riding the trolley from there to Dollywood for only $0.50. Days and hours of operation vary throughout the season; check the website or call for details.

Dollywood's Splash Country

Dollywood's Splash Country (2146 Middle Creek Rd., Pigeon Forge, 865/428-9488, www.dollywoodssplashcountry.com, May–Sept. daily 10 A.M.–6 P.M.) is one among several water parks in the Sevierville and Pigeon Forge area, but it is easily the largest. The park features a 25,000-square-foot wave pool, 29 wild water slides, a lazy river, 7,500-square-foot leisure pool, and three interactive children's water play areas. There are also, of course, concessions and a gift shop. Check the website for rates.

Dolly's Family Reunion stage at Dollywood in Pigeon Forge

© FRENCH C. GRIMES

Titanic **Pigeon Forge**

The *Titanic* Pigeon Forge (2134 Parkway, 866/488-5104, www.titanicpigeonforge. com) is not the first replica *Titanic* to show up in a landlocked town. (There is also one in Branson, Missouri.) But this one is bigger—30,000 square feet, in fact—consisting of three decks with 20 galleries containing genuine *Titanic* artifacts salvaged from the famous sinking ocean liner. The museum showcases exact reproductions of the original *Titanic*'s Marconi wireless room, its grand staircase, a first-class suite, and a third-class cabin. On boarding this vessel, anchored in water, you'll receive a boarding pass with the name of a real *Titanic* passenger, and you'll follow their journey through a 90-minute self-guided tour, learning your fate—rescue or death in icy water—at the tour's end. Kids will especially enjoy the mini-decks where they can test their balance against the real-life slope of the ship's decks as she sank into the ocean in 1912.

© FRENCH C. GRIMES

steam engine at Dollywood in Pigeon Forge

Tennessee Museum of Aviation

The Tennessee Museum of Aviation (135 Air Museum Way, Sevierville, 866/286-8738, www.tnairmuseum.org, Jan.–Feb. Mon.–Sat. 10 A.M.–5 P.M., Sun. 1–5 P.M., Mar.–Dec. Mon.–Sat. 10 A.M.–6 P.M., Sun. 1–6 P.M., adults $12.75, seniors $9.75, children 6–12 $6.75, 6 and under free) is located on the grounds of the Gatlinburg Pigeon Forge Airport and features a 35,000-square-foot hangar full of historic aircraft, including two flyable P-47 Thunderbolts and several Russian MiGs on static display. The museum also has exhibits on the history of aviation, and you might get to see an impromptu flight by one of the historic WWII warbirds. The museum has a large gift shop carrying books on aviation, aviation-related toys, posters, prints, aircraft models and kits, insignia, patches, and pins, as well as T-shirts and caps. The museum is also home to Tennessee's Aviation Hall of Fame.

Dolly Parton Statue

Located on the courthouse lawn in downtown Sevierville is a bronze statue of Sevier County's favorite daughter—Dolly Parton. The statue (125 Court Ave.) was sculpted by local artist Jim Gray and unveiled in 1987. It features the legendary songstress seated with her guitar and that big famous smile spreading across her face. The statue is, quite understandably, a popular photo spot.

SHOPPING
◖ Old Mill Square

Pigeon Forge is full of less "touristy" surprises if you know where to look between the wild rides, hotels, and mini-golf courses. One example is **Old Mill Square** (175 Old Mill Ave., Pigeon Forge, 865/428-0771, www.old-millsquare.com), situated off Pigeon Forge's main strip at traffic light #7 along the Little Pigeon River. This both restored and re-created historic area has a collection of shops showcasing Appalachian crafts as well as stone-ground flour and grains. **The Old Mill & General Store** (865/453-4628, Mon.–Sat.

8:30 A.M.–9 P.M., Sun. 9 A.M.–8 P.M.) is located in an 1830 gristmill that has been in continuous operation for 180 years. The mill produces flour and meal, which is available for purchase along with old-fashioned glass-bottled sodas, candy, and gift items.

My favorite place in Old Mill Square is **Pigeon River Pottery** (865/453-1104, Mon.–Thurs. 9 A.M.–8:30 P.M., Fri.–Sat. 9 A.M.–9 P.M., Sun. 9 A.M.–8 P.M.), where you can actually see potters at work in the studio behind the shop. For a signature souvenir, pick up a member of the potters' Mighty Bear series, a collection of handcrafted bears in various shapes and sizes fired right here in the studio and representative of the Smokies' beloved mascot—the American black bear.

The **Old Mill Toy Bin** (865/774-2258, Sun.–Thurs. 9:30 A.M.–8 P.M., Fri.–Sat. 9 A.M.–9 P.M.) carries a host of both modern and nostalgic toys, from little red wagons to tin tea sets. The **Old Mill Candy Kitchen** (865/453-7516, Mon.–Thurs. 9 A.M.–8:30 P.M., Fri.–Sat. 9 A.M.–9 P.M., Sun. 9 A.M.–8 P.M.) is another fun place to stop, kid or not. Try the chocolate-covered peanut butter–stuffed graham crackers. At **The Farmhouse Kitchen** (865/428-2044, Sun.–Thurs. 9:30 A.M.–8 P.M., Fri.–Sat. 9 A.M.–9 P.M.) you can pick up all kinds of kitchen gadgets as well as sauces and soup mixes, including the mix for the killer loaded-baked-potato soup served at The Pottery House Café and Grille just down the street.

Specialty Stores

The Christmas Place (2470 Parkway, Pigeon Forge, 865/453-0415, www.christmasplace. com, daily 9 A.M.–10 P.M.) bills itself as the South's largest and most beautiful Christmas store. I don't know the truth of either statement, but this place is pretty darn big, rambling through several Bavarian-looking buildings with grounds so coated with blooms in spring and summer that for Christmas to come and spoil the color almost seems a travesty. Whether you're into holiday kitsch or not, this store is worth checking out. In addition to

Christmas decorations by the thousands, you'll also find artificial trees, a custom floral department, candy kitchen, Vera Bradley items, and special toy and ornament galleries for kids.

If you're in the market for cowboy boots, then you definitely need to stop by **Stages Western Wear** (2765 Parkway, Pigeon Forge, 865/453-8086, www.stageswest.com, Mon.–Sat. 9 A.M.–9 P.M.), which has over 9,000 pairs of boots in stock plus everything else you need to complete your Western ensemble.

The **Tanger Outlets** (1645 Parkway, Sevierville, 865/4533-1053, www.tanger-outlet.com, Mon.–Sat. 9 A.M.–9 P.M., Sun. 10 A.M.–7 P.M.) are located at traffic light #13 in Sevierville and feature dozens of outlet shops for brand names like Polo Ralph Lauren, Nautica, J. Crew, Eddie Bauer, Old Navy, and Calvin Klein.

The Apple Barn Cider Mill & General Store (230 Apple Valley Rd., Sevierville, 865/453-9319, www.applebarncidermill. com, May–Oct. Mon.–Thurs. 9 A.M.–7 P.M., Fri.–Sat. 9 A.M.–9 P.M., Sun. 10 A.M.–6 P.M., Nov.–Apr. Mon.–Sat. 9 A.M.–5:30 P.M., Sun. 1–6 P.M.) is located on a working apple orchard just outside Sevierville, and the smell of apples is probably the first thing you'll notice upon entering the store. You can purchase freshly picked apples right off the tree, buy cider and sparkling juice, dive into a fresh-baked apple pie, or browse the country store, which also sells wine, chocolate, smoked ham, local crafts, and old-fashioned candy. The Apple Barn also has an ice cream shop. The working orchard that surrounds the farm has more than 4,000 fruit trees, bearing 14 different kinds of apples. There are two restaurants on-site as well, the Applewood Farmhouse Restaurant and the Applewood Farmhouse Grill.

ENTERTAINMENT AND EVENTS
Entertainment

There are more than a dozen theaters in Pigeon Forge offering musical entertainment, comedy, and even bison stampedes. Their offerings range from some incredibly talented performers to the downright silly, so select your pricey evening entertainment carefully. The best show in town is at the **Country Tonite Theatre** (129 Showplace Blvd., Pigeon Forge, 800/792-4308, www.countrytonitepf.com, $23–28). Don't let the over-the-top glitz fool you—people in this town can actually sing, play…and dance. Country Tonite is a prime example. This show will appeal to just about anyone, country music fan or not. Check out Mike Caldwell's incredible harmonica playing, and the fast and fancy moves of the dancers. Even Bubba the Redneck's Elvis impersonation is good! Shows are at 3 and 8 P.M. daily.

Dolly Parton's Dixie Stampede (3849 Parkway, Pigeon Forge, 800/356-1676, www.dixiestampede.com, daily, call for show times, $42–47) is the most popular show in town, seating 1,000 people for each of five shows a day during peak season. It's almost impossible to describe a dinner theater with charging longhorns—you pretty much have to experience it to believe it. Every show comes with a four-course country-style meal. And among the amazing things you'll see happening in the arena before you are horses jumping through fire, a rodeo competition, charging Yankees and Confederates, lots of cowboys and cowgirls singing and kicking up their heels, and ostrich races. Yes, I said ostrich races. And bison, too. You won't leave the Dixie Stampede hungry or even bored, but you might leave scratching your head at the meaning of it all.

Events

Wilderness Wildlife Week (865/429-7350, www.mypigeonforge.com/wildlife, free) takes place in January and is the town's first major event in a year loaded with more festivals than one can possibly list. This is one of the better ones, however, because it actually involves the great outdoors in a natural way, something that is a bit of an anomaly for this town. The event is headquartered at the Music Road Convention Center. During the week there are more than 175 workshops available, all of them run by experts

who can talk about the Smokies' earliest pioneers as well as the area's special flora and fauna. There are art and music classes available as well as 40 guided hikes and field trips in the Great Smoky Mountains National Park. Wilderness Wildlife Week has a musical side, too, with one night devoted to **AppalachiaFest** (800/792-4308, www.mypigeonforge.com/music, adults $15, 17 and under $5) at the Country Tonite Theatre. The event features traditional mountain music, ranging from folk to Celtic, and typically has several award-winning artists—in the past Tim O'Brien and Boogertown Gap have performed. Interestingly enough, these two winter events make Pigeon Forge worth visiting for those, like myself, who tend to shy away from the neon lights, hordes of people, and downright ridiculous attractions that seem to dominate Pigeon Forge most of the rest of the year.

The **Annual Dolly Parade** (865/429-7350, www.mypigeonforge.com/parade) draws more than 60,000 people to Pigeon Forge in April, the main reason being that this is when Sevier County's own Dolly Parton returns to town as grand marshall. The parade usually begins at traffic light #6 and follows the Parkway to traffic light #3. You better arrive early if you want to get a good viewing spot from which to check out one of country music's biggest stars.

Sevierville's Bloomin' Barbeque & Bluegrass (888/889-7415, www.bloomin-bbq.com, free) occurs each May and features the Tennessee State Championship Barbeque Cook-Off as well as free bluegrass concerts, which have in the past featured legends Marty Stuart, Larry Cordle & Lonesome Standard Time, and Doyle Lawson & QuickSilver. There are also kids' games, mountain craft vendors, and, of course, plenty of food. You can also hear the finalists from Sevierville's Mountain Soul Vocal Competition. These folks get to compete not just for a cash prize but for a Nashville recording session. The catch is that participants have to sing one of Sevierville native Dolly Parton's songs in any style—be it country, rock, pop, or even rap!

Winterfest (www.smokymountainwinterfest.com) kicks off in early November each year and extends until February. Over four million Christmas lights make Pigeon Forge brighter than it already is, if you can believe it. Among the light displays are a scene of the Old Mill, lighted snowflakes that seem to fall from the sky, and a 40-foot-tall light monument of the U.S. Marines raising the American flag at Iwo Jima. Live music, street dancing, hayrides with Santa, and lots of hot cocoa can all be found in both Pigeon Forge and Sevierville. Visitors can board the Fun Time Trolley at Patriot Park at 6:30 P.M. Monday through Friday to take a trolley tour of the lights. The fare is $5, and you can make reservations by calling 865/453-6444.

SPORTS AND RECREATION
Zorb
You may have heard of Zorb. Like most off-the-wall, death-defying outdoor recreation experiences, it started in New Zealand. Well, now it has come to Pigeon Forge (a likely spot for sure), and it is here in the Smoky Mountains and nowhere else in North America that you can test your mettle by free-falling downhill in a giant rubber ball. **Zorb Smoky Mountains** (203 Sugar Hollow Rd., Pigeon Forge, 865/428-2422, www.zorb.com/zorb/smoky, daily 9 A.M.–5 P.M., 1 ride $37-44, 3-ride combo $81) just might give you the ride of your life. If you're brave enough to try it, here's what you'll experience: You climb into an 11-foot-tall orb-within-an-orb, and then career 750 feet downhill. By the time you think you just might die before it's over, the ride is done, and you're thinking it might be a hoot to do it again. The Zorbit ride finds you strapped into a Zorb ball so you repeatedly roll upside down or whichever other way the ball decides to send you. If Zorbit wasn't thrilling enough, you can try out Zydro, which uses the same giant ball and adds water inside with you—and you can go bouncing and sloshing down the hill with two of your closest friends inside.

Indoor Skydiving
Fly Away (3106 Parkway, Pigeon Forge, 877/293-0639, www.flyawayindoorskydiving.com, daily 10 A.M.–7 P.M., 1 flight $32, 5 flights $105, 5-flight coaching package $175) is one of the few indoor skydiving attractions in the United States. The vertical wind tunnel here allows you to defy gravity and "free fly" above the ground. Coaching is available, and even experienced skydivers will find the attraction worthwhile as a chance to practice their freefall skills.

Helicopter Tours
If you have the spare cash, it's quite a spectacle to see the Smoky Mountains from the air as well as get some perspective on the sprawl of Pigeon Forge. **Scenic Helicopter Tours** (2174 Parkway, Pigeon Forge, 865/453-6342, www.flyscenic.com, call for days and hours, $11–467) offers a variety of flights over the region. Flights range from a two-mile introductory flight over Pigeon Forge ($10) to a 100-mile flight over nearly the entire Great Smoky Mountains National Park ($396). If you plan to go, check the website for online booking discounts.

Golf
The **Gatlinburg Golf Course** (520 Dollywood Lane, Pigeon Forge, 800/231-4128, www.golf.gatlinburg-tn.com, daily, call for hours, $30–60) is actually in Pigeon Forge and accessible from Highway 441 at traffic light #8. This scenic course is laid out over a rolling landscape with the peaks of the Smokies rising in the distance. Featuring 18 holes, this Bob Cupp–designed championship layout is best known for the 12th hole, which has been nicknamed Sky Hi because it's 194 yards in length and drops 200 feet from tee to green. The golf clubhouse has a pro shop, locker rooms, and a full-service restaurant.

ACCOMMODATIONS
Hotels and Resorts
Like Gatlinburg, Pigeon Forge and Sevierville have lodging options galore and all the usual chain hotels like Best Western, Days Inn,

Clarion, Fairfield Inn & Suites, and Comfort Inn, but there are a few local standouts if you're actually brave enough to sleep in this town. My favorite is ❤ **The Inn at Christmas Place** (119 Christmas Tree La., Pigeon Forge, 888/465-9644, www.innatchristmasplace.com, rooms $119–189, suites $189–339), located on Pigeon Forge's main drag right across the street from The Incredible Christmas Place, the South's largest Christmas store. It's Christmas all year long at this beautiful turreted hotel, and the kids will love the outdoor pool with 95-foot figure-eight waterslide. The rooms—many of which have balconies overlooking the inn's beautifully landscaped grounds and flower gardens—and common areas of the hotel are all decorated for the holidays, and Christmas music plays all day long. There is an indoor pool available as well, and all guests receive a complimentary continental breakfast.

Riverstone Resort and Spa (212 Dollywood La., Pigeon Forge, 888/908-0908, www.riverstoneresort.com, 1-bedroom $109–159, 2-bedroom $139–209, 3-bedroom $160–239, 4-bedroom $220–310) offers spacious one- to four-bedroom condominiums, all with fireplaces, whirlpool tubs, luxury linens, and flat-panel TVs. Resort guests have access to a beautiful indoor atrium pool, 300-foot lazy river, day spa, fitness center, and children's playground. There is also the 18-hole Gatlinburg Golf and Country Club course next to the resort. No doubt about it—this place is a top-shelf offering. Even though it's right in town, you feel like you're miles away from everything when you reserve a room fronting the river. You don't even know that Pigeon Forge is there behind you.

Vacation Rentals

As with Gatlinburg, navigating the vacation rental market in Pigeon Forge can be a challenge since there are so many offerings. But there are a few standouts that offer consistently good service and amenity-laden options. They include **Accommodations by Sunset Cottage** (3630 S. River Rd., Pigeon Forge, 800/940-3644, www.sunsetcottage.com, 1-bedroom

$80–199, 2-bedroom $90–250, 3-bedroom $150–325, 4-bedroom $175–800), which has rentals available ranging from one to eight bedrooms, in condos, cottages, cabins, and mountain chalets. Most rentals have ample porches and decks, fireplaces, hot tubs, Wi-Fi, and pool privileges. Sunset Cottage has over 300 options from which to choose.

Alpine Mountain Village (2519 Sand Pike Blvd, Pigeon Forge, 800/405-7089, www.alpinemountainvillage.com, 1-bedroom $110–220, 2-bedroom $125–275, 3-bedroom $160–495, 4-bedroom $235–460, 5-bedroom $235–460, 6-bedroom $305–725, 7-bedroom $305–725) offers log homes only a quarter mile off the busy Parkway but seemingly worlds away because they're tucked behind a ridge. Some of the homes are luxurious, sprawling residences set up to serve a large family group.

Another excellent local vacation rental provider is **Bluff Mountain Realty and Rentals** (2186 Parkway, Pigeon Forge, 800/462-2134, www.bluffmountainrentals.com, 1-bedroom $90–145, 2-bedroom $120–267, 3-bedroom $210–267, 5-bedroom $350–400, 7-bedroom $490–560). Bluff Mountain rents everything from condos to chalets and has dozens of properties available.

Eagle's Ridge Resort (2740 Florence Dr., Pigeon Forge, 866/450-1965, www.eaglesridge.com, 1-bedroom $114–129, 2-bedroom $139–149, 3-bedroom $164, 4-bedroom $204, 5 to 9 bedrooms $254–624) has one- to nine-bedroom log cabins available, many with fireplaces, hot tubs, pool tables, and Wi-Fi. Guests have access to a swimming pool and clubhouse and are only one mile away from the Parkway in Pigeon Forge.

If you want to be in on the action or just like people-watching, then **Whispering Pines Condominiums** (205 Ogle Dr., Pigeon Forge, 866/454-7150, www.whisperingpinescondos.com, $130–250) is the place to be. You can select from condominiums overlooking the Parkway, giving you front-row bleacher seats on all the activities below, or you can opt for a unit on the back side of the facility with mountain views.

This is a good option for families who need lots of space and are looking for clean and comfortable lodgings without spending a fortune.

Camping

KOA Campground (3122 Veterans Blvd., Pigeon Forge, 865/453-7903, www.pigeon-forgekoa.com, campsites $32–50, deluxe sites $75–80, cabins $55–70) is conveniently located near Dollywood and has 175 campsites, a heated pool, hot tub, Wi-Fi, fitness center, game room, playground, and laundry.

River Edge RV Park (4220 Huskey St., Pigeon Forge, 800/477-1205, www.stayriveredge.com, $28–38) has 175 sites, many of them on the Little Pigeon River. The RV park has full hookups, cable, bathhouse, laundry, and is located right next to a Fun Time Trolley stop.

Riverside RV Park (4280 Boyds Creek Hwy., Sevierville, 800/341-7534, www.riversidecamp.com, campsites $28–30, cabins $75–89, mobile home $89) is a scenic campground in Sevierville located on the banks of the Little Pigeon River. They offer 265 shaded campsites with full hookups, cable TV, laundry, pool, on-site general store with LP gas for sale, bathhouses, playground, and an arcade. Campers can fish from the campground, too. They also have rustic cabins and a mobile home for rent.

River Plantation RV Park (1004 Parkway, Sevierville, 800/758-5267, www.riverplantationrv.com, campsites $22–50, cabins $20–74) is located in Sevierville right off Highway 441, making it convenient to all the local attractions. The park has 285 sites and caters to oversized rigs. Sites feature concrete patios, full hookups, central modem hookups as well as Wi-Fi, and cable TV. The campground also has riverfront sites available, as well as cabins. Amenities on-site include three laundries, two pools, three bathhouses, a camp store, and a banquet hall.

FOOD

At ◖ **The Pottery House Café and Grille** (3341 Old Mill Ave., Pigeon Forge, 865/453-6002, www.oldmillsquare.com, Sun.–Thurs. 11 A.M.–8 P.M., Fri.–Sat. 11 A.M.–9 P.M., $5–18), located in Pigeon Forge's Old Mill Square kitty-corner across the street from The Old Mill, the food is consistently excellent. One of the best dishes here is the restaurant's signature quiche Lorraine with french onion soup and cinnamon bread with butter. The loaded-baked-potato soup with fresh baked bread is another filling comfort-food option. The soup is thick and creamy with hunks of skin-on potatoes floating and shredded cheese and scallions on top. I also recommend the homemade potato chips as well as the tender and juicy rib-eye steak. The Pottery House Café offers indoor and outdoor seating and serves their fare on dishes made next door at Pigeon River Pottery. Across the street from The Pottery House Café is **The Old Mill Restaurant** (164 Old Mill Ave., Pigeon Forge, 865/429-3463, www.oldmillsquare.com, daily 7:30 A.M.–9 P.M., $5–18), which is a family-friendly place with tables overlooking the Pigeon River. They offer traditional fare like country ham, grits, corn fritters, corn chowder, chicken and dumplings, and southern fried catfish, but, in my opinion, the food is a bit bland, service a bit haphazard, and the atmosphere a little too loud. But some folks just like the experience of eating riverside and getting huge portions of comfort food all in one casual, no-fuss kind of place.

Mama's Farmhouse (208 Pickel St., Pigeon Forge, 865/908-4646, www.mamasfarmhouse.com, daily 8 A.M.–10 P.M., $6–17) is almost like sitting down for a meal at your grandmother's house, and it's not just because of the food. The restaurant is located in a sprawling farmhouse with wide front porches loaded with rocking chairs, and there are even a couple of tractors parked out front. And there is a story behind all this: The restaurant is dedicated to the memory of the owner's great-grandmother, and many of her old-time recipes are cooked up for guests here. This is not your typical country-style restaurant. Meals are served family-style, and there is no menu—you just help yourself from heaping bowls set down on the table in front of you. You can have all you want of Mama's fried chicken, biscuits and cornbread, green beans, corn, mashed potatoes, macaroni-and-cheese—all those deep comfort foods of childhood. The restaurant serves breakfast, lunch, and dinner, and if you stop by for your first meal of the day, be sure to dig into those biscuits drenched in peach butter.

Opened in 2009, **New Orleans on the River** (2430 Winfield Dunn Pkwy., Pigeon Forge, 865/933-7244, www.neworleansontheriver.com, Mon.–Sat. 11 A.M.–2 P.M. and 5–10 P.M., $8–16) is a much needed addition to the Pigeon Forge scene. Atmosphere is hard to find in this town, but New Orleans offers it with window seating providing lovely views of the French Broad River and Louisiana-style cooking that will fire up your taste buds. Some of their offerings include chicken-and-sausage jambalaya served with corn relish and the Creole essential red beans and rice. Before digging into the main course, however, be sure to try the fondue-stuffed tomato, a fried green tomato loaded up with seafood fondue and shrimp. If you want a window seat (which you do!), make reservations in advance.

Mel's Diner (119 Wears Valley Rd., Pigeon Forge, 865/429-2184, www.melsdinerpf.com, daily 7 A.M.–close, $4–11) is a fun place to stop if you'd like to soak up some 1950s atmosphere in a restaurant that has been built to look like a classic diner. Open for breakfast, lunch, and dinner, the diner serves hamburgers piled high with lettuce, cheese, bacon, tomatoes, and onions with a stack of fries on the side, as well as breakfast plates that could probably power you through a whole day without lunch. You can order a variety of omelets sandwiched between hash browns and buttered toast. And, of course, you can order any type of soda fountain concoction you can think of, including banana splits featuring oozing syrups in three flavors and towers of whipped cream.

INFORMATION AND SERVICES
Information

The **Pigeon Forge Welcome Center** (1950 Parkway, Pigeon Forge, 800/251-9100, www.mypigeonforge.com, Mon.–Sat. 8:30 A.M.–5 P.M., Sun. 1–5 P.M.) is located at traffic light #0 on the Parkway (U.S. 441). A second visitors center, the **Pigeon Forge Information Center** (3107 Parkway, 800/251-9100, Mon.–Fri. 8:30 A.M.–5 P.M.), is located at traffic light #5, also on the Parkway.

If you're crazy enough to come into the Smokies by way of ridiculously busy U.S. 66, then the **Sevierville Chamber of Commerce Visitors Center** (3099 Winfield Dunn Pkwy., Sevierville, 888/738-4378, www.visitsevierville.com, Mon.–Sat. 8:30 A.M.–5:30 P.M., Sun. 9 A.M.–6 P.M.) is a good place to stop, not just for information on the Sevierville and Pigeon Forge area but for guidance on visiting Gatlinburg and the Great Smoky Mountains National Park, too. The Sevierville Chamber of Commerce shares space here with the **Sevierville Visitor Center of the Great Smoky Mountains Association** (888/898-9102, www.thegreatsmokymountains.org, daily 9 A.M.–5 P.M.). The national park visitors center also has a gift shop selling books on outdoor recreation, local history, and flora and fauna. The visitors centers are just south of I-40 on Highway 66.

Emergency Services

Fort Sanders Sevier Medical Center (709 Middle Creek Rd., Sevierville, 865/429-6100, www.fssevier.com) offers 24-hour emergency service. From U.S. 441 take Dolly Parton Parkway (U.S. 411) east in Sevierville, travel approximately one mile, and turn right on Middle Creek Road.

If you require police services, there are several options: **Sevier County Sheriff's Office** (106 W. Bruce St., Sevierville, 865/453-4668), **Pigeon Forge Police Department** (225 Pine Mountain Rd., Pigeon Forge, 865/453-9063), **Sevier County Police Department** (300 Gary Wade Blvd., Sevierville, 865/453-5506).

TENNESSEE FOOTHILLS

GETTING THERE

The heaviest traveled route into Pigeon Forge and Sevierville is from I-40, and this is the route you will likely take if you're coming in from the north or west. Most visitors exit the Interstate at U.S. 66 at Exit 407. U.S. 66 goes right into Sevierville and then feeds into U.S. 441 to Pigeon Forge. The two towns merge into one another, so you may not even notice you've passed from one into the other.

If you're coming in from Asheville and points east, take I-40 west to Exit 407, and follow the same route.

From the Atlanta area and points south, you can reach Pigeon Forge by taking I-85 north to I-985 north, and then following I-985 to U.S. 23, which feeds right into Highway 23/441 in North Carolina. Stay on 441 to Cherokee, and drive through the Great Smoky Mountains National Park on the Newfound Gap Road to reach Gatlinburg and then Pigeon Forge and Sevierville.

GETTING AROUND

The **Pigeon Forge Fun Time Trolley** (186 Old Mill Ave., Pigeon Forge, 865/453-6444, www.pigeonforgetrolley.org, Mar.–Oct. daily 8:30 A.M.–midnight, Nov.–Dec. 10 A.M.–10 P.M., $0.50) has more than 100 stops throughout Pigeon Forge, Sevierville, and Gatlinburg, too. The trolleys feature new propane/electric hybrid motors.

Townsend

Townsend is often referred to as the "quiet side of the Smokies," and if you're not interested in the tourist glitz of Gatlinburg and Pigeon Forge, this would be the best place on the Tennessee side to use as a home base for visiting the Great Smoky Mountains National Park. Townsend is also the closest town to Cades Cove, one of the park's most popular areas, where you can take a loop tour by car or bicycle of a once-thriving Appalachian community in one of the Smokies' most scenic valleys.

SIGHTS
Tuckaleechee Caverns

Tuckaleechee Caverns (825 Cavern Rd., 865/448-2274, www.tuckaleecheecaverns. com, Mar. 15–31 daily 10 A.M.–5 P.M., Apr.–Oct. daily 10 A.M.–6 P.M., Nov. 1–15 daily 10 A.M.–5 P.M., adults $14, children $7) was founded as a commercial cave in 1953 by two boyhood friends who had played in the undeveloped cave as children. Together they worked four years to raise money and also to prepare the cave for guests. Their labor paid off: Shortly after the cave opened to the public, members of the National Speleological Society discovered the Big Room, which at more than 400 feet long, 300 feet across, and 150 feet deep is one of the largest cavern rooms in the eastern United States. You can take a one-mile guided tour to see the Big Room, as well as the lower falls of the 200-foot-high Silver Falls.

Great Smoky Mountains Heritage Center

Great Smoky Mountains Heritage Center (123 Cromwell Dr., 865/448-0044, www.gsmheritagecenter.org, Mon.–Sat. 10 A.M.–5 P.M., Sun. noon–5 P.M., adults $6, seniors $4, children 6–17 $4, under 6 free) is the place to delve into the cultural history of East Tennessee. Exhibits, educational programs, and demonstrations showcase the history of Native Americans in the region as well as pioneer culture. You can visit several historic relocated and reconstructed buildings adjacent to the center to glimpse life as it was a century ago.

Foothills Parkway

If you'd like to enjoy a scenic drive of high-elevation vistas without going into the Great Smoky Mountains National Park, check out the Foothills Parkway. Access to the Parkway is on the left off Highway 321 5.5 miles from Townsend. There are numerous overlooks along this 17-mile stretch of parkway offering views of the western slopes of the Great Smoky Mountains National Park as well as views of the Tennessee Foothills and lakes to the west. If you stop at Look Rock, you can take a half-mile hike to an observation tower from which you'll enjoy 360-degree views.

SPORTS AND RECREATION
Horseback Riding
Davy Crockett's Riding Stables (505 Old Cades Cove Rd., 865/448-6411, www.davy-crockettridingstables.com, daily 9 A.M.–5 P.M., 30-minute to two-hour ride $15–40, half day $90, overnight $60) offers rides from a half hour to overnight trips into the surrounding mountains. Rides are first come, first served from March to November, but reservations are required in the off-season; call for further information.

Cades Cove Riding Stables (865/448-9009, www.cadescovestables.com, Mar.–Dec. 9 A.M.–6 P.M., 1-hour guided horseback ride $25, 30-minute guided carriage ride $8, guided hayride $6–8) offers trail rides along a nature trail within the cove for half- and one-hour rides. They also offer half-hour horsedrawn carriage rides through Cades Cove daily. Another option is to take a hayride through the cove. Call for times of carriage and hayrides.

Tours
Cades Cove Heritage Tours (123 Cromwell Dr., 865/448-8838, www.cadescoveheritagetours.org, daily 8:30 A.M.–5 P.M., $10–17) is a chance to leave the driving to someone else. The tour takes you in a 19-passenger van on a guided tour of Cades Cove while expert guides detail the cultural history, little-known stories, and natural beauty of the area. Tours depart Townsend at 1 P.M. daily from the Great Smoky Mountains Heritage Center.

Dual Sport Motorcycle Rentals (8457 Hwy. 73, 865/448-6090, www.gsmmotorent.com, call for days and hours, $75–148) offers

motorcycle rentals as well as guided tours into the park and the Cherokee National Forest. Explore little-traveled areas on both paved and gravel roads on a Kawasaki KLR 650 dual sport bike.

ACCOMMODATIONS
Hotels
Lodge at Valley View (7726 E. Lamar Alexander Pkwy., 800/292-4844, www.valleyviewlodge.com, rooms $45–109, suites $120–300) is a rustic lodge on 15 acres with a lovely setting beneath the Smokies. The lodge offers a variety of accommodations from simple lodge rooms to suites with fireplaces, hot tubs, and private decks. All guests can enjoy the landscaped grounds, two outdoor pools, hot tubs, and a really neat Play Village for the kids. The lodge is located on Townsend's walking and jogging trail, giving you the opportunity to stroll to dinner if you like.

Inns and Bed-and-Breakfasts
Gracehill (1169 Little Round Top Way, 866/448-3070, www.gracehillbandb.com, $250–325) is a gorgeous luxury estate home with floor-to-ceiling windows and 12-foot-high ceilings in many rooms, letting the outdoors in with a bang. The inn's rooms are incredibly spacious, offering decadent bathrooms where windows over the whirlpool tubs look onto the Smokies, antique furnishings, fireplaces, and graceful french doors leading onto private balconies. Guests can enjoy an on-site fitness center and an 80-bush rose garden, as well as breakfast each morning.

Vacation Rentals
Pioneer Cabins (288 Boat Gunnel Rd., 800/621-9751, www.pioneercabins.com, $95–175) are a good option if you plan to stay in the area a few days, want some peace and quiet, and have kids in tow. Located down a country road well off Highway 321 on a small organic farm, Pioneer Cabins offers six cabins for rent, sleeping 4–12 people. The cabins are rustic but offer fully equipped kitchens, lots of space for hanging out, ample front porches with rocking

chairs, wood-burning fireplaces, and hot tubs. The atmosphere is definitely one where you feel like it's okay not to keep a constant eye on the kids. Children will especially love the farm's petting zoo, where they can hang out with horses and donkeys. Many of the cabins, though nestled in the woods, offer lovely cut-out views of the Tennessee Foothills.

Camping

The **Tremont Outdoor Resort** (800/448-6373, www.tremontcamp.com, campsites $24–65, cabins $55–115, log homes $100–175) is the closest campground to the national park entrance at Townsend. Offering campsites with full hookups as well as cabins for rent, the campground is located on 2,000 feet over shady river. The campground also has a pool, camp store, bathhouses, game room, tubing, and river fishing available to guests. There are also log homes, situated on a terraced hillside overlooking the mountains.

Tuckaleechee Campground (7259 E. Lamar Alexander Hwy., 865/448-9608, RV sites $39–42, tent sites $35–37, primitive sites $24) has a variety of camping options, including 50 full hookup RV sites, tent sites with water and electricity, and primitive campsites. There are several shady sites next to the river.

Big Meadow Family Campground (8215 Cedar Creek Rd., 888/497-0625, www.bigmeadowcampground.com, $35–45) has full electrical hookups and some sites with concrete pads and patios. On-site is a camp store, exercise room, laundry, bathhouse, and trout fishing. Some sites are right on the river.

Look Rock Campground (Foothills Pkwy., 800/365-2267, $14) is not in Townsend but on the Foothills Parkway 18 miles west of town. This is probably the best National Park Service campground in the Smokies, as it's located high on a ridge (meaning no bugs!) with lovely views. It also tends to be sparsely populated, making it a good place for campers who prefer to enjoy complete peace and quiet, though it is an isolated spot. The campground has 69 sites available on a first-come, first-served basis.

There are no RV hookups. Reservations are not available, but the campground rarely fills up. Make sure to secure your valuables before you leave to go sightseeing for the day.

FOOD

The best place to eat in Townsend is **Riverstone Family Restaurant** (8511 Hwy. 73, 865/448-8816, $6–18), which not only serves up consistently good southern country fare but also has some surprisingly excellent live musical entertainment nightly from 5:30 to 9 P.M. You'll likely hear some good renditions of songs from Johnny Cash, George Strait, Charlie Pride, and Patsy Kline, and sometimes the diners join in the singing. This is where the locals eat, and you can tell by the full parking lot—always a good sign. The must-try items on their menu are the fried dill pickles, fried green tomatoes, and frog legs. Riverstone makes an excellent cheeseburger marinated in Jack Daniels sauce, and their smoked pork platter is also a good one. They also serve up country ham, liver and onions, pot roast, and grilled catfish, all with the down-home sides you'd expect, like pinto beans and turnip greens. The atmosphere here is totally casual, with drinks served in Mason jars. Be prepared to wait, however. Everything is home-cooked upon ordering.

Smoky Junction Restaurant (7735 Lamar Alexander Pkwy., 865/448-6881, $3–8) is the place to go for breakfast in Townsend. Not only is it cheap, but the options are seemingly endless. They serve eggs any way you like them accompanied by country ham, bacon, or sausage; you'll find all the other staples like buttermilk pancakes, french toast, omelets, pork chops, and biscuits and gravy—all serious comfort food.

Little River BBQ (8303 Hwy. 73, 865/448-2500, $3–17) offers dining on the river and the same kind of fare you'll find just about everywhere around Townsend—traditional country food, including some very good hand-pulled pork. You can order ribs for two, which comes with three side dishes and bread.

INFORMATION AND SERVICES

The **Townsend Visitor Center** (7906 E. Lamar Alexander Pkwy., 865/448-6134, www.smokymountains.org, daily 9 A.M.–5 P.M.) features both a Great Smoky Mountains Association visitors center and a visitors center for the community of Townsend.

GETTING THERE

If you're coming into Townsend from the west, take I-40 to Exit 386B at Highway 129 south, the same road on which McGhee-Tyson Airport is located. At Maryville, head north on Highway 321, which goes right through Townsend. You might want to do the same if coming from the north (take I-40 to Exit 386B and follow the same directions). While you can certainly exit at Highway 66 and come through Pigeon Forge, the traffic is likely to be heavy, so I still recommend this route for northern visitors.

If you're coming in from Asheville and points east, take I-40 west toward Knoxville, and follow the same route taking Highway 129 south.

From the Atlanta area and points south, you can take I-85 north to Highway 441. Follow 441 to Maryville, and then take 321 north to Townsend.

KNOXVILLE

While small perhaps by national standards, Knoxville is the largest city in East Tennessee, with a resident population of about 180,000 people. The city is well-known in the South for its music scene, which includes regular performances by nationally known artists at the historic Tennessee Theatre on Gay Street and the proliferation of music clubs all around downtown. More than a few big names in the industry have had roots in the city's musical culture, from the Everly Brothers to Flatt and Scruggs. And if you want to get a quick taste of the importance of music to Knoxville culture, just stop by the WDVX studio on Gay Street at noon on any given day to see live performances by area bands.

Beginning in the 1950s, the city struggled as residents and businesses abandoned the downtown area, and even though you'll notice the city's efforts to revitalize the historic district, it's still not unusual to see the area around Gay Street nearly devoid of people on a weekday in mid-summer, and there are still many empty storefronts.

That being said, however, downtown is where you want to go if you only have a day or a few hours to explore this little southern metropolis. There are dozens of historic and cultural attractions, including several homes that date back to the early years of the city's founding as well as a number of museums like the East Tennessee History Center and the Knoxville Museum of Art.

And even if there is, overall, not much shopping to be had in downtown Knoxville even today, the restaurant scene is a good one and

HIGHLIGHTS

◖ East Tennessee History Center: A downtown landmark, the East Tennessee History Center provides the best overview of the history and culture of the foothills (page 273).

◖ Knoxville Museum of Art: In a building made of native Tennessee marble, this museum features contemporary artwork from all over the world and is located in the city's World's Fair Park (page 276).

◖ Market Square: Recently revitalized, Market Square is the center of outdoor performing arts and eclectic dining downtown (page 277).

◖ Tennessee Theatre: The official state theater, the Tennessee Theatre is an architectural gem featuring live performances from national and international performing artists (page 277).

◖ WDVX Blue Plate Special: A local Knoxville radio station offers Blue Plate Specials – live performances by area bands – every day at noon (page 278).

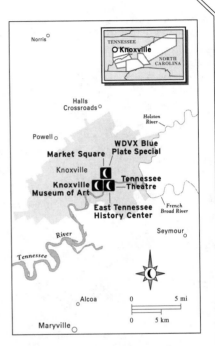

LOOK FOR ◖ TO FIND RECOMMENDED SIGHTS, ACTIVITIES, DINING, AND LODGING.

improving all the time, especially with the recent interest in revitalizing Market Square one block off Gay Street. The city's economic health today relies less heavily on tourism than it does on the fact that the city is home to the University of Tennessee as well as the Oak Ridge National Laboratory, which began as a key research site for the Manhattan Project in World War II.

HISTORY

Knoxville was first settled at the end of the 18th century, and when Tennessee joined the United States as a full-fledged state, Knoxville was made the state capital and remained so until the capital moved to Murfreesboro and then Nashville in the 1800s. The city was named in honor of the nation's first secretary of war, Henry Knox. Revolutionary War officer James White built the first house in Knoxville, which is open to the public today as James White's Fort.

The city's location at the confluence of three rivers ensured it would become a significant transportation hub and industrial center in the 19th century, and by mid-century the East Tennessee and Georgia Railroad came to town, doubling the city's population almost overnight.

During the Civil War, East Tennessee was a hotbed of Unionist sentiment with most residents of the region being both anti-slavery and anti-secession, though Knoxville had more than its share of secessionists on the whole.

KNOXVILLE

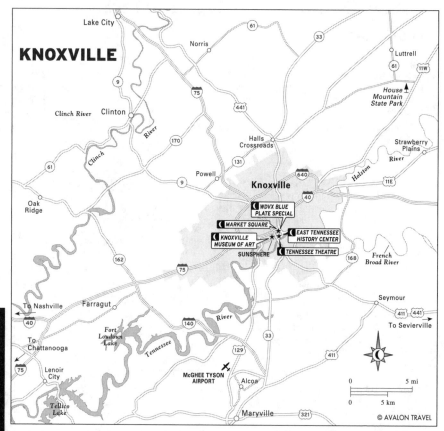

Both Confederate and Federal forces occupied the city during the war, trying to hold control of its vital rail and river connections. Unlike a lot of southern cities, Knoxville recovered quickly after the Civil War, aided by the opportunities the surrounding mountains offered for mining and timbering. The city's prosperity began to expand into the surrounding foothills with the establishment of the Tennessee Valley Authority (TVA) during the Great Depression. The building of reservoirs and dams helped control the region's historic problems with flooding, offered hydroelectric power to rural residents, and brought thousands of jobs to the area.

With the establishment of the Great Smoky Mountains National Park and then the location of the Oak Ridge National Laboratory just outside town, Knoxville's prosperity continued well into the 20th century, though the economic base shifted away from industry as railroads and river transportation grew less important in the 1950s. As with so many U.S. cities, Knoxville's downtown fell victim to the age of the automobile.

Only in recent years has the city begun working to revitalize the area, slowly bringing Gay Street to life again. The location of the World's Fair in the city in 1982 gained the city and the region further attention as a tourist destination and ultimately led to the boom of tourist industry to the south and west of the city in Pigeon Forge and Gatlinburg.

PLANNING YOUR TIME

Since you're likely coming to the area to spend most of your time in the Smoky Mountains, chances are you will hit Knoxville only if you're entering the area from the west or flying into McGhee-Tyson Airport. And even if you're flying into the area, the airport is actually well south of town, so you might just skip Knoxville altogether and keep heading south toward the Great Smoky Mountains National Park.

If you would like to see the major sights of the city in a day, your best bet is to focus on downtown, where there are a lot of offerings with regard to attractions, entertainment, lodging, and dining, all in one relatively small area, and you can take advantage of downtown's trolley service to get from place to place. The suggestions in this guide will keep you mainly in the area radiating out from Gay Street, which is easy to access from I-40.

Sights

GAY STREET
◖ East Tennessee History Center

The East Tennessee History Center (601 S. Gay St., 865/215-8830, www.east-tennessee-history.org, Mar.–Dec. Tues.–Sat. 10 A.M.–4 P.M., Sun. 1–5 P.M., adults $5, 16 and under free), as its name suggests, covers 200 years of history in East Tennessee with exhibits on the Cherokee, the American Civil War, the rise of country music, and Oak Ridge National Laboratory, which was part of World War II's Manhattan Project. The museum is also the starting point for the Cradle of Country Music Walking Tour, a self-guided walking tour throughout downtown that traces the beginnings of country music in Knoxville. Markers along the tour feature country music greats such as Roy Acuff, Dolly Parton, and Hank Williams. The museum is housed in Knoxville's old Customs House, which was built in 1874. It housed the city's federal courts, post office, and excise office until the 1930s, when the Tennessee Valley Authority took over the building for office space. TVA owned the building until 1976. The neoclassical Italianate building is built of Tennessee marble.

Emporium Center for Arts and Culture

The Emporium Center for Arts and Culture

East Tennessee History Center in downtown Knoxville

© FRENCH C. GRIMES

KNOXVILLE

(100 S. Gay St., 865/523-7543, www.knoxalliance.com, Mon.–Fri. 9 A.M.–5 P.M., first Fri. of month 9 A.M.–9 P.M., free) is only a block from the Knoxville Visitor Center and includes two light-filled art galleries as well as working artist studios. The center showcases the work of Tennessee artists and hosts rotating

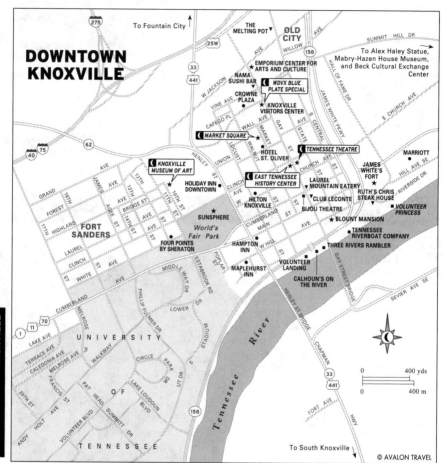

exhibits throughout the year. The center also hosts regular events, including a student art show in April to coincide with the Dogwood Arts Festival and a holiday extravaganza in December, featuring handmade gifts and artworks for sale by area craftspeople.

Blount Mansion

Blount Mansion (200 W. Hill Ave., 865/525-2375, www.blountmansion.org, Mar.–Dec. Tues.–Sat. 9:30 A.M.–5 P.M., Sun. 1–5 P.M., Jan. and Feb. by appt. only, adults $7, seniors $6, children 6–17 $4), which was built in 1792, belonged to William Blount, the state's first territorial governor and a signer of the U.S. Constitution. The house was unusual for its time in that it was built with sawn lumber when most houses in Knoxville were log. It also featured glass from Richmond, Virginia, in the windows. The house is not a mansion by modern standards; it features a main house with downstairs hall, dining room, and parlor, and two upstairs bedrooms. The two wings were added in the 19th century. The grounds of the mansion include a detached kitchen and the governor's simple clapboard office. There are guided tours every hour on the hour.

James White's Fort

Also in the downtown district is James White's Fort (205 E. Hill Ave., 865/525-6514, www.jameswhitesfort.org, Jan.–Mar. Mon.–Fri. 8 A.M.–4 P.M., Apr.–Dec. Mon.–Sat. 9:30 A.M.–5 P.M., adults $4, children under 12 $2, children under 5 free), home of the city's founder and friend to the Cherokee, James White. Built in 1876, this was the first home in Knoxville. In 1791, White parceled off 64 lots of his land for the city that would become known as Knoxville. Later a general in the War of 1812, and donor of land for the establishment of Blount College, White continued to shape the identity of Knoxville until his death in 1821. The two-story house is of simple log construction, as are the outbuildings that surround it, including a working blacksmith's shop. The restored fort features living-history demonstrations of necessary frontier skills such as fiber spinning, blacksmithing, and open-hearth cooking. The museum also occasionally hosts special events such as Cherokee Heritage Days. The Cherokee Heritage Days features a reenactment of the signing of the Treaty of Holston, an agreement between the Cherokee and the U.S. government designating the Cherokee Nation as a protectorate of the United States, plus Cherokee dance demonstrations and Native American crafts.

SUMMIT HILL AREA
Beck Cultural Exchange Center

The Beck Cultural Exchange Center (1927 Dandridge Ave., 865/524-8461, www.discoveret.org/beckcec, Tues.–Sat. 10 A.M.–6 P.M., free) is the centerpiece of African-American cultural heritage in eastern Tennessee. The center offers both a museum and research library with exhibits on the history of African Americans in Knoxville. There are particularly interesting exhibits here on the desegregation of area schools as well as on Knoxville native William H. Hastie, who became the first black

governor of the Virgin Islands in 1946, and the first black federal judge in the United States in 1950. The center also has a gift shop with a collection of books by almost every local African-American author.

Alex Haley Statue

The Alex Haley Statue at Haley Heritage Square (1600 Dandridge Ave., 800/727-8045) is located across the street from the Beck Cultural Exchange Center. The statue of one of Knoxville's most famous residents, author of *Roots,* was cast in bronze by sculptor Tina Allen. It weighs over 4,000 pounds and depicts Haley sitting down perusing a book. Adjacent to Haley Heritage Square is Morningside Park, which has playgrounds, picnic shelters, and walking trails.

Mabry-Hazen House Museum and Civil War Bethel Cemetery

The Mabry-Hazen House Museum and Civil War Bethel Cemetery (1711 Dandridge Ave., 865/522-8661, www.mabryhazen.com, Wed.–Fri. 11 A.M.–5 P.M., Sat. 10 A.M.–3 P.M., house tours adults $5, children 5–12 $2.50, under 5 free) is a Civil War–era home located a couple of blocks west of the Beck Cultural Exchange Center that served as headquarters for both Federal and Confederate troops at various points in the conflict. The home is unique in that almost all of the furnishings in it are original to the three generations of the Mabry-Hazen family that lived here from 1865 to 1987. The house's style has both Italianate and Greek Revival influences. Joseph Mabry Jr., who built the house, was a well-to-do merchant and importer who personally financed and outfitted his own regiment of Confederate soldiers at the outset of the Civil War. The house served briefly as a Confederate headquarters during the war and was later occupied by Federals when they took control of the city. In the adjacent Bethel Cemetery more than 1,600 soldiers are buried. Tours of the cemetery are available on Saturday from 10 A.M. to 3 P.M. for no additional charge.

VOLUNTEER LANDING

Volunteer Landing is a one-mile river walk and city park along the Tennessee River just below downtown's Gay Street Bridge. This scenic location offers a number of attractions, from train rides to riverboat cruises as well as restaurants, a marina, and beautifully landscaped grounds. The park has picnic tables, interactive water play fountains, playgrounds, fishing docks, and river access.

Tennessee Riverboat Company

The Tennessee Riverboat Company (300 Neyland Dr., 800/509-2628, www.tnriverboat.com, May–Oct., $14–30) offers sternwheeler cruises down the Tennessee River from Volunteer Landing with a variety of cruising options, including dinner cruises with live entertainment, sightseeing cruises, and lunch cruises.

Volunteer Princess

For a slightly different experience on the river you can board the *Volunteer Princess* (956 Volunteer Landing La., 865/633-5004, www.volunteerprincess.com, $23–50), a charter yacht that also offers public tours on the river, including champagne brunch cruises, sunset cruises, Margarita Monday cruises, and even pizza cruises. Check the website for public cruise dates.

Three Rivers Rambler

The Three Rivers Rambler (Neyland Dr., 865/524-9411, www.threeriversrambler.com, Apr.–Dec., $20–25) offers a 90-minute steam engine train ride alongside the lazy Tennessee River and the countryside of the Tennessee Foothills. If you'd prefer to see the river by boat, the **Volunteer Landing Marina** (956 Volunteer Landing La., 865/633-5004, www.themarinas.net, daily 9:30 A.M.–7:30 P.M., $5–200) offers pontoon boat, paddleboat, and aquacycle rentals.

WORLD'S FAIR PARK
🄲 Knoxville Museum of Art

The Knoxville Museum of Art (1050 World's

Volunteer Landing

© FRENCH C. GRIMES

Fair Park Dr., 865/525-6101, www.knoxart.org, Tues.–Sat. 10 A.M.–5 P.M., Sun. 1–5 P.M., free) is in World's Fair Park, one interstate exit down from Gay Street and worth a quick side trip from downtown. The museum, made of native Tennessee marble, has four galleries of international, national, and regional artwork focused on the 20th and 21st centuries. Among the internationally recognized artists featured in the museum are David Bates, Charles Burchfield, Loretta Lux, Dante Marioni, and William Morris. The museum also hosts live music every Friday night with their Alive After Five series, which costs $8 for adults and is free for children 17 years and under. The event features a wide array of music from blues and R&B to jazz and acoustic guitar. Dinner is catered, and there is a cash bar available.

Sunsphere

While you're in the area of the World's Fair, take in the view at the Sunsphere (810 Clinch Ave., Apr.–Oct. daily 9 A.M.–10 P.M., Nov.–Mar. daily 11 A.M.–6 P.M., free). This signature

Knoxville landmark was built as part of the 1982 World's Fair. At 266 feet, the Sunsphere is made of steel trussed and topped by a gold glass sphere. You can ride the elevator up the Sunsphere to the convention center level and enjoy the 360-degree view of the city.

Shopping and Entertainment

SHOPPING

Downtown Knoxville offers a wide array of shopping options, with most stores being locally owned and operated, leading to an eclectic mix of boutiques, galleries, and specialty shops.

Gay Street

The Mast General Store (402 S. Gay St., 865/546-1336, www.mastgeneralstore.com, Mon.–Wed. 10 A.M.–6 P.M., Thurs.–Sat. 10 A.M.–9 P.M., Sun. noon–6 P.M.) has always been one of my favorites, and this popular general store just keeps growing, adding more locations all the time. The Knoxville store is among the newest. Mast carries outdoors and casual clothing, hiking gear and boots, barrel candy, toys, and nostalgic gifts.

The **Art Market Gallery** (422 S. Gay St., 865/525-5265, www.artmarketgallery.net, Tues.–Sat. 11 A.M.–6 P.M., Sun. 1–5 P.M.) features the work of over 60 area artists, including painters, potters, weavers, photographers, sculptors, and jewelers, all of whom participate in maintaining and operating the gallery. The gallery was actually established for the 1982 World's Fair and then was maintained as a local artists' cooperative.

The **East Tennessee Historical Society Gift Shop** (601 S. Gay St., 865/215-8824, Mon.–Sat. 10 A.M.–4 P.M., Sun. 1–5 P.M.) carries books on Tennessee history as well as some local arts and crafts.

◖ Market Square

Market Square (800/727-8045, www.knoxvillemarketsquare.com) is a revitalized shopping and dining district one block off Gay Street. On any given day, you'll likely see street musicians gathered here, and if the day is hot, take advantage of the square's interactive fountains

for cooling off! You can tell Market Square is still trying to get its legs. Unless there is a special event taking place, this shopping and eating district can look pretty dead mid-afternoon. You have to hand it to the merchants here, however. Unlike retail shops you'll find in most downtowns, these don't bar their doors when dinnertime comes around but stay open late to catch the strolling evening diners.

Among the shops here working to eke out a living are **Bliss** (24 Market Sq., 865/329-8868, Mon.–Wed. 10 A.M.–7 P.M., Thurs.–Sat. 10 A.M.–9 P.M., Sun. 1–5 P.M.) and **Bliss Home** (29 Market Sq., 865/673-6711, Mon.–Sat. 11 A.M.–7 P.M., Sun. 1–5 P.M.), a pair of artsy and contemporary home and lifestyle shops that both do a good mail-order business.

The Village Market Place (32 Market Sq., 865/541-5050, Tues.–Thurs. 11 A.M.–5 P.M., Fri. 11 A.M.–9 P.M., Sat. 11 A.M.–7 P.M.) is one of the Ten Thousand Villages shops that carries fair trade items. This is a good place to purchase reasonably priced handmade gift items like jewelry, pottery, linens, toys, and home decor made by residents of developing nations.

ENTERTAINMENT AND EVENTS
Entertainment
◖ TENNESSEE THEATRE

The Tennessee Theatre (604 S. Gay St., 865/684-1200, www.tennesseetheatre.com, box office Mon.–Fri. 10 A.M.–5 P.M., Sat. 10 A.M.–4 P.M.) is located in a beautiful rococo-style building in the center of downtown and has been designated the official state theater of Tennessee. The theater was once a 1920s movie palace. Listed on the National Register of Historic Places, the theater is home

© FRENCH C. GRIMES

Tennessee Theatre

base for the Knoxville Symphony Orchestra and Knoxville Opera Company, and for performances by Dr. Bill Snyder on the Mighty Wurlitzer Organ. The theater hosts vintage films as well as a number of big-name musical artists throughout the year. Some of the performers here have included Willie Nelson, the Moscow Ballet, Bill Cosby, Bonnie Raitt, and Lyle Lovett. Sure to draw a sell-out crowd every year is the annual Brian Setzer Orchestra *Christmas Rocks! Extravaganza.* The Gay Street box office, located directly under the historic Tennessee theater sign, is only open on show days. The Clinch Avenue box office is open regular business hours.

BIJOU THEATRE
The Bijou Theatre (803 S. Gay St., 865/522-0832, www.knoxbijou.com) is another historic theater downtown, with 700 seats. Built in 1817, it's the fourth-oldest building in Knoxville, originally built as a hotel and tavern. The theater offers an extremely eclectic mix of music, dance, and shows from well-

known performing artists like Patty Loveless to regional imitators of Eric Clapton and then on to the Vienna Boys Choir.

◖ WDVX BLUE PLATE SPECIAL
WDVX-FM (301 S. Gay St., 865/727-8045, www.wdvx.com) is the local public radio station, with studios in the Knoxville Visitor Center. Every weekday at noon, the station hosts the Blue Plate Special, featuring a live performance by a local or regional band. The hour-long "special" is aired live on the radio and generally features Americana music, ranging from blues to jazz. Monday through Thursday the show airs live at the Knoxville Visitor Center, and on Friday it airs from Market Square at The Square Room (4 Market Square).

NIGHTLIFE
Knoxville has a number of venues for enjoying live music after dark. Among them is the **Baker Peters Jazz Club** (900 Kingston Pike, 865/690-8110, www.bakerpetersjazzclub.com, Mon.–Thurs. 4:30–11 P.M., Fri.–Sat. 4:30 P.M.–midnight), which is located in the historic Baker-Peters Mansion. The club is well known for its extensive martini menu as well as its soulful live local jazz. Also on Kingston Pike is **4620 Reinvented** (4620 Kingston Pike, 865/558-0183, www.4620reinvented.com, Mon.–Sat. 4 P.M.–3 A.M.), which has live blues and jazz as well as DJs. Along with a full bar, the club offers pizzas and tapas. If you're looking for a country music venue, then **Cotton Eyed Joe** (11220 Outlet Dr., 865/675-4563, www.cottoneyedjoe.com, daily 6 P.M.–2 A.M.) is the place to go. Considered one of the top country dance clubs in the country, the club offers dance lessons for the unschooled. On Mondays during the summer the club hosts Family Night, an alcohol-free event that children are welcome to attend. Free line dancing lessons are available.

Festivals and Events
The **Dogwood Arts Festival** (865/637-4561, www.dogwoodarts.com) gives you a chance to

enjoy trails all over the city while the dogwoods are in full bloom. Occurring each April, the event has regional art exhibitions, outdoor concerts, and craft fairs.

From April through June, **Sundown in the City** (www.sundowninthecity.com, Thurs. 7 P.M., free) takes place in Market Square with a live outdoor concert series offering rock, reggae, and jam. The live entertainment in Market Square continues with **Shakespeare on the Square** (865/546-4280, www.tenneesseestage.com, free) from July through August. The dramas are presented by the Tennessee Stage Company. The plays are free, but a small donation of $5 per patron is encouraged.

Christmas in the City (865/215-4248, www.cityofknoxville.org, Nov.–Dec.) covers eight weeks of festivities at various locations throughout the city. The activities include a Christmas parade and Regal Festival of Lights when the whole city lights up with decorations. Key events to check out include WDVX's Holiday Ho-Ho-Hoedown in Market Square, which includes some dancing from Santa, as well as ice skating on Knoxville's Holidays on Ice skating rink.

Accommodations and Food

ACCOMMODATIONS
Hotels
There are several hotels downtown, making it easy to explore the historic area while not having to go far for lodging. The **Crowne Plaza** (401 W. Summit Hill Dr., 865/522-2600, www.crowneknox.com, $120–200) has 197 rooms, indoor pool, and workout room as well as on-site dining.

A few blocks south, **Hotel St. Oliver** (407 Union Ave., 865/521-0050, www.hotelstolivertn.com, $75–225) is a beautiful small hotel in Market Square that is listed on the National Register of Historic Places. Built in 1876, the hotel now has 24 individually decorated guest rooms, all with a warm and historic feel and a certain whimsy to the decor, which mixes bold wallpapers, vibrant paint, and oriental rugs all into a single space.

Also close to downtown attractions is the **Hilton Knoxville** (501 W. Church Ave., 865/523-2300, www.hilton.com, $110–225), which has 317 rooms, an exercise facility, outdoor pool, and on-site dining and lounge. Other downtown chain options include the **Holiday Inn Downtown** (525 Henley St., 865/522-2800, www.holiday-inn.com, $113–159), with 293 rooms and indoor pool, as well as the **Hampton Inn** (618 W. Main St., 865/522-5400, www.hamptoninn.com,

$149–169), with 85 rooms, an indoor pool, and fitness room.

On the northeastern edge of the downtown area is the **Marriott** (500 Hill Ave., 865/637-1234, www.marriott.com, $120–150), which has 378 rooms as well as on-site dining and a lounge along with an outdoor pool, fitness center, and extensive meeting space. Adjacent to World's Fair Park is **Four Points by Sheraton** (1109 White Ave., 865/971-4463, www.fourpoints.com, $115–290), with 130 rooms, on-site dining, and workout room.

Bed-and-Breakfasts
If you're looking for something a little more intimate, check out downtown Knoxville's only bed-and-breakfast, the **Maplehurst Inn** (800 W. Hill Ave., 800/451-1562, www.maplehurstinn.com, call for rates). The inn has 11 homey rooms and a nice deck overlooking the Tennessee River as well as breakfast each morning.

FOOD
Gay Street
Club LeConte (800 S. Gay St., 865/523-0405, www.clubcorp.com, $22–65) offers the best dinner views in town with its dining room at the top of Knoxville's tallest building. You can even see the Smoky Mountains from here. Fine

KNOXVILLE

© FRENCH C. GRIMES

Gay Street

dining comes at a price, however: Be expected to adhere to a business casual dress code and to see a 20 percent service charge on your check in lieu of a tip. The menu is standard upscale: tiger shrimp, New York strip, tenderloin of beef, and locally harvested rainbow trout. They have a full wine list. Dining hours vary; contact the restaurant to verify availability.

Laurel Mountain Eatery (722 S. Gay St., 865/673-9135, Mon.–Fri. 8 A.M.–2 P.M., $4–8) is best known for its huge sirloin burgers as well as yummy warm sandwich wraps. As a side, be sure to order the sweet-potato fries.

Nama Sushi Bar (135 S. Gay St., 865/633-8539, www.namasushibar.com, Mon.–Thurs. 11:30 A.M.–2:30 P.M. and 4 P.M.–midnight, Fri.–Sat. 11:30 A.M.–2:30 P.M. and 4 P.M.–2 A.M., Sun. noon–9 P.M., sushi happy hour daily 4–6 P.M.) isn't just any Japanese restaurant. While they do serve traditional sushi, they mix up some entrées with a little American flair, meaning this place might appeal to you even if you're not into sushi or have never had it before. The bar takes special care to use fresh local ingredients and offers entrées for vegans.

For something a little different, try **The Melting Pot** (111 N. Central St., 865/971-5400, www.meltingpotknoxville.com, Mon.–Thurs. 5–10 P.M., Fri. 5–11 P.M., Sat. 4–11 P.M., Sun. 4–10 P.M., $18–26), a chain restaurant serving four-course meals with a fondue theme. The meal starts with a cheese fondue prepared tableside with bread, veggies, and apples for dipping. Then comes salad and a choice of fondue entrées, and the meal finishes off with a sinful chocolate fondue served with cheesecake, pound cake, strawberries, bananas, and brownies. Save plenty of room for dessert.

If you're visiting World's Fair Park, **Sunspot Restaurant** (1909 Cumberland Ave., 865/637-4663, Mon.–Sat. 11 A.M.–10 P.M., $6–15) is a fun option with mostly vegetarian fare with Southwestern, Caribbean, and Latin influences. There are a few meat-eater items on the menu, including chicken wraps and Black Angus burgers and a delectable steak salad with blue cheese crumbles.

Market Square

For a hearty breakfast, try ◖ **Market Square Kitchen** (1 Market Sq., 865/546-4212, www.marketsquarekitchen.com, Mon.–Fri. 7 A.M.–2 P.M., Sat.–Sun. 8 A.M.–3 P.M., $2–7), which serves ample servings of the usual breakfast fare, including eggs Benedict, buttermilk pancakes stacked tall, and my personal favorite, biscuits and gravy.

The Tomato Head (12 Market Sq., 865/637-4067, www.thetomatohead.com, Mon. 11 A.M.–3 P.M., Tues.–Thurs. 11 A.M.–9:30 P.M., Fri.–Sat. 11 A.M.–10:30 P.M., Sun. 10 A.M.–9 P.M., $3–25) is where the locals go, and it's easy to understand why. They serve just ever so crispy hand-tossed thin-crust pizza and house-baked bread. In addition, they offer sandwiches and salads as well as a Sunday brunch.

◖ **La Costa** (31 Market Sq., 865/566-0275, www.lacostaonmarketsquare.com, Sun.–Thurs. 4–10 P.M., Fri.–Sat. 4–11 P.M., $7–22) is one of the city's certified green eateries, serving organic vegetables and free-range meats. The cuisine here is contemporary Latin inspired but with a Southern twist. Where else could you possibly get blackened tofu with garlic-cheese grits, or a sweet-potato burrito?

Volunteer Landing

Calhoun's on the River (400 Neyland Dr., 865/673-3355, www.calhouns.com, Mon.–Thurs. 11 A.M.–10:30 P.M., Fri.–Sat. 11 A.M.–11 P.M., Sun. 11 A.M.–10 P.M., $8–22) is best known for its hickory-smoked baby-back ribs, and the Calhoun's brand has become something of an East Tennessee institution. The restaurant also serves up good old southern fried green tomatoes and fried catfish. They also have barbecue pork, steaks, chicken, and salad. And while you're licking that hot sauce from your fingers, you can take in the view of the Tennessee River rolling by. Another Volunteer Landing option is **Ruth's Chris Steak House** (950 Volunteer Landing, 865/546-4696, Mon.–Thurs. 5–9:30 P.M., Fri.–Sat. 4:30–10 P.M., Sun. 4–9 P.M., $39–80), a traditional steak-and-seafood restaurant chain.

KNOXVILLE

Practicalities

INFORMATION AND SERVICES
Information

The **Knoxville Visitor Center** (301 S. Gay St., 800/727-8045, www.knoxville.org, Mon.–Fri. 7:30 A.M.–6 P.M., Sat. 9 A.M.–5 P.M., Sun. noon–4 P.M.) is a destination unto itself. In addition to the usual brochures and maps, the visitors center has its own gourmet coffee shop and craft shop, and is also home to the WDVX radio station, which hosts daily Blue Plate Specials, live lunch-hour performances of Americana music. The visitors center also offers free Wi-Fi. While all the activity at the visitors center would seem to suggest a very dedicated focus on tourism in the city, you might have trouble finding a staff person there who can answer your questions. The front desk staff is, unfortunately, poorly trained and will often refer you to the college students working the coffee bar for directions to downtown attractions.

Fortunately, Knoxville offers several TouchKnow&Go stations (www.touchknow-andgo.com) around downtown. The stations look a little bit like ATM machines and are electronic visitor guides where you can search for and select city attractions and print out maps and information right there on the street. TouchKnow&Go, in some cases, offers better service than the visitors center. You can also access the system online or through your mobile device.

Emergency Services

There is no shortage of emergency services in

Knoxville, and the city has several hospitals. **Fort Sanders Regional Medical Center** (1901 Clinch Ave., 865/541-1111 www.fsregional. com) and **University of Tennessee Medical Center** (1924 Alcoa Hwy., 865/305-9000, www.utmedicalcenter.org) are two among more than half a dozen options.

Post Office

If you're in the downtown area, the closest post office is at 501 West Main Street (800/275-8777).

Media

The **Knoxville News Sentinel** (2332 News Sentinel Dr., 865/521-8181, www.knoxnews. com) is the city's major daily newspaper.

WDVX-FM (301 S. Gay St., 865/727-8045, www.wdvx.com) is the local public radio station that offers the Blue Plate Special at the Knoxville Visitor Center each day at noon.

Gay and Lesbian Resources

While there are no travel services in Knoxville geared specifically to gay and lesbian tourists, you can find some local information on gay and lesbian news and events in the area from the **Equality Herald** (www.equalityherald.com).

GETTING THERE
Air

McGhee-Tyson Airport (2055 Alcoa Hwy., 865/342-3000, www.tys.org) is located in Alcoa, Tennessee, on U.S. 129, about a 20-minute drive from downtown Knoxville. From I-40 take Exit 386B (only two exits west of downtown), and follow U.S. 129 for 12 miles to the airport. If you're flying into the Knoxville area for the exclusive purpose of visiting the Smokies, you don't need to go into Knoxville if you don't want to, as the airport is actually a good distance south of the city, putting you already well on your way to the Great Smoky Mountains. Just take a right out of the airport and head south on 129 towards Marysville.

Service to McGhee-Tyson is provided by AirTran (www.airtran.com), Allegiant Air

(www.allegiantair.com), American Airlines (www.aa.com), Continental (www.continental.com), Delta (www.delta.com), Northwest (www.nwa.com), United (www.united.com), and US Airways (www.usairways.com). The airport offers short-term, long-term, and economy parking. The first half hour is free in all lots. Short-term parking is $1 per half hour and $18 per day maximum. Long-term is $1 per half hour and $10 per day maximum. The economy lot is $1 per half hour with an $8 maximum daily charge.

Car

Downtown Knoxville, which is where the vast majority of the city's main attractions are located, is very easy to reach: Just take the Gay Street exit off I-40. If you're coming from the north, take I-81 south to I-40 west, and watch for the Gay Street exit if you want to go downtown. From the south, you'll take I-75 north to I-40 east to reach Knoxville.

GETTING AROUND
Car Rentals

There are seven national car rental services with counters in the McGhee-Tyson Airport: Alamo (865/342-3210), Avis (865/342-3220), Budget (865/342-3225), Enterprise (865/342-1650), Hertz (865/342-3232), National (865/342-3240), and Thrifty (865/342-3250).

Parking

Knoxville is an easy city to get into, just not an easy city to park in. Finding a parking spot on the street in downtown Knoxville can be tricky, and there is a one-hour time limit on most streets. Your best bet is to park in one of the city garages and walk or take the trolley around town. The Knoxville Visitor Center (301 S. Gay St.) offers free two-hour parking. There are also three public parking garages downtown: Dwight Kessel (900 State St.), State Street (520 State St.), and Market Square (406 Walnut St.). Parking garages charge $1 per hour with a $6 per-day limit, and you can get your parking ticket validated at many downtown businesses, allowing you to park for free. State Street and Market Square also have free parking after 6 P.M. on weekdays and all day on the weekends, excluding special events.

Public Transportation

The **Knoxville Trolley Lines** (1135 Magnolia Ave., 865/637-3000, www.katbus.com, daily 6 A.M.–6 P.M., free), which is operated by Knoxville Area Transit, offers free trolley service to dozens of downtown attractions and shopping areas, including the Knoxville Visitor Center, Tennessee Theatre, Bijou Theatre, and Historic Homes of Asheville. The trolley service has four different lines available with service running every 10 to 20 minutes from 6 A.M. to 6 P.M. on at least one of the lines. The late line runs until 3 A.M. in the summer as well. Route schedules are available at the KAT offices at 1135 Magnolia Street, the Knoxville Visitor Center at 301 South Gay Street, and the downtown library at 500 West Church Avenue. If you want to use public transportation to areas outside downtown, you can transfer from the trolley to the city bus line, known as KAT, for $0.50.

Taxis

If you require taxi service from the airport to Knoxville, there are a host of taxi companies in the Knoxville area to choose from. They include A-1/Cloud 9 (865/414-4371), A Relaxi Taxi (865/687-4016), Plus Taxi (865/970-0016), A&B Ground Transportation (865/389-0312), Benchmark Taxi (865/310-7047), Connections Taxi (888/841-8294), Discount Taxi (865/755-5143), Freedom Taxi (865/323-2594), Gold Cab (865/919-0001), Odyssey Airport Taxi (865/577-6767), Overland Taxi (865/970-4545), Selig Transportation (865/523-6284), Tennessee Taxi Service (865/984-8555), and International Taxi/Internet Taxi (865/607-8732).

KNOXVILLE

BACKGROUND

The Land

GEOLOGY

The origins of the mountains we know today as the Appalachians and of which the Great Smoky Mountains and Blue Ridge Mountains are a part began more than one billion years ago. At that time, the eastern United States was submerged under a vast sea that flooded the landscape, placing underwater the remnants of an ancient mountain range and depositing sediment on the sea floor. Over the millennia, the pressure of all this sediment compressed the soil into metamorphic rock. About 300 million years ago, the sea added limestone sediment made up of the fossilized remains of marine creatures.

About 250 million years ago came the great collision of Africa and North America, the result of tectonic plate movement. This collision made the old metamorphic rock that had formed on the sea floor rise up and then slide over the younger limestone. The long-term result would be the establishment of the Appalachian mountain range. If you look and concentrate carefully, you can still see evidence of this geologic history in the Smokies. The iconic Chimney Tops, for example, are evidence of the steep cliffs and pinnacles that were formed by this dramatic shifting of earth and rock.

During the Ice Age, the persistent freeze and thaw led some of the mountains to break apart.

© FRENCH C. GRIMES

This explains the massive boulder fields you will see in some areas of both the Blue Ridge Parkway and the Great Smoky Mountains National Park.

The Appalachian Mountains are very different today than they were millions of years ago. At one time, they would have resembled the steep slopes of some of the world's tallest mountains, like those found in the Himalayas—which are, by the way, much younger mountain ranges. The more rounded look of the southern Appalachians is the result of millennia of water erosion. That same water erosion has shaped the region's valleys. Even today, landslides continue to shape the mountains in sudden and dramatic ways. You will see the most evidence of this on the steepest slopes of the Smokies, particularly around Mount LeConte.

CLIMATE

The climate of the North Carolina Blue Ridge and the Smoky Mountains is a largely temperate one. The area has four distinct seasons with snow occurring with regularity in winter at the higher elevations. It's important to keep in mind that climate varies with elevation, and since your travel in the region will take you from a few hundred feet to well over 6,000 feet above sea level, expect temperature changes from 10 to 20 degrees Fahrenheit from the base of the valleys to mountain summits.

In spring, temperatures in the region typically range from the low 40s to low 60s, while summertime temperatures are usually in the 60s to 80s, though higher elevations will see temperatures in the 40s or lower with regularity, especially at night. Daytime autumn temperatures typically range from the upper 40s to low 60s, while winter is generally mild (save for at the highest elevations) with lows around freezing and occasional daytime highs in the 50s.

The region is quite moist, especially in the Smokies, where precipitation ranges from 50 to over 80 inches a year, depending on elevations. When winter storms hit the region, the Parkway is often closed due to snow or ice, but visitors can still enjoy the roadway by hiking or cross-country skiing. Many of the lesser roads of the Smokies are also closed in winter, particularly when the weather is poor, but the Newfound Gap Road (which is also a U.S. highway) is almost always open. For up-to-date weather and road conditions on the Parkway, call 828/298-0398. For weather and road information in the Great Smoky Mountains National Park, call 865/436-1200, ext. 630.

Flora and Fauna

The Blue Ridge Mountains and Smoky Mountains are a surprisingly diverse landscape, the result of varying elevations that bring northern climates to southern latitudes. In the Great Smoky Mountains National Park, for example, there are 100 types of trees, 1,500 different flowering plants, more than 200 species of birds, and 27 salamander species. The Blue Ridge Parkway's 81,000 acres are hardly less diverse, with 1,400 species of vascular plants. More than 75 percent of all medicinal plants found in the United States grow in the southern Appalachians, all the more reason to protect the species that live here, be they specimens we already know or ones yet to be discovered.

BLUE RIDGE PARKWAY
Birds

More than 250 different bird species have been recorded as residents or visitors (seasonal migrants) to the Parkway. Many of these birds are species one would normally find in northern climes, and they include the rose-breasted grosbeak, nuthatch, veery, black-throated green warbler, golden-crowned kinglet, and Canada warbler. So get out your lifetime list and your binoculars, and start counting. Among the species you'll see in these mountains are the northern flicker, the only woodpecker in North America that eats ants by licking them up with its tongue! It pecks on wood as a territorial signal or mating call, not, as popular myth might have it, to build a nest inside a tree trunk. The red-eyed vireo is another common bird in the forests here. Its name comes from its large red-brown eyes. And don't forget to watch for wild turkey, which are becoming almost as ubiquitous as deer.

Roadside Plants

One of the major attractions of the Blue Ridge Parkway in late spring through mid-summer are the many flowering shrubs that line the roadway. These include flame azalea, which is recognizable by its bright orange blossoms in mid-June, and the white to pink cup-like blooms of mountain laurel, which blossom in the first half of June. Catawba rhododendron fills the roadway and mountainsides with rich purple in June, while the white to pink blossoms of Rosebay rhododendron come to life in July.

Other flowers to look for include bloodroot, a member of the poppy family with white flowers and a gold center. The plant received its name from Native Americans who used its root to dye clothing red. Another pretty bloomer is dutchman's breeches, which has the appearance of a pair of bright white pantaloons. In mid- to late spring look for bluet, a lovely pale blue flower with yellow center that can be found in meadows and on grassy mountainsides.

One of my favorites is wild hydrangea, a mid-sized shrub with large clusters of snowy white blooms that can be found in the mountains all summer long. Pinxter flower is another distinctive flower with pink honeysuckle-like blooms on a rhododendron-type shrub. These bloom in early to mid-spring at lower elevations.

You'll readily recognize Turks-cap lily along Parkway roadsides as well with its tall bright orange and speckled flowers curling back toward the stem in mid- to late summer. Also look for the bright-red spiky flowers of bee balm, which you might mistake for wild bergamot. The two are similar, but bergamot is pink. Another easy-to-spot variety is large-flowered trillium, a pretty three-petal white flower you can find along roadsides in April through May.

© DEBORAH HUSO

Turks-cap lily

YOU CAN'T PICK THE FLOWERS...
BUT YOU CAN PICK THE BERRIES

The thought of gathering some of the colorful bounty of spring for display at home may sound like a nice idea, but as you enjoy wildflower displays along the Blue Ridge Parkway, remember to save the beauty of your wildflower walks for future visitors. Take pictures, but don't take flowers. Theft of wild plants, particularly rare species, is becoming increasingly common on public lands in the southern mountains, so much so that rangers no longer direct visitors to places where unusual species may be found. If you do happen upon a rare wildflower, record the experience and let the flower be so it can propagate even more native beauties and provide enjoyment for future generations of visitors.

While it's illegal to pick flowers and other plants on National Park Service lands, there are some things you can pick here without getting into trouble or potentially affecting the local ecosystem negatively. Those include wild berries and fruits like blackberries, blueberries, and raspberries, as well as nuts growing on the trees. You can pick up to a gallon of any of these per day for personal consumption... that is, if you can beat the black bears to them. So you might consider taking a pail along on that mid- to late-summer hike and finding some yummy sweet treats in the woods. Just make sure you know what you're picking. If you're in the least doubtful about what is an edible berry and what isn't, don't eat it.

GREAT SMOKY MOUNTAINS NATIONAL PARK
Park Ecosystems

Many people marvel at the diversity of the flora in the Smoky Mountains. Much of the reason so many species exist here in a relatively small land area (and yet exist nowhere else in the southeastern United States) is because these mountains were a refuge during the Ice Age for both plants and animals who were retreating from glaciers that spread from the north; the glaciers did not reach quite so far south as the Smokies. Furthermore, since the region has remained largely undisturbed by glaciers or ocean inundation for more than a million years, the park's species have had the opportunity to diversify. Many species typically found in Canadian climates found homes in the high elevations of the Smokies similar to their native northern habitats. That combined with the fact that elevations in the Smokies range from 875 feet to over 6,600 feet allows for tremendous diversity. The elevation changes make for often dramatic differences in temperature and climate from one part of the park to another, allowing for a variety of species accustomed to different environments.

The Smokies' abundant rainfall also contributes to the astounding array of life here. The park receives as much as 85 inches of rainfall a year in some places. The park's humidity and temperate climate fuel superior growing seasons, the evidence of which you can see all around you. As a result the park has about 1,500 varieties of vascular plants, 10 percent of which are identified as rare, and another 4,000 non-flowering plant species. The numbers become more astounding when it comes to trees. The Great Smoky Mountains National Park has more trees in its 500,000 acres than all of northern Europe put together. The forest landscape here is rich and thriving. All you have to do is take a short and observant walk through the woods to see it. It's because of this diversity that the Great Smoky Mountains National Park was designated an International Biosphere Reserve in 1976 and then named a World Heritage Site in 1983.

While much of the Smoky Mountain landscape was logged during the first third of the 20th century, there is virgin forest in this park. Experts estimate that as much as 25 percent of the park has been largely undisturbed by the hands of man. If you hike in the park, you'll see the evidence—old-growth forest with trees measuring up to 20 feet in circumference. These trees are likely more than 200 years old. These are forests worth marveling at for another reason as well: They have more tree species than any other national park in the United States.

The Smokies have a number of endemic species, too, and scientists are finding more of them here all the time. Rugel's ragwort and Jordan's (red-cheeked) salamander are two such species that are found here in these mountains and no place else on earth.

All Taxa Biodiversity Inventory
The ever-expanding knowledge of the park's diversity has led the National Park Service to initiate an All Taxa Biodiversity Inventory (ATBI) in the Smokies. Believe it or not,

scientists think they only know about 15 percent of the species that actually live here. Some 15,000 species are known to inhabit the park boundaries, so that means the National Park Service estimates that, in reality, some 100,000 species live here. For the last decade, scientists from around the globe have been studying the park's living creatures and constantly adding new species to the park list.

Since the study began in 1998 more than 6,000 species have been added to the inventory, including 890 that were previously unknown anywhere in the world.

You can learn more about the ATBI through the project coordinator, Discover Life in America (www.dlia.org).

Wildlife
Most visitors to the Smokies are, understandably, most intrigued by the park's mammals, especially the big ones like the black bear and

---

THE MANY FORESTS OF THE SMOKIES

Because of the Great Smoky Mountains National Park's varying elevations, it supports a wide range of forest types; there are five distinct variations in the park. Understanding the differences between the forests and the kind of plant and wildlife they support will enhance your experience of the park, particularly if you're out hiking and have the opportunity and leisure to observe the trees, plants, and even insects around you.

Pine and Oak Forest: The pine and oak forest occurs in the park's drier reaches, those receiving 55 inches of rain or less annually and a fair amount of sun exposure. Among the trees you will see in these types of forests are one or more of the park's 11 species of oaks, hickory, yellow poplar, dogwood, and pines along with an understory of rhododendron and mountain laurel thickets.

Hemlock Forest: Hemlock forest is found mostly along streams and on damp and densely shaded slopes at lower elevations. Some 25 percent of the national park is made

up of hemlock forest, though it's fading fast since the arrival of the invasive hemlock woolly adelgid.

Cove Hardwood Forest: The most diverse forest type in the Smokies, the cove hardwood forest occurs at elevations under 4,500 feet and most often in valleys and on sheltered mountainsides. Among the tree species you'll find here are sugar maple, hickory, basswood, beech, yellow birch, silverbell, and magnolia.

Northern Hardwood Forest: Above 4,500 feet, northern hardwood forest takes over, mostly with yellow birch, beech, and striped maples. It will often alternate with spruce-fir forest on the park's highest slopes.

Spruce-Fir Forest: A precipitation-dependent forest, the spruce-fir forest occurs at elevations over 4,500 feet that receive 80 inches or more of precipitation (not necessarily in the form of rain) each year. Fraser fir and red spruce predominate, though the fir component is declining all the time due to the invasive balsam woolly adelgid.

recently re-introduced elk. There are some 60 mammals in the park and about 200 species of birds, a large number of which call the Smokies home only on a seasonal basis.

The elk are a newer member of the park's ecosystem, having been introduced in 2001 from the Land Between the Lakes National Recreation Area on the border of Kentucky and Tennessee. That initial herd of 25 has since doubled in size. The best place to see them is in the Cataloochee Valley in the park's northeast corner. Elk have not lived in North Carolina since the 1700s.

Another creature that has been re-introduced to the park is the river otter. River otters were extinct in the Smokies by the 1930s due to trapping and habitat destruction. The National Park Service began restoring river otters in 1986 and by 1994 released 137 otters into the park. One of the best places to catch a glimpse of the river otter is along Abrams Creek in Cades Cove.

The peregrine falcon represents a third success story. The first pair of nesting peregrine falcons in the park since 1942 produced chicks on Mount LeConte in 1997, and the same pair of falcons continued to return to the site season after season. The birds were nearly wiped out of the eastern United States by the 1960s because of widespread pesticide use. DDT, which was banned in the United States in 1972, was the biggest culprit. While the chemical does not directly harm the birds, it interfered with their ability to develop strong shells for their eggs, which often broke, disrupting falcons' ability to reproduce successfully. In the last four decades, the falcon has made a promising comeback in these mountains. Some 13 of the birds were released here in the 1980s. Thanks to restoration and recovery efforts, the peregrine falcon was removed from the endangered species list.

Various species of lizards, snakes, and turtles make up the nearly 40 reptile species known to live in the park, and there are 43 documented types of amphibians, of which nearly 30 are salamanders! The Smokies, in fact, have the most diverse population of salamanders in the world. If you're hiking at high elevations in the park, be on the lookout for Jordan's salamander, a red-cheeked variety that is relatively easy to spot with its largely black body and rose-colored cheeks. And then there are the fish, nearly 60 different species of which call the park's streams home. Among them are the park's native brook trout, which inhabit 140 miles of the park's streams. And then there are the less common species, like the flame chub, which lives in limestone springs in Cades Cove and nowhere else in the park.

The Great Smoky Mountains National Park also has 11 different species of bats, all of which eat insects (not blood!). Bats not only roost in caves but in the crevices of trees, under bark, and sometimes even in piles of leaves. Despite popular belief, bats are not blind, though they hunt using echolocation, which involves the release of high-pitched squeals that echo and reverberate back to them, advising them as to the location of possible food sources. Bats are actually pretty good creatures to have around, as they eat a lot of the insects that drive humans crazy like mosquitoes and gnats. The park's bats are threatened, however, by the spread of white nose syndrome, a deadly disease that could potentially wipe out whole populations. To help protect the bats by preventing accidental spread of the disease, all park caves are currently closed to visitors.

As for the park's more ubiquitous creatures, white-tailed deer are the animal you're most likely to spot while here. There are about 6,000 of them in the park, and they are most easily spotted grazing in open meadows. Cades Cove and Cataloochee Valley are both excellent places for watching deer. If you spend much time along the park's streams you may encounter a muskrat or two. They're typically nocturnal, live in elaborate dens made of mud and roots, and slither in and out of the water like lean little furry race cars.

Another pretty common creature, which you likely will *not* see, is the southern flying squirrel, the smallest tree squirrel in the park. The southern flying squirrel is nocturnal. It doesn't really fly but glides from tree to tree with the

© FRENCH C. GRIMES

timber rattlesnake, one of the nearly 40 reptile species known to live in the Great Smoky Mountains National Park

help of wide flaps of skin connecting its hind legs to its fore legs. The skin almost acts like a parachute for the little critters, which are gray on top and white on their undersides.

One animal that has taken up residence on his own in the park is the coyote. Though not native to the Smokies, coyotes have started showing up here in larger numbers every year. Since the coyotes are making the migration themselves, Park Service employees are leaving them alone to let nature take its course.

Environmental Issues

ACID PRECIPITATION AND AIR QUALITY

Both the Blue Ridge Parkway and the Great Smoky Mountains National Park suffer from the effects of acid precipitation. The Great Smoky Mountains, in fact, receive more sulfur and nitrogen deposits from acid-laden precipitation, whether in the form of rain, fog, snow, or ice, than any other national park in the country. Rain on the high summits like Clingmans Dome has five to ten times the acid content of natural precipitation. Much of that acid moisture arrives here in the form of cloud cover, though Clingmans also receives an astounding 82 inches of rainfall each year.

With nearly 75 percent of the southeastern United States' spruce-fir forest existing right in the Smokies, the threats to its long-term survival are startling. And with the stress of both acid precipitation and invasive species preying on this high-elevation forest, other organisms that depend on the trees for habitat and food will also suffer. The spruce-fir forest is home to 45 species of plants and seven sub-species of birds that live in no other type of ecosystem. You'll see easy evidence of forest change in the

BRINGING BACK THE AMERICAN CHESTNUT

It's been more than 100 years since the chestnut blight, an Asian bark fungus, first appeared in New York in 1904, quickly spreading up and down the Eastern seaboard and killing off one of the most economically important and dominant tree species in Eastern forests, including the forests that now make up the Great Smoky Mountains National Park. Before the blight, American chestnuts could grow over 100 feet tall and even as large as 10 feet in diameter.

Save for isolated pockets of chestnuts still untouched by blight (but by no means immune to it), the chestnut has now disappeared from American forests. Saplings do grow back from the roots and you may find some in the park, but they, too, eventually succumb to blight before maturing enough to bear fruit. Before it was wiped out, the chestnut was king of the Appalachian forest canopy. Large, sawtooth-edged leaves characterize chestnuts, which produce creamy white flowers in early summer and produce nuts encased in a round spiny burr in fall. The chestnut is one of the fastest-growing hardwoods and grows about as quickly and as large as tulip poplars.

Before the blight, chestnuts were among the most dominant trees in Eastern forests,

growing from Maine and southern Canada to Florida. The trees provided the majority of fall foraging for deer, wild turkey, and even black bears. They were once an economic powerhouse, providing nuts that were often sold roasted on the streets of New York City and Philadelphia during the holidays and offering straight, clear-grained lumber for construction, furniture making, fences, and railroad ties. Chestnut is as rot resistant as redwood and can still be found as siding on older homes and in old fence lines throughout the East.

In the last 20 years, however, researchers around the country have made substantial progress in efforts to bring the chestnut back. The American Chestnut Foundation, for example, is backcross breeding the American with the blight-resistant Chinese chestnut in hopes of eventually creating a tree that is as much as 98 percent American chestnut but carries the blight-resistant gene of the Chinese.

By 2030, there may be viable American chestnuts repopulating the forests, and while we ourselves may never see the majesty of a full-grown chestnut in our lives, perhaps our grandchildren will. You can learn more about the project from the American Chestnut Foundation at www.afc.org.

park's higher elevations with the profusion of blackberries and other bramble-type plants that love the sun. They are taking over areas where spruce and fir trees have died and are choking out species that have long depended on these trees for survival.

It's not just precipitation that is wreaking havoc on the park's landscape—so is the air. The Great Smoky Mountains National Park has the worst air quality of any national park in the country, and not all of the haze you'll see is the natural cloud drift for which these mountains are named. Some of it is the result of air pollution from power plants and automobiles. In 1960, on an average day, visitors in the Smokies could see about 22 miles from any given overlook in the park. Today, the average

visibility is only about 12 miles. The Blue Ridge Parkway suffers similar trouble. Over the last 50 years, visibility across the board in the southern Appalachians has decreased by 80 percent in summer and 40 percent in winter.

Another thing that impacts views along the Blue Ridge Parkway, in particular, are the non-park lands that surround it. While some areas of the Parkway are surrounding by acres and acres of National Forest land, ensuring uninterrupted mountain views for miles, in a lot of places the Parkway is nothing more than a narrow strip of land sandwiched between privately owned property. Two-thirds of the land alongside the Parkway in Virginia and North Carolina is privately owned. That means that the National Park Service generally has very little control over what might end up in the Parkway viewshed in these areas.

While the problem is less prominent in North Carolina than in Virginia, you will notice some areas where development is encroaching on the Parkway views, and instead of looking into the distance to see a town nestled in a valley far below, you may see huge mountain homes parked on otherwise scenic mountaintops or buttressed against park boundaries. In an effort to maintain the Parkway's scenery and originally rural landscape, the National Park Service maintains hundreds of agricultural leases where area farmers can graze animals or hay Parkway lands. And the Park Service also maintains 21,000 acres of scenic easements in an effort to maintain the views for motorists.

INVASIVE SPECIES

Another major threat to the forests of the Blue Ridge and Smoky Mountains are invasive species. One of the most prominent invasive species whose effects you'll notice in the Smokies is the hemlock woolly adelgid. A tiny aphid-like insect, generally recognizable only by the woolly white sac in which it coats itself on the underside of eastern hemlock needles, hemlock woolly adelgid was first discovered on the East Coast in the 1950s. This invasive insect showed up in the Smokies about a decade ago and has been wreaking havoc on the park's 137,000 acres of hemlock forest. While hemlocks may not be an economically valuable tree species, their value to the forest ecosystem is substantial. A common sight along streams, hemlocks regulate ground and water temperatures year-round with their thick canopies. Native brook trout, for example, are quite dependent on hemlocks for shade and cool water. Some species of warblers are known to nest only in hemlocks.

Among the region's other major invasive threats is the balsam woolly adelgid, which has killed more than 70 percent of the Smokies' Fraser firs since its introduction 30 years ago. The loss has been tragic, as the Smokies were

HOW YOU CAN HELP PREVENT THE SPREAD OF INVASIVES

More often than not, humans are to blame for the spread of invasive species from one place to another; your attention to the problem can do a lot to prevent invasives from becoming worse or spreading to new places. For example, never bring firewood from home if you're going camping. Always purchase or pick up firewood at the place you're camping, as firewood has been found to be one of the major spreaders of non-native pests from one place to another. Also, clean your hiking boots in between trails. Soil stuck in the treads of your boots can carry weed seeds and even bugs from one environment to another. And also be sure when planting flowers and shrubs in your own backyard that you're planting something that isn't going to become a pest in the future. Focus on native plants, or talk to your local nursery or cooperative extension agent about non-native plants that are safe to grow in your area.

once home to 75 percent of all Fraser firs in the world.

Of the Fraser firs that remain alive in the park, most have already been infested by the adelgid. The pest doesn't really impact the trees until they start to produce roughened bark, which is also the time they first start to produce cones. You won't have a hard time spotting this wingless pest because they cover the bark of the tree in a white woolly mass, with as many as 50,000 of the creatures infesting any one tree. As the adelgid sticks its mouthparts into the tree's bark, it feeds on the vital sap while injecting a hormone that causes the tree's cells to harden. This eventually obstructs the flow of nutrients and water, leading the tree to die within a few years.

The Park Service is trying to save the last remaining Fraser firs by actively spraying infected trees with a fatty acid soap that is toxic to the adelgid but not to the surrounding environment. The process is labor intensive, however, as it requires the soaking of the tree's entire trunk. The Park Service uses fire pumper trucks with high pressure sprayers. This restricts treatment, however, to trees accessible by road. The Park Service is engaging in intensive control efforts in a designated area along the Balsam Mountain Road in the park's northeastern corner in an effort to preserve the Fraser fir's genetic diversity and provide sources for seeds in the future. Two places where you can readily see the effects of Fraser fir die-off are Clingmans Dome in the Smokies and Mount Mitchell along the Blue Ridge Parkway.

There are hundreds of other invasive plants whose effects aren't as prominent but which are still taking their toll on the ecosystem. For example, the beautiful flowering dogwoods, a much-beloved understory tree, are quickly being decimated by the non-native dogwood anthracnose fungus. The southern scourge, kudzu, is also encroaching on the landscape, smothering forests in its fast-growing weedy vines. Other oriental invasives include Japanese honeysuckle and oriental bittersweet.

When you think of invasive species, weeds and insects normally come to mind, but the Smokies also have a bigger bad guy. European wild hogs, which came to North Carolina in 1912 for placement on a private preserve, have become a major pest in the Great Smoky Mountains National Park. After some of the privately owned hogs escaped in the 1920s, they began to proliferate in the wild. The Park Service has worked tirelessly to control and remove them. Since 1986, nearly 8,000 have been removed. Today there 400 wild hogs in the park. They are destructive of native species ill-equipped to deal with their influx. The hogs, which root and till up the soil, destroy native plants, compete with native animals for food, and eat the park's salamanders. They pose a not-insignificant threat to the park's black bars, as they feed on the acorns and mast that are a primary source of the bears' diet.

Two other invasives that, unlike the European wild hog, were not *accidentally* introduced into the Blue Ridge and Smoky Mountains, are rainbow and brown trout. They were once intentionally stocked in these waters but are now displacing the native brook and forcing the latter to move farther and farther upstream.

History, People, and Culture

One thing it is easy to forget when exploring the Blue Ridge Parkway and Great Smoky Mountains National Park is that these parks have not always been here. Over 75 years ago, before the parks were established, the mountains and valleys that now make up their landscape were home to thousands of people as well as thriving mountain communities.

Unlike the great parks of the western United States, which were carved out of largely unoccupied landscapes, most of which already belonged to the federal government, both the Blue Ridge Parkway and the Great Smoky

Mountains National Park were formed out of settled areas. When the parks were established in the 1930s, there was no history of creating national parks out of landscapes full of farms, private logging operations, and towns. And, not surprisingly, very few of these private landowners wanted to abandon their homes or business interests in these mountains.

But by the 1920s, there was definitely a movement underway to establish one or more national parks in the southern Appalachians, where cool summers and fresh mountain air were perceived as a major attraction to people living in populous southeastern and mid-Atlantic cities like Washington, D.C. The public began to envision a park or parks that would be easily accessible to the densely populated East Coast.

In some ways, the onset of the Great Depression following the stock market crash of 1929 was a blessing in disguise, at least if you were a park supporter. The Blue Ridge Parkway and the Great Smoky Mountains National Park were built, in part, to relieve the economic woes of the mountain south during the Great Depression. Both the Public Works Administration and Civilian Conservation Corps sent workers to build roads and structures for these mountain parks, and many construction contracts were awarded to local builders, helping bring jobs to the region. Some 4,300 members of the CCC were employed in the Great Smoky Mountains National Park building roads, campgrounds, and structures during the Great Depression.

NATIVE AMERICANS

Native Americans were, of course, the first people to live in these southern mountains. It was the Cherokee who initially named the Smokies. They described them as "schaconage," which literally translated means "blue, like smoke." The Cherokee and their ancestors have lived in these mountains for at least 11,000 years. The tribe we know today as the Cherokee likely developed from a break-off of the Iroquois who moved south from New England.

At its height, the Cherokee Nation consisted of seven clans and 36,000 people occupying 140,000 square miles of territory in eight present-day southern states. Their life was agriculturally based, and they lived in towns made up of log and mud huts grouped around a central council house.

At the time of European contact in the mid-1600s, the Cherokee occupied east Tennessee, western North Carolina, northern Georgia, and southwestern South Carolina. The Cherokee were, along with the Creek, Choctaw, Chickasaw, and Seminole, considered

by Europeans to be one of the five "civilized tribes" due to their partial acculturation to western culture. By the mid-18th century many Cherokee had become farmers and sent their children to white schools, and some had even converted to Christianity.

The Cherokee believed that because of their acculturation they were safe from encroachment by white settlers, and King George III's Proclamation of 1763 confirmed this belief, as it indicated that there would be no white settlement in the Appalachian Mountains and points west. By the 1780s, however, things began to change. At that point, the U.S. Civilization Policy was in full effect with the intent of assimilating Native Americans.

With westward expansion came hunger for Cherokee land, and in 1835 Major Ridge, without full approval of the Cherokee Nation or Chief John Ross, signed the Treaty of New Echota, selling the Cherokee homeland to the federal government for $5 million and agreeing to removal westward to Indian Territory. Most of the Cherokee Nation removed to the west, including Chief John Ross, in what would come to be known as the Trail of Tears. Removal was complete by 1839, and 4,000 to 8,000 of the 16,000 Cherokee who made the journey died in the process, traveling mostly by wagon train.

Some Cherokee, however, applied to become U.S. citizens, separated from the Cherokee Nation, and occupied their own privately owned reservation. They became known as the Eastern Band of the Cherokee. The current residents of the Qualla Boundary, as the Cherokee Indian Reservation on the park's eastern border is known, are the descendants of those few Cherokee who managed to stay behind.

The Indian Reservation's largest town just outside the park's Oconaluftee River entrance, Cherokee first started coming into its own as a tourist destination in the 1950s, shortly after the founding of the Museum of the Cherokee Indian.

When compared to the Indian reservations of the American West, the Qualla Boundary is a prosperous place loaded with gift shops, restaurants, and hotels. The reservation covers 100 square miles, and some 14,000 members of the Eastern Band of the Cherokee live here.

Cherokee culture remains vibrant in the Smokies. You'll see native crafts everywhere if you visit the reservation—baskets, pottery, beadwork, and woven art made just as it has been for centuries by local craftsmen and women. As time passes, remarkably, the Cherokee's interest in preserving the arts and culture of the past grows stronger. This is especially evident in the revitalization of the Cherokee language.

In grade school you may have learned about Sequoyah, a Cherokee of mixed blood, who is the only recorded historical figure to have created a complete writing system without having first been literate in another language. Sequoyah took the Cherokee's native tongue and developed a written language from it, completing his writing system in 1821.

The Cherokee, in fact, developed their own newspaper in the written language that Sequoyah developed, and you can view an 1870 Cherokee printing press at the Museum of the Cherokee Indian in Cherokee. But the tribe's original language was nearly squelched by the English-only schools that Cherokee children attended from the late 19th century into the 1930s. In recent years, however, the Eastern Band has put major effort into revitalizing the speaking and writing of Cherokee, and many local children are now fluent in both Cherokee and English, in part due to the efforts of the Tribal Child Care Center, where children hear and speak only Cherokee.

EUROPEANS

Between the late 18th century and mid-19th century, European Americans began moving into the mountains of western North Carolina and east Tennessee, most of them subsistence farmers, though, as communities grew, many added on additional income-earning opportunities, becoming millers, blacksmiths, and shopkeepers. Leading lives based largely on agriculture, the Europeans were the first to begin large-scale clearing in the mountains to make way for crop and grazing land. They also began to actively hunt predators they perceived as pests (like wolves and mountain lions) and to take advantage of the abundance of game, including white-tailed deer, quail, and turkey.

As you travel around the Great Smoky Mountains National Park, notice how lush the mountain landscape is. It's hard to believe that this area was part of large-scale logging operations in the early 20th century. In those days, tall tulip poplar trees and American chestnuts dominated the landscape. The forest has since changed, as the chestnut was wiped out by blight 100 years ago. The Smokies are a study in recovery. Two-thirds of what is now the national park was either logged or cut over to make space for farming at the turn of the last century. Elkmont and Smokemont, both of which are now campgrounds in the park, were once logging settlements where lumber workers lived.

While the European settlers who called the southern Appalachians home for most of the 19th century made ample use of the natural resources around them, including timber, which they used to construct buildings, furniture, and fences, and also for fuel, cash cutting of timber didn't begin in earnest till the latter half of the 1800s. The voracious need for lumber in the eastern United States all but eliminated the forest landscape of the southern mountains as logging companies cleared everything they could get to. Of the few virgin forests that remain in these mountains, most were untouched simply because their landscape was just too rugged or steep to make it practicable for timbering.

Initial logging efforts were limited by the technology of the time, but by the turn of the 20th century steam-powered skidders and log loaders made the trade a more profitable one. Soon railroads were cutting into the mountains to draw out the timber.

Townsend, which is located just outside the national park near Cades Cove, was actually established at the turn of the 20th century as a company town by Little River Lumber Company, which also built the towns of Elkmont and Tremont. Little River worked in the Smokies for three decades, and Townsend is named after the company's owner. During that time the company helped take down one of the last great virgin deciduous forests in the East.

In what is now the Great Smoky Mountains National Park there were 15 logging company towns at one time and more than a dozen saw mills. Many mountain farmers left their fields to earn money in the logging industry. But by the 1930s lumber companies were slowing down, having cleared the easily accessible land. The mountains of the 1930s, when both the Great Smoky Mountains and the Blue Ridge Parkway were established, looked very different than they do today, with countless mountain slopes cleared of trees. In less than 100 years, however, the recovery has been remarkable. In most places, the untrained eye cannot even guess that these mountains were once a center of industry or home to hundreds of thriving agricultural communities.

BUILDING THE BLUE RIDGE PARKWAY

The Blue Ridge Parkway is not just a road laid across mountain ridges. It is a professionally designed landscape, much of it the responsibility of landscape architect Stanley Abbott, a gifted 25-year-old who oversaw a team of architects and engineers across more than 400 miles of roadway. Today Abbott's presence can still be seen here in the landscape architecture that has made the Parkway famous, from its roadside planted stands of rhododendron and mountain laurel to its 168 bridges designed across rivers, ravines, and valleys. Many of these bridges contain elaborate stonework, as do many Parkway guard walls and buildings, most of them constructed by the skilled hands of Spanish and Italian stonemasons or "stone setters," as they were known at the time these parks were first being built in the 1930s.

The first section of the Blue Ridge Parkway, a 50-mile stretch south of Roanoke, Virginia, opened to travelers in 1939. But it took nearly 50 more years for the Parkway to be completed. By 1968, all but eight miles in North Carolina were finished. The Parkway's final

piece, the engineering marvel of the S-curve Linn Cove Viaduct, which winds around the fragile landscape of Grandfather Mountain near Linville, was completed in 1987, opening the road, unobstructed, from its beginning at Shenandoah National Park to its end at the Great Smoky Mountains National Park for the first time.

CARVING A PARK FROM THE SMOKIES

In the 1920s, citizens of both Knoxville, Tennessee, and Asheville, North Carolina, began clamoring more loudly for public support of a national park in the Smoky Mountains. Not the least of the proponents for the creation of a park was a former librarian from St. Louis, Horace Kephart. He moved to the Smokies in 1904 and fell in love with the landscape and its people, both the Cherokee and the self-sufficient mountain folk who lived in countless little coves and communities all over the mountains. Kephart would eventually write the classic *Our Southern Highlanders,* honoring the human culture of the region in a way that had never been done previously. Kephart believed that the only way to save the Smokies from the onslaught of industrial logging was to protect them in perpetuity as a national park.

Kephart was one of the first to publicly advocate for a park, but soon Asheville, and then Knoxville, were right behind him, with citizens of both cities hoping for funds for locating a park in their states. Gradually, citizens of the two states joined forces and proposed a park in the mountains of eastern Tennessee and western North Carolina at a point that was roughly halfway between Knoxville and Asheville.

While conservationists and outdoor recreation enthusiasts were obviously proponents of building a national park in the Smokies, the newly motoring public was interested, too. As auto clubs like AAA gained members all the time as more and more Americans purchased automobiles, ordinary citizens began to think about having beautiful mountain roads on which to tour.

The National Park Service was a new kid on

the block, having been formed in 1916, and the agency was actively looking for places to establish a park or parks in the east on the order of those that had already come into the national park system in the west.

In 1926, president Calvin Coolidge signed into law a bill authorizing the establishment of both the Great Smoky Mountains National Park and also Shenandoah National Park in Virginia, with a proviso that the U.S. Department of the Interior would assume responsibility for the parks' protection and operation once at least 150,000 acres had been secured. But it was not the federal government that would fund this project but the states themselves.

Both the North Carolina and Tennessee legislatures appropriated $2 million each to go toward purchasing land for the park in the Smoky Mountains. Public fund drives, donations, and even school fundraising campaigns contributed more money to the project, and by 1928 the states had a total of $5 million available for land purchases. The Rockefeller Foundation donated another $5 million.

But the struggle to create a park was far from complete, even with ample funds in hand. There were 6,000 individual landowners in the mountains that would eventually become the Great Smoky Mountains National Park. Those tracts included both family farms and large tracts belonging to lumber and paper companies. Some mountain families left their homes eagerly and willingly, while others protested removal from their land. A few, mostly the elderly, were granted lifetime leases to their homes about to be taken into park boundaries, and others were granted shorter-term leases to their properties. One such case occurred in Roaring Fork where a farmer named M. M. Whittle had recently planted an orchard of apple trees. The National Park Service allowed him to harvest those trees for more than two decades after the park's official establishment.

The Great Smoky Mountains National Park was officially established in 1934, and then formally dedicated on September 2, 1940, at Newfound Gap, where president Franklin D. Roosevelt stood on the Tennessee–North Carolina state line at the Rockefeller Monument to deliver an address in honor of the park's creation. The park was rededicated at the same spot in 2009 on its 75th anniversary.

ESSENTIALS

Getting There and Around

AIR

While most people who travel to the Blue Ridge Mountains and Smoky Mountains drive in, if you do fly there are a few options. If you're planning to start your tour of the Blue Ridge Parkway from its northernmost point in North Carolina, then the closest airport is **Piedmont Triad International Airport** (GSO, 6415 Bryan Blvd., 336/721-0088, www.flyfrompti.com) in Greensboro. The airport is served by Allegiant (www.allegiantair.com), American Eagle (www.aa.com), Continental (www.continental.com), Delta (www.delta.com), United (www.united.com), and US Airways (www.usairways.com).

Another option is the **Roanoke Regional Airport** (ROA, 5202 Aviation Drive NW, 540/362-1999, www.roanokeairport.com), which is almost 100 miles away in Virginia, accessible by taking Route 52 north to I-77 and then I-81. The airport is served by Allegiant (www.allegiantair.com), US Airways (www.usairways.com), United (www.united.com), Northwest (www.nwa.com), and Delta (www.delta.com).

You can fly into Asheville and be right in the center of the action with the Blue Ridge Parkway just to the east and the Smokies to the west. The **Asheville Regional Airport** (61 Terminal Dr., 828/684-2226, www.flyavl.

© FRENCH C. GRIMES

com) is located at Exit 40 off I-26. The airport is served by AirTran (www.airtran.com), Continental (www.continental.com), Delta (www.delta.com), and US Airways (www.usairways.com).

You can also fly into **McGhee-Tyson Airport** (2055 Alcoa Hwy., 865/342-3000, www.tys.org), which is located in Alcoa, Tennessee, just south of Knoxville on U.S. 129. Service to McGhee-Tyson is provided by AirTran (www.airtran.com), Allegiant (www.allegiantair.com), American Airlines (www.aa.com), Continental (www.continental.com), Delta (www.delta.com), Northwest (www.nwa.com), United (www.united.com), and US Airways (www.usairways.com).

CAR

You absolutely have to have a car to explore the Blue Ridge Mountains and Smoky Mountains, so if you fly in make sure you arrange for a car rental. While some of the cities and towns have trolley service for getting you to and from various tourist areas, there really aren't any options besides having your own car for traveling around outside of one very limited area. Knoxville and Asheville both have citywide bus service, but my advice is to stick to the trolley systems each city offers for tourists. This is not New York City where everyone uses public transportation, and you might run into some seedy types on the public bus system.

Speed limits will vary widely depending on where you are. The maximum speed on interstates in North Carolina and Tennessee is 70 mph, while the speed limit on primary roads outside of cities and towns is typically 55 mph. That being said, mountain driving will often require much slower speeds, and the maximum speed on the Blue Ridge Parkway is 45 mph. In some areas it will be posted at 35 mph. Keep in mind that there are no gas stations directly on the Parkway, so be sure to fuel up before getting on the drive. Most U.S. and state highway intersections with the Parkway will have gas stations. Parking is allowed on the Parkway at overlooks and on shoulders unless posted otherwise.

The Blue Ridge Parkway frequently has temporary closures for road repairs. To avoid being disappointed or having to backtrack, call ahead for updates on road conditions. The park information line is 828/298-0398.

Recreation

BIKING

Biking is especially popular on the Blue Ridge Parkway, where bicyclists enjoy the road's 469 miles as much as motorists do. It's important to understand, however, that the Parkway is not a place to bike unless you're in good physical condition. Elevations along the Parkway range from 600 to 6,000 feet, and in some sections bicyclists will climb as much as 1,000 feet in only 3.5 miles.

To ensure your safety as you bike the Parkway, remember that all state and federal motor vehicle regulations apply to bicyclists, too. Bicycles are permitted only on paved roads and are not allowed on hiking trails. If you're bicycling with others, make sure you maintain a single file at all times, and stay to the right-hand side of the road except when passing or turning left.

Weather and temperature changes are unpredictable in the mountains, so make sure you have warm and waterproof clothing available at all times, and take plenty of water and high-energy snacks, as you may have to bike a long distance between opportunities for fresh water and concessions. For your safety, wear a helmet and reflective clothing, and avoid biking in heavy rain and fog. Bicyclists are required to display a white light or reflector visible from 500 feet away to the front and a red light or reflector visible from 200 feet away to the back when cycling in adverse weather conditions, before sunrise, after sunset, or when passing through tunnels.

To obtain more information on biking the Parkway, call 828/298-0398 or visit www.nps.gov/blri to download a brochure detailing elevation changes along the Parkway.

HIKING

One important thing to keep in mind when hiking in the mountains is that weather can change quickly, particularly when you're making hikes that involve significant changes in elevation. To make sure you're ready for whatever nature sends your way on the trail, dress in layers. That way you'll have warm clothes along for cooler mountaintop temperatures but can shed layers during hotter points of the day. Be sure to have a rain slicker, particularly when hiking in the Smokies where daily rain showers are pretty common. Wear sturdy hiking boots with ankle support, and take along at least one extra pair of socks (protected in a waterproof bag) in case your feet get wet. Bring along high-energy snacks and plenty of water for the trail.

You can find maps of the most popular trails along the Blue Ridge Parkway in the *Blue Ridge Parkway Trip Planner,* which is available for free at all Parkway visitors centers.

If you'd like to order Pisgah or Nantahala National Forest maps before visiting the area as well as trail maps and wilderness maps, contact the Cradle of Forestry in America at 800/660-0671, ext. 4, or order online at www.cradleofforestry.org.

There are very few circuit hikes in the Great Smoky Mountains National Park, meaning that on most trails you'll have to return to your vehicle the same way you came. You can remedy this issue by taking advantage of one of the many hiker shuttle services available that will pick you up and drop you off wherever you'd like in the park or even from your hotel room. That means you can park your car at one trailhead, then get the shuttle service to pick you up and drop you off at a different trailhead so you can hike through to where you left your car. Among the hiker shuttle services available are A Walk in the Woods (865/436-8283, www.

awalkinthewoods.com, daily 9 A.M.–2 P.M. or later, call in advance).

Backcountry hiking is popular in the Smokies, in large part because so much of the park is inaccessible by road. If you plan to camp overnight in the backcountry, you must have a permit and sometimes reservations. You must also use one of the park's more than 100 designated campsites or shelters. For details, call the park's backcountry office at 865/436-1297.

HORSEBACK RIDING

While horseback riding is welcome on many trails in the national forests that surround the Blue Ridge Parkway as well as in the Great Smoky Mountains, remember that horses can have negative impacts on the landscape. Stay on designated horse trails to avoid causing erosion problems. When tethering your horse, use a tree-safe strap tied between two trees. And most importantly, use weed-free feed. You don't want to contribute to the spread of invasive species. Also, be advised that any horse crossing a state line must have record of a negative Coggins test within the last year.

Remember to share the trail. It's your responsibility to yield to motorized vehicles. Bikers and hikers, however, should yield to you. If they don't, however, be polite and ask them to wait while you pass. If you camp overnight with your horse, remember to leave no trace behind, and clean up all your trash.

There are five drive-in horse camps in the Great Smoky Mountains National Park at Cades Cove, Big Creek, Cataloochee, Round Bottom, and Tow String. Horse camps are open April through early November, and you can make reservations by calling 877/444-6777. Fees range from $20 to $25. Six people and four horses are allowed at each site. Most camps have three to seven sites.

If you're not an equestrian owner but would still like to do some horseback riding in the Smokies, there are guided horseback rides available from four locations in the park—Cades Cove, Smokemont, Smoky Mountain, and Sugarlands. Rates are generally $25 per hour.

© DEBORAH HUSO

horseback riding at Moses H. Cone Memorial Park in North Carolina

BOATING

Western North Carolina and eastern Tennessee offer a variety of boating opportunities, from taking fishing trips on beautiful lakes in comfortable pontoon boats to riding white-water rapids in a raft. If you bring your own boat to the area, you will likely need a permit to use it on local waters, though plenty of area outfitters will set you up with everything from a chartered pontoon boat to a kayak. There are many white-water rivers in the region, offering rapids ranging from Class I to Class IV, and dozens of rafting companies offer guided white-water trips.

FISHING AND HUNTING

The Blue Ridge Mountains and Smoky Mountains are a paradise for fly fishermen, loaded with mountain streams and lakes that sport stocked and wild trout, musky and smallmouth bass, bream, and blue gill. Many area outfitters offer guide service on foot or by boat and will even supply you with equipment.

If you plan to do much fishing and hunting while visiting the region, it's a good idea to get the annual *Fishing, Hunting and Trapping Regulations Digest* published by the North Carolina Wildlife Resources Commission.

You can call 919/733-7291 or view and download the regulations online at www.ncwildlife.org. For information on hunting and fishing regulations in East Tennessee, contact the Tennessee Wildlife Resources Agency Region Four office at 423/587-7037 or online at www.state.tn.us/twra.

Remember that you must have a valid state fishing license from North Carolina or Tennessee to fish in each respective state. Persons under 16 can fish without a license in North Carolina. In Tennessee, anyone over 12 must have a license.

What you will catch depends on the location and altitude of where you fish. If you're interested exclusively in brook trout, then it's best to seek out the headwaters of streams above 3,000 feet, as brook trout prefer cold waters. Further downstream you'll find rainbow trout and perhaps a few brook. Where streams are wide, anglers can fish for rainbow and brown trout, and if you fish in wide rivers or lakes, you're more likely to reel in smallmouth bass and rock bass.

The Blue Ridge Parkway protects more than 100 miles of streams and also has 13 artificial lakes, offering a surprising array of opportunities to fish from this high-elevation byway.

© DEBORAH HUSO

fishing at Bass Lake in North Carolina

Only single-hook artificial lures are permitted. Regulations for trout waters as well as information on closed waters are always clearly posted. On the Parkway, fishing is allowed from one half hour before sunrise to one half hour after sunset. Catch and release is not required but is encouraged. For a list of fishing streams and lakes on the Blue Ridge Parkway, call 828/298-0398 or visit www.nps.gov/blri.

Some of the best spots to fish in the Great Smoky Mountains National Park are along Abrams Creek in Cades Cove, Big Creek at the Big Creek park entrance at I-40 on the park's northeastern corner, and the Little River near the Elkmont Campground. Before you head off into the woods with your rod and reel, request a copy of the *Great Smoky Mountains Fishing Regulations* brochure at one of the park visitors centers. It's an excellent resource, providing information on where to fish, what you'll catch, and the regulations you need to follow.

Hunting is permitted on U.S. Forest Service lands in designated seasons. Hunting is not allowed on national park lands, including the Blue Ridge Parkway and Great Smoky Mountains National Park. Firearms carried into the park must be unloaded and cased.

WILDLIFE-WATCHING

While the Blue Ridge Parkway draws visitors for its views, there is no doubt that many of the visitors to the Great Smoky Mountains National Park come to see its large mammals, mainly the black bears and elk. The best times of day for wildlife-viewing are early morning and late evening. If you're interested in seeing bear, good places for spotting them include Cades Cove, the Roaring Fork Motor Nature Trail, and Cataloochee. Just remember to keep your distance. While bears don't consider humans prey, they may charge if they feel threatened. Black bears can run up to 30 mph, and they are excellent tree climbers. In fact, trees are a good place to find bears, particularly in Cades Cove. It is actually against National Park Service regulations to approach within more than 50 yards (150 ft.) of a bear. Doing so is dangerous and could also get you fined.

One of the best times for elk viewing in terms of time of year is fall. Fall is "rutting" season; that's when they breed. There's nothing quite like sitting on the hood of your car in Cataloochee as the sunlight is fading and listening to the mournful bugling of the bulls as they compete for dominance. Remember to keep your distance, however. These animals are the largest in the park and will charge if they feel threatened.

CAMPING

Both the Blue Ridge Parkway and Great Smoky Mountains National Park offer National Park Service–operated campgrounds. Remember when camping to clean up after yourself, and leave clean campsites when you depart, removing all trash to dumpsters and recycling bins.

It's also important to store food properly when camping to prevent bear activity in campgrounds. Bears have an incredible sense of smell and can even smell food in a cooler, so any food or equipment used to prepare food should be stored in your vehicle (preferably in the trunk, as bears have been known to break car windows) or in an RV constructed of non-pliable material. Failure to follow food storage rules could result in fines.

Blue Ridge Parkway

There are nine National Park Service camp-grounds on the Blue Ridge Parkway, five of them in North Carolina. The camping season for all campgrounds runs May 1 through October 31, though winter camping may be occasionally available with limited services. No one can camp in Blue Ridge Parkway camp-grounds for more than 21 consecutive days, and all Parkway campgrounds charge $16 per night. Campsites are available on a first-come, first-served basis for the most part, though a few select sites at Linville Falls and Julian Price Memorial Park can be reserved by call-ing 877/444-6777 or reserving online at www.recreation.gov.

No more than six people can occupy any campsite, and all tents must be pitched on tent pads. No more than two vehicles are permit-ted per campsite. Dump stations are available at all campgrounds that accommodate RVs. Fires are permitted only in designated fire-places, with the exception of gas or charcoal grills and stoves. Wood gathering is allowed in the campgrounds, but only for use at park facilities and only from deadfall lying on the ground. Quiet hours at all campgrounds are between 10 P.M. and 6 A.M.

Backcountry camping is available in Basin Cove at Doughton Park (336/372-8568) and in Julian Price Memorial Park (828/963-5911), and you must have a permit to camp in the backcountry.

Great Smoky Mountains National Park

There are 10 campgrounds within the bound-aries of the Great Smoky Mountains National Park, 84 backcountry campsites, and 16 back-country shelters. All overnight hikers in the Smokies must use backcountry campsites or shelters. From May 15 through October 31, campground stays are limited to seven con-secutive days; the rest of the year the limit is 14 consecutive days. There are no utility hookups at any of the park campgrounds, though dump stations are available. Six peo-ple are permitted per campsite, and no more than two motor vehicles are allowed per site. Tents are required to be pitched on pads when available.

Fires are allowed only in provided grates, and campers can only gather wood in the park if it is dead and on the ground. Quiet hours run from 10 P.M. to 6 A.M., and use of genera-tors is prohibited from 8 P.M. to 8 A.M.

You can make reservations for sites at Elkmont, Smokemont, Cosby, and Cades Cove campgrounds in the Great Smoky Mountains National Park by calling 800/365-2267. Other campgrounds operate on a first-come, first-served basis only. For backcountry camping information, call 865/436-1297. Some back-country sites require reservations; call 865/436-1232 to reserve.

Tips for Travelers

FOREIGN TRAVELERS

While the Blue Ridge and Smoky Mountains tend to draw the vast majority of their visitors from the metropolitan areas of the Eastern United States, there are a fair number of foreign travelers exploring the mountains, too, often as part of a tour of the southeastern United States.

The National Park Service is accustomed to receiving foreign visitors, and most major visitors centers in the Great Smoky Mountains National Park and Blue Ridge Parkway will have brochures available in a number of foreign languages—just ask. This will be less likely the case outside park boundaries, so brush up on your English skills before you visit. The vast majority of U.S. citizens still speak only English, so you'll need to try hard to communicate in that language as well.

Entering the United States

Most foreign citizens coming into the United States will be required to obtain a visa, and the type of visa will vary depending on the purpose of your visit. If you're traveling for pleasure, you'll need to apply for a B-2 visa and be prepared to prove the purpose of your travel, show that you will only be in the U.S. for a limited period of time, and be able to show that your legal residence is in another country. You can apply for a visa at your nearest U.S. Embassy office. Visit the U.S. Department of State Bureau of Consular Affairs at www.travel.state.gov for more information and to find out if you're eligible for the Visa Waiver Program.

Money and Currency Exchange

If you go to any major bank in the cities of Knoxville and Asheville you'll find currency exchange services available, and most banks will also cash travelers checks and send wire transfers. Outside of banks, travelers checks are becoming so uncommon in the United States that if you try to use one at a restaurant or

hotel, the staff may not even know what it is. Rather than carry lots of cash, consider using a credit card to make large purchases.

You'll probably find it difficult to exchange currency in most other places in the region, as the towns are small and do not offer as many services, so it's best to take care of your currency exchange while still in the city. One exception is the Gatlinburg and Pigeon Forge area. In Gatlinburg and Pigeon Forge, the following banks offer currency exchange and ATMs: BB&T (811 and 912 E. Parkway, 865/430-2560), Citizens National Bank (906 E. Parkway and 110 Cherokee Orchard Rd., 800/603-2208), Tennessee State Bank (414 E. Parkway with ATMS at 130 and 727 E. Parkway, 865/436-7871).

Taxes and Tipping

Both North Carolina and Tennessee have sales tax on purchased goods, including restaurants and hotels. In North Carolina, the standard state sales tax is 7.75 percent. In Tennessee, the standard sales tax is 7 percent, 5.5 percent for food. Remember, however, that localities may have their own food and lodging taxes on top of these state-imposed taxes.

The standard rate for tipping in the United States is typically 15 percent for a sit-down restaurant. You can do 5 to 10 percent in a restaurant where they serve cafeteria style. Keep in mind it's not just waiters and waitresses that should be tipped. If you select valet parking at a hotel or have a bellboy carry your bags, you should be prepared to tip there as well. Housekeeping staff at hotels often leave an envelope for tips, though you're not required to tip. Consider it, however, if you have an especially clean and well-kept room.

North Carolina and Tennessee Laws

The maximum speed on interstates in North Carolina and Tennessee is 70 mph, while the speed limit on primary roads outside of cities and towns is typically 55 mph. Other areas, including towns and cities and curving roads, will likely have lower speed limits posted, so make sure you watch for changes in the speed limit.

Both Tennessee and North Carolina have mandatory seatbelt laws, requiring all passengers in vehicles to wear seatbelts. Children under 12 years old must be restrained in a child safety seat and/or ride in the backseat of automobiles.

A statewide law in Tennessee prohibits smoking in all enclosed public places. In North Carolina, you can no longer smoke in restaurants and bars. If you're a smoker, your options are becomingly increasingly limited. Even some hotels are now completely smoke-free. When making reservations, be sure to ask if they have smoking rooms available, as you could be charged an extra fee for smoking in a nonsmoking room.

The legal drinking age in the United States is 21. Many restaurants will ask for proof of age before serving alcohol.

TRAVELING WITH CHILDREN

Both the Blue Ridge Parkway and Great Smoky Mountains National Park welcome children, and both offer Junior Ranger programs in which your little one can participate. Stop at any visitors center to ask about the program; a ranger will help set you up with an age-appropriate Junior Ranger packet. If your child completes all the activities in the packet and turns it into a ranger, he or she will have lots of fun getting inducted as a Junior Ranger for that particular park.

Remember, however, that neither national park is a place to let your kids run around without supervision. Keep an eye on your children at all times, especially when admiring the view from steep overlooks or climbing on a hazardous trail. Children are fearless, but you shouldn't be. Teach your children to stay on designated trails and not to run ahead of you when hiking. Also, consider buying them a book about wildlife and/or plants at one of the park visitors centers. Most of the park visitors

centers have excellent selections of children's books that will help your kids not only appreciate the landscape they're visiting but will help educate them about the potential dangers of getting too close to wildlife or finding themselves in poison ivy because they strayed from the path.

Another good way to get your kids involved with nature is to sign them up for one of the many kids' or family camp programs offered at the Great Smoky Mountains Institute at Tremont or to take them to a Junior Ranger program.

If you're looking for attractions that kids will love, some of the best include Grandfather Mountain, Tweetsie Railroad, Ober Gatlinburg, Ripley's Aquarium, and Dollywood.

TRAVELING WITH PETS

Pets are a common sight in the Blue Ridge and Smokies, and most localities work hard to accommodate people traveling with pets. The larger cities and towns in the region will all have at least some lodgings that allow pets, and many localities even have restaurants and shops where pets are welcome.

Remember to bring a scooper and plastic bags along so you can clean up after your pet, and don't forget to arm your pet with flea and tick repellent just like you would yourself before taking that hike through the woods. If you plan to hike with your pooch, be sure to note which trails allow pets and which don't. Leashes are required on all pet-friendly trails in the national parks and forests.

Pets are allowed on the Blue Ridge Parkway but must be leashed at all times. Pets are not allowed on any hiking trails in the Great Smoky Mountains National Park except the Gatlinburg and Oconaluftee River Trails.

SENIOR TRAVELERS

While your Golden Age pass won't do you much good on the Blue Ridge Parkway or in the Great Smoky Mountains National Park since both are free parks anyway, you will find that almost every attraction offers discounts to seniors, so remember to ask at any place charging admission. Many restaurants also have special menus for seniors with discounted prices on popular items.

If you have mobility problems, don't worry. You'll be surprised by the number of attractions, restaurants, and lodgings that are wheelchair-accessible. Even many bed-and-breakfasts have wheelchair-accessible and first-floor rooms that they reserve for people who prefer not to contend with stairs. Again, ask. You might be pleasantly surprised by how accommodating everyone is to your special needs.

GAY AND LESBIAN TRAVELERS

While the Smoky Mountains and Blue Ridge Mountains are not going to have the same kind of atmosphere as, say, San Francisco or Key West, you might be surprised by how tolerant this region is, despite the fact that it is largely rural. That being said, the region is overall more conservative than large urban areas, so overt displays of affection might get a frown or a stare in some places. But for the most part you probably won't see most folks bat an eye. This region loves its tourists, no matter who they are.

However, if you want to find a place where you can blend in more easily, head to Asheville. Asheville is a city that prides itself on being a haven for divergent and eclectic views and has become a popular vacation getaway for gay and lesbian couples. The city has a number of gay and lesbian bars and also provides many luxurious options for gay-and-lesbian-friendly lodging. For a full listing of gay-friendly hotels, visit www.romanticasheville. com/gayandlesbian.

VOLUNTEERING

You can help support the Blue Ridge Parkway and Great Smoky Mountains National Park by giving donations and/or volunteering your services to the nonprofit organizations that help fund park initiatives. These include the **Blue Ridge Parkway Foundation** (717 S. Marshall St., Winston Salem, NC, 336/721-0260, www.brpfoundation.org), **Great Smoky Mountains Association** (115 Park Headquarters Rd., Gatlinburg, TN, 888/898-9102, www.thegreatsmokymountains.org), and **Friends of the Smokies** (160 S. Main St., Waynesville, NC, 828/452-0720 or 800/845-5665, www.friendsofthesmokies.org).

Health and Safety

WILDLIFE

One of the great pleasures of exploring the mountains is the opportunity to see wildlife in their native habitat. But it's important to remember that wild animals are just that—wild. Always maintain your distance. If a wild creature changes its behavior in reaction to your presence, you've gotten too close. It's especially important to maintain a safe distance from larger mammals like black bears and elk, both of which will charge if they feel threatened, particularly if they have young with them. If you want to watch or photograph wildlife up-close, use binoculars or a zoom lens.

Also remember never to feed wildlife and to always dispose of trash appropriately. Feeding animals or giving them access to human food sources by not properly disposing of food waste habituates them to humans. And animals that are habituated to humans, particularly when they're predators like bears, are dangerous animals. Some bears in the Smokies have been euthanized over the years because they attacked humans or domestic pets or became problem animals in campgrounds. More often than not, humans were more to blame than the bears.

If the potential harm you could cause to yourself or to the animals is not enough to deter you from feeding them, perhaps other consequences will: Feeding wildlife on National Park Service lands could subject you to a $5,000 fine and six months in prison.

There are two kinds of poisonous snakes in these mountains, timber rattlesnakes and northern copperheads. If you spend a lot of time hiking, in particular, you're likely to see one sooner or later. Rattlesnakes, if mature, are easily recognizable by their tails, and they'll warn you if you get too close. Copperheads are pale tan to pinkish tan with dark bands on their bodies. While poisonous snakes generally have large broad heads, it may not always be easy to tell a poisonous from a harmless snake, especially if you're keeping the distance you should when observing them. So to be on the safe side, don't antagonize any snakes you see in the woods, and keep your distance. Also be wary of putting your hands and feet near rocks or logs where you can't easily see what might be underneath or hidden in crevices, as these are favorite hangouts for snakes.

INSECTS AND POISONOUS PLANTS
The mountains of North Carolina and Tennessee don't have any bugs and plants that are likely to kill you (as long as you exercise some common sense), but they will annoy you if you're not prepared. Ticks are a common pest, and in addition to latching onto your skin and sucking your blood for lunch, they can also be disease carriers, so be sure to wear insect repellent when spending time in the woods. This will also protect you from mosquitoes, which can also carry disease. Unfortunately, few bug repellants will deter gnats, which can be one of the most annoying pests in the woods, as they like to fly around your face and dive into your eyes, nose, and ears. The best defense is to wear a broad-brimmed hat and sunglasses.

There are a number of plants in the woods that can cause you irritation as well, the most common being poison ivy, poison oak, and stinging nettles. Contact with any of these plants will cause your skin to itch or burn, and you'll likely develop a rash that may bother you for days. You can generally avoid encounters with irritating plants like these by staying on designated trails and wearing long pants and enclosed shoes when hiking.

WEATHER
The Smokies and Blue Ridge Parkway region are busiest in summer and in fall color season, with the peak visitation months being July and October. If your goal is to avoid crowds, go in winter or early spring. While the weather will definitely be cooler (and probably downright cold at high elevations), winter and early spring will give you the opportunity to enjoy more long-distance views while there are no leaves on the trees.

Be prepared for quick changes in weather and temperature due to elevation changes and, in the case of the Smokies, the generally rainy climate. Always have rain gear handy, dress in layers, have sturdy shoes if you plan to hike, and carry a lot of hiking, energy snacks, and water.

To obtain weather reports for various areas along the Blue Ridge Parkway, call 828/298-0938. This line will also give you reports on road closures. For updated weather and road condition reports in the Great Smoky Mountains National Park, call 865/436-1200.

EMERGENCIES
If you have an emergency you can always call 911, but keep in mind that cell phone service is unpredictable in the mountains. If you require assistance while visiting the Blue Ridge Parkway or need to report uncontrolled fires, accidents, safety hazards, or emergencies, call 800/727-5928.

For emergency services in the Great Smoky Mountains National Park, call park headquarters at 865/436-9171. You can also contact the Cherokee Police Department at 828/497-4131, or the Gatlinburg Police Department at 865/436-5181.

Information and Services

TOURIST INFORMATION
Blue Ridge Parkway
The Blue Ridge Parkway has a number of visitors centers along its length in North Carolina at Moses H. Cone Memorial Park (Milepost 294.1), Linn Cove Viaduct (Milepost 304.4), Linville Falls (Milepost 316.4), the Museum of North Carolina Minerals (Milepost 331), Craggy Gardens (Milepost 364.6), the Folk Art Center (Milepost 382), Blue Ridge Parkway Visitor Center (Milepost 384), and Waterrock Knob (Milepost 451.2). All of these staffed visitors centers have maps and brochures available. If you would like to obtain information about the Parkway before visiting, you can write to Blue Ridge Parkway, 199 Hemphill Knob Rd., Asheville, NC 28803; call 828/298-0398; or visit www.nps.gov/blri.

Great Smoky Mountains National Park
The Great Smoky Mountains National Park has three visitors centers. The Oconaluftee Visitor Center is the only one on the North Carolina side of the park and is located just inside the park entrance near Cherokee on the Newfound Gap Road (Hwy. 441). The Sugarlands Visitor Center is located on the Newfound Gap Road as well but on the Tennessee side, just inside the park near Gatlinburg. Not quite so easy to access is the Cades Cove Visitor Center, which is located halfway around the 11-mile Cades Cove loop auto tour southwest of Townsend. To obtain information about the Great Smoky Mountains National Park before visiting, you can write to Great Smoky Mountains National Park, 107 Park Headquarters Rd., Gatlinburg, TN 37738; call 865/436-1200; or visit www. nps.gov/grsm.

COMMUNICATIONS
Cell Phone and Internet Service
If you're accustomed to being able to use your mobile devices anywhere you go, prepare yourself before you head to the mountains of North Carolina and Tennessee. While all major cities and most towns of decent size have cell service available, you will likely not have service at all while in the Great Smoky Mountains National Park and only occasionally along the Blue Ridge Parkway. Don't depend on your cell phone to get you out of a bad situation if you're along on a trail four miles from the nearest road—you likely won't have service. That's why it's especially important to use common sense and always be prepared before setting off on hikes or back-road driving trips. You may be entirely on your own.

Most lodging facilities in the Blue Ridge and Smokies region have high-speed Internet and/or Wi-Fi available, including bed-and-breakfasts, and even some vacation rentals do. More and more campgrounds are including Wi-Fi as part of their amenity offerings as well. If it's important to you to stay in touch while you're on vacation, make sure to call ahead and ask about Internet service availability before booking a room or campsite.

RESOURCES
Suggested Reading

FLORA AND FAUNA

Alderman, J. Anthony. *Wildflowers of the Blue Ridge Parkway.* Chapel Hill: The University of North Carolina Press, 1997. A handy reference guide with detailed flower descriptions organized by color, the book also features full-color plates in the back.

Alsop, Fred J., III. *Birds of the Smokies.* Gatlinburg: Great Smoky Mountains Association, 1991. A guide to bird-watching in the Smokies, including where to find them and a complete checklist.

Catlin, David. *A Naturalist's Blue Ridge Parkway.* Knoxville: University of Tennessee Press, 1984. A traveler's handbook to the geology, plants, and animals to be found along the Blue Ridge Parkway.

Kemp, Steve. *Trees of the Smokies.* Gatlinburg: Great Smoky Mountains Association, 1991. A pocket-sized field guide to the trees of the Smoky Mountains, including full color photos, fall color guide, and checklist.

Simpson, Marcus B. *Birds of the Blue Ridge Mountains: A Guide for the Blue Ridge Parkway, Great Smoky Mountains, Shenandoah National Park, and Neighboring Areas.* Chapel Hill: The University of North Carolina Press, 1992. An excellent resource, Simpson's book is organized by region and includes recommendations (and maps) for some of the area's best birding hikes.

White, Peter. *Wildflowers of the Smokies.* Gatlinburg: Great Smoky Mountains Association, 1996. Full-color guide to wildflower identification in the Smokies, organized by color.

HIKING

Adkins, Leonard. *Walking the Blue Ridge: A Guide to the Trails of the Blue Ridge Parkway.* Chapel Hill: The University of North Carolina Press, 2003. The most comprehensive listing of hikes accessible off the Parkway, including mileage, mile-by-mile descriptions, and author recommendations.

Hiking Trails of the Smokies. Gatlinburg: Great Smoky Mountains Association, 2003. A comprehensive guide to the 800 miles of trails in the Great Smoky Mountains National Park, including elevations, distances, and detailed trail descriptions. A must-have resource for the serious hiker.

Hubbs, Hal, Charles Maynard, and David Morris. *Waterfalls of the Smokies.* Gatlinburg: Great Smoky Mountains Association, 1992. A full-color guide to over 40 waterfalls in the Great Smoky Mountains National Park, including hiking directions and descriptions.

Johnson, Randy. *Hiking North Carolina.* Guilford, CT: Falcon Guides, 2007. A comprehensive guidebook to the hiking trails of North Carolina with trail descriptions, elevations, and directions.

HISTORY

Dunn, Durwood. *Cades Cove: The Life and Death of a Southern Appalachian Community, 1818–1937.* Knoxville: University of Tennessee Press, 2004. A complete and entertaining history of the former community of Cades Cove in the Great Smoky Mountains National Park.

Finger, John F. *The Eastern Band of the Cherokees, 1819–1900.* Knoxville: University of Tennessee Press, 1984. Recounts the often-overlooked history of the Cherokee who remained behind following the Trail of Tears.

Jolley, Harley. *The Magnificent Army of Youth and Peace: The Civilian Conservation Corps in North Carolina.* North Carolina Office of Archives and History, 2007. The story of the Civilian Conservation Corps in the Great Smoky Mountains National Park and on the Blue Ridge Parkway.

Kephart, Horace. *Camping and Woodcraft: A Handbook for Campers and Travelers in the Wilderness.* Knoxville: University of Tennessee Press, 1988. The classic outdoorsman's guide from naturalist and national park advocate Horace Kephart, whose advice was based on years of living among the Cherokee and mountain people of the Smokies.

Kephart, Horace. *Our Southern Highlanders: A Narrative of Adventure in the Southern Appalachians and a Study of Life Among the Mountaineers.* Knoxville: University of Tennessee Press, 1976. Another Kephart classic, this book chronicles the famous naturalist's life among the mountain folk in the years before the establishment of the Great Smoky Mountains National Park.

Weals, Vic. *The Last Train to Elkmont.* Olden Press, 1993. A history of the logging industry in the Little River area of the Smokies.

FICTION

Frazier, Charles. *Cold Mountain.* New York: Vintage Books, 2006. The Civil War–era story that made Cold Mountain, along the Blue Ridge Parkway, famous.

Frazier, Charles. *Thirteen Moons.* New York: Random House, 2006. The fictionalized story of the Eastern Band of the Cherokee who avoided the Trail of Tears.

Internet Resources

GENERAL TOURISM INFORMATION
North Carolina Department of Commerce's Division of Tourism, Film and Sports Development
www.visitnc.com

North Carolina's tourism division website offers a comprehensive guide to the entire state. The site is a bit of nightmare to navigate, however. You can't just select a region to explore but have to go through an elaborate search function to find what you need. Nevertheless, if you want information on the mountains of western North Carolina, select "Mountains" when conducting your searches of area attractions, lodging, and recreation.

Tennessee Department of Tourist Development
www.tnvacation.com

Tennessee's official state tourism site is a lot more user-friendly. If you want to check out all there is to do in the mountains of East Tennessee, including the Smokies, just select "East Tennessee" under the "Regions" heading. From there an interactive clickable map will take you wherever you want to go.

Blue Ridge Parkway Association
www.blueridgeparkway.org
A nonprofit association of businesses promoting tourism along the Blue Ridge Parkway and in the Smoky Mountains, the Blue Ridge Parkway Association offers a lot of handy tools on their website, including a milepost-by-milepost listing of all the hiking trails accessible from the Parkway, a bloom schedule for favorite Parkway flowers, and a calendar of annual events and festivities occurring in the communities that surround the Parkway.

Blue Ridge Natural Heritage Area
www.blueridgeheritage.com
The Blue Ridge National Heritage Area was designated by Congress and the president in 2003 in recognition of the unique character, culture, and beauty of western North Carolina and their significance to the history of our nation. The designation recognizes the region for having its own distinctive culture. If the history, music, and arts of the southern mountains is what interest you, then check out this website, which has an excellent searchable directory of mountain artists.

Smoky Mountain Host
www.visitsmokies.org.com
A regional tourism organization promoting western North Carolina's seven westernmost counties, Smoky Mountain Host has an easily navigable site that allows you to search by location or activity. This is a great centralized place to go for information on the North Carolina counties southwest of Asheville.

NATIONAL PARK INFORMATION
Blue Ridge Parkway
www.nps.gov/blri
As with most National Park Service websites, the Blue Ridge Parkway's site provides everything you need to plan your road trip down this famous drive, including downloadable PDF maps, hiking trail maps, and information on the Parkway's history as well as flora and fauna.

The home page usually prominently notes any current or impending road closures as well.

Blue Ridge Parkway Foundation
www.brpfoundation.org
The Blue Ridge Parkway Foundation is the Parkway's primary fundraising organization, providing funding and support for everything from capital improvement projects to watershed preservation initiatives. The foundation also has an online store where you can purchase books, maps, and guides for planning your trip as well as Blue Ridge Parkway merchandise.

Great Smoky Mountains National Park
www.nps.gov/grsm
The Great Smoky Mountains National Park website provides a comprehensive resource for exploring the park before your visit, including extensive information on the history of the people before the park and loads of material on the park's natural features, flora, and fauna and the threats the landscape is facing in the present and the future. You can download maps here as well.

Great Smoky Mountains Association
www.smokiesstore.org
The nonprofit partner of the Great Smoky Mountains National Park, this association serves as the park concessionaire, providing guidebooks, maps, and logo hats, T-shirts, and sweatshirts. This is a great place to order those hiking books or field guides in advance of your trip.

Friends of the Smokies
www.friendsofthesmokies.org
Established in 1993, Friends of the Smokies is a nonprofit organization that works closely to raise funds for park initiatives, trail maintenance, invasive species control, and a host of other needs. If you enjoy your visit to the Smokies, you might want to consider lending this group some aid, whether through a donation of time or money.

NATIONAL FORESTS
Pisgah and Nantahala National Forests
www.cs.unca.edu/nfsnc

Both the Pisgah and Nantahala National Forests hug the Blue Ridge Parkway for much of its journey through North Carolina and also take in the Smoky Mountain range. Likely much of the outdoor recreation you will enjoy on your trip will take place on national forest lands. The website for the national forests in North Carolina is a bit convoluted, but if you're patient you can find a lot of material here to help you plan your trip, including downloadable maps and camping information.

Cherokee National Forest
www.fs.fed.us/r8/cherokee

On the Tennessee side of the Smokies, it's the Cherokee National Forest that meets up with the Great Smoky Mountains National Park on both its southern and northern borders. Check out the forest website before traveling to learn about opportunities for outdoor recreation outside the national park. The website has an extensive section on white-water rafting.

OUTDOOR RECREATION
North Carolina Wildlife Resources Commission
www.ncwildlife.org

For information on hunting, boating, and fishing in North Carolina, the state's Wildlife Resources Commission site offers everything you need to know, from how and where to obtain a fishing license to hunting seasons for various game.

North Carolina Division of Parks and Recreation
www.ncparks.gov

In addition to plying its way through national forest land, the Blue Ridge Parkway also brings you alongside or close to a number of North Carolina's state parks. Learn more about them before you visit at the website of the North Carolina State Parks system.

Tennessee Wildlife Resources Agency
www.tennessee.gov/twra

Anglers, boaters, and hunters visiting Tennessee should check out the state's Wildlife Resources Agency website for information on the latest regulations related to outdoor sporting activities.

Index

List of Maps

Acknowledgments

For Grandma, who taught me storytelling.

First and foremost, I must thank my research assistant, Dorothy Stephenson, without whose help I could not have put this book together in the incredibly short span of just under four months. Her tireless fact-checking efforts were invaluable, as was her patience with calling nearly every listing in this book to verify contact information, admission fees, and days and hours. She put in a number of late nights and weekends to help ensure the accuracy of information on these pages.

I must also thank my husband, French, who spent many weeks over the course of the summer driving from one destination to another while I took notes or typed away on my laptop and who also took many of the photographs in this book, allowing me to concentrate on writing.

I would like to thank Nancy Gray with the Great Smoky Mountains National Park, who spent many hours verifying factual information about the park and providing insights on park recreation and sights. I owe a similar thank you to Peter Givens with the Blue Ridge Parkway, who was consistently available to fact-check information on America's favorite drive.

Jim Davis and Walter Yeldell with the Gatlinburg Department of Tourism and Convention Center were both invaluable in providing the latest news on attractions and amenities in Gatlinburg; they are among the finest media relations representatives I have ever met in their responsiveness to my inquiries and willingness to assist me with travel itineraries.

Tom Adkinson with Bohan Ideas was a great resource in helping me navigate the overwhelming number of offerings in and around Pigeon Forge. I would also like to thank Jennifer McLucas with The Goss Agency, who helped ensure my enjoyment of all the cultural attractions of Cherokee.

I owe a special thanks to Charles and Ellen Snodgrass of Deep Creek Arts in Whittier, North Carolina, longtime friends and designers of about half the tourism websites in western North Carolina. Their generosity in sharing insider tips on new attractions and good eats were invaluable.

Additionally, I would like to extend my gratitude to Landis Wofford with Grandfather Mountain, Amanda Lugenbell with the Blowing Rock Tourism Development Authority, Dodie Stephens with the Asheville Convention & Visitors Bureau, and LeeAnn Donnelly with Biltmore.

Thanks also to all of the attractions and lodging facilities who made me feel welcome as well as to the many excellent restaurants who unknowingly fed this travel writer great meals. I wish I could name everyone, but many of you know who you are. I could not have completed this project without your insights, hospitality, and kind cooperation.

www.moon.com

DESTINATIONS | ACTIVITIES | BLOGS | MAPS | BOOKS

MOON.COM is ready to help plan your next trip! Filled with fresh trip ideas and strategies, author interviews, informative travel blogs, a detailed map library, and descriptions of all the Moon guidebooks, Moon.com is all you need to get out and explore the world—or even places in your own backyard. While at Moon.com, sign up for our monthly e-newsletter for updates on new releases, travel tips, and expert advice from our on-the-go Moon authors. As always, when you travel with Moon, expect an experience that is uncommon and truly unique.

MOON IS ON FACEBOOK—BECOME A FAN!
JOIN THE MOON PHOTO GROUP ON FLICKR

MAP SYMBOLS

▦	Expressway	◖	Highlight	✗	Airfield	⚲	Golf Course
▦	Primary Road	○	City/Town	✗	Airport	▣	Parking Area
▦	Secondary Road	◉	State Capital	▲	Mountain	⬟	Archaeological Site
▦	Unpaved Road	⊛	National Capital	✦	Unique Natural Feature	⚑	Church
-----	Trail	★	Point of Interest			⛽	Gas Station
··········	Ferry	•	Accommodation	⧹	Waterfall		Glacier
▦	Railroad	▼	Restaurant/Bar	▲	Park		Mangrove
▦	Pedestrian Walkway	■	Other Location	▣	Trailhead		Reef
▦	Stairs	Λ	Campground	⛷	Skiing Area		Swamp

CONVERSION TABLES

°C = (°F − 32) / 1.8
°F = (°C x 1.8) + 32
1 inch = 2.54 centimeters (cm)
1 foot = 0.304 meters (m)
1 yard = 0.914 meters
1 mile = 1.6093 kilometers (km)
1 km = 0.6214 miles
1 fathom = 1.8288 m
1 chain = 20.1168 m
1 furlong = 201.168 m
1 acre = 0.4047 hectares
1 sq km = 100 hectares
1 sq mile = 2.59 square km
1 ounce = 28.35 grams
1 pound = 0.4536 kilograms
1 short ton = 0.90718 metric ton
1 short ton = 2,000 pounds
1 long ton = 1.016 metric tons
1 long ton = 2,240 pounds
1 metric ton = 1,000 kilograms
1 quart = 0.94635 liters
1 US gallon = 3.7854 liters
1 Imperial gallon = 4.5459 liters
1 nautical mile = 1.852 km

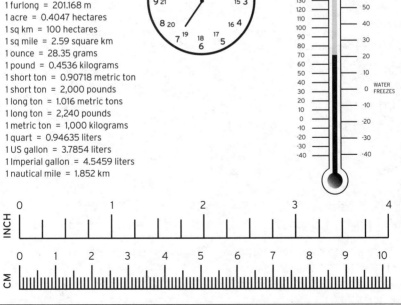

**MOON BLUE RIDGE &
SMOKY MOUNTAINS**

Avalon Travel
a member of the Perseus Books Group
1700 Fourth Street
Berkeley, CA 94710, USA
www.moon.com

Editor and Series Manager: Kathryn Ettinger
Copy Editor: Amy Scott
Graphics and Production Coordinator:
   Lucie Ericksen
Cover Designer: Lucie Ericksen
Map Editor: Brice Ticen
Cartographers: Kat Bennett
Indexer: Greg Jewett

ISBN: 978-1-59880-532-1
ISSN: 2154-2309

Printing History
1st Edition – June 2010

5 4 3

Front cover photo: Sunset light beams flood
   mountains and forest in fall colors in the Great
   Smoky Mountains. © Nancy Rotenberg/Jaynes
   Gallery/Danita Delimont.com
Title page photo: © French C. Grimes
Other front matter photos: pages 4–5, 6 bottom,
   7 top-left & bottom, 8–11, 13–14, 17, 19–22, 24:
   © French C. Grimes; pages 6 top, 7 top-right, 12,
   15–16, 18, 23: © Deborah Huso

Printed in Canada by Friesens

KEEPING CURRENT

If you have a favorite gem you'd like to see included in the next edition, or see anything
that needs updating, clarification, or correction, please drop us a line. Send your
comments via email to feedback@moon.com, or use the address above.